June 14/2009

Leadership for Social Justice

Promoting Equity and Excellence Through Inquiry and Reflective Practice

Dear Carol

For the commemoration. Thank you for the continued to serve as that have continued to refocus our thinking catalysts to refocus our thinking on how education have become social justice advocates and social justice activists. Enjoy!

Love
Tony

A volume in
Educational Leadership for Social Justice

Series Editor:
Jeffrey S. Brooks, *Auburn University*

Educational Leadership for Social Justice

Jeffrey S. Brooks, Series Editor

Leadership for Social Justice:
Promoting Equity and Excellence Through Inquiry and
Reflective Practive (2008)
edited by Anthony H. Normore

Leadership for Social Justice

Promoting Equity and Excellence Through Inquiry and Reflective Practice

edited by

Anthony H. Normore
California State University—Dominguez Hills

Information Age Publishing, Inc.
Charlotte, North Carolina • www.infoagepub.com

Library of Congress Cataloging-in-Publication Data

Leadership for social justice : promoting equity and excellence through inquiry and reflective practice / edited by Anthony H. Normore.
    p. cm. -- (Educational leadership for social justice)
 Includes bibliographical references.
 ISBN 978-1-59311-997-3 (pbk.) -- ISBN 978-1-59311-998-0 (hardcover) 1. Social justice. 2. Leadership. I. Normore, Anthony.
 HM671.L43 2008
 303.3'72--dc22

                                               2008037764

This volume is jointly sponsored by the Office of Research on Teaching in the Disciplines at the University of Alabama.

Printed in the United States of America

CONTENTS

SERIES EDITOR'S PREFACE

I am pleased to serve as series editor for this book series, *Educational Leadership for Social Justice*, with Information Age Publishing. The idea for this series grew out of the work of a committed group of leadership for scholars associated with the American Educational Research Association's (AERA) Leadership for Social Justice Special Interest Group. This group has actually existed for many years before being officially affiliated with AERA, and has benefitted greatly from the ongoing leadership, support, and counsel of Dr. Catherine Marshall (University of North Carolina-Chapel Hill). It is also important to acknowledge the contributions of the AERA SIG's first President, Dr. Ernestine Enomoto (University of Hawaii at Manoa), whose wisdom, stewardship, and guidance have helped ease a transition into AERA's more formal organizational structures that were at times difficult to reconcile with a group that largely identified itself as a group of nontraditional scholars and continues to push toward innovation rather than settle for the status quo. I am particularly indebted to my colleagues on the SIG's publications committee: Dr. Denise Armstrong, Brock University; Dr. Ira Bogotch, Florida Atlantic University; Dr. Sandra Harris, Lamar University; Dr. Whitney Sherman, Virginia Commonwealth University; Dr. George Theoharis, Syracuse University. This committee has been a joy to work with and I look forward to future collaborations as we seek to provide publication opportunities for scholarship in the area of leadership for social justice.

It is appropriate that this first book in the series, *Leadership for Social Justice: Promoting Equity and Excellence through Inquiry and Reflective Practice*, is an edited volume of diverse scholars approaching topics germane to social justice from a number of perspectives. I am personally pleased that

Dr. Anthony H. Normore, a scholar and friend whom I hold in the highest regard, is editor of this volume. The authors in this collection of peer-reviewed chapters confront myriad issues in multiple contexts and struggle to position themselves in the fuzzy space between research and activism. I invite you to consider their work as an edited volume of discrete studies, but also as a collection with many conceptual and empirical connections.

Again, welcome to the first book in this Information Age Publishing series, *Educational Leadership for Social Justice*. You can learn more about the series at our Web site: http://www.infoagepub.com/products/series/s4810de4a49015.php. I invite you to contribute your own work on equity and influence to the series. We look forward to you joining the conversation.

Dr. Jeffrey S. Brooks, Auburn University President,
American Educational Research Association Leadership for
Social Justice Special Interest Group (2008–2010)

EDITOR'S PREFACE

Anthony H. Normore

I am pleased to serve as editor for this first book of a series sponsored by American Educational Research Association (AERA) Special Interest Group Leadership for Social Justice. This book features a diverse group of scholars who have produced important scholarship on leadership for learning about issues of social justice over the last decade.

Recent commemorations of the 50th anniversary of the *Brown v. Board of Education* (i.e., the 1954 decision of the U.S. Supreme Court took scientific research into account in issuing this landmark ruling for desegregation of schools across America) and the 40th anniversary of the Civil Rights Act (i.e., the 1964 Civil Rights Act made racial discrimination in public places illegal in America, and required employers to provide equal employment opportunities) have emphasized how movements for social justice helped to define American history. Throughout the years, these commemorations have continued to serve as catalysts to refocus thinking on how educational leaders have become social justice advocates and activists. Discussions about social justice in the field of education have typically framed the concept of social justice around several issues including race, diversity, marginalization, equity, access, ethics, class, gender, spirituality, ability, and sexual orientation.

Within this book *Leadership for Social Justice: Promoting Equity and Excellence Through Inquiry and Reflective Practice* the contributors provide a variety of rich perspectives to the social justice phenomenon from the lens of empirical, historical, narrative, and conceptual designs. These designs reiterate the importance of bridging theory and practice while simultaneously producing significant research and scholarship in the field. Collectively, the authors seek to give voice to empowering, social justice-focused research—an area that continues to garner much interest in the areas of educational leadership research, teaching, and learning. In conjunction with the "theme" of this issue, the chapters offer research from an American perspective and offer suggestions, and implications for the field of educational leadership on both a national and international level. The collection contributes to research, theory and practice in educational and community settings.

The book is comprised of 14 chapters and organized into four parts. Each part focuses on a specific theme. Part I is centered on "Commitment to Social Justice, Equity, and Tolerance" and contains four chapters. In the first chapter, Gaetane Jean-Marie and Anthony H. Normore examine the experiences of four African American women leaders in historically Black colleges and universities (HBCUs) in a Southeastern state. When the 1954 ruling of *Brown v. Board of Education* by the U.S. Supreme court declared that schools should be desegregated with all deliberate speed, these four women were among the freedom fighters who integrated public schools, and later pursued higher education and professional careers. The authors catalogue how these four women, committed to social justice and racial uplift, connect their professional work with social and political activism in the quest for access, equality, and social justice for African Americans—and all people.

In chapter 2, Jonathan D. Lightfoot expands his research by arguing that modern educational reform owes much to the legal team and educational leaders who fought to make equal educational opportunity a reality for Black students in the United States. Their efforts helped to dismantle American apartheid; also know as, Jim Crow, a system of allocating human and civil rights according to assigned or assumed "racial" classifications. Lightfoot questions commonly held wisdom that promotes the idea that if things are separate they must be unequal. He argues that seeking integration to overcome segregation without addressing racism does not solve the problem of unequal educational opportunity.

In chapter 3, Autumn Tooms and Judy A. Alston used the "Attitudes Towards Lesbians and Gay Men Scale" to study attitudes of two groups of graduate students in graduate level leadership preparation programs. Findings reveal that a majority of the population (61%) tend to have more tolerant attitudes toward members of the queer community while 35% of respondents were neutral about issues concerning equity.

In chapter 4, Gerardo López and Vanessa Vàsquez focus on the attitudes and perceptions of school administrators, teachers, and other school personnel in one Latino-impacted school district in a Midwestern state. The authors argue that certain practices of language and cultural assimilation reinforce a subtle, but powerful, form of benevolent racism: where "good intentions" and compassionate altruism reproduce and reify a highly racialized discourse.

Part II contains three chapters that focus on "Promoting Social Justice Pedagogy." In chapter 5 Jeffrey S. Brooks and Mark Miles present an historical overview of pedagogical orientations of school leadership in the United States. These authors discuss issues facing contemporary educational leaders in this context with a consideration of the early influence of Frederick Taylor and ends in the present day, a time when the fields of practice and scholarship in educational leadership collectively stand at a critical, yet not unprecedented, crossroad—the intersection of social justice and scientific management.

In chapter 6, Kathleen S. Sernak examines school reform and the challenges presented to educational leaders working toward social justice. Sernak uses Freire's concept of conscientization, possessing a conscious understanding of one's lived reality, as a framework by which to analyze two particular reforms, *Success for All* and *Professional Development Schools*. She suggests that educational leadership that seeks to liberate students to make social changes creates space for trust, and nurtures participatory, equitable and just relationships rather than simply managing programs and services, and facilitates "the opportunity for empowerment rather than 'delivering it.' "

Mary John O'Hair and Ulrich C. Reitzug expand their research in chapter 7 by examining the K20 Oklahoma Science Initiative for Rural Schools that targets low-income, rural schools serving diverse populations in Oklahoma. One-third of all U.S. school children attend school in rural settings and are much poorer than urban America. Equity is a concern not only in terms of race, class, gender, disability, and sexual orientation, but also in terms of being geographically located in a rural area. These researchers assert that "rural teachers are often not certified in their teaching areas, with one in four rural science teachers lacking in academic preparation or certification."

Part III is presented in three chapters on "Collaborative Partnerships for Social Justice: Communities, Youth, and School-Linked Services." In chapter 8 Lionel H. Brown, Judith I. Larsen, Ruth Britt, Donna M. Ruiz, and Rachel Star trace the collaborative efforts of community educators/ leaders in Cincinnati, following violence in the city in 2001. These authors examine how such efforts might help break the cycle of frustration, failure, and violence that shadow many disadvantaged inner-city African American students. As emphasized in the chapter, "persistent, race-based inequities in urban areas are a major factor in this syndrome and the causes are proposed to be disparity in education, housing, economic opportunity, and political representation."

Chapter 9 draws on the parallel literature on increasing student voice in the field of education and on building youth-adult partnerships in the youth development field. Dana Mitra examines the place of young people in efforts to increase social justice in school settings. Through an examination of 13 youth-adult partnership initiatives, it considers the ways in which students and adults can collaborate to examine issues of equity and injustice that they experience in their lives, in their schools, in their communities, and in broader society. The findings identify that the groups' intended goals focused on addressing issues of equity and social justice on three levels— the system level by focusing on issues of intolerance and injustice, the organizational level by advocating for school change, and the individual level by fostering youth leadership and peer helping.

In chapter 10 Anthony H. Normore and Roger I. Blanco posit that schools must realize that their strength is found in the services they provide for students, parents, and the community members, not as an exclusive academic island unto themselves. These authors suggest that school leaders and their communities commit to collaborative partnerships through school-linked services and delivery systems for the plight of the poor. A review of literature revealed a growing rate of poverty among youth in American inner cities – a poverty which engulfed one in seven youth in 1970, one in six in 1980, one in five in 1990, and one in four in 2000. Research asserts that today, approximately 47 million Americans have no health insurance and out of the 48 million school children in the United States, more than thirteen million are poor.

In Part IV four chapters are presented with focus on "Ethical Leadership and Principles of Social Justice." In chapter 11 Pauline Leonard uses narrative research to share a journey of reflections about one College of Education team's struggle for authenticity in the development of a new educational leadership program. However, the journey takes a turn in light of renewed deliberations about authenticity in the wake of Hurricane Katrina. In the process, relevant ethical leadership and social justice principles are applied to examine, critique, and evaluate this struggle for authenticity. The narrative captures the multifaceted human dimensions embedded in the successes, achievements, challenges, and frustrations of striving for personal and professional integrity.

Chapters 12–14 focus on a movement known as the New DEEL (Democratic Ethical Educational Leadership). Each author presents a different focus. Chapter 12 is presented by Steven J. Gross. Gross describes the emergence of the New DEEL and the role it attempts to play in confronting the excesses of the current accountability movement typified by massive standardized testing and No Child Left Behind (NCLB) legislation in the United States. This chapter depicts the choice facing the field of educational leadership that pits a top-down control regime, modeled after corporations on the one hand against a progressive, democratic-ethical alternative on the other hand. A brief account of the historic traditions of the latter and its ties to the cause of social justice are offered.

In chapter 13 Valerie A. Lee Storey and Thomas E. Beeman argue that New DEEL does not refer to a specific policy or reform, but rather to an ideology, unencumbered by international borders and domestic politics. These authors identify the rhetoric of New DEEL and social justice, and the reality of its implementation in schools today especially in light of NCLB. Specifically, Storey and Beeman postulate that NCLB is a major current impediment to New DEEL and social justice and propose implementing a structure which expands the notion of pedagogy from the four walls of the classroom to a personalized, school-wide strategy.

Joan Shapiro addresses the ethical and social justice implications of New DEEL in chapter 14. Shapiro emphasizes the ethical underpinnings of this movement by focusing on the paradox of control versus democracy. This important paradox is developed through a discussion of the profound contradictions between the accountability thrust and the democratic emphasis in schools, particularly in the United States. Shapiro presents the inconsistencies within the paradox and provides some suggestions for coping with the challenges of blending these two very different and opposing concepts together to illuminate what a New DEEL moral educational leader might value. Focus is in the area of social justice and how an educational leader might guide an organization.

ACKNOWLEDGMENTS

This book could not be made possible without the support of Dr. J. Kent Donlevy (former editor) and Dr. Pamela Bishop (current editor) of the *International Electronic Journal for Leadership in Learning* who granted permission for the reprint of these articles. Sincere gratitude also goes to each of the authors who contributed to this book as well as to those who helped review the original manuscripts. I also wish to thank my friend and colleague, Dr. Jeffrey S. Brooks, President of AERA's Leadership for Social Justice Special Interest Group (SIG) and the executive members of the LSJ SIG for their support and encouragement throughout the development process. Finally, I offer many thanks to Information Age Publishing for the ongoing diligence throughout the publication process. Our hope is that these chapters will serve as catalysts for further discourse about research on leadership, teaching, and learning for social justice. Please feel free to make contact with any of the authors. Their contact information is provided accordingly. On behalf of all contributors, thank you.

Anthony H. Normore, PhD, Associate Professor and Program Development Coordinator of Doctoral Program in Educational Leadership, Graduate Education Division, College of Education, California State University, Dominguez Hills 1000 E. Victoria Street, Carson—Los Angeles California 90747
Phone: 310-243-3925
Fax: 310-516-3326
E-mail: anormore@csudh.edu

PART I

COMMITMENT TO SOCIAL JUSTICE, EQUITY, AND TOLERANCE

CHAPTER 1

A REPOSITORY OF HOPE FOR SOCIAL JUSTICE

Black Women Leaders at Historically Black Colleges and Universities

Gaetane Jean-Marie and Anthony H. Normore

The 1954 ruling of *Brown v. Board of Education* by the U.S. Supreme Court impacted the social lives of African Americans. The primary purpose of this research was to examine the experiences and struggles for social justice in education and educational institutions as viewed from the context of historically Black colleges and universities (HBCU) in one Southeastern state. A corollary purpose was to document and catalogue how four Black female leaders at HBCUs committed to social justice and racial uplift, connect their professional work with social and political activism in the quest for access, equality, and social justice for all. HBCUS are defined as Black academic institutions that were established prior to 1964 whose mission was and continues to be to educate African Americans (Garibaldi, 1984). Through the use of narrative inquiry the personal and professional experiences of four African American women leaders at HBCUs were highlighted. The key findings exemplify how these female leaders survived the struggles of integration, triumphed over barriers in educational settings, and are committed to

Leadership for Social Justice: Promoting Equity and Excellence Through Inquiry and Reflective Practice, pp. 3–35
Copyright © 2008 by Information Age Publishing

advocating for social justice in their roles as transformative leaders at HBCUs.

INTRODUCTION

The social movements over the last 50 years have been tumultuous and turbulent for people of color in the United States (Jean-Marie, 2006). Since *Brown v. Board of Education* in 1954, whereby the decision of the U.S. Supreme Court took scientific research into account in issuing this landmark ruling, negative social attitudes and the status of ethnic and racial groups have been challenged and undergone change (Cottrol, Diamond, & Ware, 2004; Valverde, 2003). Within those 50 years, African Americans, among other groups, confronted obstacles on what they could be and do. African Americans experienced harsh treatments (i.e., racism, sexism, and denied access to formal schooling and higher education) in educational institutions and had to develop unconventional ways to advocate for themselves and those in their community (Jean-Marie, James, & Bynum, 2006). When the 1954 ruling declared that schools should be desegregated with all deliberate speed (Valverde, 2003), the four African American (used interchangeably with Black) women in this study were among the "freedom fighters" who integrated public schools, and later pursued higher education and professional careers (Jean-Marie, 2005).

The primary purpose of this research was to examine the experiences and struggles for social justice in education and educational institutions as viewed from the context of HBCU in one Southeastern state. A corollary purpose was to document and catalogue how four Black female leaders at HBCUs committed to social justice and racial uplift connect their professional work with social and political activism in the quest for access, equality, and social justice for all. HBCUs are defined as Black academic institutions that were established prior to 1964 whose mission was and continues to be to educate African Americans (Garibaldi, 1984).

Consistent with previous research (Morris, 1984), the women leaders in this study came from a tradition of protest across generations by older relatives, Black educational institutions, churches, and protest organizations (Jean-Marie, 2005). The participants' commitment to social justice and racial uplift is related to their own experiences—born, educated, and started their educational career in a segregated America, both *de jure* and later *de facto* (Valverde, 2003).

This paper is organized in the following manner: first, we present a theoretical framework of Black feminist thought, leadership, and social justice, and Foster's (1986, 1989) critical model of leadership; this is followed by the research design (i.e., narrative research). Next, we present findings from the research followed by a summary discussion and conclusions.

THEORETICAL FRAMEWORK

The historic ruling of *Brown v. Board of Education* redefined what public education (i.e., kindergarten to Grade 12 and higher education) should be for people of color in a time when "separate but equal" permeated and dominated social institutions in the United States. The ruling was met with White resistance but African Americans persisted in their struggle to end social injustices by dismantling institutional practices and structures that hindered their advancement in society. As active participants in the Civil Rights Movement, African Americans established commitment and resilience in taking a stand for the ideals of equality and democracy (i.e., school desegregation, voting rights) (Jean-Marie, 2005, 2006; Loder, 2005; Valverde, 2003). Based on the resilience for social justice and racial uplift of African Americans during the Civil Rights era, we present a theoretical perspective that draws from Black feminist thought, leadership, and social justice (see Benham, 1997; Benham & Cooper, 1998; Collins, 1989, 1990; Davis, 1989; Dorn, O'Rourke, & Papalewis, 1997-98; hooks, 1994), and Foster's (1986, 1989) critical model of leadership. Foster offered a lens to analyze the kind of leadership models needed by HBCUs to fulfill its mission. Foster's model is based on: (a) critical leadership as it relates to the symbolic and educational significance of HBCUs, (b) transformative leadership in support of racial uplift and African American women's involvement, and (c) educative and ethical leadership as understood and embedded in the practice of social justice leadership.

Race and Gender: The Black Female Experience

Finding no place in the existing movement and wanting to respond to the racism of White feminist and sexism of Black men, Black women formed separate "Black feminist" groups (hooks, 1981). They sought to create new understanding about African American women to "formulate and rearticulate the distinctive, self-defined standpoint of African-American women" (Collins, 1996, p. 225). They also sought to change the one-dimensional perspectives of women's reality (hooks, 2000). For example, sexism in institutionalized systems, accompanied by disenchantment with the White-dominated feminist movement and Black male scholars' exclusive concern with racial issues (Schiller, 2000) during the Civil Rights Movement, heightened Black women's interest in liberation.

Through these efforts, African American women positioned themselves to engage in critical analysis by articulating their "voices to express a collective, self-defined Black woman's standpoint" (Collins, 2000, p. 99). Voice defines who they are, assists in how ideas are articulated, interprets what their experiences are, and help analyze their coping mechanisms for survival (Jean-Marie, 2004). Consequently, African American women have developed a double consciousness (Collins, 2000) that empowers them to move in and out of public and private spaces. As more African American women continue to make inroads into professions and occupations previously dominated by Euro American women (Mullings, 1997), they will likely impact the representation of African American women of all echelons (i.e., social, financial).

Feminist Consciousness and Afrocentric Epistemology

Women share a history of patriarchal oppression. The persistence of sexism contributes to the exploitation of women (Davis, 1989; Dorn et al., 1997-98). Furthermore, the degree of exploitation is related to social class, race, religion, sexual orientation, and ethnicity (Collins, 1996). Women have a body of knowledge that corresponds with feminist consciousness and epistemology. To understand how Black women's consciousness evolved, an understanding of Afrocentric epistemology (Collins, 2000) is vital. Black women's Afrocentric epistemology contributes to the richness of their African roots that inform what they believe to be true about themselves and their experiences. In an American society that often devalues heritage (see Jean-Marie, 2004), Black women draw from common experiences that historically connect them to the fundamental elements of an Afrocentric epistemology. Because Black people share a common experience of oppression resulting from colonialism, slavery, apartheid, imperialism, and other systems of racial domination (Collins, 1996, 2000), these shared material conditions cultivate Afrocentric values within Black communities throughout the diaspora. As a result, they seep into the family structure, religious institutions, and communities. "The collective history of people of African descent from Africa, Caribbean, and South and North America constitutes an Afrocentric consciousness that permeates through the framework of a distinctive Afrocentric epistemology" (Collins, 2000, p. 228).

Because African American women have access to both the feminist and the Afrocentric epistemology, an alternative epistemology is used to rearticulate Black women's standpoint that reflects elements of both traditions

(Collins, 2000). Black women's epistemology represents a specialized knowledge that provides opportunities to express Black feminist concerns:

> The experiences of African-American women scholars illustrate how individuals who wish to rearticulate a Black women's standpoint through Black feminist thought can be suppressed by prevailing knowledge validation processes. (Collins, 2000, p. 254)

African American women's epistemology deconstructs dominant ideologies that justify, support, and rationalize the interests of those in power (Mullings, 1997). Foster (1986, 1989) advocated a leadership that promotes democratic process and calls for political activism that leads to social justice. As a result, this practice of leading is or can be critical, transformative, educative, and ethical. These elements deserve further analysis to identify the important work involved in a critical perspective of leadership.

Reflection and Reevaluation: Critical Leadership and HBCUs

Foster (1986) proposed that the work of an educational leader involves the building of an inclusive organizational learning community with the central focus on community and culture within the organization. A critical component of this learning community is the development of the organization's ability to engage in self-reflection for purposes of analyzing its *raison d'être*, objectives, goals, and value systems. The leadership Foster (1986, 1989) advocated is one that promotes democratic processes and calls for political activism for social justice. When leadership practices support democracy and action-orientation these become critical, transformative, educative, and ethical (Jean-Marie, 2004). These elements bear further analysis to tease out the important work involved in a critical model of leadership. Based on Foster's (1989) research, critical leadership is defined as a continued analysis of what occurs in an organization with a commitment by those involved to engage in critical reflection and reevaluation of current practices.

During the period when higher education opportunity was almost nonexistent for African Americans, HBCUs played a significance role in the lives of African Americans who wanted to pursue higher learning. They continue to be a driving force for social change and racial uplift (Jean-Marie, 2004, 2006). According to Roebuck and Murty (1993), HBCUs are Black academic institutions that were established prior to 1964, cultural repositories, and educational (Sims, 1994). Their principal mission was, and continues to be, the education of African Americans. Since their inception which dates back to 1854 (Garibaldi, 1984), HBCUs' mission was threefold in their first century. First, they provided education to newly freed slaves that were rich in Black history and tradition. Second, they delivered educational experiences that were consistent with the experiences and values of many Black families. Third, they provided a service to the Black community and the country by aiding in the development of leadership, racial pride, and return service to the community (Sims, 1994). Located throughout the United States, HBCUs symbolize models that educate underserved and underrepresented individuals who traditionally do not have access to institutions of higher learning (Heath, 2001; Verharen, 1996). Making higher education accessible for every capable individual without compromising quality is an important imperative for HBCUs that continues today (Jean-Marie, 2006).

Verharen (1996) argues that a college education is the right of every competent citizen and HBCUs pave the way through outreach programs and educational resources to make higher learning obtainable to African Americans. In an era of increased standardization where potential limits regarding who should have access to higher learning, other factors beyond traditional criteria (i.e., SAT scores, grade point average, class ranking, financial resources, etc.) ought to be considered to make "quality education available for those who would not otherwise have the opportunity" (Verharen, 1996, p. 53). Among institutions of higher learning, HBCUs seek to bridge the gap between the haves and the have-nots by engaging in critical leadership practices (Jean-Marie, 2006). These practices should center on the diverse needs of their student population (financial and educational resources, and other institutional challenges that impact students' success). Many university leaders draw from past experiences to change practices that have deterred the success of students and the progressivism in the Black community.

Beyond universal education for all, HBCUs continue to serve as educational citadels and cultural repositories for the African American community, as well as centers for social and political development of students, faculty and communities, regions and states in which they are located (Sims, 1994). Although HBCUs were established to serve the educational needs of African Americans, today they serve students from a wide range of cultural, racial, ethnic, and socioeconomic backgrounds. HBCUs not only have racially diverse student populations but many also have a racially diverse faculty and administration. With respect to their enrollment and staff, HBCUs are presently more racially desegregated than historically White institutions (Roebuck & Murty, 1993).

Given the limited research on the significance of HBCUs in higher education, Verharen (1996) proposes a renewed charge for HBCUs in their second century. He states:

HBCUs are strong enough to accept their higher mission: to design models that make radical departures from mainstream education. The radical nature of the problems faced by members of communities that make the existence of HBCUs possible justifies these new models. (p. 53)

Racial Uplift and the African American Woman: Transformative Leadership

Transformative leadership is about social change with a belief that transformation is a process that occurs over time (Avolio & Gibbons, 1988; Bass, 1985; Burns, 1978; House, 1976; Leithwood, Jantzi, & Steinbach, 1999; Tichy & DeVanna, 1990; Weber, 1947). The transformation is not only in structures but also with leaders and participants. Foster (1989) asserts that transformation encourages and supports a willingness to examine one's life, ideas, and causes to develop a critical framework for leadership. The Civil Rights Movement was transformative and heightened awareness of access, equality and social justice. Many researchers (Foster, 1986, 1989; Grogan, 1994; Jean-Marie, 2006; Leithwood et al., 1999; Tichy & DeVanna, 1990; Weber, 1947) reiterate that transformative leaders are needed at HBCUs to be the voice of social change and influence policy decisions (Shakeshaft, 1993) that impact who can and cannot have access to higher education. The transformation is not only in structures but also with leaders and followers. The Civil Rights Movement campaigned for equal rights for people of color and women, securing equal opportunity for employment, and providing access to education. HBCUs, as a social institution, have provided transformative leadership throughout African American history. Verharen (1996) emphasized the use of institutional power by educational leaders in HBCUs: "Choosing the un-chosen must come from individuals rather than institutions ... we must make sure every member of the community is welcomed in the community ... we must make sure that someone is joyfully awaiting every infant" (p. 54).

When the U.S. Supreme Court ruled in *Brown v. Board of Education* that segregation in public schools was illegal, Blacks were confronted with the opportunity and responsibility to lead and seek the racial integration of public schools and higher education. For many, it was not a matter to deliberate; it had to be done, thus the beginning of their commitment to advance social justice. In the history of African Americans, many men and women emerged as leadership figures to fight against decades of oppression and injustices that people of color encountered in American society. Among the men included in the movements for racial solidarity and Black Nationalism were Curtis Hayes, Willie Peacock, MacArthur Cotton, Charlie Cobb, Bob Moses, Thurgood Marshall, Amzie Moore, Malcolm X,

and Martin Luther King, Jr. (Normore, 2006). Black communities organized for change as a force to transform race relations in America (Gordon, 2000; Jean-Marie, 2005; Morris, 1994). However, historical accounts
too often excluded the contributions of African American women in the
social movements. Although the contributions of African American
women sometimes went unrecorded, significant progress has been made
highlighting the contributions and leadership of African American
women such as Emma Bell, Ida Mae "Cat" Holland, and Mateo "Flookie"
Suarez (Hine, 1994; Normore, 2006) in these movements.

Valverde's (2003) interviews exploring the perspectives of young African American men in White programs of study conclude that their strong
character building was informed by their early life experiences:

> A major character-forming experience for these African-American higher
> education leaders was their involvement in the Civil Rights Movement dur-
> ing the 1960s. Their early values and hopes nurtured by family, church, and
> teachers as role models were reinforced by leaders of the Civil Rights Move-
> ment. (p. 77)

Similarly, African American women's characters were also informed by the
Civil Rights Movement. Many became deeply involved in social change
activities and were committed to the ideals of equality and democracy
(Hine, 1994; Robnett, 1997; Valverde, 2003). When educational institutions provided inferior equipment and inadequate facilities, many African
American women took the initiatives to make up the difference. They
used their creativity and knowledge of the world, inside and outside formal educational processes, to mentor African Americans in their communities so that they can be successful, educated, and respected (Jean-Marie,
2006; Jean-Marie et al., 2006). Young African Americans did not only
learn the standard curriculum, but they were taught community ethics,
racial pride, and how to protect themselves from the potential brutality
that await them in a White dominated society.

African American women have gained more opportunities to be
appointed leadership roles in higher education institutions. Lee and
McKerrow (2005) assert there is a renewed interest in social justice and
many women in leadership are advancing its causes:

> As women achieve positions of influence and participate in policy decisions,
> they have opportunities to open up access to knowledge and resources to
> those with less power. Women from all levels of the social hierarchy, not just
> those with official status positions, have a role in social justice leadership. As
> social justice leaders, women work to alter the undemocratic culture and
> structure of institutions and society, improving the lives of those who have
> been marginalized or oppressed. (p. 1)

While a review of the literature on leadership and/or social justice does not present a clear definition of social justice, there is a general framework for delineating social justice leadership. Lee and McKerrow (2005) offer such framework in two dimensions. First, social justice is defined "not only by what it is but also by what it is not, namely injustice. By seeking justice, we anticipate the ideal. By questioning injustice, we approach it. Integrating both, we achieve it" (p. 1). The second dimension focuses on the practice of social justice: Individuals for social justice seek to challenge political, economic, and social structures that privilege some and disadvantage others. They challenge unequal power relationships based on gender, social class, race, ethnicity, religion, disability, sexual orientation, language, and other systems of oppression.

As African American women make gains in educational attainment and inroads into professions and occupations previously dominated by Euro American women (Mullings, 1997; Schiller, 2000) and men, they continue to impact the representation of African American women of all echelons (i.e., social and financial). Their entry into these traditional settings, however, will present challenges—isolation, exclusion from informal networks, and systemic discrimination (Glazer-Ramo, 2001). Like their predecessors' (i.e., Sojourner Truth, Anna Julia Cooper, Rosa Parks, Harriet Tubman, Ella Baker) commitment to social justice and resilience to thrive in the face of adversities, these African American women leaders are vigilant but prudent and attentive in their struggle for justice. Their predecessors believed the cause was as equally important for them and generations to come. When communities were segregated by race, many African American women embraced and accepted the social responsibility of ensuring that African American children had the necessary tools to be successful in a world that would deny them a quality of life (Jean-Marie et al., 2006; Jean-Marie, 2005):

> Just as Frances Harper (1866, para. 35) declared in her speech, "We are all bound up together": "Born of a race whose inheritances has been outraged and wrong, most of my life had been spent in battling those wrongs" and Sojourner Truth's famous "Ain't I a Woman?" speech given at the Women's Rights Convention Center, so too do African-American women leaders continue the fight for social justice. How they fulfill that commitment is through their leadership practices. (Jean-Marie, 2005, n.p.)

Discourse and Democratic Values: Educative and Ethical Leadership

Also important to Foster's (1986, 1989) critical model of leadership is educative leadership. According to Foster (1986), an educative leader "presents both an analysis and a vision, and devotes time to examine [institutional] history, purpose, and responsibilities" (p. 186). Engaging in discourse involves working as a community and being willing to listen and reciprocate leadership responsibilities. Through discourse, diverse viewpoints from all members are heard; the institution, as a result moves in a direction of shared vision and practices where ethical leadership is brought to the fore. Leadership for ethics, morals, and values involves moral relationships and is intended to elevate people to new levels of morality (Foster, 1989), including maintenance of democratic values within a community. The role of a leader is to create other leaders who can assume leadership roles, and leaders can become followers when the situation calls for communal exchange. Furman and Shields (2005) argue the "need for social justice to encompass education that is not only just, democratic, emphatic, and optimistic, but also academically excellent" (as cited in Firestone & Riehl, 2005, p. 123). Leaders for social justice seek to challenge political, economic, and social structures that privilege some and disadvantage others. They challenge unequal power relationships based on gender, social class, race, ethnicity, religion, disability, sexual orientation, language, and other systems of oppression. According to Lee and McKerrow (2005):

> theory and practice, advocacy and action to counter injustice have emerged from civil rights, feminist, postmodern, critical, multicultural, queer, postcolonial, and other movements.... Grounded in these movements, social justice leaders strive for critique rather than conformity, compassion rather than competition, democracy rather than bureaucracy, polyphony rather than silencing, inclusion rather than exclusion, liberation rather than domination, action for change rather than inaction that preserves inequity. (pp. 1–2)

Lee and McKerrow (2005) postulate the necessary acts for which leaders committed to social justice ought to engage in. Whether it is at an HBCU or a predominantly White institution the purpose of education institutions is to citizens of a society to give back to that society for the greater good. HBCUs lead such efforts and challenge other institutions to fulfill similar promise. But, this mission necessitates leaders who have a moral compass to lead the way (Gordon, 2000).

In summary, the literature presented here highlights the interconnectedness of Black feminist theories, social justice, and critical leadership as applied to the advancement of women leaders of color. In light of issues facing women in the workplace, gaining access to and permission to share stories of Black women leaders at HBCUs who are leading for social justice requires a "great deal of trust ... because the process of sharing is a political action" (Lawson-Sanders, Campbell-

Smith, & Benham, 2006, p. 34). Based on the literature, this approach to generating further understanding of Black female experiences represents a fruitful way for researchers to create opportunities to examine more deeply the lives of women leaders at HBCUs and to move beyond valorizing the niceties of feminine values to a deeper embrace of feminism that attends to the issues of social justice (Benham & Cooper, 1998; Collins, 1990; hooks, 1994) and Foster's (1986, 1989) critical model of leadership.

RESEARCH DESIGN

Consistent with other research on the use of narrative (e.g., Benham & Cooper, 1998; Casey, 1993; 1995-96; Clandinin & Connelly, 1994; Lawson-Sanders et al., 2006), this study was conducted through the use of narrative inquiry by studying the life stories of four African American women. Lawrence-Lightfoot's (1994) use of narrative in her research and writing confirms its suitability for this type of study. She contends that the Black culture is rooted in stories by stating that "a strong and persistent African American tradition links the process of narrative to discovering and attaining identity ... and serves as a deep source of resonance" (p. 606). This method assumes that "people's lives are stories, and the researcher seeks to collect data to describe those lives" (Lawson-Sanders et al., 2006, p. 63) and provides the means to record and interpret (Riessman, 1993) the voices of women (Benjamin, 1997; Fonow & Cook, 1991; Gilligan, 1982, Gluck & Patai, 1992; Reinharz, 1992). The participants' backgrounds, education, experiences, church, and family that informed their identities were highlighted.

Cooper (1995), and Benham and Cooper (1998) asserted that stories speak of the power of narrative in human lives. Cooper maintained that "stories can be retold, reframed, reinterpreted and because they are fluid, open for retelling and ultimately reliving, they are the repositories of hope" (p. 121). According to Benham and Cooper "narrative methods might very well be more responsive to the researcher's and practitioner's intent to bring to the surface those experiences that go beyond superficial masks and stereotypes" (p. 7). In this study, the stories of the women's interpretations of their leadership practices revealed how they were experts and authors of their own lives. As a focus on who and a specific setting in which social justice leadership is practiced, these four African American female leaders at HBCUs provide a snapshot view of stories of justice, leadership, and racial uplift. These women leaders advance social justice, espouse the belief that democracy matters, and exemplify the torchbearers of democratic ideals. As leaders for learning in HBCUs, they provide a particular scope of the challenges, struggles and, successes they experience.

Participants and Context

The data in this study are part of an earlier study on twelve African American women leaders. For the purpose of this discussion, the analysis will focus on four African American women leaders. Pseudonyms identified participants to minimize disclosure of information about individual lives. The participants are Deans Frazier and Miller, Dr. Giddens, a former dean and department chair, and President Murphy. All of them except Dr. Giddens have taught in public schools prior to their experience in higher education. Two of the women's educational experiences were both at historically Black and White institutions; Dr. Giddens attended only historically Black institutions to pursue her studies, and Dr. Miller obtained her degrees from historically White institutions. These leaders presently serve in the capacity of deans of school of education, faculty (a former dean and department chair), and university president at four historically Black colleges in the Southeastern United States.

Because every text has a context (Casey, 1993), the personal backgrounds of the women's narratives are essential to understanding their self-definitions. These African American women participants grew up in southern parts of the United States during a period in history in which the social and political climates were in upheaval. For some, the "separate but equal" applied, while others experienced the unsettling changes in the early years of desegregation. The expectations of families and members of the African American community for Black young adults to attend college and further their education weighed heavily on these women's shoulders. One participant summed her college experience: "I felt like I was carrying the weight of my race on my back. I constantly felt that I had to do well because if I didn't, I would be letting my people down. It is a big burden to carry."

Semistructured Interview Questions

In the interviews, participants were asked an opening question: "Tell me your life story by reflecting on your personal life in relationship to your professional experiences." The ensuing story, or "main narrative," was not interrupted by further questions but was encouraged by means of nonverbal and paralinguistic expressions of interest and attention, such as "mhm" (Rosenthal, 1993). In the second part of the interview, the "period of questioning," more elaborate narrations on topics and biographical events were discussed. The interviews were one to two hours each; on occasion, another appointment was schedule to continue the interviews. This was due to time constraints relating to the participants' schedule and professional commitments.

FINDINGS

We introduce women whose elementary and secondary educational foundations were formed at the cusp of segregation in American schools (i.e., fewer resources, lack of funding, and limited teachers and classrooms). Coming of age was inextricably linked to the larger changing consciousness of these African American women who challenged the existing social order in new ways (Ladson-Billings, 1997; Robnett, 1997). Several key findings emerged from the data analysis. These findings are presented in the following sections based on the analysis of data. Within these sections, we also present subthemes. Figure 1.1 presents a diagram of how the data is reported.

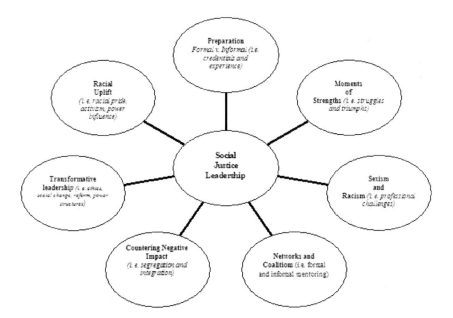

Figure 1.1.   A repository of hope: Black leaders at HBCUs.

Transformative Leadership

Preparing students to achieve their personal and professional goals was a central concern to the women in this study. Collectively, these leaders viewed their students as the children of the community. They had a particular concern regarding the overall development of their students. Having experience as department chair and dean, Dr. Giddens talked about the struggles of many of her college students:

> Since I've come there, it has always been a struggle to develop students because of the students that we serve and the environment - lack of equipment and resources, trying to work with faculty members who don't care [and] students [who] don't have initiative and drive. That has been a struggle to truly do that. It has been a struggle for me to even remain at [HBCU], knowing the potential that I have, but I stay there for the students. I could go some other place but, I truly love the students there. And the struggles, my struggles have been personal.
>
>   I look at back at a lot and I am learning to negotiate with the world that we have now, but I don't forget. I can't forget what we grew up with and what I have seen in my life and know to be real. I can't forget that, but my kids don't know that so they can't relate to it. So in a way it is good but that is the only reason I would go to a White school so I could help Blacks understand where they came from.

According to Dean Frazier,

> My students at this university are students I know that most other universities would not touch. Not because they don't have the ability, because they do and you have to reach inside and pull that ability out. But because [college personnel] have such high standards, they feel like "Well we just don't have to bother with that student." That's the kind of student that we have here. We have all kinds of students here. We also have students that have had all kinds of experiences, and I believe that there is an opportunity to give credit for a lot of experiences.

The participants also expressed concern about the lack of academic preparation students receive prior to matriculating to higher education. Many HBCU campuses are aware of their students' lack of academic preparedness and seek to provide needed resources to help them. One initiative of Dr. Murphy's, the first female president of a private HBCU, was a policy decision that would impact many students' educational experience. Although a major undertaking and with resistance from her governing board and staff, President Murphy developed a plan to attract African American students who ordinarily would not be admitted to her private university or any other higher education institution (i.e., low SAT scores and grade point average; limited to no financial resources). Her approached was:

> Next year, we're going to start what we're calling a pilot program and admit about 150 of our freshmen class. They will be kids who may not have good SAT scores or have all the credentials, but somebody in that community whether it is in the school or the church says, "This is a kid to take a chance on. Trust me. Take a chance on this kid." We are going to admit this kid and introduce them to a curriculum that is outside the box.... We are going to prove that by staying close to the mission—that is, if you provide access to education for kids, SAT scores mean absolutely nothing. It is potential that makes a difference. That is the real predictor of how well kids are going to succeed.

Garnering the support of the local community, schools, and churches, she identified and admitted 150 students who ordinarily would not have attended college. Understanding that these students would confront numerous challenges to complete their academic studies, she developed a five-year program that included year-round academic support, remedial classes, financial resources, and mentoring for the students she admitted. This act of tenacity illuminated her commitment to social justice advocacy which she started in her early teaching career. Only this time, she was in a leadership position to implement educational programs for disadvantaged African Americans. President Murphy asserted, "We're going to take a kid who nobody else thinks they ought to take a chance on except some momma, some daddy, some preacher, some teacher or some faculty member. We're going to educate them." President Murphy has taken the lead in guiding her university and constituents to a level where social inequities are addressed and access to education for all students is a priority.

When Dr. Miller, dean of a school of education, transitioned from public education as a former superintendent to dean, she was not prepared for the mismatch she saw between what her faculty taught and preservice teachers' knowledge and skills to pass the PRAXIS, a certification test for prospective teachers. Prior to her appointment, the report card and PRAXIS scores of students for the college were low. The college also lacked funding to develop and sustain initiatives for the preparation and training of preservice teachers. Similar to her previous administrative and teaching positions, she was a fearless leader and outspoken about what directions the school of education needed to go in. She admitted that this was the first position she was in that was not supportive of her leadership efforts:

> In meetings, I've had to say "That is not the right thing to do. We have to be accredited and this is what we are going to do." I have had to speak out in a

lot of meetings with administration. I had to set my priorities about [what] the school of education needed. I ran into problems.... But, through hard work we accomplished many initiatives. Our PRAXIS scores were among the first to go up for an HBCU and we turned the reputation around for this school of education. We went from a lot of weaknesses to no weaknesses on our NCATE visit. We were the only institution in this state to have the teacher quality enhancement grant. We also had the [name] scholarship program and the PreK–3 Tech Teach grant. When I came here, we had no grants. Now, we have two multi-million dollar grants.

Racial Uplift

Whether in their formal professional roles as educators in public education to their recent roles as leaders in HBCUs, the participants articulated a leadership that is tied to social change, institutional reform, and structures and processes of power and influence—what the Civil Rights Movement was about. Their involvement and ongoing interactions with students, staff, constituents at their institutions, and community characterize a social and political activism that is reminiscent of leadership practices of their predecessors of the Civil Rights Movement. For President Murphy, she described her leadership characteristic as one that involves putting together a team of people of different strengths:

> I've got to make sure I've got people working that do enjoy it and who are good at it. I am continuously encouraging others to think outside of the box. I think that I'm a leader that validates people's strengths and competencies.

Her expectations were based on high standards and quality education for students because anything less compromises the opportunities her university students seek. The ultimate goal was giving students the best education possible. Murphy held the highest ideal of education and believed 'all' students, whether they have the means or not, should be given the opportunity to succeed and become contributing members of society.

Drawing from her experiences in a large urban school district to her current role as a dean, Miller approached her leadership practices as a collective by encouraging others to be leaders. Articulating her leadership approach, she asserted:

> Often times, I bring people in and want them to initiate things. I want them to be leaders but they wait for me to bring ideas to the fore. I challenge them to bring ideas in the concept stage in our discussions. I try to bring

people who have a common vision and we know where we are going. I don't want to micro-manage people.

At times the participants challenged their administration about the direction they were going and the lack of vision on what they are to achieve. For Giddens, she raised concerns about what students were learning in the natural sciences. She stated:

> Students were allowed to graduate with Ds in chemistry and they couldn't write. Students weren't going to class and learning. I just couldn't understand it. So when I became chair, I wrote two grants. Both of them were awarded and brought half a million dollars to the school ... I didn't want any students to leave the natural sciences with anymore Ds in chemistry. I made some enemies and wasn't worried about that. I wanted to provide students with what they needed ... I had a vision for the division. The faculty was going to teach. Over time, I gained the respect of faculty and students. We started getting students into medical school and enrichment research programs all over the country.

For Frazier, she believed that HBCUs served an important purpose for students of color. She declared:

> Send them to an HBCU where people will take time to cultivate them, mold them and be a good level of comfort for them and then send them out and they are prepared with confidence to go out in the world and make contributions.

The people she referred to who will "cultivate," "mold," "comfort," and [build] "confidence" are not only performing their designated roles as teachers and administrators, but also are nurturers to the "children" [the students]. Each of the school's personnel plays an integral part in the village—rearing of African American students. The "village" concept is crucial to the development of students who attend Dean Frazier's institution. Not only is it a "village" for students but also one for the professionals to grow in as well. In recognition that many students come from "impoverished homes and backgrounds," she stated:

> We felt it was our responsibility to bring these students and help them with language, help them with basic academic skills. But equally important is to help them understand the culture and how the culture was changing because culture is dynamic.

Developing students cannot be accomplished without the contribution of the "we" and "our" of everyone included in the task. The "village" calls forth all who has a specific role to play in the development of each student. Frazier asserted,

> Bring them into that village called [HBCU] and work with them! Also prepare them to do as the eagle does the little eaglets: make you secure and warm in that environment but at some time let you know you got to go back into the larger culture. It prepares you for that larger culture by giving you good skills and then giving you a piece of confidence that says, "You can go out, you can survive."

Similar to the other participants, Frazier did not view her profession as mere work but rather as means of providing a purpose for the Black community. She displayed compassion for her students that went beyond the call of duty of an administrator. Her effort has had significance for her. The mother-tongue she used—"cultivate," "mold," "comfort," "secure," "warm," "prepare"—were descriptors of a nurturing person who is genuinely interested in the development of [Black] students. She reported building confidence into students entering the world of work and compelling them to contribute to their communities. She was continuing an African American interpretive tradition of her predecessors. Although manifested in different ways, all four of the participants continued the struggle of African Americans to achieve freedom, equity and equality.

Moments of Strengths: Personal and Professional Struggles

The African American women's experiences during the 1960s and 1970s shaped their professional work at their universities. All four of the women talked about incidences of injustices that they directly or indirectly experienced in their personal and professional lives. President Murphy's path to fight inequities and injustices was carved out soon after she graduated from college and started her first year of teaching:

> It was the first year [city] had mass busing and I taught in an elementary school. It was set on a hill in the middle of an all White neighborhood and they [school officials] bussed kids from the poorest section of [city] to one of the more affluent communities in [city]. It was a more unlikely match you could have made. Those [African American] kids endured a horrendous and horrific year. I was the youngest teacher on staff by 23 years and I was the only one of four African Americans. I watched what was happening to those kids who didn't have anyone to stand up for them. I then realized what happens to people who look like me but who didn't grow up charmed and have an advocate to address their injustices.... It was at that point I realized there was a whole population of people that didn't have an advocate.

Witnessing the struggles of disadvantaged children in the African American community, Murphy felt compelled to be the lonesome voice and risked her job to challenge the daily inequities she witnessed. Despite her failed attempts to change the conditions of these students while a teacher at the school, she became more determined to be a voice for underrepresented children and have done so throughout her years in public and higher education.

For Dean Miller, she stated that she had "a little struggle in college only in terms of race. She also talked about the lack of support she received from her now, ex-husband when she decided to pursue a career:

> I was a young mother and wife and didn't have any real career plans in those early years of my life. When my daughter was a toddler, I had this feeling of being too dependent on my husband I didn't like asking for things, getting an allowance, and not owning my own car. I announced one day that I was going back to work. My neighbor watched my daughter so I can go back to teaching…. It wasn't so much that I had this urge for a career but I had an urge for independence. The only way I knew how to have that independence and at least in my marriage, was to work.

Returning to work to teach presented many opportunities and challenges. She also went to graduate school and when she worked on her doctorate, she traveled 2 hours and 40 minutes each way, one night a week. Her determination to accomplish her professional goals prevailed. Miller not only completed her doctoral degree but her dissertation received national acclaim on the front page of *USA Today*.

Similar to Miller's personal and professional struggles, Giddens discussed the difficulty in finding work after completing her graduate studies. She later gave birth to a son and experienced a divorce in the early years of her professional career. She too received little support to pursue graduate school from her husband while they were married. She said, "When I told my husband I was going to school, he objected." But, she went anyway and took night classes. At times she brought her son to class and one professor was very supportive of her. As she recalled,

> I'll never forget Dr. [professor] who taught my biology class. He would leave his office open so I took [son] in his office and breast fed him and kept taking notes because I could hear him outside. That's how I did [it].

As a former administrator, Giddens talked about the challenges she encountered in her leadership roles. In sharing her story, she told of her unrelenting dependence on God for guidance during her years:

I wasn't the right kind of administrator, because I was very vocal and when it came to my faculty I was very outspoken. When it came to my students, I was very, very passionate. And I would just think, and know you were supposed to think about what you're going to say. But oh, if you bothered my students or if you messed with my faculty, I just forgot about this thing called diplomacy. I would pray to God, "God please help me hold my tongue or teach me to be different. I need to learn tact."

Disapproving of how administration conducted the "business as usual" she felt compelled to go "back down the hill;" a return to the college classroom. She stated:

I'm leaving this white house up here and I'm going back down the hill so I can do what I want to do and I can be effective.... So I said: I'm getting out of this mess. Anybody else wants to come up here and be crazy if they can. I don't care ... I'm not happy here. I don't like administration. I'm not able to do some things I want to do. I want to go back to the classroom so that I can do what I need to do for my students. I need to go where I know I can make a difference.

Her rhetoric on the "white house" implied how some faculty perceive the friction between administration and faculty. For example, administrators were critiqued for setting themselves apart from the members in the university community. There was very little collaboration between administration, faculty, students, and staff. Her experience led her to conclude that academics were not always a priority: "We were down on list number 8." Consequently, she has had to "defend and fight for faculty." It became too exhausting to be in a constant battle with other administrators whose agenda differed; she decided at that point, it was time for her to leave her administrative position. However, Giddens saw the classroom as the venue where she could have an effect on students. As she said, "Not everyone who is given leadership responsibilities finds it to be a rewarding experience;" fortunately, she was able to return to where she was most needed and could make a difference. Giddens said: "God told me that when you get to a place that you don't enjoy coming to work; it is time to leave. I knew then it was time for me to go."

Not only were personal tribulations of the African American leaders influential in their social justice advocacy but they also watched and observed their parents and family members' stance on injustices. These experiences also had a tremendous impact on them. Murphy called her mother and grandmother " 'crusaders' who fought a lot of causes and engaged me primarily to help fight those causes."

Countering the Negative Impact

Giddens offered a special perspective on the damage caused by deseg-regation practices. In addition to disliking administration, her reason for returning to the classroom as a biology professor was connected to what she saw as the damage caused by desegregation. Desegregation unquestionably was a detriment to Black people. She contended that many in the African American community suffered even more because of desegregation:

> For me, the reason I'm so compassionate and committed to my students and people may look at me when I say it, but I do say it, integration was not the best thing for my race. I grew up segregated, in a segregated school, but with that segregation, I had the best teachers. Teachers who knew how to talk, who knew how to teach with what they had and they taught you. You learned. They didn't skip over this and skip over that. We had second hand materials, but we were taught well and I remember that. I didn't take educa-tion for granted or didn't have this instant gratification.

She noted that a quality education was paramount to the success of Black people. "To know how to talk" which translated to formal English means acquiring proper education as the entryway to upward mobility. Black teachers during her educational experience understood the signifi-cance of providing formal education to Black children. Knowing how to read and write meant increased opportunities to further one's status in American society.

Desegregation, according to Giddens' perspective, placed African Americans at a disadvantage. The necessity to provide high-quality educa-tion to Black students was threatened. The quality of education deterio-rated for Black people because their interests were not a priority for many White teachers who taught in the Black community. Dr. Giddens com-mented:

> We get the teachers now who don't know how to teach the students and the teachers are afraid to teach the Black students. So they have developed things. They're trying to still tell us that we are not intelligent and we cannot learn so they have developed this easy way out. Like, I hate this thing called Ebonics. They are going to tell my race of children that they can't learn their own English language but you can get a foreigner to come and they learn our English language. The White students can learn the English lan-guage, but all we can do, we can speak is street talk and do Ebonics. I hate that. Then we bought into that and then we can't teach our children because we don't have the same books and we don't have this that the Whites have. Yes we can!

Giddens compared her educational experience to that of her younger brother, whose educational experience was described as going in a downward slope. "Integration was not the best thing for my people."

White people's assumptions about Black students' intellectual competence resulted in many being placed in lower level classes, thus actually causing them to drop out of school or to graduate without receiving a good education. Giddens witnessed these incidents not only in her years of teaching, but also during her younger sibling's educational experience. Her concerns, which were also her fears about the continual deterioration of Black people, carried over to her son's schooling years. She became involved in his experiences to ensure he would have an alternative outcome. She is committed to changing the conditions of students who come to her classroom. Both Giddens and Frazier suggested encouraging more African Americans to pursue the field of teaching. African Americans can retain the culture of their communities and provide quality education for all children.

Racism and Sexism

In addition to the personal and familial injustices these women experienced, they also experience challenges (i.e., racism and sexism) in their professional settings. This was a common refrain among many of the participants in the larger study on African American women administrators. According to Giddens, she encountered sexist and racist experiences among Black people and White people. In sharing her experiences as leader, she talked about some of the challenges she has had to overcome:

> As a Black woman trying to lead in an environment that is historically dominated by men, you learn quickly that negotiating with them is the best approach. And, sometimes you don't get the same recognition that a man does. It makes you mad. But, you figure out a way to press on.... Sexism is real. Racism is real. I've experience that. Some of it is subtle. Some of it is overt. But, I have tried to learn from it and process it in constructive ways, so I wouldn't let it bruise me so much that I couldn't go on.

When asked to elaborate on her life struggles, President Murphy responded:

> You know I didn't talk about those because a lot of times you can focus on the negative and loose sight of the positive. In the overall scheme of things, I encountered struggles that related to gender, race, economics, and with being a single parent. But when I look back right now, if I were to die today, I would be very happy with the life that I have had ... I really am not one to

focus on the negative. I much prefer to focus on what is good and what is possible.

Miller and Giddens also talked about challenges they faced because of their race. All four women confronted prejudices and resistance during the transitional years of integration, and encountered racists and sexists demarcations within historically Black and White institutions (i.e., as students and professionals). They credit these experiences for igniting their commitment to social justice and advocacy for all children.

Coalitions and Networks of Influence

A common refrain from the participants was the formal and informal mentoring they received as they ascended the career ladder. Miller's network of mentoring was from what she called, "a White male network" and her mobility to relocate enhanced her career opportunities:

I was in the middle of a White male network as an African American female. It started with my White dissertation advisor. The superintendent in [city] worked with me while working on my doctorate and gave me the opportunity to consult with the school district. I got a call to [city] Georgia by a White male superintendent who said I want to get to know you. He later hired me in my first senior level job as assistant superintendent for [county]. I got a called from [city] North Carolina superintendent who invited me to interview for the associate superintendent position…. I continue to be a colleague with the superintendent.

Reflecting a little more on her experience in [city] North Carolina, she indicated this was one of her best experiences. She asserted that she had a lot of autonomy to create and initiate:

[PE] was a White male and I was a Black female but we believe in certain things for the [city] schools. We believe in maintaining desegregation even at a higher risk. We believed in site-based management. We believe in disaggregating test scores and looking at the performance of African American and poor kids. We were ahead of times. We were doing this in 1985…. The three male assistant superintendent weren't thrilled about [PE] bringing me in over them. But, [PE] and I had a good enough working relationship to get things done.

Later in Miller's career, her name was referred to a search firm by a former superintendent and she was recruited to become superintendent of schools in [city], Ohio. She stated, "It was one of the largest, most troubled school districts in the United States."

In contrast to Miller, Dean Frazier asserted that the informal mentoring she received in her career—moving from an instructor to dean—helped shape where she is now. She stated:

Professors [at her 1st HBCU] such as Dr. [name] set a pace for me and encouraged me to develop in my career ... I was also given opportunities to advance far beyond what some other junior professors would have been able to advance, in particular at a historically White institution ... [HBCU] represented what I think of when we say a village. It was truly a village where we grew as professionals, but equally important, the students who came to [HBCU] also excelled, graduated and went out to make a difference in the lives of others. Just like my mentors set high expectations for me, I do the same for my students ... I have evolved throughout my professional career ... worked closely with AACTE and NCATE.

Similarly, Giddens asserted:

I started as an instructor of biology in [HBCU] and moved up to assistant professor. Then I was told I couldn't advance any further until I had my doctorate. I said, 'when somebody gives me some money then I'll go get my doctorate'. Dr. [name] encouraged me to go. I was nervous to go back to school. He told me, "I was good as anybody else." So, I went to pursue my doctorate.

Murphy talked about her mentors who helped her to progress in her professional career. One person she credited in particular was an African American woman:

I met a woman named [EJ] who became a mentor and got me into consulting. For about five or six years, I worked constantly doing diversity workshops for the American Association of School Administrators, Association for Supervision, Curriculum and Development and, others. I did workshops for [state], which really got me on the circuit and I met a lot of people that way. But [EJ] was a person who believed that you should always replace yourself. She was an advocate for African American superintendents and other administrators. She put people and networks together. She was just an extraordinary person. She gave me my first turtle as a symbol of the risk taker.... In order to progress, you must be willing to stick your neck out and put your tail on the line.

Frazier also credited the church for mentoring her and influencing her as an adolescent growing up. She expressed the importance of the Black church:

And what I suspect that I had coming out of the Black church—that children don't have now—is an opportunity for *speaking*, for *making presentations*, for *learning how to present ideas and activities* that we probably don't have at this time. And that is the missing part, I think, for young children who are developing in the African American community.

The Black church has been a central figure in the lives of many Black people during tumultuous periods in history. Church was the opportunity for large masses of people to congregate, not only for religious and spiritual purposes, but also for social activities, community building, and intellectual exchange. A deterioration of the Black church's influence in the lives of African Americans is associated with the changing times after desegregation. A number of Black families have moved away from "Black" neighborhoods because of upward social mobility.

African American women, whose foundations are strongly tied to their religious traditions, link the declining presence of the Black church in the lives of African Americans to the decline of Black communities. All four women in the study made reference to the opportunity to pass on the "culture," "traditions," "heritage," "legacy," and "intellectual capital" of the Black community and how this is threatened because of the disconnection between church and community. Church is likely to be the only institution where large masses of African Americans from different socioeconomic backgrounds congregate. The church may provide models of successful Black people for children.

DISCUSSION AND CONCLUSIONS

As leaders of HBCUs, the African American women in this study have committed themselves to guiding marginalized students of all races to a level of academic and personal success. Consistent with previous research (e.g., Benham & Cooper, 1998; Jean-Marie, 2006; Valverde, 2003), the imprint they wanted to leave on students is for them to become academically competent in their professions, intellectually informed about social issues, culturally knowledgeable, and socially attentive to their own community as well as to the larger society. In accepting the responsibility to lead at their universities, these women integrated new critical awareness, reflective inquiry, and discourse to transform practices that hinder students from equitable access to education. They articulated an ethic of care and support of students; they embody a collective mission borne out of their advocacy for social justice, thus to not let the past be repeated. Furthermore, they used their creativity and knowledge of the world, through the formal and informal education processes, to show adolescents in their institutions that they can be successful, educated, and respected. Their students do not only learn the standard curriculum of school, but they are taught community ethics, racial pride, and how to protect themselves from the brutality that awaits them in a White dominated world.

For the African American women leaders in this study, being first in their families to obtain a higher education and represent the African American community is indicative of what altered the economical, intellectual, and social capital of African Americans. The discrimination experienced by these women was present in their pursuit of terminal degrees, in their teaching profession, and in administrative roles. Some encountered racism and sexism within historically White and Black institutions by White men, White women, and Black men. Racism and sexism may be so fused in a given situation that it is difficult to tell which is which (Moses, 1997). Despite these deliberate encounters, women "stood their grounds" in order to "break down the walls" of repressive structures (hooks, 1981). In theorizing about Black leadership, Gordon (2000) purports, "in the quest for freedom, racial equality, civil and political rights, and economic and educational advancement, Black Americans, both during and after slavery, responded to the proposals and rhetoric of leaders drawn from their own ranks" (p. 1). HBCUs lead such efforts and challenge other institutions to fulfill similar promise. This mission necessitates leaders who have a moral compass to lead the way. The participants in this analysis embody this kind of leadership in their quest to lead.

With the culmination of their lived experiences and conscious awareness as African American women who grew up in a segregated society, they were determined to impart knowledge, wisdom, and a critical stance that enable young African Americans to be agents of change. In similar documented research by Foster (1989), concerned with change and creating opportunities for all students, these women critically assess the limits society imposes on groups and the paths to remove those limits. Through a collective voice, African Americans in academic settings such as these female leaders give attention to discriminatory practices that emerge inside and outside academia. In so doing, they confront injustices and inequities (Lee & McKerrow, 2005). These women's leadership practices seek to advance social justice by challenging social and educational structures that have a direct impact on the African American community. They bring these concerns to their institutions, raise the consciousness of the school community, and implement structures to improve educational opportunities.

The formal leadership role of the women leaders at HBCUs was very apparent. These administrators were careful to point out that without HBCUs many of their students would not be considered worthy of a college education. These professionals actively engaged in academic environments, and viewed education as one of the most important assets for the economic success and survival of African Americans. Historically,

HBCUs were established to challenge the general practice of exclusion based on discriminatory policies that explicitly or implicitly kept many from having access to education. Higher education institutions, whether historically Black or White institutions are challenged to be more inclusive of individuals of diverse racial, ethnic, class, and gender background. To combat that, Verharen (1996) asserts, "the populace must be more educated to defend itself against professional expertise, even to the point that a college education has become the right of every competent citizen" (p. 48). If only a few have access to quality education and increased knowledge, will an egalitarian republic tolerate this kind of elitism?

Lee and McKerrow (2005) observe that over the last few years, there has been a renewed interest in social justice. The key lies in how to translate social justice theory into practice. It needs to be pursued with actions that deconstruct institutional practices and structures that oppress people. For the African American women leaders in this study, their faith is the focal point of their personal and professional lives. Everything they do is interpreted and defined from their spiritual connection to God. Their religious relationships exist on two dimensions. The first is the personal relationship with God these women openly shared in telling their life stories. For them, this relationship is the source of their strength to help them "negotiate" the world. Throughout their life experiences, they rely on that spiritual connection to overcome the injustices they have encountered. Second, while these African American women leaders relied on their faith to overcome the prejudices, they also embraced the family and communal value of racial uplift. Like HBCUs situated in the heart of Black communities, Black churches too serve an integral role. HBCUs and churches symbolize hope, aspiration, and refuge for the Black community. Black churches have been pivotal in revolutionary movements in the social and economic development of Black people. The women leaders whose foundations are strongly tied to their religious traditions express concerns about the declining presence of the Black church in the lives of Black people.

As the Black women leaders reflected on their lived experiences and how these experiences shaped their professional work, they continue to articulate their commitment to provide quality education to students and examine institutional practices to improve upon them and the social conditions of the Black community. As Foster (1986) emphasized, "a leader's work involves the establishment of community and culture within an [institution] and the development of an [institution's] self reflective ability to analyze its purpose and goals" (p. 10). These African American women leaders practiced leadership that was closely aligned to Foster's (1986) critical perspectives of leadership. They were distinguished by their commitment to improve social conditions, empower others and support democratic participation through their roles. As reiterated by Mullings (1997), African American women have been involved not only in work outside the home, but also in transformative work, individual, and collective action to improve social justice conditions throughout their history.

While Foster (1986) did not specifically use the term social justice, principles of social justice can be found in his seminal work that focus on the application of moral, transformative, and socially just leadership conceptualizations and practices. Foster's work illuminates one of the premises of critical theory—that organizations and institutions of thought regularly generate and reproduce power inequities. Implied in the idea of transformative leadership is the exchange of new and theoretical frames and practices for the more celebrated profession-forming ones that have traditionally informed the field of educational leadership. Inherent also are the concepts of individual and institutional change (Dantley & Tillman, as cited in Marshall & Oliva, 2006).

To return to Foster's (1989) critical framework model, critical leadership is an ongoing analysis of what occurs in an institution with a commitment by those involved to engage in critical reflection and re-evaluation of current practices. Evidence of how these women leaders engaged in critical reflection centers on their discussions about the diverse needs of students who attend HBCUs, the lack of resources, and other institutional challenges that impact students' success. In their leadership practices, these women emphasized how they draw from past experiences to change practices that deter the success of students and progressivism in the Black community. Such reflection helped them to learn about and enact leadership practices that create visions of possibilities. In being critical, then, "leadership is oriented not just toward the development of more perfect [institutional] structures, but toward a re-conceptualization of life practices where common ideals for freedom and democracy stand important" (Foster, 1986, p. 52).

Dantley and Tillman (as cited in Marshall & Oliva, 2006), and Foster (1986), assert that another component of critical leadership merits highlighting: transformative leadership. Transformative leadership is about social change with a belief that transformation is a process that occurs over time. The transformation is not only in structures but also with leaders and followers. The aim is to cultivate a willingness to examine one's life, ideas, and causes to develop a critical framework for leadership. The African American women leaders in this study were among those who integrated public schools and higher education. Over the course of their professional careers, they confronted other issues of inequity. As leaders in HBCUs, they continue their efforts because they recognize that their students are the hope and future of the Black community. Therefore, the preservation of the Black community rests on them. They resolve to impart the knowledge, wisdom, and critical stance that will enable their students to be agents of social change (Jean-Marie, 2006).

Foster (1986) further explores the importance of an educative leader who "presents both an analysis and a vision, and devotes time to examine [institutional] history, purpose, and responsibilities" (p. 186). Engaging in discourse involves working as a community and being willing to listen and reciprocate leadership responsibilities. By engaging in such a discourse, diverse viewpoints from all members are heard with the likelihood that the institution will go in a direction of shared vision and practices. Finally, ethical leadership involves moral relationships and is intended to elevate people to new levels of morality (Foster, 1989), including maintenance of democratic values within a community. The role of a leader is to create other leaders.

Participants can assume leadership roles, and leaders can become followers when the situation calls for communal exchange. For these African American women leaders, their belief and commitment to a quality education is realized in the experiences they provide for every student who attends their university. Their interest in each student's success begins with developing an authentic relationship between administrator and student. Recognizing that they are in a position to make a difference, the administrators are guided by a vision for young African Americans to develop their talents and gifts to become contributors to their community and society. The success of one child is seen as an advancement of the community.

In summary, this collective group of women exemplifies how they survived the struggles of integration, triumphed over barriers in educational settings, and are committed to advocating social justice. Looking back on their life's journey, they shared the significance of their religious and spiritual faith and identified the present struggles of students, the community, and church. An important message conveyed by these Black women leaders to members within and outside academia is that they, as leaders are not to be discounted in the collective project of working towards social change. For many of them, HBCUs are where they are supposed to be and can have the most impact on students, administrative decisions, and educational reforms. Although many of their struggles go unrecorded, only when these stories are told can individuals within and outside the Black community understand the sacrifices of African American women who fought against injustices and continue to pave the way for generations to follow in their lead. Understanding their purpose, they stand firm on the promise to lead HBCUs to a level of excellence despite the challenges of students and institutional practices and policies. One might say that as advocates for social justice leadership, these African American women leaders are making revolutions in education.

REFERENCES

Avolio, B. J., & Gibbons, T. C. (1988). Developing transformational leaders: A life span approach. In J. A. Conger, R. N. Kanungo, & Associates (Eds.), *Charismatic leadership: The elusive factor in organizational effective* (pp. 276–308). San Francisco: Jossey-Bass.

Bass, B. M. (1985). *Leadership and performance beyond expectations*. New York: Free.

Benham, M. (1997). Silence and serenades: The journey of there ethnic minority women school leaders. *Anthropology and Education Quarterly, 28*(2), 280–307.

Benham, M., & Cooper, J. (1998). *Let my spirit soar: Narratives of diverse women in school leadership*. Thousand Oaks, CA: Corwin Press.

Benjamin, L. (1997). *Black women in the academy: Promises and perils*. Gainesville: University Press of Florida.

Brown v. Board of Education, 347 U.S. 483. (1954)

Burns, J. M. (1978). *Leadership*. New York: Harper & Row.

Casey, K. (1993). *I answer with my life*. New York: Routledge.

Casey, K. (1995–96). The new narrative research in education. *Review of Research in Education, 21*, 211–253.

Clandinin, D. J., & Connelly, F. M. (1994). Personal experience methods. In N. K. Denzin & Y. S. Lincoln (Eds.), *Handbook of qualitative research* (pp. 413–427). Thousand Oaks, CA: SAGE.

Collins, P. H. (1989). *Towards a new vision: Race class and gender as categories of analysis and connections* (A publication for the Research Clearinghouse and Curriculum Integration Project Center for Research on Women). Memphis, TN: Memphis State University.

Collins, P. H. (1990). *Black feminist thought: Knowledge, conscious, and the politics of empowerment*. New York: Routledge.

Collins, P. H. (1996).The social construction of Black feminist thought. A. Garr & M. Pearsall (Eds.), *In women, knowledge and reality: Explorations in feminist philosophy* (pp. 222–248). New York: Routledge.

Collins, P. H. (2000). *Black feminist thought: Knowledge, consciousness, and the politics of empowerment*. New York: Routledge.

Cooper, J. E. (1995). The role of narrative and dialogue in constructivist leadership. In L. Lambert, D. Walker, D. Zimmerman, J. Cooper, M. Lambert, M. Gardner et al. (Eds.), *The constructivist leader* (pp. 121–133). New York: Teachers College Press.

Cottrol, R. J., Diamond, R. T., & Ware, L. B. (2004, Summer). NAACP v. Jim Crow: The legal strategy that brought down "separate but equal" by toppling school segregation. *American Educator*, 9–11.

Dantley, M. E., & Tillman, L. C. (2006). Social justice and moral transformative leadership. In C. Marshall, & M. Oliva (Eds.), *Leadership for social justice: Making revolutions in education* (pp. 16–30). Boston: Pearson Education.

Davis, A. (1989). *Women, culture and politics*. New York: Random House.

Dorn, S. M., O'Rourke, C. L., & Papalewis, R. (1997-98). Women in education: Nine case studies. *National Forum of Educational Administration and Supervision Journal, 14*(2), 13–22.

Firestone, W. A., & Riehl, C. (Eds.). (2005). *A new agenda for educational leadership.* New York: Teachers College Press.

Fonow, M. M., & Cook, J. A. (Eds.). (1991). *Beyond methodology: Feminist scholarship as lived research.* Bloomington: Indiana University.

Foster, W. (1986). *Paradigms and promises: New approaches to educational administration.* Buffalo, NY: Prometheus Books.

Foster, W. (1989). Toward a critical practice of leadership. In J. Smyth (Ed.), *Critical perspectives on educational leadership* (pp. 39–62). New York: The Falmer.

Furman, G. C., & Sheilds, C. M. (2005). How can educational leaders promote and support social justice and democratic community in schools? In W. A. Firestone & C. Riehl (Eds.), *A new agenda for educational leadership* (pp. 119–137). New York: Teachers College Press

Garibaldi, A. (Ed.). (1984). *Black colleges and universities: Challenges for the future.* New York: Praegar.

Gilligan, C. (1982). *In a different voice: Psychological theory and women's development.* Cambridge, MA: Harvard University Press.

Glazer-Ramo, J. (2001). *Shattering the myths: Women in academe.* Baltimore: John Hopkins University.

Gluck, S. B., & Patai, D. (Eds.). (1992). *Women's word: The feminist practice of oral history.* New York: Routledge.

Gordon, J. U. (2000). *Black leadership for social change.* Westport, CT: Greenwood.

Grogan, M. (1994, April). *Aspiring to the superintendency in the public school systems: Women's perspectives.* Paper presented at the annual meeting of the American Educational Research Association, New Orleans, LA.

Harper, F. (1866). *We are rising as a people: Frances Harper's radical views on class and racial equality in Sketches of Southern Life.* Retrieved on August 18, 2008 from, http://goliath.ecnext.com/coms2/summary_0199-4918647_ITM

Heath, S. B. (2001). Ethnography in communities: Learning the everyday life of America's subordinated youth. In J. A. Banks & C. A. M. Banks (Eds.), *Handbook of research on multicultural education* (pp. 114–128). San Francisco: Jossey-Bass.

Hine, D. (1994). *Hinesight: Black women and the re-construction of American history.* New York: Carlson.

House, R. J. (1976). A 1976 theory of charismatic leadership. In J. G. Hunt & L. L. Larson (Eds.), *Leadership: The cutting edge* (pp. 189–207). Carbondale: Southern Illinois University.

hooks, b. (1981). *Ain't I a woman: Black women and feminism.* Boston: South End Press.

hooks, b. (1994). *Teaching to transgress: Education as the practice of freedom.* New York: Routledge Press.

hooks, b. (2000). *Feminism is for everybody: Passionate politics.* Cambridge, MA: South End Press.

Jean-Marie, G. (2004). Black women administrators in historically black institutions: Social justice project rooted in community. *Journal of Women in Educational Leadership, 2*(1), 37–58.

Jean-Marie, G. (2005). Standing on the promises: The experiences of Black women administrators in historically Black institutions. *Advancing Women in*

Leadership Online Journal, 19, 1–14. Retrieved April 23, 2006, from http://www.advancingwomen.com/awl/fall2005/19_3.html

Jean-Marie, G. (2006). Welcoming the unwelcomed: A social justice imperative of African-American female leaders. *Educational Foundations, 20*(1–2), 83–102.

Jean-Marie, G., James, C., & Bynum, S. (2006). Black women activists, leaders, and educators: Transforming urban educational practice. In J. L. Kincheloe, k. hayes, K. Rose, & P. M. Anderson (Eds.), *The Praeger handbook of urban education* (pp. 59–69). Wesport, CT: Greenwood.

Ladson-Billings, G. (1997). For colored girls who have considered suicide when the academy's not enough: Reflections of an African American Woman Scholar. In A. Neumann & P. L. Peterson, (Eds.), *Learning from our lives: Women, research, and autobiography in education*, (pp. 52–70). New York: Teachers College.

Lee, S. S., & McKerrow, K. (2005, Fall). Advancing social justice: Women's work. *Advancing Women in Leadership Online Journal, 19,* 1–2. Retrieved on April 26, 2006, from http://www.advancingwomen.com/awl/fall2005/preface.html

Leithwood, K., Jantzi, D., & Steinbach, R. (1999). *Changing leadership for changing times.* New York: Open University Press.

Loder, T. L. (2005). On deferred dreams, callings, and revolving doors of opportunity: African-American women's reflections on becoming principals. *The Urban Review, 37*(3), 243–265.

Lawrence-Lightfoot, S. (1994). *I've known rivers: Lives of loss and liberation.* Reading, MA: Addison-Wesley.

Lawson-Sanders, R., Campbell-Smith, S., & Benham, M. K. P. (2006). Wholistic visioning for social justice: Black women theorizing practice. In C. Marshall, & M. Oliva, M. (Eds.), *Leadership for social justice: Making revolutions in education* (pp. 31–63). Boston: Pearson Education.

Marshall, C., & Oliva, M. (2006). *Leadership for social justice: Making revolutions in education.* Boston: Pearson Education.

Morris, A. D. (1984). *The origins of the Civil Rights Movement: Black communities organizing for change.* New York: Free.

Moses, Y. T. (1997). Black women in academe: Issues and strategies. In L. Benjamin (Ed.), *Black women in the academy: Promises and perils* (pp. 23–37). Gainesville, FL: University Press of Florida.

Mullings, L. (1997). *On our terms: Race, class and gender in the lives of African American women.* New York: Routledge.

Normore, A. H. (2006). From a pivotal Civil Rights activist to radical equations: Grassroots leadership and lessons for educational leaders. A conversation with Robert Moses. *UCEA Review, University Council of Educational Administration, XLVl1l*(1), 19–22.

Reinharz, S. (1992). *Feminist methods in social research.* New York: Oxford University.

Riessman, C. K. (1993). *Narrative analysis.* Newbury Park: SAGE.

Robnett, B. (1997). *How long? how long?: African American women in the struggle for Civil Rights.* New York: Oxford University.

Roebuck, J. B., & Murty, K. S. (1993). *Historically black colleges and universities: Their place in American higher education.* Wesport, CT: Praeger.

Rosenthal, G. (1993). Reconstruction of life stories: Principles of selection in generating stories for narrative biographical interviews. In R. Josselson & A. Lieblich (Eds.), *The narrative study of lives*. (pp. 59–91). Newbury Park, NJ: SAGE.

Schiller, N. (2000). A short history of Black feminist scholars. *The Journal of Blacks in Higher Education*, *29*, 119–125.

Shakeshaft, C. (1993). Gender equity in schools. In C. A. Capper (Ed.), *Educational administration in a pluralistic society* (pp. 87–109). Albany: State University of New York Press.

Sims, S. J. (1994). *Diversifying historically black colleges and universities: A new higher education paradigm*. Westport, CT: Greenwood.

Tichy, N. M., & DeVanna, M. A. (1990). The transformational leader (2nd ed.). New York: Wiley.

Valverde, L. A. (2003). *Leaders of color in higher education: Unrecognized triumphs in harsh institutions*. New York: Rowman & Littlefield.

Verharen, C. (1996). Historically black colleges and universities and universal higher education. In. J. A. Ladner & S. Gbadegesin (Eds.), *Ethics, higher education and social responsibility* (pp. 45–58). Washington, DC: Howard University.

Weber, M. (1947). *The theory of social and economic organizations* (T. Parsons, Trans.). New York: Free.

CHAPTER 2

SEPARATE IS INHERENTLY UNEQUAL

Rethinking Commonly Held Wisdom

Jonathan D. Lightfoot

Modern educational reform owes much to the legal team and educational leaders who fought to make equal educational opportunity a reality for Black students in the United States of America. Their efforts helped to dismantle American apartheid; also known as Jim Crow, a system of allocating human and civil rights according to assigned or assumed "racial" classifications. The 1954 Supreme Court concluded that the doctrine of "separate but equal," initiated in 1896 under *Plessy v. Ferguson* (Delgado, 1995), has no place in public education and separate educational facilities are inherently unequal. Since the 1954 decision of *Brown v. Board of Education Topeka*, Kansas "separate is inherently unequal" has been the mantra used by advocates of desegregated schools. The purpose of this research is to question commonly held wisdom promoting the idea that if things are separate, they must be unequal. Integration, it follows, is then sought as the solution to the problem of inequality. I argue that we abandon such reductive logic and focus our energies on battling the racism that results in segregation. Seeking integration to overcome segregation without addressing racism does not solve the problem of unequal educational opportunity.

Leadership for Social Justice: Promoting Equity and Excellence Through Inquiry and Reflective Practice, pp. 37–59
Copyright © 2008 by Information Age Publishing
37

SEPARATE IS INHERENTLY UNEQUAL:
RETHINKING COMMONLY HELD WISDOM

In 1954 the Supreme Court under Chief Justice Earl Warren concluded that the doctrine of "separate but equal," initiated in 1896 under *Plessy*, has no place in public education, and separate educational facilities are inherently unequal. Since the 1954 decision of *Brown v. Board of Education Topeka*, Kansas "separate is inherently unequal" has been the mantra used by advocates of desegregated schools. I argue that separate and equal are not mutually exclusive terms conceptually. In theory it is possible to have separation and equality exist at the same time. The difficulty in achieving such in practice, given the historical evidence from 1896 to 1954 where the American education system tried to adhere to *Plessy's* mandate, is what I believe prompted the Warren Court to conclude that it was not possible. The rationale behind this impossibility seems to have been that the essential nature of separateness precluded achievement of equality of condition. Perhaps the social, political, and economic realities of competing resources in one society is what prevents theoretical possibilities from becoming practical realities. Interpreting the *Brown* decisions as the solution to a long history of marginalization and inequitable education for Black people is simplistic and was not, I posit, the intent of the civil rights advocates working toward desegregating schools. The categorization of "separate but equal" as bad and the use of "separate as inherently unequal" as the solution is problematic for at least three reasons. The first most obvious reason is that prior to 1954, "separate but equal" does not accurately describe education in the United States. We do not need to look far for evidence that Black schools were not funded equally to White schools (Anderson, 1988; Anderson, 2001; Walker, 1996). Schools are unequal when they are unequally supported. Instead of busing Black students to White schools, Anderson (2001) declares that the Supreme Court should have "bused" more money, better instructional materials, trained staff, and newer equipment to Black schools.

Second, research on the benefits of desegregation is mixed at best (Schofield, 1995). Research has shown that separate (segregated) environments, when constructed for the benefit of those being educated, can *increase* learning opportunities and result in improved academic achievement. Some females do better in content areas when all their classmates are female (Sadker & Sadker, 2004). Other examples of separate models that have had at least some degree of success include some African-centered schools (Pollard & Ajirotutu, 2000) and schools providing language instruction in the home language for immigrants for large portions of the school day (Olneck, 1995). A critical examination of research on segregated and desegregated models suggests a more complex picture than "separate is inherently unequal" implies on the surface. In advocating an educational model that meets and serves the needs of Black children, Anderson (2001) holds that the test of such a model is whether it *empowers* Black people to effectively compete, achieving success in political and economic market places.

Third, bringing diverse groups together when members of one group have wielded power over members of another group, without giving explicit attention to changing the imbalance of power and status, will not resolve conflicts (Allport, 1954). As Woodson (1933/1977) points out, sending Black students to school to be educated by their oppressors is not in the best interest of Black people. In addition, the miseducation of the White students who are taught they are superior is detrimental to both White people and Black people (Woodson, 1934/1969). An appropriate education for all groups, whether in segregated or desegregated schools, would be based on a curriculum that recognizes the histories of all groups and stresses equality, not inferiority or superiority of particular groups. My perspective on the Supreme Court ruling does not imply that the decision was misguided. The intent to overturn *Plessy* was absolutely appropriate. However, it is instructive to reflect upon the rationale and arguments that supported *Brown* as we seek solutions to closing the academic disparities between racial groups in U.S. schools and reducing barriers to full, equitable participation in society (Cummins, 2000; García, 1999; Kincheloe, Slattery, & Steinberg, 2000; Stephan, 1999).

The primary purpose of this research is to question commonly held wisdom promoting the idea that if things are separate, they must be unequal. A corollary purpose is to critically investigate the *Brown* decisions, explicitly making links between social theories (e.g., deficit theory, contact hypothesis, and the colorblind perspective) and curricula, and instructional practices and policies that continue to miseducate the nation's students. The term "mis-educate" was coined by African American historian and educator Carter G. Woodson (1933) with his classic work, *The Mis-Education of the Negro*. His premise was built around the notion that one's education should have redemptive value, for both the individual and the group. Miseducation is particularly problematic for oppressed groups who are led to believe that an education will reduce their oppressed status. The fact of the matter is that the education they receive from the oppressor only reinforces their oppression and can only be redeemed in service to the oppressor. I discuss the history of Black students' educational opportunities before and after *Brown* and purpose to answer the question: If after more than 50 years following the *Brown* decisions we still have visible, acknowledged disparity in academic achievement, levels of education, and earned incomes levels correlated with group membership, then we need to ask what, besides segregation, negatively affects the educational opportunities of Black students? How can we educate rather than miseducate Black and White people?

I maintain that the goal of the legal team who prevailed in the *Brown* decision was part of an overall larger goal articulated by Black people in Jim Crow America, which included achievement of fair and equitable treatment in all aspects of civic life. Specifically, the *Brown* dream team sought to dismantle the legal barriers that prevented Black children from attending school with White children by proving to the courts that separate but equal schooling was not possible in Jim Crow America. The children of former slaves and free Black people wanted America to live up to the ideals set forth in the Declaration of Independence and the Constitution as advanced by the 13th, 14th, and 15th Amendments. It was clear that the "truths" mentioned in the Declaration were not "self-evident" for Black people because daily reminders assured them inferior status in American society. *Brown* lawyers strategized to address the lack of institutional and legal power needed to overcome this disparity in treatment.

Were the *Brown* advocates naïve to think that dismantling the legal barriers to educational segregation would automatically or eventually dismantle the racist hegemonic forces that inspired Black and White resistance to desegregation? The rationale for resistance to integration among some Black people probably stems from experiencing the disdainful and inhumane treatment White people accorded Black people. They realized that the road to equality and full acceptance of their fellow American citizens was paved with too many bumps; bumps that would severely diminish their quality of life. It is difficult to imagine that the *Brown* legal team would think that racism would subside once Black children were able to sit next to White children in the classroom. It is equally difficult to believe they expected that Black student achievement and educational opportunity would suddenly be on par with White children once access to the *same* instruction and facilities was achieved. The *Brown* decisions were the beginning, not the solution. Our educational system has missed the real message of *Brown*—to end racist educational policies and practices. I recognize the *Brown* decisions as the beginning of a long trek towards parity and equality, not the ultimate solution to educational and civic disparity. The time to return to the unfinished business of *Brown*, that is to end the miseducation of all American students and to acquire equitable educational opportunities for Black and other students of color, is long overdue.

This chapter is organized in the following way: I first review historical accounts of Black educational opportunity in the United States beginning with a look at how legal precedence established during and after slavery set the tone for educational opportunities for future Black generations. I then assess the ways in which Black educational opportunity has been politicized in ways that have rendered true educational reform powerless to produce positive change for Black people. Next, I attempt a literal critique of *Brown* by asking whether or not separate is *inherently* unequal. In the final sections of the paper, I problematize *Brown* by engaging conditions proposed by Allport (1954) necessary for successful intergroup relations as the basis for advocating for critical curricular and instructional practices and policies that return to the intent of the *Brown* legal team. Last, I discuss specific leadership, curricular and instructional policies and practices that are empowering and antiracist, which reflect the essence of *Brown*. Fifty years of post-*Brown* research has demonstrated that racism continues to be a problem in schools and society (Spring, 1994). Forced desegregation of public school systems alone has not solved what appears to be the fundamental problem, institutionalized belief in White superiority and Black inferiority. Without a focused assault on racism in public schools and civil society, racism will continue to undermine the noblest intent of *Brown*, the promotion of the inherent equality of all peoples.

My objectives are to reanalyze the strategies that won *Brown* and propose similar strategies to disrupt the direction of education of Black people since *Brown*. This analysis of *Brown* is significant because it provides a rationale and path for future educational scholarship to honor the *Brown* legacy by accepting the baton and running in the right direction, towards antiracism in K–12 education, in teacher education programs, and in school leadership preparation. Development of anti-racist political representation and antiracist socioeconomic policy formation is what is needed to continue the legacy of *Brown*. Without a rededication to the ideals of the struggle and a recommitment to the principles and values that energized the early movement, we are destined to repeat past mistakes and not enjoy the progress that comes with learning the lessons from such mistakes. As educators, we have the tools to educate rather than miseducate *all* our students.

METHOD

The inspiration for this chapter comes from the heightened attention various academic circles directed towards the 1954 *Brown* decision at its 50th anniversary. During 2004 and 2005 many educational institutions called upon educators to revisit the landmark decision that outlawed segregation in American public schools by hosting professional conferences dedicated to the issue. Some chose themes focused on how *Brown* has impacted our current educational profile and future outlook. I attended several of these meetings and took copious notes while listening to the many veteran and neophyte scholars on the panels. The conversations and dialogue I engaged in at the meetings carried over to further discussion back at my home institution with colleagues. My research was informed by articles such as "Landing on the Wrong Note: The Price We paid for Brown" by Gloria Ladson-Billings (2004) where she poetically chimes "*Brown* is neither the panacea that we imagined, nor the problem that we experience. Rather it is the hope that landing on the wrong note does not signal the end of the music" (pp. 11–12). I became familiar with many of my sources while doing research for my dissertation 3 years ago, which I like to think, has established my academic research agenda for many years to come. By combining online query with traditional library research I have been able to expand my references related to this topic. This paper attempts to build on my primary interest in social justice critique.

HISTORICAL REVIEW OF BLACK EDUCATIONAL OPPORTUNITY

A review of United States legal history as it pertains to the social status of Africans in America serves as an instructive guide towards a better understanding of the struggle Black people face for equal educational opportunity in America prior to the 1954 *Brown* decision. Article I, Section 2 of the Constitution adopted in 1787 counted an African slave as three-fifths of a person for the purposes of representation in the new government. This proviso remained a part of the Constitution until 1868 when the 14th Amendment (Exploring Constitutional Conflicts, n.d.) was ratified, which granted whole personhood, citizenship, and due process under the law to newly freed slaves. Reconstruction was a brief period (1865–1877) during which America made monumental strides towards racial reconciliation and Black people seized unprecedented opportunities to get an education and secure political representation. However, the gains would be short lived and Black people entered a nadir, a period of time at the end of the 1800s and beginning of the 1900s (roughly 1878–1915), when Ku Klux Klan terrorism, disfranchisement, and Jim Crow segregation relegated Black people to the lowest rung of social and civic hierarchy. This social and civic position was notoriously blatant in the Southern states and more subtle in the Northern states, but no less detrimental. Constitutional amendments were rendered powerless against the aggressive White assertion of hegemony over Black people. The 1857 Supreme Court Dred Scott decision had already deemed Black people not worthy of any rights by which White people were bound to respect and paved the way for another Supreme Court ruling, *Plessy*, which established the "separate but equal" doctrine that became the key legal sanction for Jim Crow laws. *Plessy* thus became the linchpin in defense of segregated life in America including, but not limited to transportation, social affairs, civic life, and schooling.

In *Radicals and Conservatives*, Philip Rieff designates Kelly Miller (1908/ 1968) as one of the dominant intellectuals of Black America from the turn of the century to the 1930s. Miller's 1908 essay on the Negro's early struggles for education acknowledges as well known that slave owners discouraged the dissemination of literary knowledge among persons of African descent, and, in most cases, positively prohibited their being taught. But, despite the rigid regulation, Miller adds, there were many slaveholders who taught their slaves to read and write. Puritan Cotton Mather not only enjoined other masters to enlighten their slaves, but in 1717, set the example by opening a school for Native and Black people. The school was to remain open for 2 or 3 hours every night in order to instruct "Negroes and Indians in reading the Scriptures and learning their Catechisms" (Greene, 1942/1971 p. 238). Evangelical proselytizing of slaves led to some of the first attempts to provide education for them (Franklin, 1947/1969; Greene, 1942/1971; Nash, 1988). Although the work of several individuals and religious societies such as Nathaniel Pigott, John Eliot, the Quakers, and the SPG. (Society for the Propagation of the Gospel), were primarily directed at the spiritual welfare of the slaves, many paid requisite attention to secular instruction as well.

While yet a British colony in 1740, South Carolina took the lead in directly legislating against the education of people of color. Miller documents the laws there and in several other states that forbid the establishment of schools for Black people and threatened punishment for those persons teaching them to read and write. For instance, in Georgia the following law was enacted in 1829:

> If any slave, Negro, or free person of color, or any white person, shall teach any other slave, Negro, or free person of color to read or write, either written or printed characters, the said free person of color or slave shall be punished by fine and whipping, or whipping, at the discretion of the court; and if a white person so offend he, she or they shall be punished with a fine not exceeding $500 and imprisonment in the common jail, at the discretion of the court. (Miller, 1908/1968, p. 262)

Despite such laws on the books throughout many states, schools existed throughout the north and the south operating in both open and more clandestine manners. In fact, Greene (1942/1971) credits Quaker influence as largely responsible for the unique clause in the Rhode Island Emancipation Bill of 1784 making it compulsory that Black children be taught to read and write. Even though South Carolina had outlawed Black education, there were still colored schools in Charleston from 1744 to the close of the Civil War. Census records of free African Americans attending school in slave and free states in 1850 and 1860 show surprising numbers. They indicate that there were 4,414 free Black people enrolled in school in slave states in 1850 and there were 3,661 in 1860. There were 28, 627 free Black people attending school in free states in 1850 and 22, 800 in 1860.

Abraham Lincoln, when president, thought that with education, Black people would qualify for citizenship, at least on a restricted basis (Franklin, 1947/1969). W. E. B. Du Bois (1935) noted the phenomenal advance of Black people in education during Reconstruction. He considered the fact that Black people sought to prepare their own teachers as most significant. Carter G. Woodson, in his study of the *Negro Professional Man and the Community* (1934/1969), notes that the teacher was often respected as the leader of the community, receiving competition only from the preacher. With the help of abolitionists, the Freedmen's Bureau, and other missionary and church organizations, literacy rates among the newly emancipated Black people skyrocketed. Although the Bureau achieved its greatest success in education, it also organized freedmen's courts and boards of arbitration since it was felt that the interest of Black people could not be safely entrusted to local courts. The freedmen's courts had civil and criminal jurisdiction over minor cases where one or both parties were freedmen.

Frazier (1957/1962) emphasized that from its inception, the education of Black people was shaped by bourgeois ideals. The Northern missionaries established schools that taught the Yankee virtues of industry and thrift. Since practically all of these schools were supported by Protestant church organizations in the North, they sought to inculcate in their students the contemporary ideals of Puritan morality. In the pious atmosphere of the missionary schools, says Frazier, the students were found to be listless. The students obviously resented the rigid system of control but often submitted silently for fear of losing an opportunity to secure an education. The only concession made to the Black peoples' culture was that the students were required to sing spirituals for the White visitors. Finally, Frazier notes, "though the school was saturated with religious feeling, the required religious activities were designed to wean them from the religious emotionalism of the Negro" (p. 68).

Today's proponents of African-centered education (Asante, 1993; Madhubuti & Madhibuti, 1994; Shujaa, 1994) describe contemporary school scenes as does Frazier and argue against the cultural hegemony that threatens cultural genocide to millions of unsuspecting Black children and their parents. Cultural hegemony is practiced in educational systems when Black students are sent covert and overt messages that their cultural traditions contribute little or no value to their academic achievement. For example, many Black cultural traditions are rooted in churches where emotional expression via song, dance, and the spoken word is valued. The American educational system seems to find emotional expression incompatible with academic achievement. Thus students who value such traditions that reflect their heritage must discard them and adopt the cultural traditions practiced by the dominant culture to increase their chances of success.

From the early days of slavery, Black people have equated educational achievement with liberation (Scott, 1976). Slaveholders who offered religious instruction to slaves as a means of creating obedience (slaves were taught to obey their masters) did not realize, at least early on, that many slaves would develop language skills, political ideologies, and social values appropriate for organizing protest of their condition. In his oft-quoted treatise, *Miseducation of the Negro*, Carter G. Woodson (1933/1977) speaks to the notion of education for liberation. He warned in 1933, "When you control a man's thinking you do not have to worry about his actions.... He will find his proper place and stand in it" (p. 84). If in fact this is true, then it makes the struggle for liberation most difficult through educational systems designed and controlled by oppressive structures.

POLITICIZED ASSESSMENT OF
BLACK EDUCATIONAL OPPORTUNITY

Paulo Freire (1970/1993) reminds us that there is no such thing as a neutral educational process. Education either functions as an instrument that is used to facilitate the integration of the younger generation into the logic of the present system and bring about conformity to it, or it becomes "the practice of freedom," the means by which men and women deal critically and creatively with reality and discover how to participate in the transformation of their world (p. 74). The development of an educational methodology that facilitates this process brings to visibility tension and conflict within our society. Debate continues among conservatives, radicals, and liberals as to how education relates to the "American Dream." Alliances continue to form and dissolve depending on the particular issues and prizes at stake. Giroux (as cited by Holtz et al., 1989) and Freire identify the common bond among the shifting factions: their aggressive defense of schools as strategic sites for cultural production and economic renewal.

The most radical space of possibility in the academy is the classroom, says bell hooks (1994). She validly insists that all who care about education open their minds and hearts to enable knowledge beyond the boundaries of what is currently acceptable. To do so allows thinking, rethinking, creation of new visions, and celebration of teaching that invites transgressions where boundaries are met and surpassed. Such a movement, hooks argues, will make education a liberating "practice of freedom" (p. 13).

Many academics have long promoted education as one of the key means by which to overcome institutionalized racism (Anderson, 2001; Guinier, 1998; Scott, 1976). Scott makes an interesting point in suggesting that the difficulty people who are not Black may have in imagining education for use as a means to achieve liberation, since they generally tend to think of education as a prerequisite for economic payoff as opposed to political payoff. Education for Black people has traditionally been oriented toward political payoff well as an often-illusory economic payoff. Anderson blames structural racism for the limited employment options available to Black people, thus forcing them to use education as an empowerment tool to achieve social and civil rights before achieving economic rights. Though Black people have demonstrated spectacular educational achievement, and a total willingness to be long suffering, they have been duly challenged to translate those educational achievements into economic gains.

Liberatory education demands achievement. Madhubuti writes in his foreword to Mwalimu Shujaa's (1994) book *Too Much Schooling Too Little Education: A Paradox of Black Life in White Societies*, that Black students must have deep understandings of the political, racial, economic, scientific, and technological realities that confront the very survival of African people locally, nationally, and globally. When Black students realize that all education is foundational (intended to establish a basis for understanding and growth), they will also realize, and not be disappointed when they discover, that economic payoff is not an automatic result of their academic credentials. Madhubuti (as cited in Shujaa, 1994) further encourages student grounding in a worldview that promotes cross-cultural communication, understanding, and sharing. One must be self-protective enough to realize that the world is not fair and that one's own interests often conflict with the interests of others, especially when race is involved.

Education for liberation finds one of its most outspoken proponents in Molefi Asante (1993), an African American professor who is sometimes called the father of Afrocentricity. Asante clarifies, that Afrocentricity is not a matter of color but primarily of perspective, that is, orientation to data. That Afrocentrists use data and facts in making analyses is less significant to theory than determination of a position from which to view phenomena and gather data. Ultimately, Afrocentricity is a perspective that allows Africans to be subjects of historical experiences rather than objects on the fringes of European thought. The Afrocentrist seeks to move the African from the fringes to a centered position of thought and experience.

Historian Arthur Schlesinger challenged Asante's (1991) *Afrocentric Idea of Education* with *The Disuniting of America* (Schlesinger, 1998). Asante's basic premise holds that the traditional emphasis on White European history and culture, and the disregard of African history and culture, alienates Black schoolchildren, who find it difficult to feel attachment to the content being offered. Educational psychologist Hilliard (2001) notes that there is a vast amount of important information about African people that everyone, not only Black schoolchildren, should be aware of. Schlesinger denounces the Afrocentric movement as an extreme example of a "cult of ethnicity" (p. 20). He is supported by David Nicholson (1990) in "Afrocentrism' and the Tribalization of America: The Misguided Logic of Ethnic Education Schemes" where he argues that the sweeping call for inclusive curricula is based on untested, unproven premises. Nicholson further argues that such curricula would intentionally exaggerate differences and thus likely to exacerbate racial and ethnic tensions (Sizemore, as cited in Holtz et al., 1989, p. 95) would counter that the "tensions" Nicholson thinks are the result of an inclusive curricula are actually the harvest of the destructive seeds of racism, sexism, and poverty.

No historical account, however brief, would be complete without a review of the famous "debate" on whether Black people should pursue a classical liberal arts education or adopt an industrial education. The symbolic figures in this debate were W. E. B. Du Bois and Booker T. Washington. Around the time of *Plessy*, Booker T. Washington became the most prominent African American proponent of industrial education. Frazier (1957/1962) describes the dismal scene as one where the disfranchisement of Black people was being achieved through law. Public education for Black children was a mere mockery of education, and a legalized system of racial segregation was restricting the Black worker to common labor and domestic service. Washington's formula for the solution of the race problem, which he announced in his famous speech at the Atlanta Exposition in 1895, was to admonish freedmen to learn to dignify and glorify common labor and put brains and skill in the common occupations of life. This admonition was widely regarded by the White South as the Black people's acceptance of a subordinate position in American life.

Du Bois (1903/1993), on the other hand, is long credited with promoting the notion of the Talented Tenth: the development of the minds of the most brilliant of the African race that they may guide and uplift the masses to individual and collective progress. He later modified his focus on the top tenth, to include advocating a more egalitarian approach to education (DuBois, as cited in Lewis, 1995). Du Bois respected Washington's achievements. While careful not to disparage the importance of industrial education for some Black people, Du Bois was concerned that an industrial education was inadequate to prepare people to exercise successfully their civil and political rights. Without appropriate education, the prospects for exercising requisite political leadership for liberation would be a daunting task. Du Bois was also convinced that the Northern capitalists who were giving their support to Black education were not interested in his solution to the race problem, which required classic liberal teaching and thought. It was as important for Black people to know why as it was for them to know how according to Du Bois.

Assessing Black educational opportunity after Brown requires a multiple perspective examination. We cannot assume that Black people were eager to abandon their all Black schools and communities to attend White schools in White communities. By 1954 Jim Crow had done a thorough job of teaching Black and White folks how to stay in their respective places in society. Along with the lesson of how to stay in one's place was the lesson of why one must stay in one's place, because people have been consigned to inferior positions in society for a reason; they are not good enough to interact with those assigned to superior positions in any other way but a subservient way. That is, Black and White people can be seen together so long as it is clearly understood that the Black is in a servant role. For example, Black and White people can ride on the same train or bus but Black people must sit in the rear. Black and White people can attend the same movie theaters, but Black people must sit in the balcony. Rear door entry, separate water fountains, carryout dining only, and underemployment were constant reminders to Black people of their inferior social status. And given the possibilities of life transformation via education and schooling, it is understandable that there would be some volatile reactions to dismantling the segregated school system from both Black and White people.

Segregation negatively affects Black educational opportunity when major disparities in funding of Black and White schools leaves teachers in Black schools grossly underpaid. When Black schools cannot buy new books, working laboratory equipment, athletic gear and facilities, and maintain their physical plants, then segregation burdens Black educational opportunity. Under segregation Black schools were separate from and unequal to White schools. Resources notwithstanding, Black schools had to endure political and curricular challenges as well. Black school leaders were forced to spend more time raising funds to keep the school running than they did providing instructional leadership. It is hard to teach civics, social studies, and government when the books sent to Black schools have had the Declaration of Independence and United States Constitution removed. The rationale being, why fill Black children's heads with notions of freedom and rights to first class citizenship when their futures will provide less freedom and rights and second class citizenship. Without continual vigilance from the school leaders, teachers, and the community under segregation, overcoming the multiple factors contributing to the miseducation of Black students would have been nearly impossible.

It is difficult to come up with factors that negatively affect Black educational opportunity besides those related in some way, either directly or indirectly, to legally sanctioned separate but unequal segregation. The vestiges of slavery and the various manifestations of institutional and individual racism is what produced legally sanctioned separate but unequal segregation. When Justice Harlan, the sole dissenter in *Plessy*, argued, "our constitution is color-blind, and neither knows nor tolerates classes among citizens" (*Plessy v. Ferguson*, 1986, para. 11), he was either incredibly naïve or incredibly optimistic that American society could live out the true meaning of its constitutional creed. The expectation that without legal segregation, Black educational opportunity would be increased seems also both naïve and optimistic. Though racism and segregation are no longer legally imposed, we still witness challenges to Black education opportunity as evidenced by a persistent achievement gap, *de facto* segregation, and less enrollment in higher educational institutions.

We look for an understanding of the nature of Black resistance to desegregation first in the natural tendency of human beings to resist change, even when the current state is not so pleasant. Humans find ways to manage difficult situations and rationalize resistance to change by preferring the known problems and strategies used to deal with them as opposed to the less known problems which will require new coping mechanisms and strategies. Some Black people may have internalized the racial hatred directed towards them by White people and for all intents and purposes accepted their inferior social positions. Other Black people knew that God had made all people equal and thus felt no sense of inferiority to White people in spite of the treatments they received at their hands. This sense of equality, however, did not compel them to desire interaction with White people. They instead desired better treatment, more resources, and allowed to enjoy life in their Black community. Still other Black people felt the need to prove to White people that they were indeed equal under God and the law and welcomed desegregation as an opportunity to "get what White folks got." Perhaps they did not believe that their Black schools in their Black community would ever get the resources and respect they needed to effectively compete in the larger arena of opportunity.

Desegregation appears to have imposed the greatest burden upon Black people to make it work. They were the ones forced to leave their schools and communities and travel great distances to often-hostile White schools in White communities. Seldom, if at all, did White students leave their schools and communities and get bused to Black schools. There are numerous instances of public White schools in the South that chose to close rather than accept Black students. Seeking private schools and moving the family to another location were a few of the options used by White people who resisted school desegregation in their communities. Northern cities expressed their resistance to school desegregation in much the same way, moving to the suburbs and choosing private education for their children. Again, human resistance to change characterizes White animosity towards desegregation efforts. Those who believed in their own racial superiority did not want their children interacting with children whom they believed were racially inferior, among other concerns such as fear and cultural dissonance.

The role of schooling and education as a socializing and norming process is too important to risk the chance of their children being taught by a Black teacher, be subject to a Black authority figure, or become friends with another Black child. During the 1950s and 1960s television was coming of age and is credited with bringing the Civil Rights Movement to the national and world stage, thus expediting the cause. Who can forget the televised images of the 1957 Little Rock Arkansas Nine entering Central High School amidst a violent White crowd shouting racial epitaphs while national guardsmen tried to protect the nine Black students from harm? Another famous televised image occurred in 1963 when then governor of Alabama, George Wallace, stood in front of the door of the University of Alabama to prevent a brave Black student from entering. This change and rearrangement of social mores because of desegregation was all too complex and daunting for many who had to wrestle with its issues. Though the resistance to school desegregation is not as blatant as it was during its initial stages, the fact that desegregation efforts are now being replaced by a battle against resegregation is a reminder of the deeply rooted problem of race relations in America.

True School Integration

Is true school integration a possibility in a society that is not yet truly integrated? Authors Vivian Gunn Morris and Curtis Morris (2002) graduated with the 1959 class of Trenholm High School in Tuscumbia Alabama. Their research, while acknowledging the gains also documents the significant losses experienced by students when their school was closed and they were forced to attend a White desegregated school across town. This attempt to assess the price the Black community paid at the hands of desegregation is important because it locates the effects of school desegregation from the point of view of the students who had to endure the hardships of separation. Mrs. Morris explained that when the school building was torn down not only did the community lose a historical landmark, the people suffered emotional loss as well. The sentimental value of school memories, friendships, and pride in a central part of their community was razed along with the physical structure as well. In support of the account shared by Morris and Morris, bell hooks (1994) adds:

> School changed utterly with racial integration. Gone was the messianic zeal to transform our minds and beings that had characterized teachers and their pedagogical practices in our all-black schools. Knowledge was suddenly about information only. It had no relation to how one lived, behaved. It was no longer connected to the antiracist struggle. Bussed to white schools, we [Black children] soon learned that obedience, and not a zealous will to learn, was what was expected of us. Too much eagerness to learn could easily be seen as a threat to white authority. (p. 3)

hooks (1994) is vehement in her contempt of the "racist, desegregated, white schools" (p. 3) they were forced to attend. Whereas she once considered school sheer joy, she then lost her love of school. In addition to feeling alienated, the lessons taught by these White teachers, she says, reinforced racist stereotypes and taught her the difference between education as the practice of freedom and education that merely strives to reinforce domination.

While attending a reading of the Morris and Morris (2002) book, I asked the question: "Is it possible for schools to achieve true racial integration?" Having studied the whole segregation-desegregation-integration-resegregation process, along with my own experiences attending all Black schools and predominantly White universities in the North, I know about separate proms, yearbooks, class reunions, dormitories, and club organizations such as fraternities and sororities. Mrs. Morris said she believes that true integration is possible, but only with true commitment from all racial and ethnic groups. A White lady in the audience also chose to respond to my question. She shared her experience with desegregation, having been one of the White students who stayed at the school when the Black students were assigned there. Although many of her White classmates chose to leave the school when Black students were bused there, the ones who stayed welcomed the Black students and included them in all their activities, clubs, and organizations. And even now, she says, we make an active effort to include the Black alumni in our class reunion activities. She had no idea, I believe, of the language or tone she used which belied her "centered" position. It was still their (White) school, their community, and now their reunions; however, Black students are still welcome to be a part if they so choose.

LITERAL CRITIQUE OF *BROWN*

In my critical investigation of the *Brown* decision I inquire about the efficacy of interpreting the legally defining concept "separate is inherently
unequal" literally. Certainly there is overwhelming evidence that separate
was never equal under American Jim Crow existence. But to connect the
terms "separate" and "unequal" with the term "inherent" which speaks to
constitutional makeup, essential character, or intrinsic nature of something we posit is problematic. Quite simply and literally, separate is not
inherently unequal. However, when politically motivated acts of institutional domination such as racism, classism, and sexism, are factored into
the equation then yes, separate may always result in unequal and
inequitable treatment of the dominated group. The NAACP lawyers' legal
strategy initially focused on taking the *Plessy* standard seriously by insist-
ing that states provide a truly "separate but equal" education. The separate part was not the problem, but getting them to achieve the equal part
would prove more challenging. This strategy required fighting district by
district for Black schools to be brought up to par with their White only
counterparts without directly assaulting the *Plessy* doctrine of "separate
but equal." Realizing how daunting and time consuming that fight would
be prompted the NAACP lawyers to resolve in 1950 that nothing other
than education of all children on a nonsegregated basis would be an
acceptable outcome. It was this revelation that established the final
groundwork for what would become *Brown v. Board of Education* (Landman, 2004).

The NAACP lawyers' redirection in strategy turned what would have
been a pyrrhic victory at best to a bold assault on the very core of the
Plessy doctrine of "separate but equal," racism. The five cases joined to
comprise *Brown v. Board of Education* were explicit protests in relation to
"deprivations of public schooling for their [Black] children" (Dentler,
1991, p. 30) because they wanted their children's educational resources
and opportunities to be equivalent to White children's opportunities and
resources, not merely because they wanted their children to attend White
schools. Indeed, Dentler explains that, although Thurgood Marshall, the
leading defense attorney for *Brown*, was explicitly strategizing to "uncou-
ple the power of the state from all policies that used race as a criterion for
action or for neglect" (p. 31), his purpose in education was to force a
redistribution of resources. The logic applied by Marshall was that if White
parents had to send their children to schools with as few resources as
available in Black schools, had no transportation available to bus their
children to school, and their school facilities were as shabby as the Black
school facilities, then White parents would successfully push to have
improvements made quickly (Dentler, 1991). The logic of Marshall was

admirable, yet over 50 years post-*Brown*, there is much evidence that desegregated schools and *de facto* segregated schools have managed to continue to differentiate between resources, facilities and educational opportunities connected to race (Kozol, 1992; Nieto, 1999).

The *Brown* decision represents a monumental shift in the history of Constitutional law primarily because it removed any support for segregationist policy and practice (Landman, 2004). While commemorating the 50th anniversary of the *Brown* decision, I acknowledge that the NAACP lawyers, arguably, designed a strategy that ultimately became an assault on American racism. Further reflection should then prompt inquiry into what we have learned about racism since *Brown*.

Hilliard (2001) cites the preface of Lynd's 1970 book, *Who Needs the Negro*, in which Lynd describes Sidney Willhelm's thinking on the structural nature of racism.

> It does not follow that, because racism is economic in origin, racism can be overcome by economic change. The racism of white Americans has become a "dominant and autonomous social value." Racism expresses itself within economic limits created by white American's need for black American labor. If the white American no longer needed the black man's labor, this does not mean that the white American would no longer be racist. On the contrary ... he might feel free to express his racism more fully: not merely to exploit the black American, as in the last 300 years, but to kill him. (p. 14)

This is powerful commentary! Willhelm compares the plight of Black people in America with that of the Native American who fell out of economic usefulness to the European and was nearly annihilated. Is the American education system contributing to a genocidal conspiracy against students of color and students from economically stressed environments? Although this question may seem farfetched to some, consider the Herrnstein and Murray's (1994) reference to those in the bottom quartile of IQ as "worthless and expendable people" (Hilliard, as cited in Watkins, Lewis, & Chou, 2001, p. 15). Herrnstein and Murray (1994) expand this notion for clarification:

> In economic terms and barring a profound change in direction for our society, many people will be unable to perform that function so basic to human dignity: putting more into the world than they take out... For many people, there is nothing they can learn that will repay the cost of the teaching. (pp. 519–520)

Herrnstein and Murray (1994) represent an extreme position, but not a new position. So long as there are those in society who still believe in racial superiority and segregation we will continue to battle racial injustice and inequitable resource production and distribution. Fifty years after *Brown*, America is still witness to stubborn segregation and resegregation in many of our urban schools, retrenchment of civil rights and affirmative action policy, and repackaged methods of practicing institutional racism. Legal recourse to address these social issues has not proven sufficient to abate their effects on public education. Political, social, and economic recourse that involves every aspect of American life at the level of ideology is necessary to prevent further retrenchment of the gains achieved by the *Brown* legal scholars.

THE "PROBLEM" OF *BROWN*

Problematizing the *Brown* decision according to deficit theory, contact theory, and colorblind theory is helpful as we honor the legacy and carry out what we believe to have been its intent, remove racism and its effects from public education. The deficit thinking model (Valencia, 1997) essentially blames the victim for his or her condition. Students who fail in school are either internally deficient (cognitive and motivational problems) or products of home and community environments that do not value education and are otherwise dysfunctional. Teachers and school leaders are increasingly being held accountable for low-income and student of color failure. Many are clueless that their attitudes toward teaching or leading these students are reflective of an unenlightened view of educating across racial, cultural, and ethnic boundaries. This problem is directly connected to the rationale behind contact theory (Allport, 1954), which admonishes us to not expect equality of outcomes when two groups with power differentials are brought together without acknowledging and renegotiating the power differential.

Finally, several theories abound regarding the practice of colorblindness as it relates to people who have built their societies upon a hierarchy of skin color foundation. Supreme Court Justice John Marshall Harlan is noted for his hopes for a colorblind society in his dissenting opinion of the *Plessy v. Ferguson* decision back in 1896. There is a movement in educational circles today encouraging us to disregard skin color and treat everyone as equals in spite of the color of their skin. That, quite frankly, is easier said than done. American society has institutionalized skin color into the very fabric of society. Just as our efforts to achieve a separate but equal society failed, so is destined our efforts to achieve a colorblind one. In theory, yes, people should be judged by the content of their character, not the color of their skin. It will require a monumental deconstruction of race mythology and all of the institutions that owe their existence to the concept of color stratification. Schofield (as cited in Banks & Banks, 2005) reminds us that it is not a very great leap from the colorblind perspective, which says that race is a social category of no relevance to one's behavior and decisions, to a belief that individuals should not or perhaps even do not notice each other's racial group membership. (p. 270)

Bonilla-Silva (2003) argues that America has replaced its reliance on Jim Crow segregation to practice racism with a new form he refers to as color-blind racism. He poignantly asks how we still have persistent racial inequality in the United States without racists. No White person in proper circles is willing to admit that he or she is racist or practices racism, but yet there does not appear to be a shortage of evidence of inequity and inequality owed to racial discrimination. His research reveals colorblind racism to operate at a much more subtle and insidious level masked behind the guise of abstract liberalism (equal opportunity); naturalization (self-segregation is natural); cultural racism (Blacks don't value education); and minimization of racism (things are better now than in the past). Unless educators are prepared in ways that sensitizes them to identify forms of colorblind racism and empowers them to negate its impact on marginalized groups, we will not make progress. I believe that the recent removal of the term "social justice" from NCATE's (National Council for Accreditation of Teacher Education) glossary of dispositions amid heated controversy to be a prime example of colorblind racism. The movement toward centrality and neutrality so as not to appear ideologically persuaded does not bode well for social and educational transformation.

CONCLUSION: APPLYING THE LESSONS OF *BROWN*

Frances Fowler (2004) wants educational leaders to consider two important propositions about educational policy. First, she suggests that educational leaders need to understand power and how to use it responsibly. Policy, she says, grows out of conflict between different individuals, groups, and institutions and the outcome of these struggles reflects the balance of power among the participants. Certainly the balance of power among the participants in the *Brown* case was uneven with the NAACP lawyers representing a race and class of people who had suffered gross human indignity at the hands of a hegemonic institutionalized superstructure built on racism and classism. *Brown* was a classic case of David versus Goliath. If the lessons of *Brown* can teach us anything, it can teach us about "both the dynamics of everyday American power politics and how powerful interests use institutions and culture to perpetuate injustices based on race, gender, and class" (p. xii).

Second, Fowler (2004) believes that all public policy, especially education policy, is value laden. The schools of political scientists who think they can conduct "value-free" analysis operate from a fundamental misconception about social reality. They fail to realize that policymaking is inherently intertwined with values. Justice Warren's opinion in *Brown* echoed Thurgood Marshall's expert witnesses, stating that for Black children, segregation "generates a feeling of inferiority as to their status in the community that may affect their hearts and minds in a way that is unlikely to be ever undone" (Appiah & Gates, 2003, p. 97). When critics disparaged the emphasis on psychological and sociological evidence used to *win* Brown, Warren argued for the importance of contradicting *Plessy*, which purported that Black people had imagined any "badge of inferiority" conferred by segregation. The Warren court recognized the critical connection between policy and values by allowing value-laden evidence into a case they knew would become the source of much policymaking, educational and otherwise, for years to come. Thus *Brown* again teaches us to continue to defy conventional wisdom and chart new paths to win social justice for America's miseducated youth.

What I have gathered from the many *Brown* analysts is that the 1954 Supreme Court ruling *Brown* offered minimal definitive direction for the legal battles that have followed. It seems that the decision was more of a symbolic victory than a substantive one as far as equal educational opportunity is concerned. Article 13 of the International Covenant on Economic, Social, and Cultural Rights recognizes the right of everyone to an education that contributes to the full development of the human personality, its sense of dignity, and respect for human rights and fundamental freedoms. It further affirms that education shall enable all persons to participate effectively in a free society, promote understanding, tolerance, and friendship among all nations and all racial, ethnic or religious groups, and further the activities of the United Nations for the maintenance of peace. Intragovernmental separation of educational opportunity of both varieties, de facto and de jure, especially where "race" is the separating factor is not good policy. Internationally speaking, educational systems are separated by virtue of geography and often by ideology. To immediately conclude that all separation is inherently unequal without thorough consideration of the sometimes-complex factors that create separation is a rush to judgment. My hope is that a world, which has been made "smaller" via technology, continues to work to bring about compliance with the International Covenant's belief in the redemptive and unifying value of education in the world community.

REFERENCES

Allport, G. W. (1954). *The nature of prejudice* (Abridged ed.). Garden City, NY: Doubleday.

Anderson, C. (2001). *PowerNomics: The national plan to empower Black America.* Bethesda, MD: PowerNomics Corporation of America.

Anderson, J. D. (1988). *The education of Blacks in the South, 1860–1935.* Chapel Hill: The University of North Carolina Press.

Appiah K., & Gates, H. (Eds.). (2003). *Africana: The concise desk reference.* Philadelphia: Running Press.

Asante, M. (Spring, 1991) The afrocentric idea in education, *Journal of Negro Education, 60*(2), 170–180.

Asante, M. (1993). *Malcolm X as cultural hero & other Afrocentric essays.* Lawrenceville, NJ: Africa World Press.

Banks, J., & Banks, C. (Eds.). (2005). *Multicultural education: issues and perspectives.* Hoboken, NJ: Wiley.

Bonilla-Silva, E. (2003). *Racism without racists: Color-blind racism and the persistence of racial inequality in the United States.* New York: Rowman & Littlefield.

Brown v. Board of Education, 347 U.S. 483. (1954)

Cummins, J. (2000). *Language, power, and pedagogy: Bilingual children in the crossfire.* Clevedon, North Somerset UK: Multilingual Matters.

Delgado, R. (Ed.). (1995). *Critical race theory: The cutting edge.* Philadelphia: Temple University Press.

Dentler, R. A. (1991). School desegregation since Gunnar Myrdal's American Dilemma. In C. V. Willie, A. M. Garibaldi, & W. L. Reed (Eds.), *The education of African Americans* (pp. 27–50). New York: Auburn.

Du Bois, W. E. B. (1993). *The souls of Black folk.* New York: Knopf. (Original work published 1903)

Du Bois, W. E. B. (1935). *Black reconstruction in America: An essay toward a history of the part which Black folk played in the attempt to reconstruct democracy in America, 1860-1880.* New York: Atheneum.

Exploring Constitutional Conflicts. (n.d.). Retrieved September 15, 2006, from http://www.law.umkc.edu/faculty/projects/ftrials/ conlaw powers13th14th15th.htm

Fowler, F. C. (2004). *Policy studies for educational leaders: an introduction* (2nd ed.). Upper Saddle River, NJ: Pearson.

Franklin, J. H. (1969). *From slavery to freedom: a history of Negro Americans.* New York: Vintage Books. (Original work published 1947)

Frazier, E. F. (1962). *Black bourgeoisie: The rise of a new middle class in the United States.* New York: Collier-Macmillan. (Original work published 1957)

Freire, P. (1993). *Pedagogy of the oppressed.* New York: Continuum. (Original work published 1970)

García, E. (1999). *Student cultural diversity: Understanding and meeting the challenge* (2nd ed.). Boston: Houghton Mifflin.

Greene, L. (1971). *The Negro in colonial New England.* New York: Antheneum. (Original work published 1942)

Guinier, L. (1998). *Lift every voice: Turning civil rights setbacks into a new vision of social justice*. New York: Simon & Schuster.

Herrnstein, R. J., & Murray, C. A. (1994). *The bell curve: Intelligence and class structure in American life*. New York: Free Press.

Hilliard, A. (2001). "Race," identity, hegemony, and education: What do we need to know now? In W. Watkins, J. Lewis, & V. Chou (Eds.), *Race and education: The roles of history and society in educating African American students* (pp. 7–33). Boston: Allyn & Bacon.

Holtz, M., Dougherty, J., Michaels J., Marcus, I., & Peduzzi, R. (Eds.). (1989). *Education and the American dream: Conservatives, liberals & radicals debate the future of education*. New York: Bergin & Garvey.

hooks, b. (1994). *Teaching to transgress: Education as the practice of freedom*. New York: Routledge.

Kincheloe, J. L., Slattery, P., & Steinberg, S. R. (2000). *Contextualizing teaching: Introduction to education and educational foundations*. New York: Longman.

Kozol, J. (1992). *Savage inequalities: Children in America's schools*. New York: Harper Perennial.

Ladson-Billings, G. (2004, October). Landing on the wrong note: The price we paid for *Brown*. *Educational Researcher, 33*(7), 3–13.

Landman, J. H. (2004). Brown v. Board of Education: Looking back 50 years. *Social Education, 68*, 17–24.

Lewis, D. L. (Ed.). (1995). *W. E. B. Du Bois: A reader*, New York: Henry Holt.

Madhubuti, H., & Madhubuti, S. (1994) *African centered education: Is value, importance, and necessity in the development of black children*. Chicago: Third World Press.

Miller, K. (1968). *Radicals and conservatives: And other essays on the Negro in America*. New York: Schocken Books. (Original work published 1908)

Morris, V., & Morris, C. (2002). *The price they paid: Desegregation in an African American community*. New York: Teachers College Press.

Nash, G. (1988). *Forging freedom: The formation of Philadelphia's Black community 1720–1840*. Massachusetts: Harvard University Press.

Nicholson, D. (1990, September 23). Afrocentrism and the tribalization of America: The misguided logic of ethnic educational schemes. *The Washington Post*, p. B1.

Nieto, S. (1999). *The light in their eyes: Creating multicultural learning communities*. New York: Teachers College Press.

Olneck, M. R. (1995). Immigrants and education. In J. A. Banks & C. A. M. Banks (Eds.), *Handbook or research on multicultural education* (pp. 310–327). New York: Macmillan.

Plessy v. Ferguson, 163 U.S. 537 (1896). Retrieved from http://en.wikipedia.org/wiki/Plessy_v._Ferguson

Pollard, D. S., & Ajirotutu, C. S. (2000). *African-centered schooling in theory and practice*. Westport, CT: Bergin & Garvey.

Sadker, D., & Sadker, K. (2004). Gender bias: From colonial America to today's classrooms. In J. A. Banks & C. A. M. Banks (Eds.), *Multicultural education: Issues and perspectives* (5th ed., pp. 135–159). New York: Wiley.

Schlesinger, A. (1998). *The disuniting of America*. New York: Norton.

Schofield, J. W. (1995). Review of research on school desegregation's impact on elementary and secondary school students. In J. A. Banks & C. A. M. Banks (Eds.), *Handbook of research on multicutlural education* (pp. 597–616). New York: Simon & Schuster Macmillan.

Scott, J. (1976). *The black revolts: Racial stratification in the U.S.A. The politics of estate, caste, and class in the American society.* Boston: Schenkman.

Shujaa, M. (Ed.). (1994). *Too much schooling too little education: A paradox of Black life in White societies.* Lawrenceville, NJ: Africa World Press.

Spring, J. (1994). *The American school, 1642–1993* (3rd ed.). New York: McGraw-Hill.

Stephan, W. (1999). *Reducing prejudice and stereotyping in schools.* New York: Teachers College Press.

Valencia, R. (1997). *The evolution of deficit thinking educational thought and practice.* London: Falmer Press.

Walker, V. S. (1996). *Their highest potential: An African American school community in the segregated south.* Chapel Hill: The University of North Carolina Press.

Watkins, W., Lewis, J., & Chou, V. (2001). *Race and education: The roles of history and society in educating African American students.* Boston: Allyn & Bacon.

Woodson, C. G. (1977). *The mis-education of the Negro.* Washington DC: Associated Press. (Original work published 1933)

Woodson, C. G. (1969). *The Negro professional man and the community: With special emphasis on the physician and the lawyer.* New York: Negro Universities Press. (Original work published 1934)

CHAPTER 3

(OUT)SIDERS AT THE GATES

Administrative Aspirants' Attitudes Towards the Gay Community

Autumn Tooms and Judy A. Alston

Using the Attitudes Towards Lesbians and Gay Men Scale (ATLG) this study focused on two groups of graduate students in graduate level leadership preparation programs. Research questions that framed this study were: What are students' who are aspiring to school leadership positions attitudes toward lesbians and gays? What are students' attitudes concerning issues of equity as it relates to lesbians and gays? Findings for question one revealed that very few respondent were neutral on this issue with a majority of the population (61%) tending to have more tolerant attitudes toward members of the queer community. Regarding question two, survey responses showed a more even spectrum of responses. What is most interesting is that 35% of respondents were neutral about issues concerning equity.

INTRODUCTION

It was a typical Tuesday night in Room 107 of the College of Education, one of the oldest buildings on a large university campus in the Midwest.

Leadership for Social Justice: Promoting Equity and Excellence Through Inquiry and Reflective Practice, pp. 61–74

The aspiring school administrators enrolled in the graduate level "Women in Leadership" course were discussing issues surrounding power, oppression, and what it means to live as a member of a marginalized group. Bob, a White male in his 20s entered the conversation by saying,

> Isn't all the talk about feminism overrated at this point? I mean it's the year 2005. I love women, I don't have any issues with them, and it looks to me like they are doing well as compared to where they were in the sixties. I took this course because I don't understand why there is this sort of whining about not being treated right. I think we have come a long way towards respecting women. Hasn't everything changed in the last forty years?

Wendy, a Black woman in her 40s aspiring to open a charter school answered,

> You have no idea about my plight because you are a White male. You have never experienced what it means to be marginalized. Of course you don't get it; you can't because you haven't lived it. You don't see the struggle that I have lived.

The professor interjected, at this point, her opinion,

> The idea of unpacking privilege is what this course is all about. That's why privilege is a difficult thing to grasp because it is something that is taken for granted. And there are different kinds of privilege because there are different kinds of oppression. So tonight we have touched on the fact that White males may not understand privilege in the way that Black females do. Can anyone think of any other marginalized groups that might be wrestling with the same sorts of issues in our culture?

Morgan, a White woman in her 30s offered, "What about gays and lesbians?" Before the professor could respond, she noticed that Wendy had crossed her arms on her chest and had a frown on her face. So the professor asked Wendy to explain her body language. Wendy said,

> I just don't get that. I mean the gay thing is different than an issue of race. I mean who does the dishes in a set up like that? And why do I have to be a part of that? That's business I don't need brought in my face.

The professor responded,

> Wendy do you realize you have just expressed the same kind of view towards a marginalized group that Bob offered a few minutes ago? The same privileged and narrow sentiments that caused you to passionately respond to Bob are what you are now expressing about a different group of people that are not part of the dominant culture.

Wendy thought for a minute and said, "Well yeah, but gay is different than Black. I don't understand them." And Bob then said, "You mean just like I don't understand you?"

The above story is an account of what one of the authors experienced in her class during the fall semester of 2005. We see this is as a perfect example of the importance of addressing issues concerned with learning more about aspiring leaders attitudes towards members of the lesbian and gay community. As we continue to rethink how we train administrators to lead our schools, we must be cognizant of their intellectual experiences in terms of social justice and diversity issues. A step in this direction is to begin to understand the contextual frameworks aspiring leaders bring to their training experience in relation to a marginalized community that only recently has become part of the discussions centered on diversity.

The purpose of this study is to provide more information within the realm of leadership preparation by examining the attitudes of graduate students in school leadership preparation programs towards members of the queer community. Research questions that framed this study were:

(a) What are students' who are aspiring to school leadership positions attitudes toward lesbians and gays?
(b) What are students' attitudes concerning issues of equity as it relates to lesbians and gays?

LITERATURE REVIEW

In a historical context, attitudes towards gays and lesbians have varied. As Cabaj (1998) noted, there have been times when gay men and lesbians have been held in high esteem and other times when they have been feared and persecuted. This type of persecution has been termed homophobia (Herek, 1989). In ancient times, same-sex marriages were not only tolerated but were sanctioned by the Roman state (Rainey, 2001). When the Roman Catholic Church became the officiating body to conduct marriage ceremonies, homophobia began increasing. Laws were enacted in Rome and England that began the criminalization of homosexual behavior. However, same-sex marriages were still taking place as late as the 1500s. By the mid-1800s, psychiatry began to view homosexuality as a mental illness in direct confluence with the mores of Victorian England. This influence continues today in the form of social homophobia despite the new findings on sexuality, education of the public, and the political movements generated in the 1960s (Cabaj, 1998).

Educators all over the world continue to grapple with issues of diversity within their community. Issues of tolerance and accountability in terms of ethnicity can be traced in the American educational system to the 1954 *Brown* decision in which schools were desegregated. In terms of higher education, institutions have been called upon to recognize that a university is comprised of many different communities that must be intertwined in order to meet the needs of students from different backgrounds. Moses (1990) suggested that it is necessary to apply a model of cultural pluralism "in which diversity is valued to structure the university in a way that facilitates cross cultural learning among the many segments of the university" (p. 403). And while the student population of school has become increasingly diverse, the teacher population has remained relatively homogenous (Butler, 1994). Zimpher (1989) described the typical teacher education student as a White middle class female, who grew up in a rural or small town, attends a school which is close to home, and has limited geographic aspirations for the future. Furthermore, Alston (2004) noted that in 2001, there were nearly 3 million teachers in the public schools with approximately 2 million at the elementary level and 1.5 million at the secondary level (National Center for Educational Statistics [NCES], 2001). The majority of these teachers were White, female, and English-only speakers (Hodgkinson, 2000, 2001; Garcia, 1999). In 2001, the National Education Association (NEA) reported that among K–12 new teachers 7% were African American, 1% were Asian American, 4% were Hispanic, 5% were First Nations, and 83% were White. This is the pool of educators that become leaders in schools. Thus, many of the teachers who will become administrators have little to no experience with other cultural groups.

Moreover, our society continues to struggle with the idea that diversity speaks to issues beyond ethnicity. Sears (1992) encouraged educators to borrow from the work and experiences of those involved in antiracism workshops who engage professionals in 3 to 5 day tolerance workshops. He stated,

> There has been a tendency for those engaged in homophobia education not to collaborate with those engaged in other types of anti-oppression work, such as racism and sexism. This lack of communication contributes to the splintering of educational efforts to end prejudice and violence directed at lesbians, gay men, and bisexuals. (p. 60)

Because of this inability of our culture to embrace the idea that oppression transcends ethnicity, gender, and sexual preference, we see that the manifestations of homophobia and heterosexism experienced by gays, lesbians, and bisexuals serve as sources of conflict between the heteronormative culture that permeates the pool of administrative aspirants. An even stronger rationale for educating future school leaders about the issues surrounding homosexual oppression is that unlike gender or race, sexual orientation may not be obvious or revealed (Garnet, Hancock, Cochran, Goodchilds, & Peplau, 1991). So in essence by ignoring the issues, we continue to produce school leaders who may not seek to recognize populations that are oppressed within their own schools.

While there is body of literature that speaks to the broad topic of gay and lesbian issues in education, there is almost no empirical research that focuses specifically on lesbian/gay issues as it is related to school administration. Sears (1992) recommended four goals for research with sexual minority administrators: (a) chronicle their lives, (b) document institutional experiences, (c) attempt to understand the heterosexist/homophobic mind, and (d) through the combination of the first three, transform schools society and ourselves. Furthermore, Sears found that some gay and lesbian youth perceived school counselors and teachers to be ill-informed and unconcerned about issues centered on their sexual development. There is a reluctance to address the issue of sexual orientation in schools due in part to the fact that gay men and lesbians are often not considered to comprise a particular cultural group (Marcus, 1993). In other words, they are not considered to have developed unique values, attitudes, ways of knowing, and ways of living as a result of identifying themselves as gay or lesbian.

Conceptual Frame

Social oppression has been defined as "the systematic, socially supported mistreatment and exploitation of a group or category of people by another" (WebRef.Org, n.d.). Forms of social oppression include (but are not limited to) racism, sexism, classism, ableism, ageism, and heterosexism. All of these "isms" are based on social constructions and are internalized and reinforced by family, friends, and neighbors (Schmitz, Stakeman, & Sisneros, 2001). Additionally, Herek, D'Augelli, and Patterson (1995) noted that

> heterosexism is manifested at both the cultural and the individual levels. Cultural heterosexism, like institutional racism and sexism, pervades societal customs and institutions. It operates through a dual process: *homosexuality* [italics added] is usually rendered invisible and, when people who engage in homosexual behavior or who are identified as homosexual become visible, they are attacked by society. (p. 26)

Audre Lorde (1983) stated "that among those of us who share the goals of liberation and workable future for our children, there can be no hierarchies of oppression" (p. 22). However, as Adams (2000) noted, this does not mean that different forms of oppression do not affect people in different ways. She further notes that it is useless to argue victimhood, but it is more productive to understand the dynamics of social oppression and how they affect us as a society.

DESCRIPTION OF DATA SOURCE AND METHOD

The authors of this research chose to study two groups of graduate students in graduate level leadership preparation programs: Group I consisted of 42 graduate students enrolled in a midsize public university in the Midwestern United States. Group II consisted of 132 graduate students enrolled in a large public university in the Southern United States. The survey instrument used for this study was the Attitudes Towards Lesbians and Gay Men Scale (ATLG). Developed in 1984 by Herek, the ATLG Scale is a brief measure of heterosexuals' attitudes toward gay men and women. The ATLG treats these attitudes as one instance of intergroup attitudes, similar in psychological structure and function to interracial and interethnic attitudes. Borrowing from public discourse surrounding sexual orientation, the scale represents statements that tap heterosexuals' affective responses to homosexuality and to gay men and lesbians (Herek, 1984). The ATLG instrument has 20 Likert-type questions, 10 of which are a subscale to measure attitudes toward lesbians and ten are a subscale to measure attitudes towards gay men. Response choices on the instrument were ranked on scale from of 1 to 5 with 1 corresponding to "total disagreement" with the statement while a 5 signified "total agreement" with the statement.

A Cronbach's alpha was conducted as a measure of internal reliability. The overall alpha was .94 indicating a high level of reliability and internal consistency. Additionally, a principal component analysis was conducted to determine if there were any underlying dimensions. An independent t-test was also performed between the mean responses of Group I and the mean responses of Group II on each item on the instrument. Significant differences were found on only four items (one, five, six, and seven). Group I was significantly more tolerant one these items than Group II. However, given the relatively few differences that emerged, it was deemed appropriate by the authors to combine the two samples into one large pool for a further principal component analysis.

FINDINGS

The principal component analysis conducted with the large pool of survey responses revealed three underlying factors. These dimensions accounted for 64% of the total variance. Factor one contained question items 3, 1, 10, 8, 13, 6, 9, and 5. This factor was labeled by the authors as attitudes towards lesbians (queer females) and accounted for 26% of the variance. Factor two contained items, 18, 16, 12, 19, and 14. This factor was labeled by the authors as attitudes towards gays (queer males) and accounted for 21% of the variance. Factor three contained items 17, 11, 15, 20, 4, and 2. This factor was labeled as attitudes towards homosexuality and accounted for 17% of the variance.

Attitudes Toward the Gay and Lesbian Community

In terms of Research Question 1 ("What are students' who are aspiring to school leadership positions attitudes toward lesbians and gays?") survey responses to Factor One (Attitudes toward lesbians) and Factor Two (Attitudes toward gays) revealed that very few respondent were neutral on this issue with a majority of the population (61%) tending to have more tolerant attitudes toward members of the queer community and a minority of the population (30%) tending to have more intolerant attitudes toward the queer community. However, 61% can not be an acceptable number when we consider that this population will be charged with leading our nation's schools.

Homophobia must become a point of focus among prospective school administrators because it can directly and indirectly affect students. Given the negative relationships between knowledge and attitude, carefully planned, and implemented instruction may be helpful in changing negative attitudes towards members of the sexual minority. There is evidence in the literature that education about gay and lesbian issues can have a positive effect on homophobic attitudes (Anderson, 1981; Voss, 1980). This data serves at best as a cry for educators to again consider a curriculum that encompasses a strand focused understanding of diversity issues. Educational efforts geared towards changing homophobic attitudes have historically taken a cognitive approach, an affective approach (Pagtolun-An & Clair, 1986), or a combination of both (Rudolph, 1989).

The best way to understand the difference between these two approaches is to know that cognitive frameworks tend to focus on knowledge acquisition and transformation whereas affective frameworks focus more on feelings, emotions, and attitudes. Cognitive strategies typically include lecture, discussion, review, audiovisuals, and assigned readings (Ormrod, 1990). Affective approaches include speaker panels, role plays, simulations, small group discussions, case studies, debates, poetry, and photographs (Beane, 1990). A key focus point for these efforts centers on empathy. When we as leaders of a diverse culture demonstrate apathy toward the heteronormative nature of our society, we only increase the existing hegemony by naturalizing it. Critical work is needed to help address the issues of diversity that are not always apparent in a school community.

By employing educational intervention strategies that focus on empathy towards members of the gay and lesbian community and an understanding of the heterosexist culture, future school administrators are allowed the opportunities to build a framework of empathy and a social conscience that will empower them throughout their career. Moreover, administrators who have been enlightened to the perspectives of those in the gay and lesbian community maybe more likely to help build a culture of tolerance in their own schools.

Having a sound knowledge base may help educators respond to the emotional or "moral" arguments with logic and factual information (Sobocinski, 1990). Furthermore, Herek (1989) stated that educators can play an important role in reducing the bigotry which underlies anti-gay sentiment and action. He suggested that school staffs should "receive explicit training in sensitivity to lesbian and gay issues to prepare them to foster tolerance and reduce conflicts in their students. Additionally, such training should be reflected in licensing and professional degree requirements" (p. 954). This is not the first call for training in sensitivity and or empathy towards gay and lesbian issues for those who work in schools. Rainey (2001) agreed that there should be training of this sort when considering the professional development educators as well as those who specialize in school counseling. However, he noted that:

> There would be great difficulty in creating changes at the university level because of current attitudes held toward lesbians and gay men by society in general. The university could possibly face political and economic consequences by taking an overt stand on gay and lesbian issues. Social change would probably have to precede changes at the university level; however, this could be an opportunity for the university to affect social change. (p. 55)

The 31% of respondents who demonstrated an intolerant attitude towards gays and lesbians in this study is further evidence that homophobia is still pervasive in our culture. While we can recognize that there are strides being made towards acceptance of those in the sexual minority, this statistic serves as a further call to action for those involved in administrative preparation programs.

Attitudes Concerning Issues of Equity

Regarding Research Question 2 (What are students' attitudes concerning issues of equity as it relates to lesbians and gays?), survey responses showed a more even spectrum of responses with a significant number of neutral responses for each question in the factor. In general, 40% of respondents tended to be more supportive of equity for gays and lesbians with 25% being non supportive of equity for gays. What is most interesting is that 35% of respondents were neutral about issues concerning equity. The authors of this current research wonder if the neutrality of responses is a symptom of apathy in the pool of aspiring school leaders when considering issues centered on the sexual minority. Furthermore, these authors contend that neutrality concerning issues of equity and marginalized groups is in direct conflict with the concept of leading in a democratic society. Just as with issues related to other marginalized groups, neutrality regarding an issue of oppression is a symptom of one who has not considered thoughtfully the world in which they live. Discussions surrounding the theory and practice of how domination works are essential to helping aspiring leaders reflect on the world in which they live as well as their role in it. In becoming aware of both the positions they inhabit and the locations from which they speak, aspiring leaders are better able to take responsibility for, and transform their beliefs and actions (Popekewitz & Brennan, 1997). McIntosh (1988) attempted to articulate struggle with coming to understand the concept of White privilege when she noted that:

> whites are carefully taught not to recognize white privilege, as males are taught not to recognize male privilege. So I have begun in an untutored way to ask what it is like to have white privilege. I have come to see white privilege as an invisible package of unearned assets that I can count on cashing in each day, but about which I was "meant" to remain oblivious. White privilege is like an invisible weightless knapsack of special provisions, maps, passports, codebooks, visas, clothes, tools, and blank checks. Describing white privilege makes one newly accountable. My schooling gave me no training in seeing myself as an oppressor, as an unfairly advantaged person, or as a participant in a damaged culture. I was taught to see myself as an individual whose moral state depended on her individual moral will. My schooling followed the pattern my colleague Elizabeth Minnich has pointed out: whites are taught to think of their lives as morally neutral, normative, and average, and also ideal, so that when we work to benefit others, this is seen as work that will allow "them" to be more like us. (p. 3)

In an effort to help others interpret what a culture of White dominance and privilege means in day to day life, McIntosh (1988) generated a list of

privileges taken for granted by those who were not members of an ethnically marginalized group. She recommended the list be used by the
reader as a tool to reflect and build empathy for members of an ethnically
marginalized group. While she does mention that the lack of these
privileges transcend to other oppressed groups, there is not an in-depth
mention of specific privileges within a heteronormative framework. Seeing this list as an inspiration, we propose a list specific to the lens of leading school communities (see Appendix), as a starting point for discussions
geared towards helping students reflect on their own attitudes, or lack of
attitudes, towards members of the sexual minority. The purpose is to generate a sense of empathy among those administrative aspirants who are
members of the sexual majority by asking them to consider their professional goals through a queer lens. Furthermore, these perspectives may
assist members of the heteronormative community of school administrators to move from a place of apathy to a place of empathy in terms of
their attitudes towards members of the lesbian and gay community.

CONCLUSION

While this chapter highlights that there is work to do, it also recognizes
that with the call towards democracy, leadership, and social justice, this is
the time for that work. Now is the time for action and change in leadership preparation programs. Oft times we let things go without addressing
them, hoping that somehow they will disappear. We have reached a new
era in society where LGBT2S (Lesbian, Gay, Bisexual, Transgender, Two
Spirit) people are no longer hiding in the closet, but are out and proud,
even in public education.

Educational leadership preparation programs are charged with preparing the nation's schools leaders and these programs would be negli-
gent in that training should they not prepare future leaders who are
grounded in social justice. As educational leaders who set the tone for
staff and students in our school communities, principals must actively
work to build a respectful and inclusive school climate (Goodman, 2005).
Heterosexist attitudes and beliefs must be addressed, eliminated, and
changed in order to create safe, respectful schools for students and adults
of all sexual orientations.

As we continue on this road toward justice, we must heed the words of
Margaret Mead (1935):

> If we are to achieve a richer culture, rich in contrasting values, we must rec-
> ognize the whole gamut of human potentialities, and so we weave a less

arbitrary social fabric, one in which each diverse human gift will find a fitting place. (p. 322)

APPENDIX

Heterosexual Privilege Checklist

1. I can be pretty sure that if I live my school's community, my neighbors will be pleasant or neutral to me.
2. I can feel confident about the kind of ring I wear on the third finger of my left hand.
3. I am free to put in my office mementos and photos of my personal life.
4. I can confidently explain to my secretary that my partner or spouse gets immediate access to me when they call or visit my school.
5. I can feel confident in discussing the details of my weekend activities in a group of people
6. I can feel confident that when I hug a student or faculty member of the same sex, it is interpreted as an honest act of support or admiration.
7. If I was a successful athlete, physical education, drama, art, or dance teacher, I can feel confident that people will not assume my success is based on my sexual preference.
8. I can be confident that people do not confuse my sexual preference with pedophilia.
9. I can do well in a challenging situation without being called a credit to the group that shares my sexual orientation
10. I am free to publicly display affection for my partner, date, or spouse, when walking in a shopping mall, eating dinner in a restaurant, grocery shopping, running in a neighborhood park, or attending a school community event.
11. I am free to demonstrate that I and or my family is community minded by including my significant other and or children in school/community events such as carnivals, plays, concerts, and dance.
12. When students come to me for mentorship and counseling about their issues concerning sexuality, I am free to be honest about my own and I do not have to think twice about how I am counseling them.
13. I can dance with my partner at my school's prom.

14. I do not have to be concerned about who answers the telephone in my home if it rings early in the morning, in the evening or on the weekends.

15. If I am proposed to by my significant other, and accept, I can enjoy sharing the news with my coworkers, inviting them to my wedding and all the other ceremonies related to it.

16. I do not have to worry about insurance for my spouse because he or she is covered by my insurance.

17. I know that when I die, my spouse will receive the social security benefits that I spent a career earning.

18. I don't have to travel with a legal portfolio that grants me entrance into the emergency room and power of attorney for my partner and or our children in case there is an accident.

19. If I choose to be assertive, or emotional, my action will not be seen as the result of my sexual orientation.

20. My sexual preference will not be considered related at all to my ability to parent, or to relate to children.

21. I do not function in a space where I feel as though I am forced to choose between deceiving people about my private life and being stripped of my credibility as an educational leader.

22. I am not concerned with having to tolerantly educate people who ask insensitive and embarrassing questions specific to my sex life in an effort to understand those who share my sexual preference.

23. I can feel free to practice my religion with my partner or spouse in a church, synagogue, or temple of my choosing that is in the same neighborhood as the school district that I serve.

24. I am not made acutely aware that my choice of specialty as an educator, hairstyle, dress, or choice of jewelry will be taken as a reflection of my sexual preference.

25. I can build a culture of tolerance and fight homophobia in my school without my sexuality being called into question.

26. I can be alone with colleagues of the same sex in a locker room at the gym, or share a hotel room at a business conference, and feel comfortable.

27. If I lose credibility as the leader, I can feel confident that my sexuality is not the problem.

28. I don't have to feel uncomfortable every time I write a check (for service organization dues, donations, the sunshine fund, etc.) because my name and my partner's name are printed on it.

Note: © Autumn Tooms and Judy Alston, 2005.

REFERENCES

Adams, M. (2000). Introduction. In M. Adams, W. Blumenfeld, R. Castaneda, H. Hackman, M. Peters, & X. Zuniga (Eds.), *Readings for diversity and social justice* (pp. 5–9). New York: Routledge.

Alston, J. (2004). The many faces of American schooling: Effective school research and border-crossing in the 21st century. *American Secondary Education, 32*(2), 79–93.

Anderson, C (1981). The effects of a workshop on attitudes of female nursing students toward male homosexuality. *Journal of Homosexuality, 7*(1), 57–69.

Beane, J. (1990). *Affect in the curriculum: Toward democracy, dignity, and diversity.* New York: Teachers College.

Brown v. Board of Education, 347 U.S. 483. (1954).

Butler, K. (1994). Homophobia among preservice elementary teachers. *Journal of Health Education, 23*(6), 355–359.

Cabaj, R. P. (1998). History of gay acceptance and relationships. In R. P. Cabaj & D. W. Purcell (Eds.), *On the road to same-sex marriage.* San Francisco: Jossey-Bass.

Garnet, L., Hancock, K., Cochran, S., Goodchilds, J., & Peplau, L. (1991). Issues in psychotherapy with lesbians and gay men: A survey of psychologists. *American Psychologist, 46*(9), 964–972.

Garcia, E. (1999). *Student cultural diversity: Understanding and meeting the challenge.* Boston: Houghton Mifflin.

Goodman, J. M. (2005). Homophobia prevention and intervention in elementary schools: A principal's responsibility. *Journal of Gay & Lesbian Issues in Education, 3*(1), 111–116.

Herek, G. M. (1984). Attitudes toward lesbians and gay men: A factor analytic study. *Journal of Homosexuality, 10*(1/2), 39–51.

Herek, G. M. (1989). Hate crimes against lesbians and gay men: Issues for research and policy. *American Psychologist, 44*(6), 948–955.

Herek, G. M., D'Augelli A. R., & Patterson, C. J. (1995). Psychological heterosexism in the United States. In A. R. D'Augelli & C. J. Patterson (Eds.), *Lesbian, gay, & bisexual identities over the lifespan* (p. 26). New York: Oxford University Press.

Hodgkinson, H. (2000). *Secondary schools in a new millennium.* Reston, VA: National Association of Secondary School Principals.

Hodgkinson, H. (2001). Educational demographics: What teachers should know. *Educational Leadership, 58*(4), 6–11.

Lorde, A. (1983). There is no hierarchy of oppressions. *International Books for Children Bulletin, 14*(3-4), 9.

Marcus, E. (1993). Is it a choice? *Answers to 300 of the most frequently asked questions about gays and lesbians.* San Francisco: Harper.

McIntosh, P. (1988). *White privilege and male privilege: A personal account of coming to see correspondences through work in women's studies* (Working Paper 189). Wellesley Centers for Women, Wellesley College.

Mead, M. (1935). *Sex and temperament in three primitive societies.* New York: William Morrow/Quill.

Moses, Y. (1990). The challenge of diversity: Anthropological perspectives on university culture. *Education and Urban society, 22*(4), 402–412.

National Center for Educational Statistics. (2001). *Digest of education statistics, 2001.* Washington, DC: U.S. Department of Education.

National Education Association. (2001). *Fact sheet on teacher shortages.* Washington, DC: Author.

Ormrod, J. (1990). *Human learning: Theories, principles, and educational applications.* Columbus, OH: Merrill.

Pagtolun-An, I., & Clair, J. (1986). An experimental study of attitudes toward homosexuals. *Deviant Behavior, 7*, 121–135.

Popkewitz, T., & Brennan, M. (Eds). (1997). *Foucault's challenge: Discourse, knowledge and power in education.* New York: Teachers College Press.

Rainey, J. (2001). *Predictors of homophobia in master's level counseling students.* Unpublished doctoral dissertation, Texas A&M University Commerce.

Rudolph, J. (1989). Effects of a workshop on mental health practitioner's attitudes toward homosexuality and counseling effectiveness. *Journal of Counseling and Development, 68*(5), 81–85.

Sears, J. T. (1992). *Educators, homosexuality, and homosexual students: Are personal feelings related to professional beliefs?* Binghamton, NY: Haworth Press.

Schmitz, C. L., Stakeman, C., & Sisneros, J. (2001). Educating professionals for practice in a multicultural society: Understanding oppression and valuing diversity. *Families in Society: The Journal of Contemporary Human Services, 82*(4), 612–622.

Sobocinski, M. (1990). Ethical principals in the counseling of gay and lesbian adolescents: Issues of autonomy, competence, and confidentiality. *Professional psychology: research and practice, 2*(4), 240–247.

Voss, J. (1980). Sex education: Evaluation and recommendations for future study. *Archives of sexual behavior, 9*(1), 37–59.

WebRef.Org (n.d.). Retrieved August 15, 2008, from http://www.webref.org/sociology/s/social_oppression.htm

Zimpher, N. (1989). The RATE project: A profile of teacher education students. *Journal of teacher education, 40*(6), 27–30.

CHAPTER 4

"THEY DON'T
SPEAK ENGLISH"

Interrogating (Racist) Ideologies and
Perceptions of School Personnel in
a Midwestern State

Gerardo R. López and Vanessa A. Vàzquez

This paper focuses on the attitudes and perceptions of school administrators, teachers, and other school personnel in a Latino-impacted school district in a Midwestern state. As this district struggles to meet the educational needs of a growing number of Latino students, this research finds that school officials increasingly employ assimilationist ideologies that not only privilege the English language, but view Latino students and their families as intellectually and culturally inferior. In this paper we make the argument that these practices reinforce a subtle, but powerful, form of benevolent racism: where "good intentions" and compassionate altruism reproduce and reify a highly racialized discourse.

Public concern over the growing number of undocumented immigrants has intensified in recent years (Daniels, 2004; Graham, 2006; Perea, 1997;

Leadership for Social Justice: Promoting Equity and Excellence Through Inquiry and Reflective Practice, pp. 75–96
Copyright © 2008 by Information Age Publishing
75

Portes & Rumbaut, 2006; Suárez-Orozco & Páez, 2002; Wells & Bryne, 1999). This concern is fueled by an outpouring of American patriotism, nationalist sentiment, and a renewed esprit-de-corps that has blanketed the nation in the wake of the 9/11 attacks. Indeed, as Americans search for a common symbol of allegiance to bring them together during these troubled times, they've found such symbols in the American flag, in patriotic songs, and in pleas for a common national language (Coryn, Beale, & Myers, 2004; Freyd, 2002; Gerstenfeld, 2002; López, 2002). As our nation struggles to heal itself from the wound inflicted within its borders, it has increasingly looked outside its borders as possible sites of worry, fear and trepidation. In an effort to allay public concerns over "weakened" borders and other potential threats to national security, U.S. public policy has now focused on immigration reform and border security as solutions to protect this country from future possible attacks (Cornelius, 2005; National Public Radio, 2004; Newport, 2004).

At the same time, the threat of terrorism has fueled a need to reexamine the contours of our "American" identity—as this country has done several times throughout its history, particularly during times of economic crises, political upheaval, and international conflict (Daniels, 2004; Suárez-Orozco & Suárez-Orozco, 2001). As in the past, what it means to be "American" is often defined conterminously with the characteristics of the dominant culture (Perea, 1992, 1997, 1998). Individuals who do not fit this mold are viewed as outsiders, foreign, or alien. This often leads to xenophobic and racist reactions, as many of these "outsiders" often become the target of ridicule, disparagement, scorn, and vilification:

> It happened to the Irish of the 1850s, the Germans during WWI, the Japanese during WWII, the Mexicans during Operation Wetback, and the Russians during the Cold War. In fact, the very definition of what and who is an "American" has shifted as different "out groups" become "in groups" when the situation and historical circumstances change. (López, 2002, p. 198)

It is against this backdrop of social and political tension, with a war on terror being fought both abroad and within our borders, in which the U.S. Senate voted to make English the "national language" of the United States in May of 2006 (Hulse, 2006).

What is problematic about this political maneuver is that it happened in the wake of large-scale immigration reform. In effect, the Senate's move to "link" language issues with immigration not only positioned the English language as a linchpin of the immigration debate, but wrongly conflated issues of national security with modern-day nativism (Crawford, 2006). Moreover, by choosing the English language as a signifier of "true"

Americanism, the U.S. Senate simultaneously subscribed to a popular myth surrounding bilingualism: that is, that it is a divisive force that threatens national unity (Johnson, 2005; Stritikus & Garcia, 2003). Not only is this myth largely unfounded (Fishman, 1991), but it ignores the fact that language plurality is a "normal state of affairs in all but a few small countries" of the world (Crawford, 2006, p. 9). In other words, while the belief in a unifying national language is a powerful ideological construct, there is often much more at work than mere mastery of the English language when defining what it means to be "American" (Perea, 1992; Sekhon, 1999).

Research asserts (e.g., Cornelius, 2002, 2005) that Latinos are often viewed as a cultural "other," even among other marginalized groups. They are perceived as problem minorities, largely because of their growing presence in the United States coupled with their apparent failure to effectively assimilate into the larger social polity (Cornelius, 2002; Portes & Rumbaut, 2001; Rumbaut & Portes, 2001). The rapid growth of the Latino population, especially in regions outside the Southwest, has also been a source of tension and concern. States like North Carolina, South Carolina, Georgia, Arkansas, Missouri, Iowa, and Nebraska, are rapidly becoming destinations where Latino "newcomers" are settling (Guzman, 2001). Lured by American businesses and the desire to provide a better livelihood for their children, Latinos are now invigorating local economies in areas that have not historically attracted Latino workers (Cantu, 1995; Lazos & Jeanetta, 2002; Stull, Broadway, & Griffith, 1995; Wells & Bryne, 1999).

In scholarly circles this population trend is referred to as "the New Latino Diaspora" (Hamann, Wortham, & Murillo, 2002). This term arose from the need to address the multiple issues and circumstances facing Latinos in nontraditional regions of the United States. More often than not, issues pertaining to identity, citizenship, and "belongingness" are intensified in these emerging arenas—largely because there is little experience and first-hand knowledge in working with this population. As some research reveals, many Latino newcomers face an unwelcoming context of reception in these communities, as local residents often struggle with how to best accommodate this particular group (Lazos & Jeanetta, 2002; López & Vázquez, 2005).

While not all of the experiences of these Latino newcomers are negative, this group nevertheless remains positioned as a problem within the larger public discourse. This problem is due, in part, to predictable social forces that shape the lives of many immigrant communities, as Portes and Rumbaut (2001) conclude:

[O]n the whole, the environments created by the combination of the immigrants' human and social capital, and the context that receives them, dominate the process of adaptation and its prospects of success. Placed in an impoverished community and surrounded by a hostile world, even the most motivated individuals flounder, despite brave declarations to the contrary. (pp. 267–268)

In other words, despite their desire to overcome their social and economic position, most Latino immigrants have a difficult time assimilating into the larger U.S. society (see also Rumbaut & Portes, 2001). Consequently, Latino social mobility—particularly in second and third generations—is often segmented and dispersed, as opposed to being predictable and expected (Portes & Rumbaut, 2001). To be certain, Latino immigrants and their offspring often experience much stress as they try to adjust to life in their new communities (Cornelius, 2002; Falicov, 2002; Lazos & Jeanetta, 2002).

Such stress is often intensified when tension, apprehension, and misunderstandings arise between newcomer Latinos and local residents. Moreover, the inability to communicate across linguistic and cultural divides may only heighten this tension lead to further frustration, suspicion, animosity, distrust, and misunderstanding (Cornelius, 2002). Unfortunately, this may only reinforce the belief that newcomers are foreign, other, different and "un-American" (Hernandez-Truyol, 1998). To be certain, notions of who is/is not "American"—including the social, cultural, economic, and linguistic characteristics engendered therein—all influence how local communities interact with Latino newcomers (Perea, 1992, 1997, 1998).

This study seeks to interrogate the multiple, yet subtle, ways in which teacher and administrator perceptions of their Spanish speaking Latino students were informed by nativist and assimilationist ideologies. It emerges from the belief that ideology is a powerful force that impacts and structures our everyday perceptions of reality and that racism, as an ideological construct, permeates our organizational practices, structures, and everyday ways of thinking (Scheurich & Young, 1997; Tyson, 1998). We argue that racism is more than just the enactment of overt and explicit acts and/or deeply-held prejudicial sentiments about a particular group, but is an "integral part of our social fabric" (Delgado & Stefancic, 2001, p. 7). By looking at teacher and administrator perceptions of the Latino community, particularly perceptions of cultural and linguistic differences, this study aims to interrogate how these perceptions function as racialized constructs that reify and reproduce inequities in the larger social order.[1]

"HELP! THEY DON'T SPEAK ENGLISH"

The title of this study was taken from an educational resource manual that aims to provide teachers with lesson plans, advice, and support on how to work with Limited English Proficient students.[2] The online resource kit was produced in 1989 by a task force of migrant educators in Virginia who had received an increasing number of requests from classroom teachers, particularly in areas of high Latino growth. While the purpose of the "rescue" kit was well-intentioned, one need not be familiar with its contents in order to discern how language and cultural differences were perceived. In fact, the title alone ("Help! They don't speak English,") suggests feelings of helplessness, frustration, and despair, and connotes a general lack of knowledge and/or competence in working with linguistically and culturally diverse learners.

Moreover, this kit positions teachers as helpless victims in need of a "life-line" to rescue them from their particular dilemma. In effect, language and culture are problematically positioned as issues that overwhelm and frustrate, thus making this kit the first line of defense for teachers working with these students. This is not to suggest that working across linguistic and cultural lines is not difficult and challenging, but that the emphasis on students' shortcomings is narrowly conceptualized.

In other words, the title of the kit unilaterally blames children for their inadequacies, rather than looking at other sources (we don't speak Spanish) or at the nature of the language barrier itself (we don't understand each other) as possible sources of frustration. Not only is this discursive move problematic, but it is deeply troubling, given the current backlash against language rights in the classroom and the rise of "English only" initiatives that are gaining increased national support (Gershberg, Danenberg, & Sánchez, 2004; Piatt, 1990).

In effect the nature of deficit thinking and the ideology underpinning English language acquisition is so pervasive that even progressive educators have internalized its poisonous logic by unconsciously subscribing to a language rights discourse that views students as having linguistic deficiencies or shortcomings (Perea, 1992; Sekhon, 1999). Not only does this ontological move position English as the dominant or primordial language, but also subscribes to the ideology that academic and economic opportunities are *dependent* upon the learning and mastery of the English language. This is not to suggest that learning English is unimportant, but to separate the learning of the language from the concomitant "benefits" one gains from having mastery over the language.

To be certain, many African American and Latino communities have been "speaking English" for hundreds of years, yet most have not "made it" academically, politically, economically, or socially in society (Conchas,

2001; Heath, 1983; Johnson & Martinez, 2000). When English mastery becomes the primordial route to achieving the American dream, we make a dangerous slippage between English language mastery and educational/economic success (Heath, 1983; Krashen, 1994; Ovando, 2003; Portes & Schauffler, 1994). As an ideological construct, this belief disregards the social, economic, political, structural, and racial context which keeps all underrepresented students—second language learners and English dominant learners alike—in a subordinate position in society (Stanton-Salazar, 2001; Valdés, 2001). This is why it is critically important to interrogate the perceptions of school personnel, especially how they view, understand, and interact with under-represented language minority students, particularly those who are new or recent arrivals in their respective communities.

BACKGROUND OF STUDY

This case study emerged from a larger study based on Latino parents' perceptions about and interpretations of "involvement" (López & Vàzquez, 2005). The aim of the research was to bring to light how traditional conceptions of parental involvement overshadow the ways in which Latino parents and their extended kin network are already involved in the educational lives of their children. As part of the study, we also interviewed teachers, administrators, and other school personnel in order to understand how the larger educational community in which the Latino families participated, were defining the terrain of parent involvement.

During these interviews, however, we quickly became aware that perceptions of Latino parent involvement were intimately connected to the perceptions of the Latino community itself. Many of our respondents provided anecdotes, observations, and first-hand accounts of their interactions with Latino parents, as well as explanations and personal insights as to why they believed there was a disjuncture in meeting the linguistic and cultural needs of their Latino students. In essence, we quickly realized the school personnel held particular beliefs about Latino families—beliefs that were "noble" and/or "righteous" on the surface, but emerged from a deeper racialized logic about language and culture.

METHOD

The research methodology chosen for this study was primarily qualitative in nature. Researchers focused on schools in three counties in one particular Midwestern state that had experienced substantial Latino growth in the previous ten years according to U.S. Census and school district figures. However, because this study is still unfolding, the findings reported herein center around one particular county whose school district had a total student enrollment of 10,665 during the 2004–2005 academic year. Of particular importance is the fact that this district experienced a 500% growth in Latino student enrollment since 2001.

The school district is comprised of 11 elementary schools, two middle schools, and two high schools. In order to gain entry into these schools, researchers relied on personal and professional contacts within the district's central administration to personally introduce us to principals, teachers, and other key personnel. After spending approximately one month at schools conducting observations in classrooms, gathering field notes and interacting with parents, researchers began the interview process. We specifically focused on three elementary schools, one middle school, and one high school that served the largest concentration of Latino students according to district records.

During a 4 month period, researchers interviewed administrators, teachers, and other personnel at these schools—including counselors, social workers, teacher's aides, program assistants, and support staff who worked directly with Latino students and/or English as a Second Language (ESL) students in general.[3] Researchers interviewed a total of 14 administrators, 8 teachers, and 6 support staff. Special effort was made to interview these individuals at different times of the day in order to increase the availability of our subjects.

All of the subjects were interviewed once using a semistructured interview protocol and three participants were interviewed twice. Interviews ranged between 50–60 minutes in length, and the longest interview lasted approximately 90 minutes. All interviews were audiotaped and transcribed with the consent of the participants.

In addition, researchers conducted an informal or "unstructured" interview with each of the participants. These interviews were not audio recorded, although field notes were taken by researchers during the interview process. These unstructured interviews generally occurred after the first "taped" interview, but within the 4-month time period of this study. They provided us with opportunities to ask follow-up questions, probe for meaning/clarification, and triangulate some of our initial findings. Since many of these interviews were un-planned (though certainly not accidental or unintended), they occurred during the school day, and were held under less prescribed circumstances. They typically lasted between 7 and 15 minutes in length, and materialized during hallway conversations, cafeteria duty, planning periods, and before/after-school bus duty.

Data analysis proceeded according to the procedures outlined by Miles and Huberman (1994), Huberman and Miles (1994), Patton (1990), and Coffey and Atkinson (1996), and included interview coding according to significant themes and the utilization of case and cross-case analysis. It is important to note that our analysis was an ongoing process, where observations, interviews, field notes, and journaling informed each other by providing analytic and theoretical insights during the data collection process (Miles & Huberman, 1994; Patton, 1990). In effect, our analysis was formulated and reformulated while in the field. We found this overlapping of data collection/analysis useful, since many of the findings we uncovered—particularly those surrounding racism and assimilation—were rarely explicit or overt, but rather, were inferred from our collective insights during the interview process (Tierney & Lincoln, 1997).

Thus, we can not pretend that our findings are entirely unproblematic. In fact, as Stanfield (1993), Denzin (1997) and Lather (1993) collectively argue, there is no way of objectively interpreting the world—since we only see what our conceptual frames "allow" us to see. As with most qualitative accounts; our findings are partial, imperfect, and not ideologically—or theoretically—"pure." At best, our findings are mediated, fleeting, and constructed accounts of our own engagements at this research site, and are far from neutral or objective recollections (Geertz, 1988; Lather, 1997; St. Pierre & Pillow, 2000; Van Maanen, 1988). This is not to suggest that our findings are false, intentionally misleading, or meaningless, but that "truth" itself is multifaceted, complex, slippery and "unreliable" (Britzman, 1998; see also Lather & Smithies, 1997).

To be certain, our aim is not to provide findings that are universally true, but rather, to provide findings that are more local/situated. This is why the use of an instrumental case—as a methodological device—was chosen for this particular study (Stake, 1994). As Hamel (1993) and Yin (1994) suggest, the purpose of a case is not to "generalize" to a larger population, but to provide readers with a unique opportunity to identify how social practices are evident in the individual case.

RESULTS

Preliminary results suggest that school personnel experienced much stress when working with members of the Latino community. Most of the individuals we interviewed shared anecdotes of frustration, fatigue, and disillusionment when working across linguistic and cultural lines, and often referred to the multiple "barriers" that had to be overcome in order to adequately work with this population.

While most of these perceptions highlighted a general frustration in working with language minority students, some emerged from deeply-held racial perceptions about language inferiority and an equally powerful belief in the "melting pot" ideology of assimilation. To be certain, all of our respondents did not directly state that they viewed Latino students or their parents as inferior. Nor did any of them mention any racial hostility toward Latino students. On the contrary, much of what they provided was very positive accounts. However, when we probed deeper in our interviews—and upon a closer examination of the data—a pattern of subtle, unconscious, and restrained racial attitudes became evident.

For example, early in the interview process, it became apparent that many of our respondents spoke to us in a kind of "code" that avoided any direct mention of race or ethnicity. Instead, they described the new population with "raceless" signifiers that masked any ill-intention or negative perception of the Latino newcomers. For example, when asked to describe the types of changes had occurred in their schools over the past 5 years, many of our respondents mentioned that "things were different now" or that they had "more problems today than in the past." When prodded to elaborate on what these statements meant, they typically utilized other benign signifiers to describe those changes:

> "Our students are now more mobile. We really didn't have that problem before." (Elementary school teacher)

> "We now have students who are poorer and low-SES. That's certainly a change. I've been here for 28 years and this is the first time we've had to deal with issues of extreme poverty." (Middle school principal)

> "We have larger class sizes than we did in the past. That's a huge change!" (High school counselor).

> "There are a lot more language barriers than ever before. I think that's another major difference—and a challenge for all of us at the high school." (High school teacher)

While one could look at this evidence as harmless descriptors of the changing school context, the rapid demographic shift experienced in this school district during the past five years would indicate that they were making reference to the Latino community. Upon closer examination of the data, one might speculate that our respondents engaged in a type of racial avoidance. In other words, these signifiers indirectly made reference to how "things used to be" and juxtaposed those experiences to how radically different things now were.

In effect, our respondents reminisced about a time when students and families were less problematic, troublesome, English dominant, and middle class. It is these types of subtle, almost unconscious, racialized perceptions that permeated how our respondents perceived these Latino newcomers and their families.

Language as Barrier

A finding that consistently emerged in each of our interviews was the notion of "linguistic barriers" or the belief that there was a gap in understanding students and families because they spoke a different language. In fact, the phrase "language barriers" or some iteration thereof (e.g., "the language issue," "language differences," "language deficiency," "communication gap,") was mentioned by each of our 28 respondents during the interview process. This concept usually emerged when asked about the types of challenges they faced when working with Latino students and/or families.

In effect, all of our respondents believed that language was the primary issue that was at the heart of many of the problems, concerns, and experiences they faced when working or interacting with Latino families. They firmly believed that if the "language barrier" could be mitigated, many of the frustrations they experienced on a daily basis (e.g., discipline referrals, school performance issues, student conduct, etc.) would disappear. However, as was the case with the "emergency kit" mentioned above, many of our respondents problematically assumed that Latino families were the ones who had the "language barrier"—failing to recognize that the act of communication is bi-directional in nature. This perspective, therefore, not only blamed Latino families for their linguistic deficits, but perpetuated a problematic myth that linked English language mastery with educational success (see also Conchas, 2001; Heath, 1983; Johnson & Martinez, 2000; Krashen, 1994; Ovando, 2003; Portes & Schauffler, 1994).

The insistence that the primary problem schools surrounded the inability of Latino families to speak English was vividly expressed by one elementary school teacher:

Interviewer: With regards to Latinos, do you see parents being involved?

Teacher: [W]e are working on getting those parents to be more involved at home because to this child we're saying "you need to practice this or you need to practice that" and the Hispanic parents don't know how to help their children. Or we'll send things home, or have kids do activities at home with their parents, and we get no response [from the parents]. I remember having a conference with a Spanish-speaking dad. Dad came to the conference, mom didn't come. I think because of work. But, the student [would] say:

"My mom don't know English! My mom don't know English! My mom can't help me with my homework! My mom don't know English!"

Interviewer: Is all the work you give your students in English?

Teacher: Well, yeah. The things she needs to learn are. I mean she needs to learn her shapes in English and her letters in English, and those things. But she has an older brother [who] speaks English. So there's probably some way to work it out, you know? But we are probably going to have to meet with these parents again because that child isn't progressing. It's been really interesting to watch the [Latino] families. You know, each work it out the best they can. And, and they do show interest. They do care. But there are things that slip through the crack because of the language barrier. I don't speak Spanish. I cannot begin to write my newsletters in Spanish. And I wish I could. I wish I spoke Spanish. I wish I could translate everything because it would simplify things a lot. But, that's just not realistic.

As the interview reveals, there appears to be an unstated assumption that the "real" root of the parent involvement problem was the inability of the parents to speak English. The fact that homework assignments, newsletters, and suggested parent/child activities are not available or offered in Spanish, all seem to be irrelevant reasons for the parents inability to get involved. Adding insult to injury, the teacher adopted a somewhat paternalistic stance when she stated that it was not "realistic" for her to learn Spanish—though she did not seem to find it unrealistic for the Spanish-speaking parents to learn English.

In effect, there were particular assumptions about the nature, origin, and locus of the "language barrier" that problematically prevented communication between the home and the school. Most of our respondents did not perceive it as their obligation to have to adapt to meet the linguistic needs of students and families, primarily because such "barriers" were outside of their domain. Despite the fact that all of the educators we interviewed had gone through ESL and other diversity training—including professional development for working with language minority students— many still harbored particular feelings about the role, primacy, and centrality of the English language. Moreover, they employed an assimilationist stance that not only privileged English, but viewed

Spanish-speaking students and their families as having particular deficits for not being able to communicate in the "national language" of this country.

Need's Specialist Become "Experts"

A second theme that emerged was that school personnel heavily relied on ESL teachers, Spanish interpreters, teaching assistants, and community aides when dealing or interacting with Latino students and family members. This seemed to happen on a regular basis, regardless of whether or not there was a "language barrier" present. For example in one situation, the high school principal sought the help of a Spanish teacher to translate at a conference he was having with the parents of a Latino student. When the parents responded (in English) that they completely understood the principal and that an interpreter would not be needed, their words seemed to fall on deaf ears. The principal insisted that the Spanish teacher be present "just in case" there was a language issue that emerged during the conference.

In another example, a teacher at an elementary school specifically sought the help of a Spanish-speaking teaching assistant in order to help translate a class activity to a group of Latino students in her class. What makes this example problematic was the fact that the students appeared to have a solid grasp of the assignment in question. Nevertheless, the teacher walked out of her classroom and proceeded to the second story of the school building. She interrupted an ESL class that was in session in order to request the services of the bilingual teaching assistant. When we asked this teacher why she felt the need to have an interpreter present, she indicated that every assignment was important, and that she did not want her Latino students to feel inadequate by not knowing the material. When we indicated to her that the students appeared to have a good grasp of the assignment, she smiled and retorted "Oh they always say that! I just want to make sure that they really know what they're doing, that's all."

In effect, building personnel engaged in what appeared to be diffusive practices: circumventing direct contact with Latino students and families under the pretext of linguistic or cultural barriers. While we do not care to speculate the reason undergirding such practices in this paper, we can conclude that the net result was an overreliance on Spanish-speaking translators to negotiate the interactions between school personnel and Latino students/families.

We believe this led to a "diffusion of responsibility" in the school building: so long as there was someone in the building who could translate and/or was knowledgeable about Latino culture, that person would be called upon to perform the intermediary function. The following quote by an elementary principal provides further insights:

Interviewer: Tell me about those recess problems.

Principal: There were fights. Lots of fights. And kicking and just, I mean, you know, blows. And we had just never allowed fighting in our playground or anything like that. And they [Latinas/os] really felt like if somebody just barely brushed up against them, that you got in their space. And they felt like they wanted to solve it right there. So we had a lot of fights.

Interviewer: Was there kind of a trend?

Principal: It wasn't. It was, in a sense. But it wasn't racial or anything. I just think that Hispanic children have always been taught to stand up for themselves and if somebody doesn't fight fair—whether it be soccer or whether it be coming down the slide and someone bumps into you—then you got in their space. [But] the Hispanic children tended to stay together, so the fighting was really amongst each other and not so much, you know, with White [children]. You know, Hispanic children fighting back and forth.

Interviewer: And what did you do as a school to begin to address that?

Principal: We brought—well, again, language was a barrier—so we did bring in the ESL teacher to help us with the problem. She came out to recess duty for a while. And she worked with the Spanish-speaking kids to kind of establish procedure again. And she taught them that if somebody does take something, or bumps into you, or you don't think is playing fair, that you come and get the teacher and let them help solve the problem. She came out to recess a couple of times, and that greatly helped. It also helped that she covered some of those things within her class.

While the belief in the innate "cultural roots" of Latino dysfunctionality is problematic in itself, what is even more problematic is that the principal felt these students needed to be "educated" on appropriate playground etiquette and social skills. Gitlin, Buendía, Crosland, and Doumbia (2003) suggest that many White educators firmly believe that Latino students—particularly those who are recent immigrants—come from "rural, underdeveloped countries that are devoid of any social order" (p. 108). Consequently, many educators feel that these students need to be taught the norms, customs, traditions, and values of this country. This assimilationist logic is perhaps made even more insidious when educators actively recruit the efforts of ESL teachers and staff (who can communicate in Spanish) to perform those functions.

In short, ESL teachers and other individuals in these schools often served as interpreters, buffers, and liaisons, between full-time school teachers and administrators and the broader Latino community. By viewing and placing these individuals in this associative position, school personnel created a space between themselves and those students/families whom they serve. In essence, the ESL and Spanish-speaking staff (many of who were hired on "soft" moneys and/or on an hourly basis) became the default "go-to" persons in the building whenever translation services were needed. The irony of this approach, is that the effort to consciously mitigate the linguistic and cultural barriers, only ended up reifying them in unique and different ways.

The Construction of "Good" and "Bad" Latino Parents

The last finding in this study surrounds how teachers, administrators, and other school personnel perceived Latino parents and their involvement in their children's educational lives. These perceptions not only engender particular understandings of home and school functions, but also define the terrain of actions that circumscribe the discourse of appropriate parental behavior. Oftentimes, what is viewed as "good" involvement from the perceptive of schools only reflect and/or privilege "mainstream" involvement forms (Lightfoot, 1978; López, 2001). We believe this constitutes a deficit perspective that not only diminishes the culturally-specific perspectives of minority populations, but more importantly, deflects attention away from the professional responsibility of schools to establish effective parental involvement programs for marginalized families (Valencia, 1997).

Generally speaking, the findings in this study indicate that school personnel continue to deflect attention away from their own inadequacies to effectively reach out to all parents. Moreover, they reproduce a deficit discourse that focuses exclusively on stereotypic notions of home dysfunctionality. This was particularly true for Latino children whose parents were viewed as lacking the educational, social, and cultural, resources to have a positive effect on a child's schooling. The following exchange with a middle school teacher provides an example of this type of deficit thinking:

Interviewer: How do you think the school sees the role of the parent?

Teacher: We hope that they're making sure the homework is being done, that they're eating right, that they're going to bed at a decent time, you know? I think that's the mental image of what a parent should be. And I think that with the demographics we have here, and especially with our Hispanic students, a lot of times we don't see that. We know that's not happening in everyone's house. We know that a lot of those parents are working two, maybe three, jobs in order to put food on the table.

Interviewer: So what is it that you want from these parents when it comes to involvement?

Teacher: I think knowing, just knowing, the parents are going to be supportive. If there is a problem, are the parents are going to be there to back their children to make sure they have loving and nurturing environment to go home to? I think parents are, you know, the most important thing in the child's life. And you know, I think a lot of students here don't go home feeling that way.

This notion of what makes a "good" parent—checking homework, putting children to bed, making sure children eat right—are perceived by teachers as actions that support the overall schooling agenda. When parents are perceived as "failing" at these tasks, they are not only viewed as unsupportive by teachers, but are also seen as not providing loving and nurturing environments at the home. In effect, blaming the parent for their lack of involvement situates teachers as the "caring" adult in the Latino child's life.

Teachers, unproblematically view themselves as benevolent and compassionate caregivers who call the home, communicate with parents, and try to balance schedules—only to be met with parents who are not supportive of the overall educational agenda. However, there is a danger-ous and unexamined slippage between not getting a response from par-ents, and the parent not loving their children (de Carvahlo, 2001). This perception certainly needs to be critically examined and unpackaged, as it reproduces a very problematic—and dangerous—stereotype.

CONCLUSION AND IMPLICATIONS

We want to make it clear that the school personnel we interviewed care very deeply for the Latino children and parents with whom they work and interact on a daily basis. There is no doubt in our minds that they truly love their jobs and want to provide Latinos with the best schooling experi-ence possible. As public servants, they are fulfilling their duties in a pro-fessional manner and firmly believe that their teaching will benefit local, regional and national interests. Nevertheless, our participants held on to deeply ingrained, and dysconsious (King, 1991) racial perceptions about language, culture, and "good" parenting. These ideologies were often cloaked with good intentions: the desire to bridge the language barrier, the heartfelt need to bring interpreters to minimize misunderstanding, the desire to assimilate parents and children into the mainstream, the yearning for Latino parents to express their support in more visible and discernable ways. Yet, the harder teachers tried to bridge this gap, the more frustrated they became, and the easier it was to point the finger at perceived linguistic and cultural inadequacies.

Not only are such beliefs and perception grossly exaggerated and unfounded, but they emerge from a deep-seeded paternalism that views immigrant groups as having to shed their native language and culture in order to "melt" into an English-dominant social order (Perea, 1997). Because these beliefs are so ingrained and transparent, we often fail to recognize how much they structure and shape both our personal and pro-fessional lives.

As individuals who work with culturally and linguistically diverse chil-dren, we have an ethical duty, and moral responsibility, to interrogate our own assumptions and perspectives about language and culture— especially those perceptions that may be harmful to linguistically and cul-turally diverse students. We also have a duty to challenge our deeply-held assumptions about the dominance and supremacy of the English lan-guage, and to interrogate the role of language in defining the parameters of what it means to be "American" (Crawford, 1998; Montoya, 1998; Navarrete, 1998; Perea, 1998). Perhaps the time has come to critically examine the ideological cloth of our assimilationist ideology and highlight the various overt and hidden processes in which schools and their agents regulate, monitor, and control language differences in the larger social order. This study is but a first step in this direction.

NOTES

1. This study is heavily influenced by the theoretical underpinnings of critical race theory (CRT), which posits that racism is an endemic component of society (Bell, 1995; Crenshaw, Gotanda, Peller, & Thomas, 1995; Delgado, 1995; Delgado & Stefancic, 2001; Valdés, Culp, & Harris., 2002) and shapes our institutions, relationships, and everyday ways of thinking (see also Ladson-Billings & Tate, 1995; Parker, Deyhle, & Villenas, 1999; López & Parker, 2002). CRT scholars argue that we often fail to recognize racism because we do not see it beyond its most blatant manifestations (Delgado & Stefancic, 2001). Racism, in other words, is both explicit and hidden: it structures our actions, beliefs, and perceptions; it is omnipresent, ubiquitous, and inescapable. Thus, the aim of CRT is to unmask racism in its everyday and hidden forms and challenge dominant ideologies of racial neutrality and colorblindness that maintain a highly racialized social order (Dixson & Rousseau, 2005; Lynn & Adams, 2002; Lynn, Yosso, Solrzano, & Parker, 2002; Sólrzano & Delgado Bernal, 2001; Sólrzano & Yosso, 2002; Yosso, 2006). One such ideology is the notion of citizenship and how society defines what it means to be an American or a citizen of this country (Perea, 1997). CRT scholars argue that citizenship is much more than a legal construct, but engenders political, social, linguistic, cultural, racial, and assimilationist components (Aleinikoff, 1997; Delgado, 1997; Perea, 1997).
2. See the following URL for more information about this kit: http://employees.oneonta.edu/thomasrl/helpkit.html
3. It is important to clarify why we utilize the labels "ESL" and "Latino" interchangeably. We do not believe these categories are interchangeable. However, school personnel often switched between these terms. Therefore, we found it relevant to include all the identities used to categorize Latino students, as these are a direct manifestation of teacher perceptions at these schools.

REFERENCES

Aleinikoff, A. (1997). The tightening circle of membership. In J. F Perea (Ed.), *Immigrants out: The new nativism and the anti-immigrant impulse in the United States* (pp. 324–333). New York: New York University Press.

Bell, D. A. (1995). *Brown v. Board of Education* and the interest convergence dilemma. In K. Crenshaw, N. Gotanda, G. Peller, & K. Thomas (Eds.), *Critical race theory: The key writings that formed the movement* (pp. 20–29). New York: The New Press.

Britzman, D. (1998, April). *On tolerating the ambivalence of unreliable narrators: Literature, psychoanalysis and affect.* Paper presented at the annual meeting of the American Educational Research Association, San Diego, CA.

Cantu, L. (1995). The peripheralization of rural American: A case study of Latino migrants in America's heartland. *Sociological Perspectives, 38*(3), 399–415.

Coffey, A., & Atkinson, P. (1996). *Making sense of qualitative data: Complementary research strategies.* Thousand Oaks, CA: SAGE.

Conchas, G. Q. (2001). Structuring failure and success: Understanding the variability in Latino student engagement. *Harvard Educational Review, 71*(3), 475–504.

Cornelius, W. A. (2002). Ambivalent reception: Mass public responses to the "new" Latino immigration to the United States. In M. M. Suarez-Orozco & M. M. Páez (Eds.), *Latinos: Remaking America* (pp. 165–189). Berkeley, CA: The University of California Press.

Cornelius, W. A. (2005). Controlling "unwanted" immigration: Lessons from the United States, 1993–2004. *Journal of Ethnic and Migration Studies, 31*(4), 775–794.

Coryn, C. L., Beale, J. M., & Myers, K. M. (2004). Response to September 11: Anxiety, patriotism, and prejudice in the aftermath of terror. *Current Research in Social Psychology, 9*(12). Retrieved from http://www.uiowa.edu/~grpproc/crisp/crisp.9.12.html

Crawford, J. (1998). Hold your tongue. In R. Delgado & J. Stefancic (Eds.), The Latino/a condition (pp. 559–562). New York: New York University Press.

Crawford, J. (2006, July). *Official English legislation: Bad for civil rights, bad for America's interests, and even bad for English. Testimony before the House Subcommittee on Education Reform.* Retrieved from http://users.rcn.com/crawj/Crawford_Official_English_testimony.pdf

Crenshaw, K., Gotanda, N., Peller, G., & Thomas, K. (1995). (Eds.). *Critical race theory: The key writings that formed the movement.* New York: New Press

Daniels, R. (2004). *Guarding the golden door: American immigration policy and immigrants since 1882.* New York: Hill & Wang.

De Carvalho M. E. P. (2001). *Rethinking family-school relations: A critique of parent involvement in schooling.* Mahwah, NJ: Erlbaum.

Delgado, R., (Ed.) (1995). *Critical race theory: The cutting edge.* Philadelphia: Temple University Press.

Delgado, R. (1997). Citizenship. In J. F Perea (Ed.), *Immigrants out: The new nativism and the anti-immigrant impulse in the United States* (pp. 318–324). New York: New York University Press.

Delgado, R., & Stefancic, J. (Eds.). (1998). *The Latino/a condition.* New York: New York University Press.

Delgado, R., & Stefancic, J. (2001). *Critical race theory: An introduction.* New York: New York University Press.

Denzin, N. K. (1997). Performance texts. In W. G. Tierney & Y. S. Lincoln (Eds.), *Representation and the text: Re-framing narrative voice.* Albany, NY: State University of New York Press.

Dixson, A. D., & Rousseau, C. K. (Eds.). (2005). Special issue: Critical race theory in education. *Race, Ethnicity and Education, 8*(1), 1–127.

Falicov, C. J. (2002). Ambiguous loss: Risk and resilience in Latino immigrant families. In M. M. Suarez-Orozco & M. M. Páez (Eds.), *Latinos: Remaking America* (pp. 274–288). Berkeley, CA: The University of California Press.

Fishman, J. A. (1991. Interpolity perspective on the relationships between linguistic heterogeneity, civil strife and per capita gross national product. *Applied Linguistics, 1*, 5–18.

Freyd, J. L. (2002). In the wake of terrorist attack, hatred may mask fear. *Analysis of Social Issues and Public Policy, 2*(1), 5–8.

Geertz, C. (1988). *Works and lives: The anthropologist as author.* Palo Alto, CA: Stanford University Press.

Gershberg, A. I., Danenberg, A., & Sánchez, P. (2004). *Beyond bilingual education: New immigrants and public school policies in California.* Washington, DC: Urban Institute Press.

Gerstenfeld, P. B. (2002). A time to hate: Situational antecedents of intergroup bias. *Analyses of Social Issues and Public Policy, 2*(1), 61–67.

Gitlin, A., Buendía, E., Crosland, K., & Doumbia, F. (2003). The production of margin and center: Welcoming-unwelcoming of immigrant students. *American Educational Research Journal, 40*(1), 91–122.

Graham, O. L. (2006). *Unguarded gates: A history of America's immigration crisis.* New York: Rowman & Littlefield.

Guzman, B. (2001). *The Hispanic population: Census 2000 Brief.* Washington, DC: U.S. Census Bureau. Retrieved from http://www.census.gov/prod/2001pubs/c2kbr01-3.pdf

Hamann, E. T., Wortham, S. E. F., & Murillo, E. G. (2002). Education and policy in the new Latino diaspora. In S. E. F. Wortham, E. G. Murillo, & E. T. Hamann (Eds.), *Education in the new Latino diaspora: Policy and the politics of identity* (pp. 1–16). Westport, CT: Ablex.

Hamel, J. (1993). *Case study methods* (Qualitative Research Methods Series, 32). Newbury Park, CA; SAGE.

Heath, S. B. (1983). *Ways with words.* Cambridge, England: Cambridge University Press.

Hernandez-Truyol, B. (1998). Natives and newcomers. In R. Delgado & J. Stefancic (Eds.), *The Latino/a condition* (pp. 125–132). New York: New York University Press.

Huberman, A. M., & Miles, M. B. (1994). Data management and analysis methods. In N. K. Denzin & Y. L. Lincoln (Eds.), *The handbook of qualitative research,* (pp. 428–444). Thousand Oaks, CA: SAGE.

Hulse, C. (2006, May 19). Senate votes to set English as national language. *New York Times,* p. 1.

Johnson, E. (2005). Proposition 203: A critical metaphor analysis. *Bilingual Research Journal, 29*(1). Retrieved (INSERT DATE), from http://brj.asu.edu/content/vol29_no1/art4.pdf

Johnson, K. R., & Martinez, G. A. (2000). Discrimination by proxy: The case of proposition 227 and the ban on bilingual education. *UC Davis Law Review, 33*(4), 1227–1276.

King, J. E. (1991). Dysconscious racism: Ideology, identity, and the miseducation of teachers. *Journal of Negro Education, 60*(2), 133–146.

Krashen, S. D. (1994). Bilingual education and second language acquisition theory. In C. F. Leyba (Ed.), *Schooling and language minority students: A theoretical framework* (pp. 47–75). Los Angeles: California State University, Evaluation, Dissemination, and Assessment Center.

Ladson-Billings, G., & Tate, W. F. (1995). Toward a critical race theory of education. *Teachers College Record, 97*, 47–68.

Lather, P. (1993). Fertile obsession: Validity after poststructuralism. *Sociological Quarterly, 34*(4), 673-693.

Lather, P. (1997). Creating a multilayered text: Women, AIDS, and angels. In W. G. Tierney & Y. S. Lincoln (Eds.), *Representation and the text: Re-framing narrative voice.* Albany, NY: State University of New York Press.

Lather, P., & Smithies, C. (1997). *Troubling the angels: Women living with HIV/AIDS.* Boulder, CO: Westview Press.

Lazos, S. R., & Jeanetta, S. C. (2002). *Cambio de colores: Immigration of Latinos to Missouri.* Columbia, MO: MU Extension, University of Missouri-Columbia.

Lightfoot, S. L. (1978). *Worlds apart: Relationships between families and schools.* New York: Basic Books.

López, G. R. (2001). The value of hard work: Lessons on parent involvement from an (im)migrant household. *Harvard Educational Review, 71*(3), 416–437.

López, G. R. (2002). From sea to shining sea: Stories, counterstories, and the discourse of patriotism. *Qualitative Inquiry, 8*(2), 196–198.

López, G. R., & Parker, L. (Eds.). (2002). *Interrogating racism in qualitative research methodology.* New York: Peter Lang.

López, G. R., & Vàzquez, V. A. (April, 2005). *Parental involvement in Latina/o-impacted schools in the Midwest: Effective school leadership for a changing context.* Montreal, Canada: American Educational Research Association.

Lynn, M., & Adams, M. (Eds.). (2002). Special issue: Critical race theory in education. *Equity and Excellence in Education, 35*(2), 87–199.

Lynn, M., Yosso, T. J., Solórzano, D., & Parker, L. (Eds.). (2002). Special issue: Critical race theory and qualitative research. *Qualitative Inquiry, 8*(1), 1–126.

Miles, M. B., & Huberman, A. M. (1994). *Qualitative data analysis: An expanded sourcebook.* Thousand Oaks, CA; SAGE.

Montoya, M. E. (1998). Law and language(s). In R. Delgado & J. Stefancic (Eds.), *The Latino/a condition* (pp. 574–578). New York: New York University Press.

National Public Radio. (2004, September). *Immigration in America: Report on a national survey.* Retrieved from http://www.npr.org/news/specials/polls/2004/immigration

Navarrette, R. (1998). A bilingual-education initiative as a Prop. 187 in disguise? In R. Delgado & J. Stefancic (Eds.), *The Latino/a condition* (pp. 563–565). New York: New York University Press.

Newport, F. (2004, January). Americans worried about immigration, oppose Bush plan. *Gallup News Service.* Retrieved from http://www.npr.org/news/specials/polls/2004/immigration/]

Ovando, C. J. (2003). Bilingual education in the United States: Historical development and current issues. *Bilingual Research Journal, 27*(1), 1–24.

Parker, L., Deyhle, D., & Villenas, S. (Eds.). (1999). *Race is race isn't: Critical Race Theory and Qualitative Studies in Education.* Boulder, CO: Westview Press.

Patton, M. Q. (1990). *Qualitative evaluation and research methods* (2nd ed.). Newbury Park, CA: SAGE.

Perea, J. (1992). Demography and distrust: An essay on American languages, cultural pluralism, and official English. *Minnesota Law Review, 77,* 269–373.

Perea, J. F. (Ed.). (1997). *Immigrants out: The new nativism and the anti-immigrant impulse in the United States.* New York: New York University Press.

Perea, J. F. (1998). American languages, cultural pluralism, and official English. In R. Delgado & J. Stefancic (Eds.), *The Latino/a condition* (pp. 566–573). New York: New York University Press.

Piatt, B. (1990). *Only English? Law and language policy in the United States.* Albuquerque, NM: University of New Mexico Press.

Portes, A., & Rumbaut, R. G. (2001). *Legacies: The story of immigrant second generation.* Berkeley, CA: University of California Press.

Portes, A., & Rumbaut, R. G. (2006). *Immigrant America: A portrait* (3rd ed.). Berkeley, CA: University of California Press.

Portes, A., & Schauffler, R. (1994). Language and the second generation: Bilingualism yesterday and today. *International Migration Review, 28*(4), 640–661.

Rumbaut, R. G., & Portes, A. (2001). *Ethnicities: Children of immigrants in America.* Berkeley, CA: University of California Press.

Scheurich, J. J., & Young, M. D. (1997). Coloring epistemologies: Are our research epistemologies racially biased? *Educational Researcher, 26*(4), 4–16.

Sekhon, N. (1999). A birthright rearticulated: The politics of bilingual education. *New York University Law Review, 74*(5), 1407–1446.

Solórzano, D. G., & Delgado Bernal, D. (2001). Critical race theory, transformational resistance, and social justice: Chicana and Chicano students in an urban context. *Urban Education, 36,* 308–342.

Solórzano, D. G., & Yosso, T. J. (2002). Critical race methodology: Counter-story telling as an analytic framework for educational research. *Qualitative Inquiry, 8*(1), 23–44.

St. Pierre, E., & Pillow, W. S. (2000). *Working the ruins: Feminist poststructural research and practice in education.* New York: Routledge.

Stake, R. E. (1994). Case studies. In N. K. Denzin & Y. L. Lincoln (Eds.), *The handbook of qualitative research* (pp. 236–247). Thousand Oaks, CA: SAGE.

Stanfield, J. H. (1993). Epistemological considerations. In J. H. Stanfield & R. M. Dennis (Eds.), *Race and ethnicity in research methods* (pp. 16–36). Newbury Park, CA: SAGE.

Stanton-Salazar, R. D. (2001). *Manufacturing hope and despair: The school and kin support networks of US-Mexican Youth.* New York: Teachers College Press.

Stritikus, T. T., & Garcia, E. E. (2003). The role of theory and policy in the educational treatment of language minority students: Competitive structures in California. *Education Policy Analysis Archives, 11*(26). Retrieved from http://epaa.asu.edu/epaa/v11n26/

Stull, D. D., Broadway, M. J., & Griffith, D. (1995). *Any way you cut it: meat processing and small-town America.* Lawrence, KS: University Press of Kansas.

Suárez-Orozco, M., & Páez, M. M. (2002). *Latinos: Remaking America.* Berkeley, CA: University of California Press.

Suárez-Orozco, C., & Suárez-Orozco, M. (2001). *Children of immigration*. Cambridge, MA: Harvard University Press.

Tierney, W. G., & Lincoln, Y. S. (1997). Introduction: Explorations and discoveries. In *Representation and the text: Re-framing narrative voice*. Albany, NY: State University of New York Press.

Tyson, C. (1998). Coloring epistemologies: A response. *Educational Researcher*, 27(9), 21–22.

Valdés, G. (2001). *Learning and not learning English: Latino students in American schools*. New York: Teachers College Press.

Valdés, F., Culp, J. M., & Harris, A. P. (Eds.). (2002). *Crossroads, directions, and a new critical race theory*. Philadelphia: Temple University Press.

Valencia, R. R. (1997). Conceptualizing the notion of deficit thinking. In *The evolution of deficit thinking: Educational thought and practice*. London: Falmer Press.

Van Maanen, J. (1988). *Tales of the field: On writing ethnography*. Chicago: University of Chicago Press.

Wells, B., & Bryne, J. (1999). The changing face of community in the Midwest U.S.: Challenges for community developers. *Community Development Journal*, 33(1), 70–77.

Yin, R. K. (1994). *Case study research: Design and methods*. Thousand Oaks, CA: SAGE.

Yosso, T. J. (2006). *Critical race counterstories along the Chicana/Chicano educational pipeline*. New York: Routledge.

PART II

PROMOTING SOCIAL JUSTICE PEDAGOGY

CHAPTER 5

FROM SCIENTIFIC MANAGEMENT TO SOCIAL JUSTICE ... AND BACK AGAIN?

Pedagogical Shifts in the Study and Practice of Educational Leadership

Jeffrey S. Brooks and Mark T. Miles

"One faces the future with one's past."

—Pearl S. Buck

This chapter presents an historical overview of pedagogical orientations of school leadership in the United States, and then considers issues facing contemporary educational leaders in this context. Our survey begins with a consideration of the early influence of Frederick Taylor and ends in the present day, a time when the fields of practice and scholarship in educational leadership collectively stand at a critical, yet not unprecedented, crossroad—the intersection of social justice and scientific management.

INTRODUCTION

In the United States, school leadership underwent a profound transformation over the course of the twentieth century. Prior to World War II, the

Leadership for Social Justice: Promoting Equity and Excellence Through Inquiry and Reflective Practice, pp. 99–114
Copyright © 2008 by Information Age Publishing
99

likes of Elwood Cubberly, George Strayer, and others in the Frederick Taylor-influenced first wave of scientific management, shaped a nascent and under-conceptualized knowledge base. After 1945, an explosion of scholarly activity in educational leadership and the emergence of university-based preparation programs helped buoy several significant pedagogical movements that had profound implications for educational leaders. In particular, two mid-century movements, one devoted to the creation and testing of administrative theory and another centered on the application and exploration of social science research methods, shaped the thirty years preceding 1980 and continue to exert significant influence on the field today. The 80s saw the study of educational leadership take a "postmodern turn," as a cadre of influential scholars and practitioners reconceived leadership by conducting inquiry through conceptual lenses grounded in various forms of ethical critique, critical and feminist theories, pluralistic multiculturalism, and social justice. Yet, for over a century's worth of practice, inquiry, and interest in educational leadership, practitioners and scholars seldom look backward for guidance as they consider the future.

The purpose of this chapter is twofold. First, we seek to examine pedagogical trends in educational leadership toward the goal of identifying patterns that have historically shaped the field. Second, given this historical perspective, we consider issues and contingencies that confront a field of practice and scholarship standing collectively at a crossroads. As a second wave of scientific management gathers strength, scholars and practitioners alike must consider how concepts such as social justice will inform, transform, or have marginal impact on the preparation and practice of a new generation of leaders.

In order to ground subsequent discussions in an historical context, we begin this chapter with a review of literature that chronicles certain historical trends in educational leadership. It is important to note at the onset that we consider this review broader than it is deep; we posit zeitgeist rather than expounding subtleties within specific eras. After establishing broad themes that have informed formal educational leadership during various eras, we then turn from the past to the present and consider how these themes inform the practice, preparation, and study of educational leadership.

PEDAGOGICAL TRENDS IN EDUCATIONAL LEADERSHIP IN THE UNITED STATES: PRE-WORLD WAR II

The First Wave of Spiritual and Social Leadership

At the onset of the twentieth century many community members viewed school leaders as having a few primary concerns, including the promotion of traditional spiritual values and the development of strong social contacts within the school community. The social contact element dealt with enlisting the cooperation of faculty members in finding solutions to institutional problems and "accurately sensing" the social problems of the student body (Johnston, Newlon, & Pickell, 1922). Upon sensing problems and "correcting" them, principals were then expected to actively promote appropriate moral and spiritual values among school community members. School leaders of this era embraced a pedagogy grounded in the belief that humans could be molded into a particular vision of "perfectibility" (Mason, 1986). However, sensing social problems and applying an uncomplicated (and uncompromising) moral functionalism as a salve was soon not enough for a field moving quickly toward professionalism and systematic preparation.

The First Wave of Scientific Management

It is hard to overstate the importance and influence of several key individuals and a single institution on the development programs and processes of educational leaders in the first 4 decades of the twentieth century. With regard to institutional significance, the Teachers College at Columbia University stands alone. From 1904–1934, over half of all dissertations completed on topics related to educational administration were conducted at the "temple of Educational Administration in the Pre-World War II era" (Campbell, Fleming, Newell, & Bennion, 1987, p. 180). This generation of Columbia-educated pioneers included Dutton and Snedden (1909) who published one of the earliest textbooks on educational administration, *The Administration of Public Education in the United States*, an exhaustive 600 page text which "left nothing unexamined" (p. 176).

English (2002a) notes that early Columbia generation writers were "infatuated with the rhetoric and publicity surrounding the work of Frederick Winslow Taylor" and accordingly, "the 'new' mission for education colleges was to scientifically prepare educational leaders" (p. 110). Campbell et al. (1987) lent further support to this analysis, pointing out that the assumptions of scientific management are evident throughout Dutton and Snedden's (1909), *The Administration of Public Education in the United States*, as evidenced in part by the "Problems of Active Interest" that the authors list including:

1. The centralization of administrative functions;
2. The determination of the most effective areas of local administration, according to the type of education under consideration;

3. The most effective distribution of functions between lay and ex-official administrators, on the one hand, and experts on the other;
4. Supervision of instruction in non-urban areas; and
5. The development of new agencies of control for new types of educational activity (p. 176).

These administrative goals and functions are consistent with principles of scientific management, in that they reveal an overarching concern with protocol and procedure, and a penchant for efficiency, control, and effectiveness. Other textbooks were generally in keeping with this orientation (e.g., Cubberly, 1922; Strayer & Thorndike). While Dutton and Snedden (1909) had an influence on early administrative thought, their students Elwood Cubberly and George Strayer continued Columbia's history of influence by shaping several subsequent generations as textbook writers.

The emerging view of the 1920s principal as scientific manager dominated the scholarly writing of the 1930s. The spiritual element of the principalship became less important, and the conception of schools as businesses with the principal as an executive became more popular. Business values and rhetoric gained acceptance within school systems, and as leaders of the schools, principals became business managers responsible for devising standardized methods of pupil accounting and introducing sound business administration practices in budgeting, planning, maintenance, and finance (Strayer, Engelhardt, & Elsbree, 1927).

School organization and supervision of employees were critical components of educational leadership. Leaders concerned themselves with designing school systems where expertise and efficiency governed the organization. University-based educators contributed to the development of educational leadership as a professional occupation by creating degree programs and special courses of study to prepare educational leaders (Tyack & Hansot, 1982). Beck and Murphy's (1993) research revealed that these preparation programs commonly included courses such as finance, business administration, organization, and administration of school curriculum, and management of school records and reports.

Human Relations and Social Policy

By the late 1930s, even early proponents of scientific management began to turn their interest from Taylorism. Cubberly (1922) himself integrated human relations concepts into a revised version of public school administration in order to acknowledge the dynamic and complex nature of educational administration. Newlon (1934), another Columbia

University professor, added to the field's sudden ontological pluralism by adding an influential book titled *Educational Administration as Social Policy* which suggested the role of administrators was actually as developers and implementers of educational policy rather than site-based authorities. Importantly, Newlon implicitly predicted what was to become the intellectual thrust of one of the most influential postwar movements in educational administration when he noted that school leaders must "look to the emerging social sciences, not to the physical sciences, for its methods of inquiry" (Campbell et al., 1987, p. 178). Newlon had predicted the theory movement.

THE SEARCH FOR AN INTELLECTUAL AND THEORETICAL BASE FOR EDUCATIONAL ADMINISTRATION

Democratic and Theoretically Based Leadership Preparation

World War II had a profound effect on educational leadership in the United States. Society expected their school leaders to be the leaders of the war effort on the home front by promoting and instilling in their students distinctly "American" values. With this idea came a different social purpose for schooling, particularly at the building-site level; principals were expected to provide democratic leadership enabling students and teachers to more actively engage and understand decision making processes as they sought to lead a productive life. Involvement of various stakeholders in decision-making processes became important. Farmer (1948) and Reber (1948) suggested that an effective principal understood the community and provided for positive community relations to ensure the success of the educational organization. Leadership preparation became concerned with curriculum development, group coordination, supervision, and personnel development (Barnard, 1938; Campbell et al., 1987).

In addition, a host of structural and organizational issues influenced educational leadership during the early postwar years. Universities began offering administrator training courses on a larger scale; society became more centralized; the United States began to play an increasing role in international affairs; technology advanced rapidly; and schools themselves became more crowded and more complex (Pulliam & Van Patten, 1995). As a result of these factors, educational leaders were expected to draw insights from educational, psychological, sociological, and business research.[1] When schooling practices were challenged, principals were expected to defend those practices with empirical and theoretical findings from behavioral science disciplines (Campbell, 1981). However, concurrent to these shifting societal and topical emphases, another substantive change was taking place.

The administrative theory movement began in the late 1940s and continued through the 1950s. Proponents of this movement advocated that educational leaders develop and test theories like researchers in other scientific disciplines. Buoyed by widespread acknowledgement among influential educational administration organizations and from strong philosophic influences outside the field (Culbertson, 1995), educational administrators and the professors who prepared and trained them embarked on a journey of conceptual exploration, popularly called, the "Theory Movement." The goal of the movement was to create a single, unified science of educational administration grounded in the tenets of logical positivism that could guide inquiry, and ultimately practice (Brooks, & Miles, 2006; Culbertson, 1995). Again, educational administration scholars looked outside their ranks to find conceptual inspiration, methodological processes, and epistemological perspective, this time turning to "the applied field of public administration" (Culbertson, 1995, p. 38).

Examples of important contributions to the theory movement included Getzel's (1952) "social process" of administration, Shartle's (1956) theory of behavior in organizations, Hemphill and Coons' (1957) theory of group leadership, and a broad range of contributions set forth by Daniel Griffiths (Culbertson, 1995). As the field of educational administration sought to develop theory, several strains of inquiry rooted in various social sciences emerged and continue today. In particular, researchers adopted anthropological (Callahan, 1962; Conant, 1964; Wolcott, 1970), sociological (Lortie, 1975), and political science (Scribner & Englert, 1977) methods and theories to investigate educational administration-related phenomena.

EDUCATIONAL ADMINISTRATION AND SOCIAL TURBULENCE

Leadership for Social Equilibrium

As a result of the social and political unrest of the 1960s, principals and academics made efforts to maintain stability and a sense of normalcy in schools. Theorists and administrators upheld conceptions of schools as rational, goal-driven systems and investigated ways educational leaders might promote institutional and social equilibrium. In particular, theorists relied heavily upon Max Weber's concept of organizations as rational bureaucracies. As a result, administrators and those who prepared and trained them came to believe that this type of governance structure was appropriate for schools and began to stress bureaucratic images and structures in their work (Douglass, 1963; Noar, 1961).

With the proliferation of this belief in rationality, educational leaders were expected to support the educational bureaucracy by protecting their own authority, respecting the position of superiors, and guarding against appropriation of power by teachers (Beck & Murphy, 1993). In addition, principals became on-site researchers as categorical, quantitative, and empirical terms dominated discussions of the principals' work. Principals were asked to use increasingly sophisticated, scientific strategies for planning and measuring (Glass, 1986). The belief that proper techniques and modern technology would produce increased outcomes resulted in principals being held accountable for their decisions and school activities in a way they never had been before. Because of this pressure and related macropolitical demands, many principals felt vulnerable and confused about role expectations (Austin, French, & Hull, 1962).

Educational Administration as a Humanistic Endeavor

External factors exerted a heavy influence on administrators' preparation and practice in the 1970s. Increased federal involvement in local schools and the growing number of special interest groups altered many tasks of educational leaders. As a result of a renewed emphasis on community, leaders were expected to build alliances to ensure that schools and the community connected in meaningful ways (Burden & Whitt, 1973). More than ever, the professional success of educational leaders hinged on the support of stakeholders outside the school organization. In the 1970s, principals were also expected to see that meaningful educational experiences were offered to students, teachers, staff, and community members (Macdonald & Zaret, 1975). This emphasis on the human side of schools-as-open-systems also led to the expectation that principals would engage in and encourage positive, supportive interpersonal relationships. Theorists called for principals to adopt a human resource model of administration (Sergiovanni & Carver, 1973).

As a result of these expectations, educational leaders balanced many roles including interpersonal facilitators, information managers, and decision makers. As interpersonal facilitators, principals acted as figureheads, leaders, and liaisons. As information managers, they were monitors, disseminators, and spokespersons. And finally, as decision makers, principals became entrepreneurs, disturbance handlers, resource allocators, and negotiators (Mintzberg, 1973). The roles educational leaders were to assume and the duties to which they were beholden had expanded to an almost untenable list.

THE POSTMODERN TURN IN EDUCATIONAL ADMINISTRATION

During the 1980s and 1990s educational administration took a "postmodern turn" (English, 2003). That is, a proliferation of ideas, perspectives and pedagogies entered the field to provide fresh insight. In particular, the introduction and application of various forms of critical and feminist theory cast a doubting eye over much of the terrain that had previously been identified as the "knowledge base" that undergirded the field (English, 2003; Foster, 1986; Marshall, 1997). Other important conceptual advances included pluralism (e.g., Capper, 1993), multiculturalism (Banks, 1993), a second wave of ethical (e.g., Beck & Murphy, 1993) and spiritual leadership (e.g., Dantley, 2005), and the emergence of several loosely-coupled strains of inquiry called social justice (English, 1994; Young & Laible, 2000). The last of these, social justice, incorporates elements of many of these "postmodern" ideas, and is a movement that prompts scholars and educational leaders to assume an activist stance in practice and urges them to practice liberation and emancipatory pedagogy in all facets of their work.

LEADERSHIP FOR SOCIAL JUSTICE

Social justice is studied by legal scholars, social scientists, and in professional fields such as journalism and education (Ayers, Hunt, & Quinn, 1998; Cohen, 1986). Finding conceptual inspiration and guidance in notions of equity and equality, and in critical, feminist, and ethical theories, social justice scholars have largely rejected the rational-technical and efficiency-focused conceptions of leadership that form the balance of the field's traditional knowledge base (English, 2002b; Marshall & Gerstl-Pepin, 2005; Marshall & Oliva, 2006). While not altogether eschewing managerial, administrative, organizational, and leadership theory, social justice scholars have critiqued and expanded them as they developed a pedagogy of leadership based on an ethic of care and the moral imperative of improving "practice and student outcomes for minority, economically disadvantaged, female, gay/lesbian, and other students who have not traditionally served well in schools" (Marshall & Oliva, 2006, p. 6). Over the past several decades, educational leadership researchers and practitioners who have embraced this calling—this pedagogy of social justice—have drawn from and contributed to emergent multi- and interdisciplinary lines of inquiry in thought and action (Marshall & Oliva, 2006). As a result, several rich veins of research have emerged and phenomena previously ignored (e.g., the influence of leadership activity on institutional racism, gender discrimination, inequality of opportunity, and inequity of educational processes) have gained currency and attention. In particular, scholars have noted a need to raise awareness of social justice issues in pre-service educational leadership preparation programs and to understand how school leaders can promote equity at the building-level (Brooks, 2006).

In order to understand, promote, and enact social justice, school leaders must first develop a heightened and critical awareness of oppression, exclusion, and marginalization. According to Freire (2004), critical consciousness, or *conscientizacāo*, "refers to learning to perceive social, political, and economic contradictions, and to take action against the oppressive elements of reality" (p. 17). This orientation is taught overtly in some pre-service educational leadership programs, learned on-the-job or in professional development by other leaders, and likely never learned by others.

However, awareness of social injustices is not sufficient, school leaders must act when they identify inequity. School leaders are not only uniquely positioned to influence equitable educational practices, their proactive involvement is imperative. As Larson and Murtadha (2002) note, "throughout history, creating greater social justice in society and in its institutions has required the commitment of dedicated leaders" (p. 135). Without leadership, schools are more likely to perpetuate status quo hegemony rather than advance liberation (Apple, 1979). Thankfully, the proactive leader has a number of options should they choose to pursue external support for meaningful reforms that can substantively and positively change what might be longstanding traditions of inequity in their schools. In addition to increased federal funding through such programs as Title I, school leaders may also apply for additional funding from an unprecedented variety of federal, state, local, and philanthropic programs. Depending on their particular situation, school leaders may also be able to adopt a comprehensive or programmatic school reform designed to ameliorate a particular social and/or educational need (Brooks, Scribner, & Eferakorho, 2004). Other options available to leaders seeking to enact social justice include introducing and supporting democratic and ethical organizational processes, reforming, aligning, and expanding curricula to better meet the needs of a particular population, promoting understanding of multicultualistic pluralism, practicing difference-sensitive instructional leadership and providing professional development opportunities that focus on how educators can better serve traditionally underrepresented and poorly served peoples (Capper, 1993; Marshall & Oliva, 2006). Contemporary leaders have a variety of tools and techniques at their disposal that can help them identify social injustice in schools. For example, school leaders can:

1. conduct equity audits using aggregate or disaggregated student achievement data (Scheurich & Skrla, 2003);
2. examine allocation of instructional and curricular resources among school personnel and programs to determine if traditionally disadvantaged populations are receiving equitable disbursement of goods and services (Dantley & Tillman, 2006);
3. form meaningful and vibrant communications networks that include and validate the perspectives of students, families, and community members in addition to educational professionals who serve the school (Merchant & Shoho, 2006).

Leaders who develop this perspective and adopt a social justice stance have been characterized as:

1. *Transformational public intellectuals*, who "believe that the pedagogy in schools must be focused on morally impacting ends" (Dantley & Tillman, 2006, p. 20).
2. *Bridge people*, who are "committed to creating a bridge between themselves and others, for the purposes of improving the lives of all those with whom they work" (Merchant & Shoho, 2006, p. 86).
3. *Critical activists*, who will deconstruct political, social, and economic inequity and organize school and community resources toward the central aim of providing opportunity for traditionally underrepresented and oppressed peoples (Larson & Murtadha, 2002; Larson & Ovando, 2001).

Still, numerous resources, innovative options, and outstanding individuals do not guarantee that processes will be implemented faithfully or that educational outcomes will necessarily improve.

Even when school leaders recognize inequity and conceive of an intervention, they can be forced into complicity or inaction because they fear sanctions, or even termination of employment, from "higher-ups" in the system that do not share the leader's goals and instead operate from a rational, technocratic, and "difference-blind" pedagogy (Larson & Murtadha, 2002, p. 138). Many school leaders operate in complex and conflicted bureaucracies that prevent rather than often enable the kind of proactive behavior that a social justice orientation toward leadership demands (Marshall & Oliva, 2006). Further, while internal organizational constraints can thwart attempts to promote social justice in a school, external and boundary-spanning dynamics such as poor communication with traditionally oppressed families, lack of community support and involvement, and deep-seeded mistrust of public institutions such as schools among traditionally disadvantaged peoples may likewise prove to be significant obstacles (Larson & Murtadha, 2002).

STANDING AT THE CROSSROADS OF SCIENTIFIC MANAGEMENT AND SOCIAL JUSTICE: CONTEMPORARY IMPLICATIONS

In the United States, 2002's No Child Left Behind Act (NCLB) signaled the beginning of an educational policy era marked by accountability and an emphasis on increasing student achievement. While this twin focus has been part of the foundation for the study and practice of educational leadership for some time, the advent of legislative mandate introduces a new and complicated dynamic, especially since the legal structure of education in the United States means that the somewhat ambiguous NCLB guidelines are interpreted and implemented at the state level (Cambron-McCabe, McCarthy, & Thomas, 2004). Therefore, by design, the exact manner in which these goals should be attained and the implications of these foci for educational leaders at the school and district levels are unspecified and have been a topic of much debate, consternation, and confusion. To some, the new accountability is a clarion call for a second wave of scientific management. In particular, Levine (2005), Hess (2004), and Hess and Kelly (2005) have argued for the abolishment or reconstitution of university-based educational leadership preparation programs, in part because scholars and instructors in their ranks focus on a "utopian agenda" of social justice (Hess, 2004, p. 3). Hess favors a business management, market driven, and high stakes outcome-oriented model of educational leadership. This emphasis on business-style efficiency bears an uncanny resemblance to the Frederick Taylor-inspired traditions that dominated the field throughout the 1920s–1940s. Curiously, as also happened during that era, contemporary educational leaders are considering the rise of scientific management pedagogy at a time when moral issues—social justice issues—have been at the fore of pedagogical conversations.

In light of recent trends in the scholarship and practice of educational leadership, the rise of a second wave of scientific management asks many questions of practicing researchers and leaders engaged in educational leadership for social justice. We will raise two questions in particular, and then conclude this chapter by posing others to scholars and practitioners for further consideration and exploration. First—*are social justice and scientific management mutually exclusive concepts?* At first glance, an emphasis on technocratic rationality and outcome measurements may seem completely incongruent to issues of equity, and to be sure, many researchers have argued this point at great length (e.g., Berliner & Biddle, 1995). However, other scholars (e.g., Johnson, 2002; Scheurich & Skrla, 2003) have explored techniques for promoting equity using standardized test data and other accountability measures. Exploring this tension is difficult and controversial work but extremely relevant and necessary in a maturing high-accountability policy environment. Second—*what lessons can we learn from the first wave of scientific management that are still relevant today?* To be sure, the political and sociocultural contexts of educational leadership are different from a century ago in many respects. However, certain critiques of scientific management retain relevance and are important for contemporary educational leaders to consider. For example, English (2002b), notes that a scientific management orientation "creates a demarcation line, bestowing legitimacy on those who do their work within it while discrediting all that which came before as false or trivial" (p. 111). In a time where demographic trends indicate unprecedented and increasing ethnic diversity, and educators have a heightened sensitivity toward meeting the needs of all students, educational leaders must strive to understand issues from multiple perspectives and craft a leadership pedagogy sensitive to individual and subgroup differences. The idea of creating such a line of legitimization that separates and favors some at the expense of others seems unacceptable.

Certainly there are other questions that beg askance. Given these issues, what is the next step in the evolution of educational leadership preparation? How might credentialing and/or accreditation for educational leaders develop as they seek to navigate uncharted pedagogical terrain? How do educational leaders positively impact the educational experiences of all children in schools? What, if anything, now constitutes the protean knowledge base of educational leadership? Are there signature pedagogies, sets of skills, or certain competencies an educational leader should, could, or must exhibit? Will social justice become another historical era, fondly recalled by a few and gladly forgotten by some, or a paradigm shift that actually produces the liberation pedagogy it promises? Will social justice be washed away by a second wave of scientific management? Surely, educational leaders stand at a crossroads, with critical decisions to be made about the direction of the present and the future.

While the balance of this inquiry was restricted to identifying and discussing pedagogical trends in the United States, this review and these questions touch on many enduring dilemmas and enigmas that educational leaders and scholars have addressed in many national and international contexts. As researchers and practitioners outside the United States reflect on the salience of the perspective we articulate in this chapter, we invite them to consider how these trends and issues differ or resonate to pedagogical shifts they have witnessed in their own countries. Further, as educational leaders from around the globe increasingly seek to learn from each other in their efforts to provide better educational experiences for children, it seems that unless we try and learn lessons from the history of educational leadership, regardless of political or geographic boundary, then we are doing a disservice to our profession and to the children in our charge.

NOTE

1. Of course, while the new-found emphasis on social science methods marked an important development, many researchers continued to concentrate on administrators' effective and efficient use of time and fiscal resources by focusing on details of school operations, including methods for handling daily attendance slips, change of classroom procedures, and effective ways of introducing new staff members to the school environment (Kyte, 1952).

REFERENCES

Apple, M. W. (1979). *Ideology and curriculum*. Boston: Routeldge & Kegan Paul.

Austin, D. B., French, W., & Hull, J. D. (1962). *American high school administration: Policy and practice*. New York: Holt, Rinehart and Winston.

Ayers, W. C., Hunt, J. A. & Quinn, T. (Eds.). (1998). *Teaching for social justice*. New York: Teachers College Press.

Banks, J. A. (1993). The canon debate, knowledge construction, and multicultural education. *Educational Researcher, 22*(5), 4–14.

Barnard, C. I. (1938). *The functions of the executive*. Cambridge, MA: Harvard University Press.

Beck, L. G., & Murphy, J. (1993). *Understanding the principalship: Metaphorical themes 1920s–1990s*. New York: Teachers College Press.

Berliner, D. C., & Biddle, B. J. (1995). *The manufactured crisis: Myths, fraud, and the attack on America's public schools*. Reading, MA: Addison-Wesley.

Brooks, J. S. (2006, April). *Educational leadership and justice: An interdisciplinary perspective*. Paper presented at the 2006 annual meeting of the American Educational Research Association, San Francisco, CA.

Brooks, J. S., & Miles, M. (2006). Logic, history, use of. In F. W. English (Ed.), *SAGE encyclopedia of educational leadership and administration* (pp. 623–625). Thousand Oaks, CA: SAGE.

Brooks, J. S., Scribner, J. P., & Eferakorho, J. (2004). Teacher leadership in the context of whole school reform. *Journal of School Leadership, 14*(3), 242–265.

Burden, L., & Whitt, R. L. (1973). *The community school principal: New horizons*. Midland, MI: Pendell.

Callahan, R. E. (1962). *Education and the cult of efficiency: A study of social forces that have shaped administration of the public schools*. Chicago: University of Chicago Press.

Cambron-McCabe, N. H., McCarthy, M. M., & Thomas, S. B. (2004). *Public school law: teachers' and students' rights*. Boston: Pearson.

Campbell, R. F. (1981). The professorship in educational administration: A personal view. *Educational Administration Quarterly, 17*(1), 1–24.

Campbell, R. F., Fleming, T., Newell, L. J., & Bennion, J. W. (1987). *A history of thought and practice in educational administration*. New York: Teachers College Press.

Capper, C. A. (Ed.). (1993). *Educational administration in a pluralistic society*. Albany, NY: SUNY.

Cohen, R. L. (1986). *Justice: Views from the social sciences*. New York: Plenum Press.

Conant, J. (1964). *Shaping educational policy*. New York: McGraw Hill.

Cubberly, E. P. (1922). *Public school administration*. Boston: Houghton Mifflin.

Culbertson, J. (1995). *Building bridges: UCEA's first two decades*. London: UCEA.

Dantley, M. E. (2005). Faith-based leadership: ancient rhythms or new management. *International Journal of Qualitative Studies in Education, 18*(1), 3–19.

Dantley, M. E., & Tillman, L. C. (2006). Social justice and moral transformative leadership. In C. Marshall & M. Oliva (Eds.), *Leadership for social justice: Making revolutions in education* (pp. 16–30). Boston: Pearson.

Douglass, H. R. (1963). *Modern administration of secondary schools: Organization and administration of junior and senior high schools*. New York: Blaisdell.

Dutton, S. T., & Snedden, D. (1909). *The administration of public education in the United States*. New York: McMillan.

English, F. W. (1994). *Theory in educational administration*. New York: Harper Collins.

English, F. W. (2002a). *The fateful turn: Understanding the discursive practice of educational administration*. Huntsville, TX: NCPEA.

English, F. W. (2002b). The point of scientificity, the fall of the epistemological dominos, and the end of the field of educational administration. *Studies in Philosophy and Education, 21*(2), 109–136.

English, F. W. (2003). *The postmodern challenge to the theory and practice of educational administration*. Springfield, IL: Chalres C. Thomas.

Farmer, F. M. (1948). The public high school principalship. *Bulletin of the National Association of Secondary School Principals, 32*(154), 82–91.

Foster, W. (1986). *Paradigms and promises: New approaches to educational administration*. Buffalo, NY: Prometheus Books.

Freire, P. (2004). *Pedagogy of the oppressed*. New York: Continuum Press.

Glass, T. E. (1986). Factualism to theory, art to science: School administration texts 1955–1985. In *An analysis of texts on school administration 1820–1985: The reciprocal relationship between the literature and the profession* (pp. 93–114). Danville, IL: Interstate.

Getzels, J. W. (1952). A psycho-sociological framework for the study of educational administration. *Harvard Educational Review, 22*, 235–246.

Hemphill, J. K., & Coons, A. E. (1957). Development of the leader behavior description questionnaire. In R. M. Stogdill and A. E. Coons (Eds.), *Leader behavior: Its description and measurement*. Columbus, OH: Bureau of Business Research, Ohio State University.

Hess. F. M (2004). *Common sense school reform*. New York: Palgrave-McMillan.

Hess, F. M., & Kelly, A. P. (2005). *Learning to lead: What gets taught in principal preparation programs*. Retrieved May 9, 2005, from http://www.ksg .harvard.edu/pepg/PDF/Papers/ Hess_Kelly_Learning_to_Lead_PEPG05.02.pdf

Johnson, R. S. (2002). *Using data to close the achievement gap: How to measure equity in our schools*. Thousand Oaks, CA: Corwin Press.

Johnston, C. H., Newlon, D. H., & Pickell, F. G. (1922). *Junior-senior high school administration*. Atlanta, GA: Charles Scribner's Sons.

Kyte, G. C. (1952). *The principal at work*. Boston: Ginn.

Larson, C. L., & Murtadha, K. (2002). Leadership for social justice. In J. Murphy (Ed.), *The educational leadership challenge: Redefining leadership for the 21st century* (pp. 134–161). Chicago: University of Chicago Press.

Larson, C. L., & Ovando, C. J. (2001).*The color of bureaucracy: The politics of equity in multi-cultural school communities*. Belmont, CA: Wadsworth.

Levine, A. (2005). *Educating school leaders*. Retrieved May 9, 2005, from http:// www.edschools.org/reports_leaders.htm.

Lortie, D. C. (1975). *Schoolteacher: A sociological study*. Chicago: University of Chicago Press.

Macdonald, J. B., & Zaret, E. (Eds.). (1975). *Schools in search of meaning: 1975 yearbook of the Association for Supervision and Curriculum Development*. Washington, DC: Author.

Marshall, C. (1997). Dismantling and reconstructing policy analysis. In *Feminist critical policy analysis* (pp. 1–40). London: Falmer Press.

Marshall, C., & Gerstl-Pepin, C. (2005). *Re-framing educational politics for social justice*. Boston: Allyn & Bacon.

Marshall, C., & Oliva, M. (2006). *Leadership for social justice: Making revolutions in education*. Boston: Pearson.

Mason, R. (1986). From idea to ideology: School administration texts 1820–1914. In T. E. Glass (Ed.), *An analysis of texts on school administration 1820–1985: The reciprocal relationship between the literature and the profession* (pp. 1–21). Danville, IL: Interstate.

Merchant, B. M., & Shoho, A. R. (2006). Bridge people: Civic and educational leaders for social justice. In C. Marshall & M. Oliva (Eds.), *Leadership for social justice: Making revolutions in education* (pp. 85–109). Boston: Pearson.

Mintzberg, H. (1973). *The nature of managerial work*. New York: Harper & Row.

Newlon, J. H. (1934). *Educational administration as social policy*. San Francisco: Charles Scribner's Sons.

Noar, G. (1961). *The junior high school: Today and tomorrow*. Englewood Cliffs, NJ: Prentice-Hall.

Pulliam, J. D., & Van Patten, J. (1995). *History of education in America*. Englewood Cliffs, NJ: Merrill.

Reber, D. D. (1948). The principal interprets his school. *Bulletin of the National Association of Secondary School Principals, 32*(152), 73–80.

Scheurich. J. J., & Skrla, L. (2003). *Leadership for equity and excellence: Creating high-achievement classrooms, schools, and districts*. Thousand Oaks, CA: Corwin Press.

Scribner, J. D., & Englert, R. M. (1977). *The politics of education*: An introduction. In J. D. Scribner (Ed.), *The politics of education* (pp. 1–29). Chicago: University of Chicago Press.

Sergiovanni, T. J., & Carver, F. D. (1973). *The new school executive: A theory of administration*. New York: Dodd, Mead.

Shartle, C. L. (1956). *Executive performance and leadership*. Englewood Cliffs, NJ: Prentice-Hall.

Strayer, G. D., Engelhardt, N. L., & Elsbree, W. S. (1927). *Standards for the administration building of a school system*. New York: Bureau of Publications Teachers College, Columbia University.

Strayer, G. D., & Thorndike, E. L. (1912). *Educational administration*. New York: MacMillan.

Tyack, D. B., & Hansot, E. (1982). *Managers of virtue: Public school leadership in America, 1920–1980*. New York: Basic Books.

Wolcott, H. F. (1970). An ethnographic approach to the study of school administrators. *Human Organization, 29*(2), 115–122.

Young, M. D., & Laible, J. (2000). White racism, anti-racism, and school leadership preparation. *Journal of School Leadership, 10*(5), 374–415.

CHAPTER 6

SCHOOL REFORM AND FREIRE'S METHODOLOGY OF *CONSCIENTIZATION*

Kathleen S. Sernak

This chapter addresses school reform and the challenges presented to educational leaders working toward social justice which is not limited to only academic achievement. Social justice as used here is education for emancipatory social change resulting in freedom to, that is, the opportunity for individuals to pursue work they value, and, ultimately, to discover and create a life of worth for self and community. To examine such reform and the implications for educational leadership, I use Freire's (1989) concept of conscientization, possessing a conscious understanding of one's lived reality, as a framework by which to analyze two particular reforms, Success for All and Professional Development Schools. From that analysis, I suggest that educational leadership that seeks to liberate students to make social changes creates space and spaces for trust; and nurtures participatory, equitable and just relationships rather than simply managing programs and services, and facilitates "the opportunity for empowerment rather than 'delivering it'" (Grinberg, as cited in Larson & Murtadha, 2001, p. 8).

Leadership for Social Justice: Promoting Equity and Excellence Through Inquiry and Reflective Practice, pp. 115–149
Copyright © 2008 by Information Age Publishing
All rights of reproduction in any form reserved.

Administrators, internationally, and particularly in the United States, have embraced various whole school reforms (WSR) since the 1980s as a way to assure students, particularly those in poor, urban districts, of academic success. Not all schools with WSR are poor and urban, however, a vast majority are. Although I discuss WSR from the perspective of the United States and particularly analyze two WSR in a elementary school in New Jersey, I believe that school leaders internationally will benefit from the discussion of school reform and social justice. Urban schools internationally have significant populations of students not of the dominant culture who present new challenges, based on race, ethnicity, culture, and religion, to educators. Like the United States, standardized, high-stakes tests also play a major role in what is considered student "success." My intention, therefore, is to consider the goals of school reform, how Freire's (1989) methodology of conscientization, and caring power can enable leaders to guide schools in a socially just manner.

INTRODUCTION: WHOLE SCHOOL REFORM AND MARKET GOALS

In the past several years, WSR has been the watchword for better schooling in economically disadvantaged districts. Unlike previous reforms that tinkered with individual aspects of the curriculum, pedagogy, or governance, WSR implies systemic change within a school. Ideally, the result is transformation—rethinking teaching and learning that encompasses strategies to enhance children's academic progress, and, depending on the particular reform, emphases on professional development for preservice and in-service educators; curriculum articulation; community building, within and outside the school; creating and maintaining relationships built on trust; collaboration with the university; and a governance structure that supports those modifications.

WSR in many cases, however, have not reached—nor are they necessarily reaching for—the ideal. School reforms are driven by a "preoccupation with academic quality" (Mintrom, 2001, p. 615), and build "on proposals to bolster the economy and promote 'traditional' values" (Toll, 2001, p. 1). They, as such, do little to advance the function of social justice, and continue to pursue academic quality as a means to ensure economic efficiency. Without denigrating school reforms, Mintrom and Toll examine them, respectively, from the perspective of a need for education for democracy, and emancipatory social change. In both analyses, the authors explore the goals of the reforms and ask whether different questions regarding purposes and outcomes should be asked, questions that get at the link between schooling and social change that offers *freedom* to individuals to pursue work they value, and, ultimately to discover and create a life of worth for self and community. They question the current reality of public education that is valued primarily from an exchange perspective. That is, the driving force of schooling is to teach individuals to participate in the market or market-related activities. The result is reproduction and maintenance of current socioeconomic classes (Bowles & Gintes, 1976), with some being privileged and many not having access to the knowledge and power that would advantage them in the larger society.

Economic exchange models play out differently, depending upon the perspectives of the culture in power and the individuals/groups exercising that power. Whole school reform established on a free market approach emphasizes the honing of academic skills for the brightest students, and "back to the basics" and "functional literacy" programs for children of racial and ethnic minorities in low socioeconomic status (SES) schools and districts (Toll, 2001). The curricula for children living in poor areas tend to be "overtly utilitarian" (Lankshear, 1993, p. 91) and based on the assumption that the students are less able and need to learn how to become incorporated into the "established economic and social values and practices" (p. 91) of the dominant society. The goal for functional skills programs is for students to become employable and to integrate into and adjust to the norms of society, while programs for students of the dominant culture encourage them to develop the abilities and skills needed to develop the standards that will direct and power the social and economic order.

Other economic models of WSR stress excellence rather than equity of access and opportunity, and individualism over the common good. School choice that includes private and religious, as well as public schools, and ability tracking are among the WSR models that illustrate those goals. Both often militate against the children the reforms were intended to serve.

There are efforts affecting WSR that blend the free market approach with government intervention that set the direction for schools, yet continue to have exchange value at their core. National standards and high stakes testing provide the framework for increased expectations for all students, but do not take into consideration that not all students have the same background advantages that privilege children in school. Testing and national standards limit teacher control of content and curricula, advocate uniformity among schools and students, and, most importantly, reduce the attention given to difference, tolerance (Toll, 2001), and valuing the Other.

Mintrom (2001) and Toll (2001) speak to issues of democracy and social justice that must be more than rhetoric; they must form the foundation that will not only improve teaching and learning, but also will contribute to significant changes for the public good. Those concerns and topics form new—and necessary—ways in which the purpose and any discussion and analysis of WSR require examination. Among those concerns are the lack of respect and value for difference, equity of opportunity and access to the same knowledge, and focus on "emancipatory social change" (Toll, 2001, p. 4). Finally, Toll and Mintrom do not denounce the importance of the exchange value of education. They call attention, however, to the failure of current reforms to connect economics and education "to the empowerment of the individual to create rewarding work" (Toll, 2001, p. 4), and to the value of "communitarian"[1] benefits that derive from civic engagement" (Mintrom, 2001, p. 618).

Nevárez-La Torre and Sanford-DeShields (1999) note that school reforms often do have aspects of social justice as their focus. Achieving equity in education for all students, especially, racial and ethnic minorities, is a goal in virtually all school reform efforts. However, the concentration is on participation and/or access "without facilitating a process [emphasis added] to support effectively the academic performance of participants" (p. 245). Without a process for taking advantage of the opportunities for access and of participation, there is limited improvement in academic success, thereby, limiting the exchange value, education for economic advancement, of poor and minority students. The ultimate result is that students' learning to question and challenge the current reality of their lives, and to know they have the freedom—and the abilities—to make liberating changes in the social structure does not occur. Despite equal opportunity for and access to the same education for all students, without a course of action to support students' learning, schools continue to maintain and reproduce social and class hierarchies based, in large part, on difference in cultural values, beliefs, and traditions.

Leadership that questions the purpose and goals of WSR will consider success not solely from an academic perspective, but also from the viewpoint of school as a microcosm of a socially just society and what that entails. Academic excellence, accountability mandates, and integration into, and adjustment to, the norms of society are just the tip of the proverbial iceberg of WSR. Leadership that seeks social justice in order to liberate students creates space and spaces for trust; and nurtures participatory, equitable, and just relationships rather than "managing programs and services [whole school reform models] within a mere and colonizing public relations approach.... [T]he role of leadership is, therefore, that of facilitating the opportunity for empowerment rather than 'delivering it' " (Grinberg, as cited in Larson & Murtadha, 2001, p. 8).

In the next section, I describe the ways in which I use the concepts of social justice, conscientization, and power relations as those terms relate to WSR.

SOCIAL JUSTICE, *CONSCIENTIZATION*, AND CARING POWER

Social Justice

WSRs generally promote more than academic success, having as goals improved parent-school-community relationships that not only enhance students' academic progress, but encourage collaboration for the well-being of the community. Those latter goals, combined with academic success, have the potential to achieve social justice, which I interpret as emancipatory social change through which students learn the concept of "freedom to," that is,

> the relation between freedom and the consciousness of possibility, between freedom and imagination—the ability to make present what is absent, to summon up a condition that is not yet ... to seek out openings in their (students') lived situations, to tolerate disruptions of the taken-for-granted, to try consciously to become different than they are. (Greene, 1988, pp. 16–17)

In order to experience "freedom to," school leaders need to determine how to put WSR into practice so reform will benefit students who, in turn, will improve society by working for equity, cultural understandings, and placing value on all persons because they are human beings (Kant, 2003). Too often we, as educators, get caught up in teaching a static curriculum to students whom we view as bright, privileged, disabled, part of a minority, non-English speakers, poor, average, Muslim, or having behavior problems, rather than as the human beings with minds, hearts, and souls who need to be educated to live in and work with a continuously transforming society, world, and galaxy.

Social justice is not equality, but equity, allowing more to some and less to others depending on their needs. It is not a deficit model, in which nonhegemonic students are considered "in need" rather than having different knowledge. It is not patronizing students whose first language and culture are not American English. It is not limiting gifted and talented classes to only academically successful students. It is acknowledging one's own biases and prejudices and how they affect teaching and learning. It is teaching what is "expected" in order to be successful in society, and dialoguing with, not inculcating, students regarding their perspectives on those expectations. It is educator's belief that they have much to learn from all students. It is caring for each student.

Social justice requires school leadership to challenge the "interiorities of school" (English, 2005, p. 7) and of WSR. Leaders question the legitimacy of goals dealing with knowledge, skills, and dispositions to be successful in adulthood; learning that is research-based and, therefore, is "thorough and efficient" (New Jersey Educational Standards); the idea of a safe environment for students and staff; and a vision that is "shared and supported by the school community" (p. 6) as lacking for they do not provide the moral strength and support from which to make the necessary changes to achieve a society in which people are willing to listen to and learn from one another; to view compromise as owning together rather than giving up; to live in harmony, not necessarily in unity; and to transcend the self through a synthesis of self and other. Or, as English suggests, school leaders need to concern themselves more with the exteriorities of school, the assumptions, the institutional biases ingrained in the general society.

Conscientization

Children who live in poverty and/or who are minorities racially or ethnically need more than a "banking" education (Freire, 1989). They need to learn for liberation and freedom, that is, they need to question the answers, not answer the questions, in order to take control of their own lives.

Conscientization is the possession of critical consciousness, that is, understanding and addressing the reality one lives and, simultaneously, one's consciousness of that reality (Lankshear, 1993). Fundamental to attaining critical consciousness is dialogue, for it opens the spaces for free, creative exploration of complex and subtle issues (Senge, 1990), thus, requiring critical thinking. It is this dialogue that is necessary to address the exteriorities of schooling. It is not telling the community what is needed in schools, but it is the deliberative dialogue that Gutmann (1987/1999) notes is essential to dealing with the various beliefs and assumptions people have about one another and that affect the ways in which we school our children. Without a leader's willingness to deal with dialogue, assumptions, and biases, differences continue to be ignored. The power structure, hegemonic and hierarchical, continues as is; schools, despite the rhetoric of vision, researched pedagogy, and community-shared and supported educational goals, remain the same.

Shor (1993) explained conscientization as having four qualities: power awareness, critical literacy, desocialization, and self-organization/self-education (I will use these qualities later in the paper to structure the discussion and analysis of two WSRs: Success for All and Professional Development Schools).

Power awareness. Shor (1993) described power awareness as "knowing that society and history can be made and remade by human action and by organized groups; knowing who exercises dominant power in society for what ends and how power is currently organized and used in society"

(p. 32). As schools and districts consider reforms for the liberation and freedom of students, teaching them to use their power positively is a critical component. "Power is a necessary and positive feature of social relations that allows human beings to attain a degree of sovereignty and control over their lives" (Wartenberg, 1990, p. 194). Power often is thought of as negative, as control or "power over." However, "if power is in everything, as Foucault advocates, then power *per se* isn't bad" (Grimshaw, 1993, p. 55). Leadership for school reform must embrace the positional power that affords opportunities to guide the education of students to an understanding that they have the power to take control of their lives, and to the development of skills that enable them to use their personal and collective power to benefit them individually and collectively.

Power used in social justice leadership transforms people and schooling; it does not dominate. The issue is not *who* has power, but what are the *patterns* of the exercise of power. The basis of transformative power is trust, and the heart of trust is vulnerability (Wartenberg, 1990). The school leader is key in establishing a climate in which taking risks and feeling exposed can occur without fear. Teachers need to trust that an administrator will support their work to teach students to question and challenge the givens of society and the place of minorities in it, and to question the answers, not answer the questions (Shor, 1993). Faculty put themselves in a vulnerable position when they challenge the hidden curriculum, or when they expose the oppression in a whole school reform model. As important, is the leader's inviting, seeking, not only community input, but the questions that challenge everyone to look beyond the externality of societal policies, rules, regulations, and goals, to the realities of who benefits from them and why.

Administrators and teachers need to risk credence in order to attend to the externalities of schooling. They need to attend to knowledge that is not valued, that is, they appreciate the importance and worth of the learning that students bring to the classroom. They are willing to hear them *outside* the framework of some "true knowledge," and, therefore, are willing to suspend truth as a possible concept (Shor, 1993, p. 92). Teachers further their risk-taking by choosing the standpoint from which they view the students. That is, they acknowledge their political choice to change the site from which traditionally they have viewed the generation of knowledge to put themselves into the students' sites so they can share that place with the students in order to know the students (Cain, 1993, p. 93). School leaders, therefore, provide the support and facilitate this process. By so doing, they challenge the accepted norm.

Likewise, students need to trust teachers to accept their challenges to schooling and society. They also need to trust that faculty, staff, and administrators will use their power to help them in fundamental ways. If knowledge is empowering as well as power over, then students must be provided with and have access to more structured forms of knowledge. Not acknowledging or explaining that to students can be construed as failing to provide resources for empowerment that some have and some do not (Grimshaw, 1993). Students' experience of acquiring new types of consciousness may be disorienting, as old guidelines for behavior and practice become open to question and old interpretations become subjects for students' deep-seated doubt (Bartky, 1990). Trust requires that students, those in subordinate positions, allow themselves to be in control of teachers and administrators, those in stronger positions, believing that the latter will use their control to enable them to grow in strength and positive use of their own power. The challenge is to engender that trust. To do so requires educational leaders to deconstruct who they are, to be willing to engage in conflictual dialogue with teachers, community members, and politicians. It will necessitate leaders to lead, not simply to comply, in order to deal with the "elephant in the room."

Trust requires dialogue, the free, creative exploration of complex and subtle issues (Senge, 1990). In all schools, but particularly in those with minority and poor students, communication that indicates concern for and interest in the students and their community is paramount to any reform effort. Deep listening to students by school staff and the ability of staff to suspend their own views are vital to understanding the buried truths so that there can be negotiation of shared purposes within a diverse community. Dialogue is essential, for power that transforms cannot be required; it can only be accepted (Wartenberg, 1990). Power that transforms ultimately is necessary for building trust that is fundamental to students' liberation and freedom.

Critical literacy. Shor (1993) explains critical literacy as analytic habits of thinking, reading, writing, speaking, or discussing which go beneath surface impressions, traditional myths, mere opinions, and routine clichés; understanding the social contexts and consequences of any subject matter; discovering the deep meaning of any event, text, technique, process, object, statement, image or situation; applying that meaning to your own context (p.32).

Critical school leadership[2] is that which enables educational communities—teachers, students, parents—to pursue justice and equity for children who are economically poor, and who may be different in race, ethnicity, gender preference, religion, physical, or mental ability. Social justice leaders provide guidance when embarking on curricular or whole school reform models by asking the questions: Who benefits? Who dominates? Who defines how the organizational re-structuring that needs to occur accommodates the changes necessary to successfully implement the reform efforts? How must caring actions ultimately come about as a result of improved teaching and learning, that is, how will the educational community exceed the demands of efficiency in order to generate acts of caring (Noddings, 1992; Sernak, 1998; Shields, 2001)?

Freire (1989) advocated that education for poor children should be about human and community development, about understanding who the children are, personally, culturally, and socially. It is about becoming visible to self and others. David Whyte (2001), poet, eloquently illustrates this sentiment: "To be human is to become visible while carrying what is hidden as a gift to others" (p. 190).

Social justice leadership seeks whole school reform that bases teaching and learning on students' creation of knowledge that will liberate and free them from the ways in which they "have already been classified and identified by dominant discourses. This means discovering new ways of understanding [themselves] and one another, refusing to accept the dominant culture's characterizations of [their] practices and desires, and re-defining them from within resistant cultures" (Sawicki, 1991, p. 44). Through problem posing and solving, students learn to question which knowledge is valued and why; they examine their access to opportunities for intellectual, economic, and social advancement; and they learn to reach an understanding of knowing that they know.

As the children learn and grow in understanding of self and society, so does the community. Critical leadership, therefore, emphasizes schooling that addresses the needs, interests and concerns of the children and parents. Incumbent upon the critical school leader is facilitating choice by focusing discussion of the reform models on the children's lives and values, the school personnel's understandings and perceptions of the values of the school and children, and the gaps between and among their own, the school's, and the children's cultures. In other words, to improve teaching and learning, difference must be acknowledged, accepted, and respected in order for students to be liberated and to experience freedom, for as Whyte (2001) reflects, "In freedom is the wish to belong to structure in our own particular way" (p. 233).

Although it is important for educators to reflect and advocate their own and the school's values, it is of equal importance to support the values of the community and to see that the curriculum and policies are consistent with those values (Power & Makogon, 1996). If they are not considered, or only peripherally noted, the response to who benefits? would be, "Not the children," for their needs and concerns would not dominate. "Freedom," as Sawicki (1991) notes, "lies in our capacity to discover the historical links between certain modes of self-understanding and modes of domination" (p. 44). The school reform implemented would aid in that discovery and liberate students to develop knowledge about themselves and their place in society that provides them with the *freedom* to—to access what has traditionally been denied to them, deny the categories into which they have been put, celebrate the values and knowledge of their own cultures, and achieve. Leadership needed to interpret and implement school reform for social justice outcomes would facilitate reflection for teachers and students so that students learn to act with intentionality toward the world, that is, they would engage "in action upon the world informed by their reflection upon it" (Lankshear, 1993 p. 96). Reflection resulting in intentionality would become the basis of teaching and learning for individual and collective liberation. In order for that to happen, however, educational leaders must be willing to open the doors to contentiousness and conflict, to risk being viewed as not nice, to deal with their own and others' ingrained biases which have become beliefs. Change in schools that liberates cannot come about without dealing with all that keeps certain groups in chains.

Critical leaders direct educators to reforms that open the spaces for school personnel to question not only why students do not read at home or why parents do not read to their children. They encourage teachers and staff to ask, "What are the social circumstances behind the limited or lack of academic success?" Rather than determine the feasibility of what might be done, social justice leaders focus reforms on what should be done, that is, educational change becomes the framework to diagnose the deprivation in order to establish what ideally should be done if the resources were available. The leaders then use the reforms to guide teachers not simply to improve the achievement of the students, but to provide the freedom for children to achieve (Larson & Murtadha, 2001).

Such leadership creates space and spaces for trust; nurtures participatory, equitable and just relationships rather than "managing programs and services [whole school reform models] within a mere and colonizing public relations approach ... the role of leadership is, therefore, that of *facilitating the opportunity* [italics added] for empowerment rather than 'delivering it' " (Grinberg, as cited in Larson & Murtadha, 2001, p. 8). Such leadership asks the why questions behind the facades of equity and oppression. Then there is action to change, which is a continuous process of dialogue, decision making, action, change, evaluation, all the while continuing dialogue.

Desocialization. Shor (1993) explains desocialization, integral to *conscientization,* as

> recognizing and challenging the myths, values, behaviors, and language learned in mass culture; critically examining the regressive values operating in society, which are internalized into consciousness—such as racism, sexism, classism, homophobia, a fascination with the rich and powerful, hero-

worship, excess consumerism, runaway individualism, militarism, and national chauvinism. (p. 33)

In the language of whole school reform, "community" is most often a goal. The term "learning community," usually perceived as homogeneous, rarely is discussed regarding its meaning how or to achieve it. Learning communities in virtually all instances are composed of differences of thought. Communities made up of children from many different ethnic, racial, religious, and social backgrounds especially need to be viewed as non-homogeneous, and from the perspective of "cross-cultural leadership" (Shields, 2001). Shields discusses the need for critical leaders to respect all perspectives relating to difference, and to work with those differences to create a community with shared norms and values that are dynamic and continuously renegotiated as the community ebbs and flows; it is a harmonious community rather than a united one.

> In a community of difference, the commonalities are values of inclusivity, respect, and a desire to understand diverse perspectives; the norms are commitment to reflection, critique, and dialogue. Such norms do not merely reflect the customs of an already powerful or established group, but are constantly subject to re-examination and renegotiation to best address the needs of all members. (p. 5)

There are no prescriptions for community because all are different. In each context, communities are created and recreated. The critical leader, through exercise of transformative power and understanding of the necessity to reach beyond the efficiency goals of reform to that of caring acts, uses dialogue between and among students, teachers, staff, parents, and neighborhood community members. Dialogue establishes the foundation for trust building which engenders inclusivity, esteem, deliberation, and analysis, ultimately resulting in negotiated norms and values by which societal members may live in accord.

In communities of difference, a significant task for social justice leaders is to consider the "extra-discursive" as it affects racial and ethnic minority students, for it is fundamental to narrowing the gap between and among educators', students', and school cultures. The "extra-discursive" is "an intransitive relationship pre-existing its possible utterance" (Cain, 1993, p. 83). That is, it is the experience of something prior to its having a name or of being understood and explained; it is having knowledge without the ability to discuss. How is it possible to know a reality that is pre-discursive?

Reality and the knowledge of it are separated by capacities of the knowers who are limited and species-specific. In communities of difference, members of various groups of difference may have pre-discursive knowledge of other difference groups, for the creation of that knowledge emanated from their particular group. That is, the knowledge of the Other is limited by their own capacity and experience based on and limited by their own culture.

- Capacities for knowing are culture-specific, depending on the modes of thought and discourse.
- Capacities are historically or relationally specific, depending on the site occupied by the knower in a relational nexus which provides social vantage point (professions, race, class, religion, age) (Cain, 1993).

Unless there is social justice leadership, the differences among and between groups may remain in the pre-discursive mode, each group knowing the Other and themselves through their own cultural experiences.

Developing and maintaining a community of difference requires attention to the individual as well as to the community. Social justice leadership, committed to apprehending the ideals of community and mutuality need to be cognizant of "preserving the forms of autonomy, individuality and care for self" (Grimshaw, 1993, p. 69). That is particularly important in the creation and sustenance of a community of difference, where the focus is understanding the Other in terms of cultural group, and finding commonalities among norms and values of various groups in order to form a community of difference. Within whole school reform, the individuality of each student requires recognition and consideration; the personal and common good need to be balanced unless they become as constraining and coercive as forms of individualism that community seeks to replace (Grimshaw, 1993).

Communities of difference include economically poor children. Because WSR largely targets schools in poverty areas, education for the children is more than academic. Education necessary for such students is political as it includes the context and circumstances that affect children's external options, as well as their choices, hopes, and goals (Noddings, 1992; Nussbaum, 2000). The children see and experience a world of drugs, poverty, and sickness; inordinate health problems; inequitable access to educational opportunities; unjust expectations of school and society; and the lack of instruction in how to use the power they have to liberate and free themselves (Freedman, 1991; Kozol, 1991, 1995, 2000; McLeod, 1987; Tronto, 1993). Those experiences influence what they love, value, fear, and feel capable of doing. The children's schooling and education, therefore, necessitate considerations of health, physical and emotional; freedom from humiliation and violence; and attention to the inner spirit (Noddings, 1992; Nussbaum, 2000).

For the success of WSR to be tied solely to accountability systems is unreasonable. Although accountability may be necessary to sustain the bureaucracy of schooling, to expect all children to learn the same things at the same time despite the disparities in their freedom to achieve (Sen, 1992) flies in the face of all that educators know and believe. Furthermore, state and national accountability systems do not take into account communities of difference: language, family priorities, social and economic opportunities or limitations, and other group values. In essence, accountability systems narrow what children learn, despite the increased knowledge of how children learn (Larson & Murtadha, 2001).

School leaders need to be more like community organizers and less like corporate executives. Larson and Murtadha (2001) note that

> the problems that limit the educational opportunity and life chances of many children must be resolved through community-wide initiatives where the purposes of education and the needs of the communities of color and communities of poverty are central to discourse, policy, pedagogy, and practice. (p. 15)

For social justice leadership to facilitate the implementation of WSR in communities of difference, the following questions serve as a guide:

- Does WSR seek liberation and human development for marginalized and oppressed children?
- Does WSR emphasize possibilities rather than problems?
- Is there obvious commitment to the value of the children they are intended to serve? (Larson & Murtadha, 2001).
- Do WSR models reflect traditional and historical behaviors and worldviews of White males? Do they hold up for females and people of color?
- Does WSR promote harmony within difference?
- Does WSR encourage—insist on—focusing on our children rather than children at-risk?
- Is the foundation of WSR's commitment to difference in unity, that is, to working in harmony? To ethical behavior?

Self-organization/self-education. Last, Shor (1993) indicates that self-organization or self-education is critical to the methodology of conscientization. He describes this as "taking the initiative to transform school and society away from authoritarian relations and the undemocratic, unequal distribution of power; taking part in and initiating social change projects; overcoming the induced anti-intellectualism of mass education" (p. 33). This final stage of *conscientization*, is the actual implementation, the action resulting from the deliberative dialogue, critical thinking, and reflection. It is Freire's (1989) notion of the people identifying what it is they need, not being told, and taking the actions to acquire those needs.

The role of social justice school leaders is critical, for it is at this stage where "apprehensions of the complex of contradictions" (Freire, 1989, p. 106) must be considered in order to develop and implement educational pedagogies suitable for all students and educators. At this point, school leaders need to work with the school community, including teachers, students, parents, and community members, to address the self-identified educational needs of various groups, acknowledge and respect the professional knowledge of teachers, meet the political mandates, and bridge the gaps between teachers' and students' cultural understandings that affect teaching and learning. In other words, the social justice leader is asked to have the wisdom of Solomon!

At this juncture, power relationships are forefronted. Caring power is necessary to facilitate and implement schooling that will educate students to become positive social change agents, but the site for caring power is the traditional organization of school: bureaucratic, hierarchical, and domineering.

Power[3]

In addition to the discussion of power awareness associated with conscientization, I offer my further understandings of power and caring power, and schooling. Social justice leaders need caring power, that is, the recognition that caring for an organization requires the positive use of power, power of position and of authority to provide the room for moral debate concerning particular needs vis-à-vis principles of fairness and justice. Such a leader uses positional power to respond "to the particular, concrete, physical, spiritual, intellectual, psychic, and emotional needs" (Tronto, 1989, p. 174) of the total organization.

> Implementing school reform requires the power associated with people and places of domination in order to merge public and private spheres. It means seeking out and developing leaders from nonhegemonic cultures whose roles and power most often are ascribed as informal and unofficial, uninstitutionalized, that is not publicly acknowledged. An understanding and ability to care, merged with official power to teach and model caring becomes caring power. (Sernak, 1998, p. 156)

Caring power needs leadership to support thinking and doing, demands time, resources, skills and knowledge. Social justice leaders see power in terms of not having all the answers, but willingly using their power to struggle with ambiguity and to make hard decisions, despite knowing that they will not always be right and may, unintentionally, make a decision that is not in the best interests of a student or group of people. However, they know how to regroup, to dialogue, to know when it is appropriate to show weakness and when it would be damaging to others in their care. Their vision is clear enough to guide others, but does not dictate, leaving space open for the development of collective imagination. Finally, the caring power of social justice leaders functions to maintain a "delicate balance of care, justice, and power" (Sernak, 1998, p. 161).

A STUDY OF TWO WHOLE SCHOOL REFORM MODELS: SUCCESS FOR ALL AND PROFESSIONAL DEVELOPMENT SCHOOLS

In this section, I examine two WSR models, Success for All and Professional Development Schools and their implementation in one elementary school in New Jersey. I suggest that although neither has claimed as its purpose to achieve social change through social justice, that both—and all other WSRs—be examined in that light. Though higher academic achievement and accountability for the academic success of students traditionally underserved are certainly worthwhile goals, it is essential for leaders of WSR to ask why those goals carry such importance. In other words, it is critical that leaders ask what the overarching purposes of schooling are, and how WSR will help students achieve those outcomes. To that end, I open a discussion about Success for All (SFA), a highly structured whole school reform model, and the Professional Development School paradigm (PDS); a collaboration between P–12 schools and universities, using questions presented by scholars invested in social justice: Whose reform is it? Who benefits? Who dominates? Will our society benefit as a whole? (Starratt, as cited in Shields, 2001; Toll, 2001). With those questions as my guide, I turn to Freire's notion of conscientization as a framework from which to examine the two reforms in order to begin dialogue on the potential for WSR and the leadership necessary to impact the reality of children whose cultures and traditions are not those of the hegemonic society and who live in poverty.

SFA

Power awareness. Weber maintained that bureaucracy leads to excessive rationality, numbing feeling and producing a loss of spiritual vitality. Modern society becomes an "iron cage" in which "specialists without spirit, sensualists without heart" (Weber, as cited in Wexler, 2000, p. 6) live. Whole school reform too often becomes embroiled in bureaucracy, power that manipulates and controls, that seeks efficiency over and at the expense of caring. There is more talk about "reform" and not enough effort to "reform" our educational system.

The State Department of Education in New Jersey maintains a power position—owning, benefiting, and dominating—in regard to whole school reform. It mandated that all Abbott[4] districts must choose and implement a whole school reform model from among the many available. It highly recommended that elementary schools with especially low scores on the state standardized fourth grade test elect to use SFA, a highly structured program with many of its own materials, training programs for teachers, and evaluation procedures for each school. Although the program has components in the four major subject areas (reading, mathematics, social studies, and science), reading is by far the area most developed and for which there are the most extensive materials, training and evaluation. If a school chose SFA, it received "perks" from the state, usually in terms of more money for technology.

SFA would be appealing to the state because it is, in Weber's (as cited in Wexler, 2000) terms, excessively rational. There are minutely detailed teachers' manuals, series of books for each reading level, standardized tests for each level, record-keeping materials, extensive initial training and annual follow-up training for all teachers, a coordinator who receives initial and continuous training, and regular evaluation by SFA-employed staff. The program requires management of the ways in which it prescribes its materials to be used. It provides a rational way to assess all students.

Although the trainers say that teachers can substitute materials for theirs, few teachers do, nor are they encouraged to do so because that would require rethinking time-use and assessment.

The state maintained control over education in the whole school reform selection process. Teachers in PS (public school) 3 did have a choice regarding which reform model they wanted to use, but they were not in effect, empowered to do so. The choice was forced, in as much as they were given a limited number of models from which to choose and an even a more limited amount of time to consider them.

When I asked teachers whether they based their choice on the culture of the students, the answer was, "No." Their selection was based almost entirely on the "sales pitch" they received from the SFA sales representatives. SFA is an example of what Toll (2001) calls the "neo-liberal" approach to reform: educational entrepreneurs who design programs that limit teacher control in pedagogy and content, advocate uniformity among students through the use of the same instructional methods, and reduce attention to difference and tolerance with the standardized materials. The program fit the technical rational understandings common to bureaucratic functioning, thus maintaining a power over structure.

SFA reflects not a remaking of society, but a repetition of the past. Listening to the children during their rigidly controlled lessons, I immediately was taken back decades to Distar, the rote learning reading program designed for children with learning difficulties and often used with poor, minority children. When I perused the materials, I also was reminded of the highly scripted Houghton Mifflin series of the 1980s—the big books, the little series books, and the unison responses to questions. The SFA model mirrors the past, and perpetuates the historical stereotype of economically deprived students who often are not of the dominant culture: they are capable of primarily rote learning which will continue nondeliberative social reproduction (Bowles & Gintes, 1976; Gutmann, 1987/1999). Rarely, if ever, would SFA be the whole school reform of choice in middle and upper-class schools where developing critical thinking and analytical ability is of high priority (Anyon, 1981). Students maintain the traditional authority-dependency position in the SFA process, thus, rehearsing their futures as passive citizens and workers by learning what is told to them and accepting that as having learned (Shor, 1993).

Critical literacy. SFA is essentially a functional literacy program that emphasizes reading at the expense of writing. Common teacher complaints center on the lack of time to attend to writing because it is not part of the scheduled 90-minute SFA block. Writing is to take place in the students' classroom during another literacy period, which may or may not occur. A concern for teachers is that during the SFA reading block, students are homogeneously grouped by reading ability, not by grade level. Each teacher is assigned and trained to teach a particular SFA reading level. When the students return to their home classrooms, they are in a heterogeneous literacy group. That presents difficulties to the teachers, who are secure in the strategies for their homogeneous reading group, but are not necessarily confident basing writing strategies on the SFA reading techniques that would have to span a number of reading levels to accommodate the children in their classes. By controlling the content and pedagogy, the SFA program limits the teachers' perspectives to only the content within the parameters dictated by the SFA materials. Teachers are aware of the need for students to write, but not in terms of critical literacy, of having students discover deep meanings of events or situations and applying them to their own lives.

SFA is, for the teachers, the vehicle to improve student scores on standardized tests. If, as Foucault (1987, 1990) declares, knowledge is empowering as well as power over, then not providing and making accessible more structured forms of knowledge can be construed as failing to provide resources for empowerment that some have and some do not (Grimshaw, 1993). This program does provide resources and accessibility for students to learn how to read words, that is, to recognize and to be able to figure out what a group of letters says and stands for. The SFA model does afford students a basic structure for reading for meaning, let alone critical thinking.

However, students' achieving the ability to understand social contexts and their relation to them has not been integral to teachers' training in SFA. There, in essence, has been no dialogue. SFA is a process that teachers learned to follow. The product is student achievement, not the *freedom* for students to achieve (Larson & Murtadha, 2001). Writing enables students to learn to express themselves in ways that will initiate needed change to overcome their economic and social standing. Without or with only limited writing experience, students' access to education for liberation and freedom is compromised.

Deep understanding occurs through dialogue emanating from reflection. In SFA, there is little dialogue, which Freire indicates is the basis for transforming the world through self-knowledge gained by reflection. In a program based on rote learning and response, teachers have little or no time to work with children to understand themselves and their reality mediated by society. Dialogue "is the encounter between humans, mediated by the world, in order to name the world" (Freire, as cited in Lankshear, 1993, p. 96). To name the world is not just to have knowledge, but it is to know that one is knowing. For poor and minority students to know they are knowing is critical to their liberation and freedom, in essence, to their humanization.

To engage in dialogue requires time and patience, a spiral of time to reflect and time to think. Critical thinking is subverted by the need to have instant "knowledge" so that students can demonstrate "learning" on standardized tests. SFA provides the salve for those in power to feel as though they have prescribed methods by which children who have not learned sufficiently in the past now know. By scores on regularly administered tests constructed by the SFA corporation, teachers, administrators, and politicians can point to instant learning. Yet, there are critical teachers and leaders who question:

The success of the reading program in this study (SFA) depends on the design of the assessment and the curriculum. The curriculum basically teaches to the test. However, based on the grade summary report the percentage of students tested at grade level increases with more experience in the Reading Program. Teaching to the test is definitely not the way to create success in our schools....

Discovering how the assessment tool caters to the program was an important developmental outcome. The intern gained knowledge about the assessment tools and how important it is to research the assessment tools along with the curriculum. Teaching to the test sometimes appears to be a hidden agenda. This process helps some students, but it does not promote true success to me![5]

Critical literacy and thinking happen over time with guidance. Teachers know and understand that, but their actions are mediated by the social climate and the needs and wants of those in power. No matter what educators perceive, there is too often the reality of having that knowledge compromised over time without the consciousness that it has been changed.

There is a sublimated social vision, a reality-based envisioning of possibility in the mystical, dimly articulated space of the social unconscious, which the depth and rapidity of current social change churns to the surface by grinding its defenses down quickly in the path of instant productivity. (Wexler, 2000, p. 12)

Desocialization. Parental involvement is important to SFA. The program "encourages and trains parents and other community members to fulfill numerous volunteer roles within the school, ranging from providing a listening ear to emerging readers to helping in the school cafeteria" (Slavin & Madden, 2001, p. 12). To create a community of difference, it is important that parents be involved in the school. The key word to consider in the SFA philosophy, however, is "train." Like the teachers, parents are "trained;" they are not "educated" to think about, to question, and to enter into discourse and dialogue with each other and educators. Consider the assumptions made. If the parents were middle class or above, or if they were not racial or ethnic minorities, would there be the expectation that they needed to be "trained" to work in classrooms, or would the assumption be that they would know how, or would be able to "figure out" what they should do? Nor are teachers, administrators, and staff educated to work with parents. Is there the assumption that educators do not need to understand the cultures of their students in order for students to learn? Nothing in the SFA materials takes into account the cultural backgrounds of the students and their parents, the teachers, and the school.

How are "poor" and "poverty" understood in connection with the goals of SFA? "When a child fails to read well in the early grades, he or she begins a downward progression.... Failing students begin to have poor motivation and poor self-expectations, which lead to continued poor achievement, in a declining spiral that ultimately leads to despair, delinquency, and dropout.... The commitment is that SFA will do "whatever it takes to see that every child becomes a skilled, strategic, and enthusiastic reader by the end of the elementary grades" (Slavin & Madden, 2001, pp. 4–5). Imposed values may lead to low-self-esteem if the children are unable to meet the expectations of others. Educators who believe that WSR is to liberate children would have to question why students would despair and ultimately drop out of school because they had trouble reading. What does "doing whatever it takes" mean? Are poverty, homelessness, teachers' divergent cultures and beliefs considered in the students' "failure?" Nowhere does SFA specifically discuss how the program addresses those issues. Nor does SFA account for continuous student transfers in and out of the building, for the lack of substitutes because of a district's inability to pay competitive wages, for SFA tutors not meeting their students because of having to cover classes where there are no substitutes, for poor teacher attendance because of low morale caused by budget cuts and increased responsibility, and for conflicting teacher-student cultures. To reiterate Sen's (1992) sentiment, do all children need to learn the same things, in the same way, and at the same time?

The SFA program maintains the myths and beliefs of the dominant culture by what it does not overtly espouse, namely the freedoms the children will achieve.

Discussing why educators ought to consider using the SFA program with children who have been traditionally underserved, Slavin and Madden (2001) use value-laden words traditionally used in the mass culture to refer to children living in low-income areas and who often are racial and ethnic minorities: learning deficits, failing students, poor motivation, poor self-expectations, poor achievement, delinquency, and children at risk. In their discussion, they do not attempt to define or describe what those words and phrases mean. Are the children at risk because, as Kozol (1991, 1995) points out, they have a high incidence of asthma among them? Because they do not have enough to eat or sufficient clothes to wear? Because they have to assume responsibilities that many adults would not take? Because they do not read about people like themselves? Because they are not taught to question, but are rewarded for compliance? How or in what are they delinquent—in not doing homework? In behavior? Will reading alone raise poor self-expectations? As stated before, there is little in SFA that promotes self-reflection mediated with the realities of society to allow students to learn how to transform their situations in the world.

The myths of poor, minority children and what they need from school continue to abound in SFA through the attention given to reading, a ninety-minute block, and mathematics at the expense of science and social studies. In kindergarten, the entire day must be devoted to some form of reading pedagogy; there is no time for activities of the past that were valuable learning experiences for the children. In middle- and upper-class schools, children delight in learning to use the computer and find science experiments fascinating. Through a breadth of learning experiences encompassing a variety of disciplines, those students learn that a much bigger world is open and accessible to them than to the children in poor districts. The SFA "whole school reform" does not involve the whole; it revolves around only a minute part, continuing to de-privilege the poor and the minorities.

Yet with all my criticism of SFA, the program has dispelled some of the myths and stereotypes about poor, minority children for some teachers. Some teachers who previously believed that "those" children cannot learn, have begun to change their perception as they see that through SFA evaluations the students' test scores have increased. Because there seems to be "proof" that the students are learning, some of the teachers who doubted now have higher expectations for the children.

Self-organization/Self-education. Because of the highly structured nature of SFA, and the premise that it was created by experts who provided the process by which it should be implemented, there is no reason to think that it would encourage self-organization and self-education to transform schools. In fact there is no reason to believe that the goal of SFA is to transform school and society. It is an impersonal movement emanating from the current power elite to maintain school and society as it is.

PDS

Power awareness. The PDS model unites schools and/or school districts, and a university to establish a collaboration that blends theory, research, and practice to enhance teaching and learning, P–16, through continuous professional development. The PDS philosophy and organization are based on five standards emanating from the national accrediting body, North Central Association of Teacher Education (NCATE): (a) learning community, (b) collaboration, (c) accountability and quality assurance, (d) diversity and equity, and (e) structure, resources, and roles. Each of the standards is applied according to the needs of the individual school and/or district and university; building and sustaining relationships within and outside the school are an important aspect of the reform. Integral to the standards are content, pedagogy, and disposition, the latter highlighting the importance of attitude and feeling, soft and often unwieldy qualities that make assessment of outcomes difficult, but that are important in the overall commitment to relationships. There is no program per se, nor are there specific materials. The PDS model has not been endorsed as a whole school reform by the state of New Jersey, but has been chosen by some schools as a supplement or additional WSR model.

The primary difference between SFA and the PDS model regarding power awareness is that PDS has the potential to reconfigure the pedagogy and structure of schooling so that people have the opportunities to use their power to affect how educators and students learn, and how knowledge is created. That is, effort spent to establish collaborative relationships that lead to shared decision making within schools—in classrooms, as well as within the institution of school—and between P–12 schools and the university in research and in the preparation and continuing professional education of teachers and administrators is fundamental to the reform.

Unlike SFA whose focus is on delivering instruction to students via material, strategies, and assessments designed by experts, PDS concentrates on improving teaching and learning for educators in all positions, as well as for students. The emphasis is on collaboration, working together to construct continuously improved pedagogy through research, theory, and practice. No one entity is *the* expert; each person or body contributes knowledge and experience to develop the best practices until they, from a Kuhnian perspective, become insufficient because there is new content and pedagogical knowledge that has been found to supercede them.

Although the intent of PDS is to reform schooling by refocusing power, P–12 and university educators are not always capable of changing their own historical perceptions and actions. Collaboration should start with commitment, not only to creating a collaborative between the university and a P–12 school, but also to changing the structure of schooling. "This commitment must go beyond the desire to build a collaborative. It must include a strong desire to deal with structural inequalities due to status differentials in our society and with personal conflicts that arise when people work together" (Sandoval, 2001, pp. 25–26).

Gallego, Hollingsworth, and Whitenack (2001) describe two PDS partnerships, one that was successful and one that was not. That which was not resulted from the inability of the participants from the P–12 school to rethink their roles in terms of equity and equality, to question power differentials, and to avoid the discomfort of conflicting thoughts and ideas. The school personnel viewed the university liaisons as the experts, looking to them for ideas and or approval. Collegiality, connoting harmony, that is, no contentiousness, at all costs, was preferable to vulnerability and risk-taking that might result in feeling pain in the process of growth and change which could lead to social justice. They preferred to keep their distance from one another by maintaining politeness.

The successful PDS included personnel who challenged the university staff, who debated and argued issues that traditionally had not been discussable. They were willing to expose their ideas, values, and beliefs in order to create the trust necessary to develop an equitable relationship among themselves and between themselves and the university liaisons. In relation to the university liaison, they initiated ideas and actions and did not seek approval or even necessarily want approval. The teachers challenged the university staff and were comfortable being challenged. Furthermore, they looked at the structure of their school and proactively sought ways to change it that would accommodate better ways of teaching, and that would seek to limit inequity and inequality among staff and between staff and administration. They challenged the assumptions connected with WSR, in general. As the teachers experienced the growing trust that supported equity among them, they were able to understand the benefits of sharing decision making with their students and creating classrooms and a school that sought equity for all.

For PDS partnerships to be authentic, they need to derive from conviction, not convenience (Gallego, Hollingsworth, & Whitenack, 2001). At this time, the PS 3 partnership with the university is largely a convenience, particularly since there is funding from a Title II grant. Teachers and administrators see PDS more as a way to "get help" without having to pay for it, rather than as a partnership in which there is commitment to improve the structure, function, and equity of schooling. Like SFA with its perks from the state, PDS carries its own perks through its offers to support professional development through workshops for beginning teachers and for teachers who would mentor student teachers. Additionally, the university sponsors graduate courses at the school that are tuition-free. Administrators and teachers view those benefits from personal perspectives of improving the school in the eyes of the community, or of doing what has been mandated by the state (teachers working toward their 100 hours requirement[6]).

Although a formal contract exists between the College of Education, the district and PS 3, the teachers were not really involved in making the decision to take part in PDS. As with SFA, PDS became a reality because of decisions made by those in formal power positions in the bureaucratic hierarchy with the intent of doing what would be best for the children. Unlike SFA where there are distinct guidelines to follow, PDS requires deep thinking and whole-hearted involvement. Many of the teachers at PS 3 are open to collaboration, routinely sharing ideas and materials with one another, or offering a listening ear or helping hand. However, there is minimal understanding concerning the commitment to a partnership that is ongoing—even after the grant expires—for continuous improvement of teaching, learning, and equity in power and cultural relationships, the latter two not in teachers' or administrators' consciousness.

Teaching for student success requires restructuring the organization of school for caring, for bringing social justice into conscious awareness, and for serious learning. PS 3 has already made strides to do that with its "family halls" of Grades 1–5, and with the attempt to keep class sizes small, around 20 or fewer students. Although one teacher does not have the same class for more than 1 year, teachers come to know the students because they are in the same family for 5 years. The students also feel comfortable as they progress from grade to grade. Lunch time is arranged so that students are able to be with their age-peers for that time, as well as teachers having time to visit and collaborate informally with other teachers at that grade about their students and their teaching. They also have scheduled times once a month for grade-level meetings. However, issues such as poverty—why there is poverty—among the students, cultural gaps between educators' and students' lives, and differences between communal, cultural, and school values are not considered.

Such restructuring mirrors some of the ways in which Howey (1999) advocates PDS partnerships might do a better job of teaching children. Yet, what is missing in the previous description of the reorganization is the dialogue among the teachers and with the administrators that provides the opportunity to question and analyze how and to what degree they perceive the effectiveness of that configuration. The power to restructure and to maintain it remains in the hands of those in power, most often those external to the schools.

The university wants PDS to become a whole school reform accepted by the state. At this time, the objections revolve around the lack of "hard" data to corroborate success. The state wants data that will indicate rising test scores on the standardized tests. There is firm belief that will happen through PDS, but the change will not be instant because the model is holistic, attempting to create and sustain community; address children's mental, physical, and emotional health; create an equitable environment; and equalize power. That will take time. Those in power want instant results.

Critical literacy. Emphasis in PDSs is on "best practices" in teaching that lead to increased learning. Like any other model, the interpretation of the standards and of the rhetoric will drive the particular program in a specific situation. The teachers discuss their pedagogy in terms of how it helps the children increase their learning to pass the state standardized tests. Little discussion or conversation involves student's understanding of the deeper meaning of learning: who they are and what have they internalized about themselves from society's assumptions, how they can change their lives, how their past history is important to understanding what they can do for themselves and their community in the future, why and how the content areas affect their immediate lives.

For critical literacy to occur requires that teachers and school leaders not fear taking risks. An example in PS 3 is that of a teacher who chooses to show the television movie, "Roots" to her class each year during African American History month. The video is listed in the district as unacceptable viewing for elementary school children. The teacher in question, however, has decided that the children she works with need to know and understand their history as it happened and as it continues to affect their lives. She shows the video to the children and asks them what they know about slavery, if they had any relatives who were slaves, and what they know about those relatives. She then talks about what slavery was and how some of their lives continue to imitate slavery in certain ways. The teacher commented that parents have thanked her for those lessons, and that students have brought bits and pieces of those conversations up throughout the remainder of the school year. There are two issues at hand: the teacher went against district policy at risk to her tenure; the administrator passively allowed her actions by not acknowledging—not seeing—what she did. Significant change in attitudes and beliefs about particular nonhegemonic cultures cannot occur within passivity.

In many PDSs affiliated with our university, teachers are becoming more aware and committed to students' connecting schooling to the social context of their lives. One of the ways that has occurred is through teacher study groups using the book, *The Teaching Gap* (Heibert & Stigler, 1999), based on the TIMMS study of mathematics teaching in the United States, Japan, and Germany. Through their study, teachers have responded to the deep learning that happens in Japanese schools in which there are fewer topics covered, but far more in-depth study.

Although PDS promotes deep understanding, that is not always what PS 3 teachers do. There is strong concern and much pressure for teachers to get through the explicit curriculum set before them by the district and state. To take the occasion to show "Roots," interspersed and followed by deep discussion, takes time away from covering the mandated coursework. Assessment and evaluation of teacher work stresses curriculum completion as much as possible, therefore, indicating teacher and student success, albeit a narrow interpretation. To spend more time on deep learning rather than on coverage of the surface issues is to put oneself—and students—in jeopardy of less than satisfactory reviews.

The accountability system has narrowed what children learn despite our increased knowledge of how students learn (Larson & Murtadha, 2001). The SFA program meets the expectations of the system in an immediate perspective more so than PDS. Rather than teach for children to achieve over the long term, accountability systems tend to focus on narrow perceptions and understandings that too often are not part of racial minority children's lives. The PDS model attempts to focus on developing the students' freedoms and capabilities to learn, as well as providing the fundamental knowledge that is needed for them.

Creation of knowledge by the students is critical to the PDS philosophy. Much of PDS teaching and learning is based on constructivist thinking whereby students determine how they know what they know. Constructing knowledge takes time. Although teachers may choose to have children learn through that pedagogical method, the structure of their school may not support it. Critical literacy and power awareness must occur simultaneously. A bigger concern is whether educators know how to encourage students to create knowledge that goes beyond what they have experienced and internalized from society.

Desocialization. Freire (1989) talks about the necessity to know oneself in order to know the self in relation to others and to society. Although there is the tendency to focus on curricular issues because of the often painful anxiety and complexity of the process of learning about oneself, that is less than compassionate teaching. Without knowledge of the self, educators contribute to distancing and manipulating students. The PDS model, through its emphasis on building community, intimates the importance of being personally present to others or in the situations of their lives. Teaching and learning are reciprocal, therefore, there is a need for active problem solving regarding an awareness of who one is, as well as how one learns.

In the learning community graduate course at PS 3, as we dialogue about culture, the teachers are continuously asked to consider how they think about particular issues. For instance, when we discussed standardized tests and how they affected the children they taught, I asked how they would change the tests to better assess their students. Their solution was to test primarily on basic skills. The next question, then, was what did that say about their expectations for their students, despite the fact they all said that they told the children "they could be anything they wanted to be?" A poignant conversation resulted in the conflicting thoughts they carried about who they wanted to be and how they acted in reality. The possibility to cover the critical area of the self is present through PDS; however, how the liaisons from the university and school choose to interpret the learning community standard determines whether that will occur.

Through the diversity and equity standard, PDS implies a commitment for equity on behalf of children. A commitment *to action* for equity on behalf of children is even more important. There is personal safety and reward in compliant teaching/leadership, but that will not ensure action to liberate and free culturally diverse students. In the learning community class, teachers examine aspects of the children's lives that they feel are inequitable and are making action plans for change. One of the changes they are considering is the notion of expectations: if they believe the children can be anything they want to be, what are they, as teachers, going to do to work with the children to reach their goals?

Bilingualism and cultural understanding need to be an integral part of PDS. A deep understanding of school culture and of the children in the context of their community needs to be a critical component of preservice teacher education (Howey, 1999). Despite the diversity and equity standard for PDS, few teacher education programs prepare students to work with children of different cultures, and rarely is there an effort to positively socialize new teachers into the culture of the students. Teachers in PDSs, as those involved in other WSR, want to help the children succeed. Yet the question arises, are the teachers' understandings of the children and their cultures, including gender, patronizing or valuing? In the context of a learning community, one of the PDS standards, how are teachers encouraged to help others learn to collaborate with others who are different from them? At this point, that learning is not consistent, but dependent upon the university liaisons' understandings and abilities to facilitate the development of such knowledge and action, as well as the teachers' and administrators' receptivity to it. Knowing about the social culture is a necessary component to promote and strengthen high academic performance learning. It is essential to critical literacy and power awareness.

Although there is a standard for diversity and equity, little emphasis is given to gender equity. There is an increased awareness of the discrimination associated with race and class, but less attention is placed on gender bias and gender preference. For PDSs to be viewed as a whole school reform that seeks to address and remediate unjust practices in schooling and ultimately in society, desocialization in the education of girls and young women cannot not be ignored.

Self-organization/self-education. Considering the goals and standards of the PDS model, the similarity is striking. Consider Shor's (1993) list of values for critical pedagogy, which are essential to *conscientization*: "participatory, situated, critical, democratic, dialogic, desocialization, multicultural, research-oriented, activist, and affective" (pp. 33–34). Compare those to the PDS standards: learning community, collaboration, accountability and quality assurance, diversity and equity, and structure, resources, and roles.

Viewing the goals, it is important to note from a critical pedagogy perspective, that situated, democratic, dialogic, desocialization, and affective are not specifically listed in the standards for PDS. The affective component is a criterion by which to assess the outcomes of the PDS standards. However, the other components were not addressed in the standards' norms. The concepts of democracy and of dialogue are most important in establishing a learning community, and to accomplish collaboration, and diversity and equity. Desocialization is critical to the concept of multiculturalism and diversity and equity. Until a group is desocialized of its prior beliefs and biases about and toward different cultures, diversity and equity will be difficult, if not impossible, to attain.

PDSs have the potential to transform society, but will have to take a hard look at their relationship to "the standards." Both the NCATE and the National Board of Professional Teacher Standards provide a reasonable guideline and framework by which to put the PDS model into service. However, those standards, depending upon interpretation, can become a stranglehold on the efforts to teach for social justice. How we view the learning community; collaboration, diversity, and equity; accountability and quality assurance; and structures, roles, and resources will determine how socially just the PDS model is. A major concern is that context will not be taken into account in the pursuit of the standards; however, the school site is important in the interpretation and accomplishment of the goals. If site is considered, then it will be possible to argue that PDS is striving for self-organization and self-education that will change schooling and society. Through collaboration, creation and sustenance of learning communities, shared vision, and the valuing of diversity, PDSs have the potential to institutionalize vision and imagination, sensory practice (linking schooling and life experience), and the union of diverse cultures and thought as a reintegration of education into society (Wexler, 2000).

For self-organization and self-education to become a reality, PDS will have to question and challenge the political nature of schooling, assumptions about minority cultures, and context of the curriculum. There will have to be the willingness to risk exposing the hidden agendas and the powers that control. In order to do that, those who implement the PDS model will have to know and understand themselves and be amenable to asking the hard questions of self-knowledge to others. Diversity and equity can happen only with that knowledge. Finally, and most importantly, there has to be the commitment to action. All the knowledge and dialogue in the world will not change society unless it is put into actions that seek to bring equitable access and opportunities for life experiences.

IMPLICATIONS AND CONCLUSIONS

Implications for Social Justice Leadership and WSR

Whole school reform models are just that, models. Each has a particular thrust and design to guide a school to reform itself for the benefit of improving teaching and learning. Their success in achieving social justice, however, in large part depends on school leadership and the way in which the intent of the models is interpreted and put into practice. Some models, such as the Comer model or coalition for essential schools, provide a strong foundation for positive social change by emphasizing strong connections between parents, students, educators, and the communities at large, as well as efforts to bridge the cultural gaps among those groups, in order to improve schooling for all students. Should those models achieve success, students would be educated to become citizens ready to work in a dynamic society in continuous need of change and reevaluation of change. However, the success of those models, as the ones I studied, are dependent upon school leadership. Are the leaders asking the big questions and dealing with the complexities of interweaving and opposing values, understandings, and cultural beliefs of the different groups of people involved their schools?

As I reflect on SFA and PDS in PS 3, my thoughts concern the school leader and what his role was in the implementation of the reforms. Did he consider power awareness as using caring power to address questions and complexities resulting from differences; critical literacy to consciously facilitate students' and teachers' understanding of themselves and the cultural, racial and ethnic, economic, and religious gaps among students and school personnel, as well a between school community goals and national and state mandates; desocialization to consciously work with students and teachers to rethink ingrained and institutionalized beliefs concerning different cultures; and self-education to work with students and community to blend the needs and wants of different cultural groups and the national and state mandates for education to lead beyond what is to what can be?

The success of SFA and PDS in PS 3 to work toward social justice would have required much more involvement, directly and indirectly, by the school leader. He would have had to question what the children actually learned through the call and response and rote learning of SFA reading materials. Instead he satisfied himself with increased test scores as proof of learning and improved teaching, although the SFA materials are teacher proof.[7]

When teachers initiated projects that addressed critical literacy and desocialization, there needed to be more than tacit support. He would have had to use his caring power to rearrange schedules so innovative teachers could implement their creations through which they and their students learned about difference. Teachers involved with PDS designed projects that involved team teaching and students not in the mainstream, a regular second grade class paired with a bilingual class to learn about and from each other, and a special education teacher and art teacher who co-taught a behaviorally challenged class the four basic subject areas through art. They all received approval from the leadership, but had to plan "on the fly" because they had no common time to meet.

He would have had to take a risk to fight for a qualified bilingual teacher rather than settling for a personable teacher from Venezuela who had limited English and was assigned to teach children from Mexico who spoke no English. He would have worked with the PDS facilitator to find ways to integrate the teacher and the students into the school, rather than avoiding the bilingual room altogether.

To actively support social change, he would have encouraged the teacher to show "Roots," not just looked away so he did not know she violated policy. He may have invited other principals to discuss the policy in light of the benefits and drawbacks it had regarding students' learning to question who they think they are and who they really are and can be.

Collaboration with parents was having them sign a notebook that they listened to their child read each night, an SFA requirement, then keeping a tally of how many signed each week or month. Having a pizza party or spaghetti supper for parents and children once a semester had value via the opportunity for him to visit with the parents together with their child or children on an informal basis and not connected to a discipline issue. However, handing the parents a paper with upcoming events was not dialoguing with them regarding the education of their children.

Dialoguing with, not telling teachers what had already been decided was totally lacking, despite efforts by PDS facilitators to encourage this and to ask for meetings to discuss topics brought up by teachers. There were no faculty meetings other than the initial beginning-of-the-year one in which teachers were treated to a continental breakfast and 2 hours of requirements and expectations for the year. Information and discussion occurred much like the game, telephone. The original information or topic was much distorted because it was communicated and discussed in multiple venues in and out of the school among various individuals and groups. What resulted was not attention to multiple understandings of a topic, but polarizations of one group against another.

Because there was no dialogue, there was no way to uncover the values (Shields, 2002) of the teachers and administrators. Consequently, there was no overt understanding of where the teachers, individually and collectively, stood regarding SFA and PDS. As a PDS facilitator, the administrator gave me 10 minutes at the beginning-of-the-school year meeting to explain PDS. The school leader had no follow-up other than to say that if anyone had questions s/he should see me after the meeting.

He would have to have been open to teachers' questions about the curriculum and how they wanted to change it, rather than his telling them what the changes were for any give semester or year.

Most importantly, he needed to understand the climate *outside* his building. The community denigrated the students in his school; the district lines were redrawn so that the poorest students in the community and from projects known to harbor drug dealers attended PS 3; all the students were primarily African American with a growing Latino population. Teachers did not volunteer to go to PS 3. The school itself was not visible from the street, but was accessible only from a alley-like drive. There was not community understanding of the reform models, nor was there support. He led in a vacuum except for quantifiable data, which were highlighted each year his students came in last on state standardized tests.

The above are just snippets of what a school leader would need to do in order for a school reform to address social justice issues. In essence, working with a reform model toward social justice requires more than management and efficiency or following the model protocol. The reform model is only as good as its leader and those who choose to follow him/her. A school leader must want to work with and in a community of difference, understanding that the dynamic nature will require constant work to maintain a positive tension. A leader must want to collaborate with teachers, parents, and community members, knowing that the process is often messy and contentious. For a community of difference to thrive, dialogue is necessary, although time-consuming. Efficiency may, therefore, be sacrificed. A school leader desiring social change as an outcome of a reform model needs to know him/herself in order to open dialogue with others to facilitate their self-growth. Ultimately, a school leader needs to see whole school reform as a microcosm of the larger society, that is, to understand that reforming teaching and learning is the beginning of social change.

Conclusion

When I began this paper, my intent was to examine the success of whole school reform and two models, specifically, in terms of addressing social justice issues through schools. I end this paper realizing that WSR are only new and, maybe, improved tools for school leaders to use in working for positive social change, that is, successful living within communities of difference. The values and beliefs of the leader (who may be in an informal leadership position) are critical to the achievement of social justice. Most of all, school leaders must view their position of influence out of the school as well as inside it; s/he has to acknowledge and act on the biases and prejudices from without.

I believe that of primary importance is the consideration of the "continuing impact of social structure on our lives" (Wexler, 2000, p. 10) and the "determinative power of organized social life, social structure, and technology to affect not only meaning and identity, but also the conditions of experience and, perhaps most importantly, to set the terms for opposing, transforming, and transcending the social present" (Wexler, 2000, p. 11). School reformers who work toward social justice will have to be cognizant and vigilant in working within situated life experiences, within the externalities of schooling, in order to strive for change that is transformative. Unquestionably, attention needs to be paid to social injustices; however, while educational leaders have to work towards social justice by rooting out discriminatory patterns and practices which represent prejudice and scientism, we have to attack the core of the problem which is anchored in our culture and the attendant mythologies which define and support them. (English, 2005, p. 56)

And, as important, we must "remain constantly aware of the ways in which new modes of resistance and self-understanding run the danger of reinstating, in some way, aspects of that against which they have been struggling" (Grimshaw, 1993, p. 59).

NOTES

1. Mintrom's (2001) notion of communitarian benefits stems from his discussion of exchange perspectives on democratic governance. Because businesses, professional associations, unions, and political interest groups control a great deal of political clout, there is the assumption "that interests and resources are fixed and, hence, exogenous to the political process" (p. 618). Mintrom disputes that theory citing as potential communitarian benefits the shaping and results of policy debates through dialogue and exchange among politicians, scholars, and others from a wide variety of paradigms and perspectives. Additionally, other benefits as they pertain to the goals of WSR would include collective problem solving and decision making that has the potential to lead to respect for how decisions are made and for the participants, themselves; educational policy based on and supporting democratic practices, leading to more student behavior influenced by democratic tradition and the greater the likelihood of students and adults engaging in the customs and procedures of democracy; mutual respect for self and others by working through differences using dialogue; and education that is nondiscriminatory, nor is oppressive.
2. I use critical school leader or leadership interchangeably with social justice leader or leadership, as I believe they share the same qualities.
3. The following is a summary of my beliefs regarding caring for a collective using caring power. For an extensive discussion of the connections between caring and power, (see Sernak (1998), in this volume, chapters 9 & 10).
4. As a result of the court case, *Abbott v. Burke*, economically disadvantaged school districts, as determined by the state, receive increased state funding in the attempt to equalize the education for children in poor districts with those in moderate to wealthy ones.
5. Taken from an administration student intern's conclusion of a study of SFA in her elementary school, 2001–2002.
6. Teachers in New Jersey are required to have 100 hours of professional development beyond their BA.
7. The SFA program provides for regular monitoring, during which time SFA trainers spend a day in the school to observe classes and to make sure the

teachers are following the script. If there were deviations from it, the school would receive a lower rating, which was reported to the Central Administration. It was common knowledge that when the teachers knew the monitors were coming they prepared their lessons to follow the script exactly, which many of the more skilled teachers rarely did.

REFERENCES

Anyon, J. (1981). Social class and school knowledge. *Curriculum Inquiry, 11*(1), 3–42.

Bartky, S. L. (1990). Towards a phenomenology of feminist consciousness. In *Femininity and domination: Studies in the phenomenology of oppression* (pp. 11–21). London: Routledge.

Bowles, S., & Gintes, H. (1976). *Schooling in capitalist America*. New York: Basic Books.

Cain, M. (1993). Foucault, feminism and feeling: What Foucault can and cannot contribute to feminist epistemology. In C. Ramazanoglu (Ed.), *Up against Foucault: Explorations of some tensions between Foucault and feminism* (pp. 73–86). London: Routledge.

English, F. W. (2005, November). *Towards a theory of social justice/injustice: Learning to lead in the social cage*. Paper presented at the 2005 Convention of the University Council of Educational Administration, Nashville, TN.

Foucault, M. (1987). *The history of sexuality* (Vol. II): *The use of pleasure*. Harmondsworth: Penguin.

Foucault, M. (1990). *Michel Foucault: Politics, philosophy, culture: Interviews and other writings 1977–1984* (A. Sheridan, Trans.). London: Routledge.

Freedman, S. G. (1991). *Small victories: The real world of a teacher, her students, and their high school*. New York: Harper Perennial.

Freire, P. (1989). *Pedagogy of the oppressed*. New York: Continuum.

Gallego, M. A., Hollingsworth, S., Whitenack, D. A. (2001). Relational knowing in the reform of educational cultures. *Teachers College Record 103*(2), 240–266. Retrieved March 12, 2004, http://spweb.silverplatter.com/c5773

Greene, M. (1988). *The Dialectic of Freedom*. New York: Teachers College Press.

Grimshaw, J. (1993). Practices of freedom. In C. Ramazanoglu (Ed.), *Up against Foucault: Explorations of some tensions between Foucault and feminism* (pp. 123–146). London: Routledge.

Gutmann, A. (1987/1999). *Democratic education*. Princeton, NJ: Princeton University Press. (Original work published 1987)

Heibert, J., & Stigler, J. (1999). *The teaching gap*. New York: Free Press.

Howey, K. R. (1999). Professional development schools: Looking ahead. *Peabody Journal of Education, 7*(3/4), 322–334. Retrieved March 12, 2004, from http://spweb.silverplatter.com/c5773

Kant, I. (2003). Good will, duty and the categorical imperative. In J. Ciulla (Eds.), *The ethics of leadership* (pp. 94–109). Belmont, CA: Thomson/Wadsworth.

Kozol, J. (1991). *Savage inequalities: Children in America's schools*. New York: Crown.

Kozol, J. (1995). Amazing grace: *The lives of children and the conscience of a nation*. New York: Harper Perennial.

Kozol, J. (2000). *Ordinary resurrections: Children in the years of hope*. New York: Perennial.

Lankshear, C. (1993). Functional literacy from a Freirean point of view. In P. McLaren & P. Leonard (Eds.), *Paulo Freire: A critical encounter* (pp. 90–118). New York: Routledge.

Larson, C. L., & Murtadha, K. (2001, November). *Leadership for social justice*. Paper presented at the University Council for Educational Administration Convention 2001, Cincinnati, Ohio.

MacLeod, J. (1987). *Ain't no makin' it: Aspirations and attainment in a low-income neighborhood*. Boulder, CO: Westview Press.

Mintrom, M. (2001). Educational governance and democratic practice. *Educational Policy, 15*(5), 615–643.

Nevárez-La Torre, A. A., & Sanford-De Shields, J. S. (1999). Strides toward equity in an urban center: Temple University's Professional Development School Partnership. *The Urban Review, 31*(3), 243–262.

Noddings, N. (1992). *The challenge to care in schools: An alternative approach to education*. New York: Teachers College Press.

Nussbaum, M. (2000). *Women and human development: A capabilities approach*. New York: Cambridge.

Power, F. C., & Makogon, T. A. (1996). The just-community approach to care. *Journal for a Just and Caring Education, 2*(1), 9–24.

Sandoval, P. A. (2001). Inequity as a source of the cultural gap in an urban school-university collaborative. *The Urban Review, 33*(1), 1–26.

Sawicki, J. (1991). *Disciplining Foucault: Feminism, power and the body*. London: Routledge.

Sen, A. (1992). *Inequality reexamined*. Cambridge, MA: Harvard University Press.

Senge, P. M. (1990). *The fifth discipline: The art and practice of the learning organization*. New York: Doubleday/Currency.

Sernak, K. (1998). *School leadership: Balancing power with caring*. New York: Teachers College Press.

Shields, C. M. (2001, November). *Cross-cultural Leadership and Communities of Difference: Thinking About Leading in Diverse Schools*. Paper presented at the University Council for Educational Administration Convention 2001, Cincinnati, Ohio.

Shields, C. M. (2002, October). *Towards a dialogic approach to understanding values*. An address presented to the 7th annual conference of Values and Leadership, Toronto, Ontario.

Shor, I. (1993). Education is politics: Paulo Freire's critical pedagogy. In P. McLaren & P. Leonard (Eds.), *Paulo Freire: A critical encounter* (pp. 25–35). London: Routledge.

Slavin, R. E., & Madden, N. A. (Eds.). (2001). Success for all: Research and reform in elementary education. Mahwah, NJ: Erlbaum.

Toll, C. A. (2001). Critical and postmodern perspectives on school change. *Journal of Curriculum and Supervision 16*(4), 345–367. Retrieved March, 12, 2004, from http://spweb.silverplatter.com/c5773

Tronto, J. C. (1993). *Moral boundaries: A political argument for an ethic of care*. New York: Routledge.

Tronto, J. (1989). Women and caring: What can feminists learn about morality from caring. In A. M. Jagger & S. R. Bordo (Eds.), *Gender/body/knowledge: Feminist reconstructions of being and knowing* (pp. 172–187). New Brunswick, NJ: Rutgers University Press.

Wartenberg, T. E. (1990). *The forms of power: From domination to transformation*. Philadelphia: Temple University Press.

Wexler, P. (2000). *The mystical society: An emerging social vision*. Boulder, CO: Westview Press/Perseus Books Group.

Whyte, D. (2001). *Crossing the unknown sea: Work as a pilgrimage of identity*. New York: Riverhead Press.

CHAPTER 7

A NEGLECTED DIMENSION OF SOCIAL JUSTICE

A Model for Science Education in Rural Schools

Mary John O'Hair and Ulrich C. Reitzug

One-third of all U.S. school children attend school in rural settings. Rural America is often much poorer than urban America, with most of the poorest counties in the United States located in rural areas. Equity is a concern not only in terms of race, class, gender, disability, and sexual orientation, but also in terms of being geographically located in a rural area. Rural teachers are often not certified in their teaching areas, with, for example, one in four rural science teachers lacking in academic preparation or certification. This chapter describes the K20 Oklahoma Science Initiative for Rural Schools that targets low-income, rural schools serving diverse populations in Oklahoma. The K20 Initiative helps reduce the professional, cultural, and social isolation and lack of professional development in rural schools. The objectives of the initiative are to improve teacher quality and student success through three research-based strategies which are described in the chapter.

Leadership for Social Justice: Promoting Equity and Excellence Through Inquiry and Reflective Practice, pp. 151–167

Rural America, representing one-third of all U.S. schoolchildren, is much poorer than urban America, with 59 of the 66 poorest counties located in rural areas (Gates, 2004). Rural school districts, serving nearly 10 million children (Johnson & Strange, 2007) are at a disadvantage when competing for resources for professional development and attracting qualified teachers, with one in four rural science teachers lacking in academic preparation or certification (National Science Board [NSB], 2006). More than 400,000 educators teach in rural schools, representing 31% of all public school teachers (National Center for Education Statistics 2002). Compared to their nonrural counterparts, rural teachers average 13.4% less in salary, live in substandard housing, experience professional, cultural, and social isolation, and receive little if any professional development (Beeson & Strange, 2003; Darling-Hammond, 2000; Education Trust, 2003; Jimerson, 2003). Rural principals and superintendents feel ill-prepared for challenges that face them (Lamkin, 2006). Thus, although social justice is often discussed in terms of race, class, gender, disability, and sexual orientation, it may also be an issue of location—in this case, being located in a rural area.

The purpose of this chapter is to call attention to a neglected dimension of social justice—social justice for rural schools and, particularly, for the education of the students who attend these schools and the professional development of the educators who serve in them. We do this by describing the kindergarten through graduate education (K20) Oklahoma Science Initiative for Rural Schools, a program within the K20 Center for Educational and Community Renewal at the University of Oklahoma. The Oklahoma Science Initiative for Rural Schools [K20 SCIENCE] targets low-income, rural schools serving diverse populations in Oklahoma, including the 22,000 Native Americans who attend rural Oklahoma schools. K20 SCIENCE is one initiative that helps reduce the professional, cultural, and social isolation and lack of professional development in rural schools. The initiative is focused on science education due to the dire need in that area. The NSB (2006) reports that "the critical lack of technically trained people in the United States can be traced directly to poor K–12 mathematics and science instruction" (p. 2).

Research on professional development finds that teacher learning is greater when professional development utilizes an embedded professional development approach, linked directly to student achievement (e.g., lesson study, authentic research experience for teachers, professional learning communities), rather than the traditional workshop or conference format (Garet, Porter, Desimore, & Birman, 2001). Similarly, Fullan (2001, 2003) notes that to significantly improve student learning, *teachers* must be learning. Based on this knowledge, the K20 Center at the University of Oklahoma and the Oklahoma Science Project (OSP) developed an embedded professional development model. For 12 years, OSP has provided authentic research experiences for rural science teachers with 48 teachers (4 per year) completing the program. The K20 Center for Educational Renewal and Community Development has, for 10 years, promoted systemic "whole school" reform through a school-university network designed to transform conventional schools into professional learning communities (PLCs) using peer coaching, regional networking, and the IDEALS systemic change framework[1] (O'Hair, McLaughlin, & Reitzug, 2000). In recent years, over 500 rural schools have participated in this effort.

This chapter describes a professional development model that moves beyond a conceptual framework to one that is evidence-based and which combines strengths of OSP and K20 to promote exemplary science instructional practices in seventh–twelfth grade rural classrooms.

THE K20 SCIENCE INITIATIVE FOR RURAL SCHOOLS

The objectives of K20 SCIENCE are to improve teacher quality and student success through two main components: interactive instruction and embedded professional development. Merging these well-established approaches, the K20 SCIENCE Initiative for Rural Schools deepens teachers' content knowledge while impacting large numbers of rural teachers and classrooms across the state.

Interactive Instruction

The most prominent theories on how students develop understanding are based on the ideas that learning is active (Bransford, Vye, Bateman, & Brophy, 2004), involves the acquisition of organized knowledge structures and social interaction (Piaget, 1972; Vygotsky, 1978; Greeno, 1997), and relates new information to existing cognitive structures in order for learning to be meaningful (Blumenfeld, Soloway, Marx, & Krajcik, 1991; Good & Brophy, 2000; Hannafin & Land, 1997; Jonassen, 1999). Additional research has documented substantial achievement benefits for *all* students, regardless of school level, size, context, ethnicity, or socioeconomic status (SES), when students are exposed to the kinds of teaching characterized as interactive instruction producing authentic intellectual work (Smith, Lee, & Newmann, 2001). This type of teaching results in students producing intellectual artifacts that are worthwhile, significant, and meaningful, such as those undertaken by successful adults (i.e., scientists and other professionals) who apply basic skills and knowledge to complex problems (Newmann, 1996; Newmann & Wehlage, 1995). Educational researchers have developed instructional strategies based on experiential learning, meaningfulness, and reflection, in order to facilitate the development of knowledge that can be applied more flexibly to different contexts and problems (e.g., Blumenfeld et al., 1991; Bransford, Brown, & Cocking, 2000).

Authentic assignments using interactive instruction require students to (a) construct knowledge involving organizing, interpreting, evaluating, or synthesizing prior knowledge to solve new problems; (b) engage in disciplined inquiry (i.e., use of a prior knowledge base; striving for in-depth understanding rather than superficial awareness; and expressing one's ideas and findings through elaborated communication); and (c) provide value beyond school for the learning. "These three criteria—construction of knowledge, through the use of disciplined inquiry, to produce discourse, products, or performances that have value beyond school—form the foundation for standards to assess the intellectual quality of teaching and learning" (Newmann, Bryk, & Nagaoka, 2001, p. 14). Recent research supports that interactive instruction producing more authentic intellectual work improves student scores on conventional tests (Newmann et al., 2001), student motivation to learn (Greene, Miller, Crowson, Duke, & Akey, 2004; Roeser, Midgley, & Urdan, 1996), and is linked to student success in high school science and mathematics (Lee, Croninger, & Smith, 1997). The effectiveness of interactive methods is supported by substantiated theory on how students learn (Bransford et al., 2000; Good & Brophy, 2000; Hannafin & Land, 1997; Jonassen, 1999).

Concerns about the reluctance of teachers to implement interactive instruction are not new (e.g., Blumenfeld et al., 1991). For students to receive interactive instruction that engages them in authentic intellectual work, teachers must learn new teaching methods and acquire more subject matter knowledge as well. After studying 2,017 assignments from 277 teachers, Newmann and colleagues (2001) concluded that asking teachers to effectively implement authentic intellectual work necessitates providing resources for integration and assessment and professional networking opportunities.

The K20 SCIENCE model, described next, combines three strategies linked to accelerating and supporting change from didactic to interactive pedagogy: authentic research experiences for teachers, lesson study, and professional learning communities.

Embedded Professional Development

The embedded professional development component of K20 SCIENCE is grounded in three research-based strategies:

1. Deepening the content knowledge and comfort with inquiry-based teaching of rural secondary science teachers through *authentic research experiences*. Authentic research experiences for teachers deepen understanding of scientific inquiry while enriching substance and process (Kincheloe, 1991; Newmann, 2000).

2. Transferring and sustaining teachers' authentic research experiences into classroom practice through *lesson study* (credited with Japan's evolution in mathematics and science teaching; National Research Council [NRC], 2002).

3. Creating PLC that provide meaningful learning experiences for teachers and students. Professional learning communities, including peer coaching and regional networking, reduce the remoteness and isolation which affects rural teachers' learning (Malhoit & Gottoni, 2003) and support authentic intellectual work which has been associated with higher levels of student achievement (Lee & Smith, 1996).

The goals of K20 SCIENCE address specific needs through research-based strategies emphasizing interactive instruction.

Goal 1: Deepening Content Knowledge and Comfort With Inquiry-Based Teaching of Rural Secondary Science Teachers through Authentic Research Experiences

Need

Research connects increased student achievement in science with teaching for understanding of both science disciplinary content *and* the centrality of inquiry in science (Pasley, Weiss, Shimkus, & Smith, 2004). Developing high quality mathematics and science teaching requires deepening teachers' content knowledge through sustained professional development (NSB, 2006). The National Science Education Standards identify more attention to inquiry as the hallmark of good science instruction (NRC, 2002). Teachers who have not experienced inquiry-based, interactive instruction are ill-equipped to employ this instructional strategy in their classrooms (Newmann, King, & Youngs, 2000).

Research-Based Strategy: Authentic Research Experiences for Teachers

Authentic research experiences for teachers provide sustained opportunities for teachers to experience an instructional strategy while they study, experiment with, and receive helpful advice on scientific content; collaborate with professional peers both within and outside of their schools; have access to external experts (i.e., research scientists); and have influence on both the substance and the process of their professional development (Newmann et al., 2000). Experiences of the OSP program over the past 11 years found that teachers readily gained the essentials of scientific inquiry, including confidence in their ability to carry through a rationally conceived research project from beginning to end, when provided authentic research experiences and guidance (Silverman, 2003). In addition to confidence in research ability, teachers' mastery of the scientific content increased significantly through the research experience (Slater & Cate, 2006). As an added bonus, mentor research scientists improved their teaching and communication skills through authentic pedagogy that encouraged critical reflection and knowledge construction through social interaction (Tanner, Chatman, & Allen, 2003).

Implementation

The K20 SCIENCE Summer Research Institute (SRI) engages teachers in scientific discovery with scientists from the University of Oklahoma and assists them in teaching for conceptual understanding. The SRI involves an in-depth, 5-week summer research experience for rural teachers, including:

1. An introduction to scientific research, research methods, and experimental materials.
2. The designing and conducting of original authentic research with guidance from scientists.
3. The translation of research experiences into classroom practices that focus on conceptual understanding.

Teachers utilize wireless-enabled laptop computers and scientific probes to gather, record, and analyze data. During and following the SRI, teachers work in lesson study teams (see Goal 2 discussion below). Upon completing the SRI, teachers submit a summary presentation of their research, reflections on the SRI, and formal lesson plans generated by lesson study teams. The K20 SCIENCE network is available for teachers to seek assistance and advice from other teachers, K20 SCIENCE staff, and research scientists. In addition, teachers completing the SRI have the opportunity to return as mentors for subsequent SRIs in order to support new teacher participants and add to their own research experience.

Goal 2: Transferring and Sustaining Teachers' Authentic Research Experiences Into Classroom Practice Through Lesson Study

Need

For 8 years, researchers at the Wisconsin Center for Education Research (WCER) National Center for Improving Student Learning and Achievement in Mathematics and Science (NCISLA) have worked with teachers and schools to create and study classrooms in which compelling new visions of mathematics and science are the norm. NCISLA found that fundamental reforms in learning and teaching are most likely to be achieved through professional development grounded in teacher inquiry and student conceptual understanding. Huffman and Hipp (2003) similarly found that teachers transfer their learning to the classroom and ultimately to student learning when they network with each other using processes, such as lesson study, designed to create mutual respect and trustworthiness among staff members.

Research-Based Strategy: Lesson Study

Lesson study originated in Japan and has been credited with Japan's evolution of effective mathematics and science teaching (Lewis, 2002a, 2002b; Lewis & Tsuchida, 1997; National Research Council, 2002). Lesson study is an iterative process focusing on what teachers want students to learn rather than on what teachers plan to teach (Lewis, 2002a; Stigler & Hiebert, 1999; Yoshida, 1999). A group of teachers develop a lesson together; one group member teaches the lesson while the others observe student learning; the group reconvenes to debrief, analyze, and if needed revise the lesson to incorporate the observations; and the teaching process begins again with a new teacher. This process of inquiring about their own teaching permits teachers to examine and adapt their practice, resulting in authentic achievement for students (Stewart & Brendufer, 2005). Through creating a culture of inquiry and demanding rigorous work, lesson study provides the opportunity for lifelong learning by teachers and a model for the students (Chokshi & Fernandez, 2004).

Implementation

Using the process of lesson study, the SRI staff guides and assists participants in integrating scientific research processes into classroom practices whose objective is teaching for conceptual understanding. Teachers collaborate (during and after their SRI experience) to craft and refine lessons that utilize the principles of inquiry they have practiced during their research experience. With support from the K20 SCIENCE staff, teachers work with their teams throughout the school year to reflect on, revise, and refine the lessons and instructional strategies from the SRI experience.

The purpose of lesson study is not simply the improvement of a single lesson. Rather lesson study provides teachers with an opportunity to examine their teaching in a way that results in the transfer of new knowledge acquired during the SRI research experience directly to their classrooms, ultimately resulting in the improvement of student achievement (Lewis, Perry, & Hurd, 2004). Teachers completing the SRI experience also engage in lesson study to share their learning with colleagues in their schools. Lesson study teams of four to six teachers, either within a school or within a region, meet for a full day monthly, using release time or stipends, to cooperatively build and script a science lesson and carry out the lesson study process. K20 SCIENCE staff members or outside experts are available during these meetings in a consulting capacity. During the lesson study process, the teachers collaborate to consider core and cross curricular strategies, analyze student learning, and develop small communities of practice. A teacher subsequently teaches the lesson to his/her own class, while the other team members (and K20 SCIENCE staff) carefully observe how the students are learning the concepts and skills. Following the lesson, observers report to the teacher and the team revises the lesson consistent with the feedback. Subsequently the revised lesson is re-taught by a different teacher. The debriefing and revision process continues until the teachers are satisfied with the lesson and feel that it exemplifies inquiry learning standards and maximizes student conceptual understanding.

Goal 3: Creating PLCs that Provide Meaningful Experiences for Learners

Need

An early OSP evaluation indicated the lack of sustaining variables such as teacher networking throughout the school year to deepen learning and accelerate the change process in science classroom practices (McCarty, 2003). In that program, teachers generated curriculum documents at the conclusion of their research experience that were posted on the OSP Web site. Subsequent interviews with OSP teachers revealed that these documents were rarely used after the initial SRI experience (Slater & Cate, 2006). Teachers indicated that although the curriculum documents were important, isolation and lack of peer interaction and support reduced their use of the documents.

PLCs

Researchers (Atkinson, 2005; Williams, 2006) have found that professional learning communities and technology integration (TI) provide supportive conditions that foster peer interactions and changes in classroom practices leading to interactive teaching that enhances authentic intellectual work of students. Early constructivist research (Dewey, 1938; James, 1958) supports the work of recent theorists (Dufour, Eaker, & Dufour, 2002; Hord, 1997; Senge, 2000), who report that PLCs, an approach to engaging school staffs in meaningful learning, leads to increased student achievement (Huffman & Hipp, 2003; Lee & Smith, 1996). Research reveals that a strong sense of community not only increases persistence, but also enhances information flow, learning support, group commitment, collaboration, and learning satisfaction (Rovai, 2002; Wellman, 1999). How successfully a science innovation travels across diverse conditions and geographical areas depends on the extent to which a teachers' academic support network is established (Carpenter, 2004). Technology helps expand teachers' access to a larger community of learners, and as noted by the National Staff Development Council (2001), allows teachers to exchange ideas with each other and leading experts in their content areas, visit classrooms of exemplary teachers, receive coaching from their mentors via internet conferencing, and access online virtual libraries (Loucks-Housley, Love, Stiles, & Mundry, 2003). Schools functioning as PLCs promote collective responsibility for student learning, develop norms of collegiality among teachers, and have been associated with higher levels of student achievement (Lee & Smith, 1996; Little, 1993; Louis, Marks, & Kruse, 1996). Not only is students' achievement significantly higher in schools that function as professional learning communities, but those gains also are also distributed more equitably. That is, the achievement gap between students of lower SES and students of higher SES is narrower (Lee & Smith, 1994). Developing PLCs and networks among rural educators decreases the remoteness and isolation that often plagues rural teachers (Malhoit & Gottoni, 2003) and improves rural teacher quality and student success while ensuring sustainability beyond direct K20 Center involvement (Hamlin, 2007; O'Hair, Williams, Wilson, & Applegate, in press). As rural schools incorporate characteristics of professional learning communities, a commensurate increase of TI into their practices, including student use for learning, has been documented (Atkinson, Williams, O'Hair, & O'Hair, 2008). Research findings suggest that this kind of organizational learning with continual renewal increases professional learning community development and school capacity to support and sustain change (Dufour et al., 2002; Hord, 1997; Huffman & Hipp, 2003; O'Hair, 2008; Sergiovanni, 1994).

Over the past 4 years, the state of Oklahoma's barometer for academic success (Academic Performance Index—API) has recorded significant improvement in K20 partner schools (74% higher than the state's average increase; Williams, Atkinson, O'Hair, & Applegate, 2007). Although other factors may impact API gains, the only attribute shared by participating schools is their involvement in the K20 Center's systemic reform model. These results may well extend into higher education and industry as students complete a multitude of degrees, particularly STEM-related, and enter the work force. K20 SCIENCE efforts support a strong foundation designed to support and nurture rural schools and to respond to "America's urgent challenge to remain a world leader in science and technology" (NSB, 2006, p. 1).

Implementation

A professional learning community can be as small as an individual classroom or as broad as a network of schools across a state. Within a classroom, the PLC is focused on effectively implementing K20 SCIENCE instructional strategies to increase student achievement in science and includes interactive instruction and authentic intellectual work standards (Newmann, 1996; Smith et al., 2001). Classroom practice considers students' prior knowledge and encourages construction of new knowledge based on experiments, demonstrations, extensive written and oral communication, problem-solving, and real world connections. Authentic, high-quality science lessons provide opportunities for students to interact purposefully with science content and focus on the overall learning goals of the concept.

At the school level, the PLC strategy expands learning of teachers to include the entire school community, creating a collaborative, sustaining culture to improve the school's capacity to help all students learn at high levels (Dufour et al., 2002). K20 SCIENCE teachers equipped with internet based video-conferencing capabilities are encouraged to network and collaborate on classroom projects with other rural teachers and scientists. Video-conferencing collaborations have received exceptionally positive feedback from students and teachers.

Additional opportunities for networking include the K20 network of 500 rural school leaders and their school boards. K20 SCIENCE strategies are introduced, studied, and discussed in initial 2-day leadership seminars for administrators wishing to join the K20 schools network; professional meetings with partner organizations such as the state's school boards association, administrator and teacher associations; and K20 regional cluster meetings designed for ongoing professional development.

CONCLUSIONS AND IMPLICATIONS

Low-income, rural students and their teachers are the forgotten under-represented group. Students living in rural areas of the U.S. achieve at lower levels and drop out of high school at higher rates than their non-rural counterparts (Roscigno & Crowley, 2001). Additionally, in Oklahoma, the state in which the K20 SCIENCE model is based, the poverty rate substantially exceeds the national poverty level (Bishaw & Stern, 2006). Nearly 25% of Oklahoma students drop out of high school between ninth and twelfth grade and too many Oklahoma high school students fail to learn higher levels of science that lead to college graduation and scientific and technical careers. Particularly disadvantaged are Native Americans. According to the National Assessment of Educational Performance assessments from 1996 through 2003, Native American students nationally are scoring below other students at fourth, eighth, and twelfth grade levels. In addition, approximately 22% fewer Native American students complete the core coursework in high school.

Teachers in rural areas are often not prepared or certified in the subjects they are teaching. This is particularly true in science education where 24% of rural science teachers lacked academic majors or certification compared to 18% of teachers in nonrural settings (NSB, 2006). The K20 Center network of 500 rural schools provides an extensive infrastructure from which to design, implement, test, revise, and share results of rural education innovation. The K20 SCIENCE Initiative for Rural Schools described in this chapter directly impacts these low-income, rural schools. Although early in its implementation, participating rural teachers report strengthening of their own scientific understanding and how students develop scientific understanding; making complex changes in pedagogy to foster that development; and reinventing their practice in such a way as to reflect authentic intellectual work both in themselves and their students.

While the K20 SCIENCE Initiative directly impacts rural schools in the state of Oklahoma, the initiative has broad implications for schools nationally and perhaps internationally. CNN Polling Director Keating Holland examined U.S. Census data and identified 12 key statistics—four that measure race and ethnicity, four that examine income and education, and four that describe the typical neighbourhood in each state—and calculated how distant each was from the figures for the average state on each measure. Oklahoma ranked sixth nationally in the CNN poll of the most representative state in the country—the state that is a microcosm of the entire country (Preston, 2006). If Oklahoma is representative of the United States, the K20 SCIENCE Initiative has broader impacts than Oklahoma rural schools.

While equity in the United States is lacking for rural schools, other countries may or may not provide greater resources and support to their rural schools. Additionally, in some countries, the geographical setting at which inequity occurs may be different—for example, in some countries suburban and urban settings may be short-changed. The implication for governmental and educational leaders across the globe is that it is important to examine social justice and equity across geographical settings.

Although not every student will become a working scientist, all students, including rural students, need to make informed decisions as citizens about crucial science issues involving health, environment, energy, spending, and ethics (Conn, 2004). K20 SCIENCE advances social justice in rural schools through new conceptions of teacher professional development that enhances learning and prepares citizens for democratic participation.

NOTE

1. The K20 Center's programs, including K20 SCIENCE Initiative, are committed to the promotion of the democratic education **IDEALS—Inquiry, Discourse, Equity, Authenticity, Leadership, and Service,** and are grounded in the knowledge bases on school and community partnerships, teacher quality, and student success.

ACKNOWLEDGMENTS

The authors gratefully acknowledge support from Perri Applegate, Linda Atkinson, Jean Cate, Janis Slater, Leslie Williams, and Scott Wilson, researchers and staff of the K20 Center for Educational and Community Renewal, University of Oklahoma. This research was supported by the Oklahoma Medical Research Foundation through a Howard Hughes Medical Institute grant and the National Science Foundation's Research and Evaluation on Education in Science and Engineering (REESE) program (REC-0634070). Opinions reflect those of the authors and do not necessarily reflect those of the granting agencies.

REFERENCES

Atkinson, L. K. (2005). *Schools as learning organizations: Relationships between professional learning communities and technology-enriched learning environments*. Norman, OK: University of Oklahoma.

Atkinson, L. K., Williams, L. A., O'Hair, M. J., & O'Hair, H. D. (2008). Developing and sustaining schools as technology enriched learning organizations. *I-managers Journal of Educational Technology, 3*(4), 17–33.

Bass, H., Usiskin, Z. P., & Burrill, G. (Eds.). (2002). *Studying classroom teaching as a medium for professional development.* Proceedings of a U.S.-Japan workshop. Washington, DC: National Academy Press.

Beeson, E., & Strange, M. (2003). *Why rural matters 2003: The continuing need for every state to take action on rural education.* Randolph, VT: Rural School and Community Trust Policy Program.

Bishaw, A., & Stern, S. (2006). *Evaluation of poverty estimates: Comparison of the American Community Survey and the Current Population Survey.* Washington, DC: Poverty and Health Statistics Branch, U.S. Census Bureau. Retrieved August 15, 2008, from http://www.census.gov/hhes/www/ poverty/acs_cpspovcompreport.pdf

Blumenfeld, P. C., Soloway, E., Marx, R. W., Krajcik, J. S., Guzdial, M., & Palincsar, A. (1991). Motivating project-based learning. *Educational Psychologist, 26*(3/4), 369–398.

Bransford, J. D., Brown, A. L. & Cocking, R. R. (Eds.). (2000). *How people learn: Brain, mind, experience, and school committee on developments of science of learning.* Washington DC: National Academies Press.

Bransford, J., Vye, N., Bateman, H., Brophy, S., & Roselli, B. (2004). Vanderbilt's AMIGO^3 project: Knowledge of how people learn enters cyberspace. In T. M. Duffy & J. R. Kirkley (Eds.), *Learner-centered theory and practice in distance education* (pp. 209–234). Mahwah, NJ: Erlbaum.

Carpenter, T. P. (2004, Spring). Scaling up innovative practices in math and science. *WCER Research Highlight, 16*(2), 1–8.

Conn, S. S. (2004, February 11). A new teaching paradigm in information systems education: An investigation and report on the origins, significance, and efficacy of the agile development movement. *Information Systems Education Journal, 2*(15). Retrieved June 22, 2005, from http://isedj.org/2/15/

Chokshi, S., & Fernandez, C. (2004). Challenges to importing Japanese lesson study: Concerns, misconceptions, and nuances. *Phi Delta Kappan, 85*(7), 520–525.

Darling-Hammond, L. (2000). Teacher quality and student achievement: A review of state policy evidence. *Education Policy Analysis Archives, 8*(1). Retrieved May 19, 2004, from http://epaa.asu.edu/epaa/v8n1/

Dewey, J. (1938). *Experience and education.* New York: Simon & Schuster.

Dufour, R., Eaker, R., & Dufour, R. (2002). *Getting started: Reculturing schools to become professional learning communities.* Bloomington, IN: National Educational Service.

Education Trust. (2003). *Education watch: The nation.* Retrieved May 8, 2006, from http://www2.edtrust.org/edtrust/summaries2004/USA.pdf

Fullan, M. (2001). *Leading in a culture of change.* San Francisco: Jossey-Bass.

Fullan, M. (2003). *Change forces with a vengeance.* New York: Routledge.

Garet, M. S., Porter, A. C., Desimore, L. M., Birman, B. T., & Yoon, K. S. (2001). What makes professional development effective? Results from a national sample of teachers. *American Educational Research Journal, 38*(4), 915–945.

Gates Foundation. (2004). *Southern governors committed to high performing rural schools*. Retrieved April 2, 2005, from http://www.gatesfoundation.org/Education/Announcements/Announce-042104.htm

Good, T. L., & Brophy, J. E. (2000). *Looking in classrooms* (8th ed.). New York: Longman.

Greene, B. A., Miller, R. B., Crowson, H. M., Duke, B. L., & Akey, C. L. (2004). Relations among student perceptions of classroom structures, perceived ability, achievement goals, and cognitive engagement and achievement in high school language arts. *Contemporary Educational Psychology, 29*(4), 462–482.

Greeno, J. G. (1997). On claims that answer the wrong questions. *Educational Researcher, 26*(1), 5–17.

Hamlin, G. (2007). *An evaluation report to the Oklahoma Educational Technology Trust-concerning sustainability of Grants to Schools*. Oklahoma City, OK: OETT.

Hannafin, M. J., & Land, S. M. (1997). The foundations and assumptions of technology-enhanced, student-centered learning environments. *Instructional Science, 25*(3), 167–202.

Hord, S. M. (1997). *Professional learning communities: Communities of continuous inquiry and improvement*. Austin, TX: Southwest Educational Development Laboratory.

Huffman, J. B., & Hipp, K. K. (2003). *Reculturing schools as professional learning communities*. Lanham, MD: Scarecrow Education.

James, W. (1958). *Talk to teachers*. New York: W. W. Norton.

Jimerson, L. (2003). *The competitive disadvantage: Teacher compensation in rural America*. Washington, DC: Rural School and Community Trust.

Johnson, J., & Strange, M. (2007). *Why rural matters 2007: The realities of rural education growth*. Arlington, VA: Rural School and Community Trust.

Jonassen, D. H. (1999). Designing constructivist learning environments. In C. M. Reigeluth (Ed.), *Instructional design theories and models: A new paradigm of instructional technology* (Vol. 2, pp. 215–239). Mahwah, NJ: Erlbaum.

Kincheloe, J. L. (1991). *Teachers as researchers: Qualitative inquiry as a path to empowerment*. London: The Falmer Press.

Lamkin, M. L. (2006). Challenges and changes faced by rural superintendents. *Rural Educator*. Retrieved June 5, 2007, from http://findarticles.com/p/articles/mi_qa4126/is_200610/ai_n16840815

Lee, V. E., & Smith, J. B. (1994, Fall). High school restructuring and student achievement: A new study finds strong links. *Issues in Restructuring Schools, 7*, 1–16.

Lee, V. E., & Smith, J. B. (1996). Collective responsibility for learning and its effects on gains in achievement for early secondary school students. *American Journal of Education, 104*(2), 103–147.

Lee, V. E., Croninger, R. G. & Smith, J. B. (1997). Course-taking, equity, and mathematics learning: Testing the constrained curriculum hypothesis in U.S. secondary schools. *Educational Evaluation and Policy Analysis, 19*(2), 99–121.

Lewis, C. (2002a). Does lesson study have a future in the United States? *Journal of the Nagoya University Education Department, 1*(1), 1–24.

Lewis, C. (2002b). *Lesson study: A handbook of teacher-led instructional change*. Philadelphia: Research for Better Schools.

Lewis, C., & Tsuchida, I. (1997). Planned educational change in Japan: The case of elementary science instruction. *Journal of Educational Policy, 12*(5), 313–331.

Lewis, C., Perry, R., & Hurd, J. (2004). A deeper look at lesson study. *Educational Leadership, 61*(5), 6–11.

Little, J. (1993). Teachers' professional development in a climate of educational reform. *Educational Evaluation and Policy Analysis 15*(2), 129–152.

Loucks-Horsley, S., Love, N., Stiles, K., Mundry, S. & Hewson, P. (2003). *Designing professional development for teachers of science and mathematics* (2nd ed.). Thousand Oaks, CA: Corwin.

Louis, K., Marks, H., & Kruse, S. (1996). Teachers' professional community in restructuring schools. *American Educational Research Journal, 33*(4), 757–798.

Malhoit, G., & Gottoni, N. (Eds.). (2003). The rural school funding report. *The Rural Education Finance Center, 2,* 12.

McCarty, R. (2003). Specified ignorance: A pedagogical and cognitive tool for learning the nature and process of science. *Teaching and Learning, 17*(3), 113–132.

National Center for Education Statistics. (2002). *The nation's report card: Mathematics 2000, NCES 2001–517*. Washington, DC: U.S. Department of Education, Office of Educational Research and Improvement.

Bass, H., Usiskin, Z., & Burrill, G. (2002). Studying classroom teaching as a medium for professional development. In *Proceedings of a U.S.-Japan workshop*. Washington, DC: National Academy Press.

National Science Board. (2006). *Science and Engineering Indicators 2006*. Washington, DC: National Science Foundation.

National Staff Development Council. (2001). *NSDC Standards*. Retrieved May 19, 2004, from http://www.nsdc.org/standards/index.cfm

Newmann, F. M. (1996). *Authentic achievement: Restructuring schools for intellectual quality*. San Francisco: Jossey-Bass.

Newmann, F. M. (2000, Fall). Authentic intellectual work: What and why? *Research/Practice 7,* 1 Retrieved March 16, 2004, from http://education.umn.edu/carei/Reports/Rpractice/Fall2000/default.html

Newmann, F. M., Bryk, A. S., & Nagaoka, J. K. (2001). *Authentic intellectual work and standardized tests: Conflict or coexistence?* Chicago: Consortium on Chicago School Research.

Newmann, F. M., King, M. B., & Youngs, P. (2000). Professional development that addresses school capacity: Lessons from urban elementary schools. *American Journal of Education, 108*(4), 259–299.

Newmann, F. M., & Wehlage, G. G. (1995). *Successful school restructuring: A report to the public and educators*. Madison, WI: Center on Organization and Restructuring of Schools, University of Wisconsin.

O'Hair, M. J., McLaughlin, H. J., & Reitzug, U.C. (2000). *Foundations of democratic education*. Fort Worth, TX: Harcourt Brace.

O'Hair, M. J., Williams, L. A., Wilson, S., & Applegate, P. (in press). Addressing social justice in rural schools: The K20 Model for systemic educational change and sustainability. In P. Woods & G. Woods (Eds.), *Leading alternative in education*. London: Palgrave Macmillan.

Pasley, J. D., Weiss, I. R., Shimkus, E., & Smith, P. S. (2004). Looking inside the classroom: Science teaching in the United States. *Science Educator, 13*(1), 1–11.

Piaget, J. (1972). *The psychology of the child*. New York: Basic Books.

Rovai, A. P. (2002). Building sense of community at a distance. *International Review of Research in Open and Distance Learning, 3*(1), Retrieved August 1, 2006, from http://www.irrodl.org/index.php/irrodl/article/view/79/152

Preston, M. (2006, July 27). The most "representative" state: Wisconsin. *Politics: The Morning Grind*. Retrieved August 22, 2006, from http://www.cnn.com/2006/POLITICS/07/27/mg.thu/index.html

Roeser, R. W., Midgley, C., & Urdan, T. (1996). Perceptions of the school psychological environment and early adolescents' self-appraisals and academic engagement: The mediating role of goals and belonging. *Journal of Educational Psychology, 88*(3), 408–422.

Roscigno, V. J., & Crowley, M. L. (2001). Rurality, institutional disadvantage, and achievement/attainment. *Rural Sociology, 66*(2), 268–293.

Senge, P. (2000). *Schools that learn: A fifth discipline field book for educators, parents, and everyone who cares about education*. New York: Doubleday.

Sergiovanni, T. J. (1994). *Building community in schools*. San Francisco: Jossey-Bass.

Silverman, P. (2003). The origins of molecular biology: A pedagogical tool for the professional development of pre-college science teachers. *Biochemical Molecular Biology Education, 31*(5), 313–318.

Slater, J., & Cate, J. M. (2006, April). *Cognitive dissonance as a perspective in the transfer of learning from authentic teacher research experiences to inquiry instruction in the classroom*. Paper presented at the American Educational Research Association Annual Conference, San Francisco.

Smith, J. B., Lee, V. E., & Newmann, F. M. (2001). *Instruction and achievement in Chicago elementary schools*. Chicago: Consortium on Chicago School Research.

Stewart, R. A., & Brendufer, J. L. (2005). Fusing lesson study and authentic achievement. *Phi Delta Kappan, 86*(9), 681.

Stigler, J. W., & Hiebert, J. (1999). *The teaching gap: Best ideas from the world's teachers for improving education in the classroom*. New York: Summit.

Tanner, K. D., Chatman, L., & Allen, D. (2003). Approaches to biology teaching and learning: Science teaching and learning across the school-university divide—Cultivating conversations through scientist-teacher partnerships. *Cell Biology Education, 2*(4), 195–201.

Vygotsky, L. S. (1978). *Mind and society: The development of higher mental processes*. Cambridge, MA: Harvard University Press.

Wellman, B. (1999). The network community: An introduction to networks in the global village. In B. Wellman (Ed.), *Networks in the global village* (pp. 1–48). Boulder: Westview Press.

Williams, L. A. (2006). *The relationships of technology integration and high school collaboration through the development of a professional learning community: A mixed methods study*. Unpublished doctoral dissertation, University of Oklahoma.

Williams, L., Atkinson, L., O'Hair, M. J., & Applegate, P. (2007, April). *Improving educational quality through technology-enriched learning communities for success in the global economy.* Paper presented at the meeting of the American Educational Research Association, Chicago.

Yoshida, M. (1999). *Lesson study: A case study of a Japanese approach to improving instruction through school-based teacher development.* Unpublished doctoral dissertation, University of Chicago.

PART III

COLLABORATIVE PARTNERSHIPS FOR
SOCIAL JUSTICE: COMMUNITIES, YOUTH, AND
SCHOOL-LINKED SERVICES

CHAPTER 8

A COLLABORATION OF COMMUNITY EDUCATORS FOLLOWS CRISIS IN CINCINNATI

Two Museums and a University Join Forces to Promote Understanding

Lionel H. Brown, Judith I. Larsen, Ruth S. Britt, Donna M. Ruiz, and Rachel Star

This paper focuses on how community educators might collaborate to help break the cycle of frustration, failure, and violence that shadows many disadvantaged inner-city African American students. It suggests that persistent, race-based inequities in urban areas are a major factor in this syndrome. These causes are proposed to be disparity in education, housing, economic opportunity, and political representation. The paper suggests that a deeper understanding of these ongoing issues is a key to educating these particular students. Specifically, it explores a collaboration between Cincinnati Museum Center, The Arts Consortium of Cincinnati, and the

Leadership for Social Justice: Promoting Equity and Excellence Through Inquiry and Reflective Practice, pp. 171–194
Copyright © 2008 by Information Age Publishing
171

University of Cincinnati College of Education following violence in the city in 2001, and it traces some impacts of that effort.

INTRODUCTION

Nearly 4 decades ago, in June 1967, Black Cincinnati exploded. Riots took place in eight separate African American communities within the city. According to Taylor (1993),

> The anger and deep frustration that led to the "fires, acts of hoodlumism, looting and anarchy" are best captured in Langston Hughes's poem, Harlem: "What happens to a dream deferred? Does it dry up like a raisin in the sun? or does it explode?" Inquiries into the causes of the riots pinpointed unemployment, bad housing, poor neighborhood conditions, and the lack of political representation. (p. 20)

These causes—inequalities in education/employment opportunities and substandard housing/living conditions, as well as disproportionate Black representation in civic government—have persisted from the 1960s until today, giving rise to generation after generation of disadvantaged and disenfranchised, alienated Black youth. In spite of legislated efforts to improve opportunities for African Americans (e.g., affirmative action initiatives), factors remain that have contributed to the persistence of inequality between Black and White people today. And while White treatment of Black people has been the target of public policies and intervention efforts, deeper understanding of Black frustration has not yet resulted within many sectors of the White community (Ogbu, 1994).

The 60s was a decade of social, cultural, and political upheaval. The Civil Rights Movement, student activism, and antiwar movements, political assassinations, race riots, the "hippie" counterculture, the sexual revolution, the beginnings of feminism and the environmental movement, the movement toward Black Pride and Black Power, and the rise of the drug culture all challenged traditional respect for authority and the law. And yet, amidst all this upheaval, according to Taylor (1993):

> Race and class [still] defined the position of blacks in Cincinnati's plural but unequal society. Prejudicial thinking, discrimination, segregation and location on the economic margin determined the life chances Americans at every stage in Cincinnati's social, economic and political order. Blacks marched, demonstrated, picketed, harangued, and worked behind the scenes to educate, plead their case, and negotiate, but to little avail.[1] (p. 20)

The momentum of the previous decade's civil rights gains led by Martin Luther King, Jr. carried over into the 1960s, but for most Black people, the tangible results were minimal. Only a tiny percentage of Black children actually attended integrated schools; and in the South, Jim Crow practices barred Black people from jobs and public places. New groups and goals were formed, and new tactics were devised to push forward for full equality of the races—but as often as not, White resistance resulted in violence. For Cincinnati, mid-June 1967 marked the beginning of a series of riots in the city. Soon hundreds of national guardsmen and city policemen armed with rifles, pistols, and machine guns were patrolling Black sections of Cincinnati. In the words of Taylor (1993) "armored tanks roared up and down the streets, and as angry young blacks burned, looted, and marauded, it seemed significant how much things had changed yet remained the same" (p. 20).

Issues raised by rioting and political action in the 60s are still having a profound impact upon today's society—as evidenced by the continuing Civil Rights Movement and by the struggle for racial equality and better race relations in America.

Why have the longstanding, underlying causal conditions of racial unrest not changed? It appears that institutionalized conventions persist in the Cincinnati inner city, and in other similar communities throughout the country that have made it hard for Black people to advance and increase their chances for success. Physical and social segregation within the city has exacerbated the problems. Disparities remain between Black and White people in both educational and economic outcomes. Both the national and local Cincinnati NAACP (National Association for the Advancement of Colored People) listed the achievement gap as a prime educational concern. Kati Haycock, director of the Education Trust, stated that "the gap is established by the time students enter kindergarten and the gap widens as students progress through school" (Mrozowski & Kranz, 2002, p. A1). It is important, therefore, to understand the relationship of early educational achievement during elementary and secondary school years and later academic and economic success. Recent longitudinal studies investigating the relationship between early educational achievement and subsequent academic and economic outcomes used multiple datasets from the years 1972, 1980, and 1992 to explore this relationship (National Center for Education Statistics, 2002). The researchers found that educationally disadvantaged Black people also fared more poorly in the labor market and were much more likely to be unemployed than White people with better educational opportunities and early success.

This paper explores the place where the efforts of community educators and urban educators intersected in their mutual quest to understand the underlying causes of racial unrest in the inner city. It should be noted that in Cincinnati it is understandable that racial concerns have dealt mainly with the interactions between the Black and White populations, since according to 2003 census figures, the African American population is 43%, while Native Americans, Asian, or Hispanic/Latino were each under 2%. This paper proposes that the causes for unrest, and causes for persistent, complex problems in educating urban Black youth are the same, and suggests that a more informed approach to educating this population may be one of the keys to change for these students' futures. The authors propose that a more informed pool of educators can be a key to open the door of communication between people of different races isolated from one another in different economic and social situations. This key could help open a world of opportunities for those who are living largely without hope. But to operate this key requires a deeper understanding on the part of community educators.

"Community educators," as used in this paper, includes not only teaches, local and district administrators, and college professors, but also, parents and caregivers, religious leaders, social workers, and police and juvenile justice system workers. Each single strand in the web of community education has power and strength, but the entire web is needed to prevent urban Black youth from falling through the cracks of society.

EXAMINING ROOTS OF
RECURRING RACE CONFLICT IN CINCINNATI

Background and "Trigger" for the 2001 Unrest

Following the shooting of an unarmed, fleeing young Black male by a young White policeman in April of 2001, the streets of one underprivileged, largely Black inner city neighborhood in central Cincinnati burst into violent protest. The shooting incident was the culmination of a string of seemingly race-biased acts committed against Cincinnati's Black population by city police. In a 5-year period, 15 Black males were killed by Cincinnati Police. Circumstances surrounding a number of these deaths seemed to justify forceful defensive action by police. It is significant, however, especially to the African American community, that no White people were killed by Cincinnati police during that same 5-year period. Previous efforts by the Black community at peaceful communication with city leaders and police about this perceived inequity had been unsuccessful. In 1999, the Sentinel Police Association, which represents the city's Black police officers, compiled a report that urged city leaders to take immediate action, warning that something must be done to "quell the very tense and volatile atmosphere that currently exists between the police and the community" (Horn, 2001, p. A6). That warning went unheeded. Three times—on May 31, November 8, and November 13 of the year 2000—African Americans protested at City Hall concerning young Black males killed during their arrests by Cincinnati police. On March 14, 2001, Black activists and the American Civil Liberties Union sued the city of Cincinnati, asking a federal court to end what they said had been 30 years of unchecked discrimination by police officers (Goetz, 2001).

The crucial April 2001 shooting incident that triggered the violence looked very different from different eyes. Was the killing of this Black man an excuse by antisocial young Black males to stir up things in the city? Or was the resulting violence the act of desperate people needing to be heard and reacting to the last straw in a series of police acts that seemingly singled out African Americans? Both of these views are over simplifications of what happened. Neither view addresses the underlying causes. Calm has returned to Cincinnati. Under the surface, however, serious problems remain.

Race Riots in the 1960's/Unrest in 2001: The Same Root Causes? A First Person Comparison

University educator, Dr. Lionel H. Brown, offers a personal reflection on the 1967 race riot in Cincinnati and the 2001 civil unrest in the city. He compares and contrasts the two events and proposes that the root causes have remained distressingly similar, although decades of social upheaval and striving for equality separate the two.

Cincinnati—1967

On a mid-week summer evening in 1967, I was driving down Reading Road on my way home from the University of Cincinnati where I was a junior in the college of design, art, and architecture. I had been working late that night in the design lab. As I passed the intersection of Rockdale Avenue and Reading Road, I noticed a large unruly crowd in the middle of Rockdale. People were running out of their houses and a nightclub. As I slowed my car, there was a loud explosion. Flames leaped into the air to the right and left of my car. I heard shouts of "Black power" and "power to the people." I turned onto Lexington Avenue and came to a stop. To my far right, I heard another thunderous explosion. I realized it was in the vicinity of Model Laundry where my grandmother worked during the day as a shirt press operator. I could hear loud angry voices of crowds moving in all directions and the sound of glass breaking and smaller explosions. There was the sound of bricks crashing through car windows and frightened screams from inside the automobiles. I sped off down Lexington Avenue, turned onto Victory Parkway, past Walnut Hills High School. As I turned right onto Gilbert Avenue, there was another loud explosion further up Gilbert near the Thompson Cadillac showroom. I hurried onto Bresford Avenue. As I turned onto Kerper Avenue and drove to my house, I could see flames leaping higher into the air as Model Laundry burned. (Gilbert Avenue, Reading Road, and Victory Parkway are major thoroughfares extending like spokes from the central city.)

The next day as I drove the same route, I saw that Model laundry—a plant that employed hundreds of people—was burned to the ground. Thomson's Cadillac, where new cars were displayed daily, was damaged badly. Large plate glass windows that had previously allowed passers-by to look through and be tempted by shiny new cars now were replaced with wooden boards. Reading Road and Rockdale Avenue were a complete shambles—debris everywhere, stores damaged beyond repair. Windows that had managed to survive thrown bricks, trashcans, and Molotov cocktails the night before were now boarded up. A curfew was enacted but similar acts of destruction went on until the National Guard was called in, arriving in full riot gear, driving military jeeps, to protect the city from rioters and looters.

One night later in the week as I was again driving home from University of Cincinnati, I was pulled over by the National Guard. I was ordered out of my car, directed to lean spread-eagle against the car, and searched with a bayonet pressed against my backside. My car was also searched. Riot conditions that started that night in early June of 1967 lasted for the remainder of the summer (Amos, 2004).

Cincinnati—2001

In April 2001, a group of fifth and sixth graders and I were returning from a college tour. These students were participants in GEAR UP (Gaining Early Awareness and Readiness for Undergraduate Programs). As the last group of students stepped off the bus at Parham School not far from the city's center, the custodian told me there had been a disturbance in downtown Cincinnati. Later that evening, I drove to the downtown post office and passed a large crowd of angry people moving down Vine Street and another large crowd moving up Central Parkway (urban thoroughfares located in a central part of the city). Violence had erupted. Windows were broken; food carts were overturned; a few buildings were looted and set afire. The next night a curfew was enacted. Once again, as many years earlier, I drove home from the University of Cincinnati, this time not as a student but as a research associate, and not to Kerper Avenue, but to an area outside the city—a quiet area unaffected by the unrest and civil disobedience. The April 2001 unrest lasted for several days and a curfew was enacted, but it was lifted in less than a week (Thompson, 2001; Vulliamy, 2001b).

Differences Between the 1967 Riots and the Unrest of 2001

What the city and I experienced in the 60s and what we experienced in April 2001 were not the same. The riots of the 60s were a forest fire, and the unrest in 2001 was the threatening flame of a match. However, in the 60s, in spite of the fact that violence and physical harm were much greater, city government and activists were willing to seek common ground for discussions. In contrast, in 2001, city government and activists were unwilling to sit down together to look for common ground that can lead to solutions. Subsequently, Cincinnati Black United Front leaders and others called for a boycott that continued into 2004 (Aldridge, 2004). A proportion of the Black population felt that the boycott was the only bargaining chip available to them to keep attention on the problems in the city. Those who opposed them refused to negotiate while the boycott was still in place. The boycott did keep millions of dollars in convention and entertainment business away from downtown Cincinnati; consequently the city and its economy have suffered (Aldridge, 2004). The image of the city is sorely damaged and the racial divide remains and grows larger.

There are a number of general underlying reasons that could be contributing to this lack of progress in communication. Many of the "deeply held grievances" listed by the Kerner Commission when it investigated causes for the 1960's riots have still not been addressed.[2] In addition, recent recalls of some affirmative action initiatives have been interpreted by some as a movement to turn the clock back and remove gains made by Black people. Even the right to vote and the promise of a voice in a democratic society often seem to be a waste of time. Why vote when it appears to many that a good portion of those elected can't see a voter's worth beyond a campaign promise? Franklin Raines, first Black CEO of a Fortune 500 corporation, has observed that Blacks are "so suspicious of the establishment that, until the establishment demonstrates it will do something, the assumption is that it will not [italics added] do something" (Cose, 2002, p. 35).

Two of Cincinnati's current problems, for example, police profiling of Black men, and apparent targeting of Black youth, are both symptoms of a much greater problem of racial attitudes that have persisted from generation to generation. The 2001 shooting of the young Black male was just the match that ignited issues that have been smoldering over time.

Sadly city leaders, government officials, and influential community members still cannot seem to find ways to bring about systemic change.

EDUCATORS MUST HELP BRIDGE THE GAP

It is beyond the scope of this paper to discuss the many factors that influence the educational success of Black males. For example, some have suggested that desire for an education among this group has been replaced by an attitude that excellence in achievement is akin to "acting White" and is a symbol of femininity, while other theorists dispute the real meaning of that phrase (Harpalani, 2003). In addition, it is impossible to look at race without a consideration of other influences such as class (Horvat, 2003). Nevertheless, a current view of the success rates of students in Cincinnati public schools shows that the task of improving educational outcomes is daunting. High rates of suspension and expulsion coupled with a dismal attitude toward education have brought the Black male's journey from poor attendance to high school dropout. Poor scores on standardized tests and huge gaps in achievement between Black and White students diminish hope among Black students that college can be apart of their lives. Low expectations and hopelessness cause Black males to trade classroom chairs for street corners and eventually for jail cells when they turn to crime, violence and self-destruction. As Cose (2002) has said,

> Public schools in poor urban communities are often nothing but factories for failure. Instead of taking black and brown children seriously, instead of treating them as human beings fully capable of great success, they frequently treat them like dullards simply marking time until they are ready to collect welfare or go to prison. (p. 91)

One local African American minister, active in efforts to bring about change in the urban core of the city, cites another often discussed idea. He believes that the standard, 13-year education in our schools presents only a "Eurocentric" viewpoint without acknowledging other cultures. African American children (and children of other cultural and racial minorities) are hard-pressed to develop a sense of self worth and self determination, and conversely, White students often cannot understand the African American perspective. The two groups not only live in different worlds, they see the same events very differently. Education from a multi-cultural perspective could be one key to supporting future dialogue and understanding within our city and others.

Exploring the Lack of Understanding Between Black and White People

One fundamental obstacle to communication and change became clear as the events of 2001 unfolded: how can our diverse communities begin to face and address the city's problems together when often we come from separate worlds and separate understandings? Cincinnatians are segregated by race. For the most part, African Americans and Caucasians live in separate parts of the city. In fact, the current city manager recently repeated a description of Cincinnati as the "6th most segregated city in America" at a "Hope in the Cities" December 2003 meeting in Richmond, Virginia.[3] Lionel Brown, one of the authors of this paper, was deputy superintendent at the time of a 1976 NAACP judgment against school segregation in Cincinnati. His view quoted recently in a local newspaper was that

> It is now nearly impossible to end school segregation ... [in Cincinnati]. There are fewer students in the district overall and, of greater import, fewer white students. Lack of resources, poor discipline and underachievement have taken their toll on the district's demographics. (Amos, 2004, p. A16)

People in Cincinnati are also segregated by economics, as most cities are, but does this separation also have a racial component? Even though the Black middle class is growing, is it still harder for African Americans to make the climb out of poverty and escape a bleak future?

COMMUNITY AND URBAN EDUCATORS BECOME INVOLVED

Two educational institutions were among the first to promote communication and understanding. Realizing the complexity of the problem and the need for understanding on both sides, Cincinnati Museum Center (CMC) and the Arts Consortium of Cincinnati took on the challenge to provide historical perspective on the racial violence of 2001 to show as many viewpoints and voices from the community as possible, to present the issues for consideration, and to provide a safe place for dialogue and options for individual involvement. The two museums came together, combining their physical and human resources, to produce an exhibit to educate and to encourage dialogue.

Cincinnati Museum Center, located close to the center of the disturbed area, felt it was within its mission to document the events as part of its historical museum/library. In a move that went beyond this mission, CMC decided to partner with the Arts Consortium of Cincinnati (an African

American institution also located in the same area) to produce the exhibit. The exhibit also went far beyond the mission of the Arts Consortium of Cincinnati and represented a perilous step for both.

Very quickly, the University of Cincinnati College of Education added its strong support to the effort. Several education professors and their graduate student classes toured the exhibit and participated in discussion groups, and students wrote papers on the exhibit. The experience became a unique, first-hand and personal way for students to absorb the complexities of the racial inequalities in the city and to see how the situation impacts inner city students. It is significant that the graduate students most involved with the exhibit were doctoral candidates in one of the few programs in the United States that offers a degree in urban education leadership. One education graduate student, who was teaching in a Cincinnati suburban school at the time, struggled with the realization that, even though she believed she was caring and unprejudiced, true understanding was difficult because her social world did not intersect with African Americans who felt injustice. She had to agree, saying in effect, we are segregated—our worlds do not cross.

Historical Perspective: A Necessary Foundation

As preparations for the exhibit "Civil Unrest in Cincinnati: Voices of Our Community" proceeded, research showed that basic economic conditions and opportunities for poorer inner city dwellers had not changed much since the riots of the 60s. Lack of proportionate African American representation in the city leadership, disproportionate unemployment, excessive poverty, unequal educational opportunities, and substandard housing were still common in 2001. A study found that in 1990 almost 85% of residents in the Findlay Market District, at the center of the 2001 violence, were living below the federal poverty level (Cerveney, Haney, & Vredeveld, 1997). Cincinnati has, in fact, become a more segregated city since the 60s, with many White people living in mostly White neighborhoods and Black people living in mostly Black neighborhoods. Cerveny et al. found that within the area surrounding the violence, 83% of the residents were Black. In contrast, the overall racial make-up of the Greater Cincinnati region was found to be 87% White and 12% Black.

Educational data also show a lack of positive change for city school students. School district 2001 data showed that the high school graduation rate for African American students was under 50%. In addition, proficiency test scores were far lower in the city school district than in all of the other surrounding suburban schools of greater Cincinnati.[4] This kind of data is especially disturbing in view of longitudinal studies that link educational success with later economic success.

One panel in the completed exhibit quoted Dr. Kenneth Clark, the first witness to appear before the National Advisory Commission on Civil Disorders (later often described as the Kerner Report). After looking at previous riot commission reports on violent disturbances in the country he noted: "It is a kind of Alice-in Wonderland—with the same moving picture shown over and over again, the same analysis, the same recommendations and the same inaction" (Ashworth, 2008, para. 14). In fact, prior to the 2001 disturbance, Cincinnatian Cecil Thomas, a former policeman who now heads the Human Relations Commission, had warned that the city was "one questionable shooting away from riots" (Edwards, 2001, para. 5).

Another exhibit panel showed that nearly 1/3 of the city's children—who by 2001 were more than half African American—were still living in substandard housing in distressed neighborhoods. Unemployment among White people in the city at large stood at around 5%, but in the largely Black neighborhood of the disturbance, unemployment was over 20% (Annie E. Casey Foundation [AECF], 2001). Figures from a University of Cincinnati economic study further show that Black males represent the highest category of unemployed. Census figures from 1990, in fact, showed that 50% of Black males in the Findlay Market district (at the immediate site of the violence) were unemployed. This figure rose to over 60% unemployed when the surrounding economically distressed urban areas were included (Cerveny et al., 1997). The exhibit showed movement in city representation, but not consistent with population percentages—in 1967, not one of the 69 city officials was Black; in 2001, 11 of the 56 comparable officials were Black, but the city's Black population had grown to 43%.

Responses by city leaders to the riots in the 60s and the unrest in 2001 were distressingly similar as well. Three examples from the exhibit follow: (a) In the 1960s, "Home Visit Sundays" were held in an effort to allow Cincinnati's Black and White residents to meet in informal, social settings, small discussion groups, and book circles were created for Cincinnati's Black and White citizens and members of the police to come together informally to share ideas and experiences. In the 1960s, business leaders pledged to create jobs and job training for inner city youth ("Official city of Cincinnati publication," 1967; Trapp, 2001, para. 1). In 2001, business leaders again pledged to create 3,000 jobs for inner city youth (Rutledge, 2001a; Trapp, 2001 para. 2). From the 60s up through the crisis of 2001, city commissions, committees and panels were organized to study the problems and suggest change (Kiesewetter, 2001). As newspaper headlines in 2001 asserted, past ideas for correcting the city's problems have not been implemented, for example, "Past race reports gather dust" (Rutledge, 2001b), and "Panel to plow familiar ground" (Horn, 2001).

While there is no doubt that some progress has been made, the underlying attitudes have not only remained similar, but in the view of some informed citizens, have perhaps regressed. Reverend Fred Shuttlesworth, a legend of the Alabama Civil Rights Movement of the 1950s and 1960s, has served a congregation in Cincinnati for many years. In 2001, he said,

> Race relations haven't changed very much since those days. If anything, things are worse if everybody thinks they have changed yet, in reality, those changes are not every-vein deep.... Cincinnati ... has had time to change, but the whites have blocked progress and the police is more a prosecutor than a protector... people will rebel if they don't see ... progress. The riots happening now are the result of Cincinnati not responding to change. (Vulliamy, 2001a, para. 9, 10)

SEEKING A BROADER BASE OF
UNDERSTANDING IN THE COMMUNITY

As alliances formed in new ways between the two museums and the university and additional community educators, the influences of the collaboration multiplied. Influence within the traditional educational community was immediate and far reaching. Educational institutions at all levels contributed directly to the exhibit. Elementary students, from a school just blocks from the major violence, sent their pictures and poems. Poetry and artwork from high school students from a suburban school covered one section of the exhibit wall. In turn, any visiting teacher who requested it received transcripts of the entire text for use in their classes after visiting the exhibit, lists of children's books dealing with the topics of race relations and urban violence compiled by staff at the children's section of the Cincinnati Public Library and at the Center for Peace Education were also popular with parents and teachers alike. In addition, the exhibit drew many school groups in the short, 4-week span that it was open at the beginning of the 2001 school year.

A university student group, with a diverse membership working toward racial awareness—Racial Awareness Pilot Project—came to see the exhibit and held a discussion following their visit. In addition, the closing event for the exhibit brought together elementary African American school children who read their poetry and Caucasian students from a suburban high school who had contributed poetry and art work for the exhibit. These high school students who participated also had carried out a 2-day exchange with the inner city high school nearest the civil unrest. A community project called "Posters4Peace" headed by a university professor in the school of social work also became part of the fabric of the exhibit, since posters drawn on cardboard by citizens concerned about bringing the community together were scattered throughout the exhibit. An organization dedicated to working toward tolerance and understanding in children called the Center for Peace Education also provided hand-made masks and a display of books for children.

As previously mentioned, university education students in the University of Cincinnati's Urban Education Leadership (UEL) program became immersed in the exhibit. The UEL is a program specifically dedicated to helping education leaders tackle the difficult educational challenges in problem inner city areas. These students, therefore, are a direct link to the future of education within challenged urban areas. The coordinator of the program recognized the unique opportunity to build an action-oriented museum/education partnership using the exhibit as a focus for his students. As part of the process, he assembled a panel of community leaders who belonged to an organization "Changing Hearts and Minds One Block at a Time" to present their visions for positive change in Cincinnati to the UEL students. That panel reflected a broad spectrum of community educators—as this paper defines the phrase—including concerned business leaders, a pastor, the exhibit designers, university educators, a museum evaluator, and the publisher of the city's leading African American newspaper.

The opportunity to speak to a wider traditional educational audience arose through several presentations for leaders in education at national meetings. A panel presentation at the 2001 UCEA (University Council for Educational Administration) national convention held in Cincinnati described the education/museum partnership. Again, a group of community leaders—some formal educators, others supportive of education (all community educators)—came together to address the underlying issues facing Cincinnati and other cities. A panel of presenters from the Cincinnati collaboration also spoke in Savannah, Georgia, at the 2002 Teachers' Education Division (TED) of the Council for Exceptional Children Conference. The title of this presentation brings home the message: "Conditions affecting urban children: Street violence, the impetus for broader educational partnerships."

Both the connection to the Urban Education Leadership Department and to the educators at the TED and UCEA conferences hold much promise for the future. Administrators and educators of teachers are in a unique position to help prepare teachers to better understand communities where a history of unfavorable urban conditions has been responsible for violence and poor outlooks for children. These trained teachers can affect positive change for the outcomes of individual children and therefore can have a profound affect on the future.

A practical plan for action is also in the works, spurred on by the 2001 violence. A center called the Urban Technology Community Center (UTCC) is being planned for families from the inner city neighborhood most affected by the violence. The University of Cincinnati education department, a local organization called "Changing Hearts and Minds One Block at Time," and a number of individual business and religious leaders are raising money to open a center where young children can have access to technology and learn together with their parents. It would offer job application skill training and address health issues and community responsibility. A site has been chosen and serious planning is underway. See Appendix A for a detailed description of the proposed center.

Impacts on Informal Education

Reaction to the exhibit "Civil Unrest in Cincinnati: Voices of Our Community" also reverberated throughout the national museum community and continues to create thought and discussion. Panels, presentations, and articles in museum publications have given museum professionals the opportunity to consider wider, community-oriented missions that respond to current local issues (Larsen, 2002a, 2002b).

Presentations about the process of designing and implementing this kind of exhibit (serving the community as an immediate response to a local crisis) as well as studies looking at the lasting effect on visitors have been presented both at the 2002 African American Association of Museums Annual Conference in Washington, DC[5] and at the 2003 Visitors Studies Association Conference in Columbus, Ohio. Another indication that museums are becoming increasingly interested in this kind of community education mission is shown by trends in museum studies programs. For example, one graduate class in museum studies recently traveled to CMC from Indiana University expressly to talk with the designers, curator, and evaluator for the Civil Unrest exhibit.

A small, but direct consequence of the collaboration occurred with the museum building itself. The Arts Consortium of Cincinnati exhibit partner has been housed within the Museum Center Union Terminal building ever since the Union Terminal opened as a museum, although its board and operations have always been completely independent from CMC. After this exhibit collaboration, awareness of the programs of this African American Museum partner has increased and also recognition of the important connection it offers to contemporary local African American artists and their public supporters. For the first time its hours of operation are now listed along with CMC activities on the monthly calendars available for visitors.

Tracking the Educational Impact of the Exhibit

A key to turning emotion and sentiment into action is arming citizens with knowledge. Ninety percent of the 10,000+ visitors said that the exhibit evoked emotion and 98% felt that Cincinnati needed to change. Half of those writing about the exhibit in a journal (around 200 individuals) wrote about how much they had learned about the root causes for our city's current problems. Many visitors expressed surprise at how little has changed in the living situations and opportunities available for the people living in the area where the civil unrest occurred. They said they saw that "things hadn't changed" and that "the exhibit was thought provoking" or "opened their eyes." Another common statement was that "the exhibit should be seen by more people, stay longer, or travel."[6]

Visitors' comments also suggested opportunities for education to make a difference. In spite of the fact that open-ended questions did not direct visitors toward the topic of education, over 50 visitors specifically mentioned the need for education to help overcome the city's problems. Personal comments also showed that many felt parents are a crucial part of this educational process, describing "mentoring" and starting education at home. A few examples:

"I am educating myself and others to diversity"
"Provide the children with opportunity to learn about others"
"Find ways to 'confront' people when they say/do racist things. EDU-CATE!"
"Educate consciously and continuously. I've had enough of knee-jerk reactions. Let's be proactive."
"Improving educational opportunities and improving communication opportunities and skills are vital, I feel."
"We need direction and leadership. We also need better funding of public education and more grants and loans for post high school training."
"Yes we need to fight poverty & its consequences - our schools are vital."

Educational Initiatives Moved into the Local Community

Following the end of the exhibit run, its impact continued to be felt in the larger Cincinnati community. The following three initiatives serve as examples. First, the soundtrack from an evocative component of the original exhibit called the "Whisper Tunnel—an audio space that presented unflattering comments commonly used to describe people of another race—was borrowed for use in a Martin Luther King Day assembly. Cincinnati students from four schools were gathered for the event. The "Whisper" soundtrack played while they entered and continued until all students sat down and could hear it all the way through. Then several students who had visited the exhibit themselves spoke about their experience.

Second, on the anniversary of the civil unrest, another community educator, The Center for Peace Education, held a workshop at CMC, again using the museum as a safe place to encourage dialogue. This "Peace Day" brought representatives from the urban environments and beyond, including organizations ranging from homeless shelters to evening continuing education centers. The Poster[4]Peace professor also returned to the museum on Peace Day to involve more people in a tangible artistic expression of working toward understanding and peace.

Third, the designers of the museum exhibit have established a new arts initiative aimed at increasing diversity in the theatre community. As their awareness of the social and cultural segregation in the Cincinnati area increased, the husband and wife team, long active in community theatre groups, set out to build a bridge between Black and White communities based on this art form. Efforts progressed through several smaller presentations to the November 2003 full-length and fully-staged performance of the classic African American play *A Raisin in the Sun* in collaboration with another community theatre group. A second collaborative performance took place in March 2004. Actors trained by the African American Theatre Company of Butler County (AATC/BC) have also won parts with other, previously all-White community companies. The AATC/BC continues to train and network Black actors with the larger theatre community in the Cincinnati area, and to present its own Black-themed productions for integrated audiences.

Current Efforts in Cincinnati

The current situation in Cincinnati shows the need for continued efforts at dialogue. Although the scene seems calm on the surface in Cincinnati, serious problems remain. An observation made by *All Things Considered* cohost Noah Adams while visiting Cincinnati in 2001 noted that despite the meetings and conversations and negotiations, city officials and citizens seem far from closing the racial divide (National Public Radio, 2001). This is for the most part still true. Three main factions—the Black United Front, Cincinnati Police, and the city power structure—remain at odds and will not accept conditions set down by the others. A "Boycott Cincinnati" group is still active in the city, using boycotting as a tool to exert pressure on city administrators to address policing and other issues that fuel the climate of racial intolerance. In turn, top city officials still refuse to negotiate with boycott advocates. News headlines in 2003 suggest some community perceptions and continuing racial tensions: "Police race data filed and forgotten" (Prendergast, 2003a) and "Black firefighters accuse union" alleging hostility by White colleagues (Prendergast, 2003b).

Meanwhile, dialogues sponsored by the Cincinnati Human Relations Commission still continue between residents and police. In addition, a number of organizations formed at the time of the outbreak of violence carry on the fight. A commission started at the time of the violence, Cincinnati CAN (Community Action Now), has disbanded but several initiatives are continuing, including a program to accelerate minority businesses and a community-police partnering center. The Women's City Club, League of Women Voters, and Grassroots Leadership Academy have combined forces to present programs supporting community problem oriented policing. The more that groups like these interact and combine their efforts, the better the chance for change. The question remains: will all of these heartfelt efforts make a long-term difference or will the city once again come full-circle to another violent event.

Another positive change in the scene is the inclusion of more African Americans in positions of leadership in the city government, with both a Black city manager and vice mayor. An African American has also been chosen as head coach of the local professional football team—a first in Cincinnati. There has been strong community support for the National Underground Railroad Freedom Center (NURFC), soon to open in the city. NURFC is already partnering with CMC and the Cincinnati Art Museum, to design an exhibit about an African American Cincinnatian who was a highly successful daguerreotype photographer in the city around the time of the Civil War. In addition, several community school centers are being developed in Cincinnati, combining health centers, police subunits and local arts or cultural organizations with traditional education. Both CMC and the Arts Consortium of Cincinnati are each currently in partnership with one of these centers.

CONCLUSION

Cincinnati, like many other cities, needs to face its current problems, but also desperately needs to help overcome problems for future generations—to stop the cycle of inequality, frustration and violence from repeating. There are many areas in which attention is necessary if the chronic conditions discussed in this paper—disparity in employment/education opportunities, substandard housing, and lack of representation in civic government based on race—arc to undergo change. But communication and the opportunity to see problems from the perspective of the 'other' side are also crucial. Traditional educators and political, religious, social, and business leaders must work with community leaders to increase understanding, with the goal of creating a society made stronger by its diversity.

Perhaps a large part of the success of the museum-university partnership in "Civil Unrest in Cincinnati: Voices of Our Community" was that it became a catalyst that brought together the efforts of many, already-existing community groups, helping to give a focus to their similar goals. Other initiatives that hopefully will carry on this spirit of collaboration, building on the collective strengths of other community institutions are: community education centers combining traditional schools with health, law enforcement, and cultural organizations, the University of Cincinnati's Urban Educational Leadership doctoral program taking students from theoretical foundations in educational leadership to actual practice in urban schools and communities, and finally, a proposed UTCC that would provide a safe welcoming center where children and their parents can go to learn, interact casually with police officers, and have access to technology that could change their future prospects. See Appendix B for details about UTCC and examples of collaborations in other cities.

At the most fundamental level, urban community educators must recognize ongoing, underlying conditions faced by urban youth, especially young Black males, and pool their resources in addressing them on a daily, one-to-one basis. Obviously solutions to ongoing, long-standing social, economic, and political problems are not up to educators alone, but they can play a vital part in creating the new citizens armed for future grass roots change.

The causes of racial crisis and conflict in Cincinnati are similar to those in surrounding communities and cities across our country. The authors of this paper hope that readers of this paper will reflect on the causes of racial civil unrest and find ways to help educational organizations in their own cities join together to address these problems with solutions. Community educators are in a unique position to respond on a very basic level in a way that could change lives and the cities in which we live forever.

NOTES

1. Taylor notes that his statements are based on discussion in Lewis (1991)
2. The National Advisory Commission on Civil Disorders, chaired by Otto Kerner, Jr., known as the Kerner Report was released February 29, 1968. The first seven grievances in descending order of intensity were (1) police practices, (2) unemployment and under-employment, (3) inadequate housing, (4) poor recreation facilities and programs, (5) ineffectiveness of the political structure and grievance mechanisms, (6) disrespectful White

attitudes, (7) discriminatory administration of justice. Researchers on the Cincinnati Historical Society staff found many of these to still be problems in Cincinnati at the time of the 2001 violence in the city.

3. *Hope in the Cities* (2004). This is the newsletter of an organization based in Richmond, Virginia, that is dedicated to race reconciliation. The current name of the organization is: Initiatives of Change International, accessible at http://www.iofc.org

4. Demographic and educational information from AECF, KIDS COUNT Cincinnati Web page http://www eccensus.cgi, and http://www.aecf.org. Additional data from Children's Defense Fund-Ohio and the Ohio Department of Education, retrieved August 2005 respectively from: http://www.cdfohio.org, 2005 Ohio County Factsheets and Federal Poverty Guidelines and http://www.ode.state.oh.us/

5. African American Association of Museums 2002 Conference abstract:

> Immediately following racial and political unrest in the streets of Cincinnati in April 2001, Cincinnati Museum Center collaborated with the Arts consortium of Cincinnati to present an exhibit that explored past unrest in the city offered a fact-based look at the events of 2001, and challenged visitors to become part of the healing process. Presenters will discuss team building for the project and the challenge of turning a controversial subject into physical form. Examples of on-term effects of the exhibit upon groups working for peace and justice in Cincinnati will also be provided.

6. Information on the CMC museum exhibit: Civil Unrest in Cincinnati: Voices of Our Community exhibit evaluation: Over 10,000 people from 20 states visited the exhibit during its 3-month run with a demographic profile much more diverse than Cincinnati Museum Center's usual visitation. Since about 1/3 of these visitors responded about their experience in one or more ways (by writing in a journal, on graffiti boards, on a survey, or on personal pledge cards), visitor response was well documented—1,648 of these individual responses were analyzed.

APPENDIX A

The proposal for an Urban Technology Community Center (UTCC) in the Over-The-Rhine (OTR) area of the city includes a specific plan of intervention by a team of educators, clergy, and business leaders in a group called "Changing Hearts and Minds—One Block at a Time." In OTR, students and their parents represent the lowest rung of the socioeconomic ladder, facing a daily reality of drugs and crime in their neighborhoods. They also have often experienced failure in public school systems.

The Center would provide mentors for children, programs for parents, and technology training to enhance future educational and economic opportunities in a safe, welcoming center in OTR where both children and their parents can go to learn, interact casually with each other and with Cincinnati police officers, and have access to the kind of technology that can change their future prospects. The goals are:

1. Safety in the community: The approach would be holistic, encouraging families, business owners, police, clergy, and school personnel to work together to create a safe community. Implementation of neighborhood block watch programs would give residents a stake in securing the safety of their neighborhoods.

2. Respect for individual and property rights: The center (with support from local ministers and the police) would help parents improve their parenting skills to develop a sense of respect for individual and property rights in their children.

3. Joint sponsorship of neighborhood blocks with corporate and community area partnerships: Corporations will be encouraged to "adopt" housing segments and to work with the residents to renovate buildings.

4. Cleanliness of the community: The UTCC will promote programs that foster pride in a clean and renewed community

5. Job application skills: The UTCC would use technology to help older students and adults study for a GED diploma and encourage individuals to think beyond the GED toward continuing their education at a trade school or community college level. Job training and educational and vocational counseling would be provided.

6. Health and wellness issues: Community health agencies would help prevent problems through early identification of physical, emotional, social, family, or substance abuse problems and would improve knowledge in the area of nutrition.

7. Community responsibility: The UTCC would promote shared authority and responsibility by community stakeholders so that residents, business persons, clergy, and school personnel could work as equal team members toward common goals.

8. Educational & technology enhancement—reducing the digital divide: The UTCC would provide educational and technology instruction and enrichment to enable children and parents to advance academically and technologically.

Collaboration for Implementation

A creative network of public and private support would need to be tapped to fund the center and help develop the programs. Corporate support in the form of technology donations, such as laptop computers, printers, scanners, and digital cameras, also would be solicited. Local universities would be approached for architectural expertise in building restoration, medical assistance and chemical/alcohol dependency expertise, literacy and mathematics tutorial services, and technology skills training. Five components of the UTCC will be implemented in phases over several years.

1. Access to technology and technical training: A grant request submitted to the state of Ohio requests funds for desktop computers in the Center, refurbished laptops for school, access to internet at home and at the center, and training for adults and students on educational uses of computers.

2. Access to GED training for parents and older students: Once technology is in place it would be used to help older students and parents study for a GED diploma.

3. Location of a police substation at the Center: The proposed collaboration with Cincinnati police would provide the opportunity for the community and police to interact on a casual basis, allowing mentoring and tutoring relationships to develop.

4. Alternative learning and parent support center: The UTCC tutors would work with students to improve basic and test-taking skills. It would help parents assist their children with schoolwork, stressing the importance of early child development, and work to improve the parents' knowledge of technology, nutrition, budgeting, and finances.

5. Juvenile intervention: The Center would provide a safe, supervised location for police to bring children with minor offenses (e.g., truancy). It is hoped that police at the Center could then help them work out changes in their lives. Future plans include a police-student court in which students and police together evaluate negative behaviors and determine appropriate actions for offenders.

All of these interventions are designed to address specific aspects of the neighborhood residents' frustrations and combat both racial crisis and conflict. The effects of such a center would take time and only evaluation over the long term will be able to sort out possible benefits. The plan, however, holds tremendous promise.

Note: Cofounded by Dr. Lionel Brown and Randy Sandier.

APPENDIX B

Other Community Educator Partnership Examples

A variety of other community educator partnerships that deal with social problems are aimed at helping people of different backgrounds and cultures understand each other and providing tools for better personal success. Education is very much a part of the mission of the institutions in these partnerships.

The Open Museum of Los Angeles formed a partnership that connected museums and the power of dialogue to address the 10th anniversary of the Los Angeles riots. In April 2001 that museum produced an exhibit that traveled around Los Angeles called "Remember the Riots," which drew upon the experiences of people who had lived through the riots of 10 years ago. A book accompanied the exhibit, full of personal accounts from individuals and produced in English, Spanish, and Korean. The museum partnered with the University of California at Los Angeles Hammer Museum, and the nonprofit organization "Days of Dialogue," which facilitated discussions at each of the venues for the exhibit.

On the opposite coast, the Lower Eastside Tenement Museum of New York (LESTM) serves as a community educator whose "pupils" (immigrants who learn English and how to cope in practical ways in big city life) often become teachers of the next new group of immigrants. The LESTM actively educates immigrants and fosters tolerance and respect for all cultures. The museum also forms partnerships with groups that carry out restoration or neighborhood improvement projects.

REFERENCES

Aldridge, K. (2004). Where boycott succeeded, and where it failed. Retrieved July 2006, from http://www.enquirer.com/editions/2004/09/19/loc_loc1aboycottb.html

Amos, D. (2004, May 16). Separate and unequal: A half-century later, racial divide persists. *Cincinnati Enquirer,* A1, A16, A17.

Annie E. Casey Foundation. (2001). *Kids count, Cincinnati, Ohio.* Retrieved August 18, 2008, http://www.kidscount.org/cgi-bin/cliks.cgi?action=rank_indicator&subset=OH&areatype=county

Ashworth, K. (2008, April 28). It doesn't help to replay the same movie. *Trenton Space.* Retrieved August 18, 2008, from http://www.trentonspace.com/Articles-c-2008-04-28-43422.113122_Lessons_unlearned_It_doesnt_help_to_replay_the_same_movie.html.

Baraka, A. (1987). A critical reevaluation: A Raisin in the Sun's enduring passion. In R. Nemiroff (Ed.), *A Raisin in the Sun and the sign in Sidney Brusrein's window*. New York: New American Library.

Cerveney, L., Haney, M., & Vredeveld, G. (1997). *Cincinnati Historical Society Papers on Cincinnati Riots, box 11, folder 9*. Cincinnati: Cincinnati Historical Society Library.

Cose, E. (2002). *The envy of the world: On being a Black man in America*. New York: Washington Square Press.

Edwards, J. (2001). Official warned city of riots for years. *Cincinnati Post*. Retrieved August 10, 2005, from http://www.cincypost.com/2001/apr/12/cecil041201.html

Goetz, R. (2001, May 19)). Racial tension in Cincinnati. *The Cincinnati Enquirer*, p. A6. Retrieved June 20, 2005, from http://www.enquirer.com/editions/2001/05/19

Harpalani, V. (2003). What does "acting White" really mean? *Perspectives on Urban Education* (Penn University edition). Retrived August 10, 2005, from http://www.urbanedjournal.org/commentaries/c0001.html

Hope in the Cities Newsletter. (2004, Spring). Retrieved from http://www.hopeinthecities.org

Horn, D. (2001, April 17). Panel to plow familiar ground. *The Cincinnati Enquirer*, pp. A6, A8.

Horvat, E. (2003). The interactive effects of race and class in educational research: Theoretical insights from the work of Pierre Bourdieu. *Perspectives on Urban Education*, 2(1). Retrieved August 18, 2008, from http://www.urbanedjournal.org/archive/Issue3/articles/article0009.html

Kerner Commission Report. (1968). *Report of the National Advisory Commission on Civil Disorders*. Washington: U.S: Government Printing Office

Kiesewetter, J. (2001, July 15). Civil unrest woven into city's history. *Cincinnati Enquirer*. Retrieved August 18, 2008, http://www.enquirer.com/editions/2001/07/15/tem_civil_unrest_woven.html

Larsen, J. (2002a). Putting the present into history: A museum challenges the community to listen to today's voices and learn from its past. *History News*, 57(1), 22–25.

Larsen, J. (2002b). Civil unrest: Voices of our community. *Hope in the Cities Newsletter*, 1(1), 5, 6.

Lewis, E. (1991). *In their own interest: Race, class, and power in twentieth-century, Norfolk, Virginia*. Berkeley, CA: University of California Press.

Mrozowski, J., & Krantz, C. (2002, March 6). Race gap evident in Ohio test scores. *Cincinnati Enquirer*, pp. A1, A11.

National Public Radio. (2001). *NPR. All Things Considered. Cincinnati: Searching for a Resolution*. Retrieved August 2005, from http://www.npr.org/programs/atc/features/2001/nov/cincinnati/011101.cincinnati.html

Ogbu, J. (1994). Racial stratification and education in the United States: Why inequality persists. *Teachers College Record*, 96(2), 264–298.

Official city of Cincinnati publication. Proceedings of City Council: Statement in RE recent violence in city of Cincinnati. (1967, June 27). *The City Bulletin*, 41(26), 3, 4.

Prendergast, J. (2003a, Sept. 7). Race data filed and forgotten. *Cincinnati Enquirer*, p. A1.

Prendergast, J. (2003b, Sept. 26). Black firefighters accuse union. Retrieved August 18, 2008, from http://www.enquirer.com/editions/2003/09/26/loc_cfddiscriminate26.html

Rutledge, M. (2001a, April 25). Jobs promised for 3,000 youths. *Cincinnati Post*, p. 1a:5.

Rutledge, M. (2001b, May 5). Past race reports gather dust. *Cincinnati Post*, p. 1a

Taylor, H., Jr. (Ed.) (1993). *Race and the city: Work community and protest in Cincinnati*, 1820–1970. Urbana, IL: University of Illinois Press.

Thompson, R. (2001, April 17). Curfew ends; Recovery begins. *Cincinnati Enquirer*, pp. A1, A9.

Trapp, D. (2001, May 17). The fire last time. *City Beat*, 7(26). Retrieved August 2006, from http://www.citybeat.com/2001-05-17/news2.shtml

Vulliamy, E. (2001a, April 15, 2001). *The Tribune. Racism stains Cincinnati*. Retrieved August 18, 2008, from http://www.tribuneindia.com/2001/20010416/world.htm#7

Vulliamy, E. (2001b, April 16, 2001). *Guardian Unlimited*. Retrieved August 18, 2008, from http://www.guardian.co.uk/print/0,,4170865-103681,00.html

CHAPTER 9

STUDENT VOICE OR EMPOWERMENT?

Examining the Role of School-Based Youth-Adult Partnerships as an Avenue Toward Focusing on Social Justice

Dana L. Mitra

Drawing on the parallel literature on increasing student voice in the field of education and on building youth-adult partnerships in the youth development field, this chapter examines the place of young people in efforts to increase social justice in school settings. Through an examination of 13 youth-adult partnership initiatives, it considers the ways in which students and adults can collaborate to examine issues of equity and injustice that they experience in their lives, in their schools, in their communities, and in broader society. The findings identify that the groups' intended goals focused on addressing issues of equity and social justice on three levels—the system level by focusing on issues of intolerance and injustice, the organizational level by advocating for school change, and the individual level by fostering youth leadership and peer helping.

Leadership for Social Justice: Promoting Equity and Excellence Through Inquiry and Reflective Practice, pp. 195–214
Copyright © 2008 by Information Age Publishing

INTRODUCTION

When considering the place of social justice in educational leadership, one must examine the concept as both a goal and a process. That is, one must think not only about whether schools can be engaged in discussions and activities on questions of equity and social change. One must also examine whose voices are included in such conversations.

REVIEW OF LITERATURE

A growing body of literature emphasizes the value of extending the notion of distributed leadership (Elmore, 2000; Lashway, 2003) to include students in the process. Such research has demonstrated that youth-adult partnerships can create a synergy that transcends what youth or adults alone can do, including sparking great strides in clarifying an organization's vision and accomplishments (Kirshner, O'Donoghue, & McLaughlin, 2003; Mitra, 2001; National Research Council, 2002; Zeldin, 2004; Zeldin, Camino, & Mook, 2005). Increasing student voice in schools can also encourage schools to more closely align their mission, goals, and activities with a social justice focus. Research indicates that young people tend to broach subjects that adults are reluctant to discuss, such as equity issues that tend to get swept under the rug by administrators and other adults in the school who would rather avoid controversy (Fine, 1991; Wehlage, Rutter, Smith, Lesko, & Fernandez, 1989). For example, by involving students in school-wide discussions about academic achievement—and particularly students failing subjects or rarely attending school—school personnel cannot easily shift the blame of failure onto the students (Mitra, 2003). Instead they must assess the problems within the school's structure and culture. Giving students a voice in such reform conversations reminds teachers and administrators that students possess unique knowledge and perspectives about their schools that adults cannot fully replicate without this partnership (Kushman, 1997; Levin, 2000; Mitra, 2001; Rudduck, Day, & Wallace, 1997; Thorkildsen, 1994).

In addition to a focus on social justice of outcomes, the process of including young people at the table also has been shown to lead to great benefits for youth. These gains include an increase in agency, confidence, attachment to social institutions, and to foster a range of competencies (Kirshner, O'Donoghue, & McLaughlin, 2003; Mitra, 2004). Increasing student voice can lead to an increase in youth empowerment (Larson, Walker, & Pearce, 2005), which can provide sources of social capital for youth that can yield opportunities for further education, employment, and other enrichment opportunities (O'Connor & Camino, 2005). In addition to the professional growth that these partnerships can facilitate, youth-adult partnerships also can benefit the adults involved by fulfilling a fundamental psychosocial need of adult development by fostering intergenerational relationships that include sharing knowledge and experiences with youth (Ginwright, 2005).

The Evolution of Student Voice in Schools

The current origins of student voice initiatives in school stem from the student empowerment efforts of the 60s and early 70s that demanded increased civil and individual rights (Johnson, 1991). During this era, students focused more directly on social justice issues, such as youth having a right to contribute to decisions about their schools and their academic preparation. In the modern context, the term "student voice" offers a less threatening notion of youth engagement than "student empowerment." The politics of the time often require a justification of student voice as a way to increase student outcomes, and particularly test scores. Legitimacy of student voice is thus gained by developing the argument that it can be an avenue toward improving student outcomes.

The recent increase in attention to student voice initiatives dovetails with a growing field of research on the importance of "youth-adult partnerships" in the youth development field (Camino, 2000; Zeldin, 2004). The literature is so similar in its findings and approach that this chapter will use the concepts of "student voice initiative" and "school-based youth-adult partnership" interchangeably to draw attention to impressive and growing research in both fields. Both of these fields describe youth-adult partnerships as spaces in which adults and young people have the potential to contribute to decision making processes, to learn from one another, and to promote change (Jones & Perkins, 2004). A focus on mutual teaching and learning develops in youth-adult partnerships as all parties involved assume a leadership role in some aspects of their shared effort (Camino, 2000). This emphasis may include youth sharing in the responsibility for the vision of the group, the activities planned, and the group process that facilitates the enactment of these activities (Jones, 2004). In school contexts, the concept of student voice has gained increasing credence as a construct that describes the many ways in which youth might have the opportunity to actively participate in school decisions that will shape their lives, the lives of their families, and the lives of their peers (Fielding, 2001; Goodwillie, 1993; Levin, 2000).

Given the history of student empowerment and the current political contexts deemphasizing individual rights and prioritizing test scores, this chapter takes a closer look at the ways in which school-based youth-adult partnerships can still raise issues of social justice. The chapter suggests that a socially just school not only trains students in a narrow academic sense but it also prepares young people to lead democratic and morally just lives. This chapter therefore examines how young people can be a voice for change in their schools and what such efforts look like.

METHODS

Sample

This chapter draws from a larger study designed to examine the process and outcomes of 13 student-voice initiatives in Northern California. The research sample was designed to identify sites that most actively demonstrated commitment to fostering youth-adult partnerships rather than to find schools with a range of student involvement in reform efforts. The sample therefore is based on representation of strong student voice initiatives rather than representation of school sites (Strauss & Corbin, 1990).

The 13 groups for this study were chosen because they all received grant funding from a local foundation in the San Francisco Bay Area to work on building a student voice initiative in their school. Schools had to apply for the funds, and seed grants of $5,000 were awarded to schools demonstrating involvement in the proposed plan and sufficient capacity to complete their proposed projects. The groups were chosen because they were identified as the strongest applicants in the pool (and indeed some were recruited because of their reputation for working on student voice issues). The staff of the foundation worked closely with potential applicants to learn more about both the goals and process of the groups. This interaction before the funding decision helped to inform the selection committee of the extent to which young people were actively involved in the grant writing process, since preference was given to applicants that actually had youth write the grant request themselves. Additionally, it is worth noting that all of the schools in the sample were situated within an urban environment—either within an inner city or a bedroom community in the Bay Area that possessed urban characteristics of the region, including a diverse population, a public school system that lacked sufficient funding, and high concentrations of poverty. The groups ranged in size from only 3 youth to over 50, with each group supervised by one or two adult advisors. Table 9.1 provides a summary of the types of activities conducted by the 13 groups in the study.

Table 9.1.   Description of the Youth-Adult Partnerships in the Sample

School/Group	Examples of Specific Projects
College Center: Unity Council	Creation of a unity council that would include representation from all ethnic groups on campus
Great Valley: End the Stereotypes	Creation of a peace park honoring students who serve as peacemakers
High Hills: Polynesian Club	Creation of a large mural reflecting Polynesian history and their roles in that community
Highland: Business Enterprise	Program offering school lunches made by local restaurants; participation in international business competitions; Income tax assistance for elderly; Student-designed business cards
Hillside: Unity of Youth	Development of a center providing social services and tutoring assistance; campaigns seeking an end to school exit exams and improving bathroom conditions
Hoover: Gay-Straight Alliance	Student-designed video of youth experiences with intolerance; annual Day of Silence.
King: Youth Voice Initiative	Youth-driven dialogues on their concerns and a subsequent focus on developing more course electives
Latin: Peer Support	Conflict mediation, peer tutoring, and peer workshops on suicide, body image, and racism
McGuire: Peer Mentoring	Peer-to-peer conflict resolution program
Midland: Campaigns for Justice	Campaigns to acquire substantive student representation on the district school board
Morgan: Peer Support	Preparation of a book describing youth experiences through poems and essays; peer education about youth rights
Sierra: Youth Taking Charge	Student-designed video of injustices in their disadvantaged community, including no lack of grocery stores, too many liquor stores, rampant drug dealing, and domestic violence.
Whitman: Student Forum	Critique of textbooks for district's adoption process; student-led community tours; participation in professional development sessions

Data Collection

Data collection consisted of two semistructured telephone interviews conducted with a minimum of two and a maximum of five individuals participating in each of the 13 groups. The interviews were conducted once within the first few months of receiving their grant funding and again a few months after the grant funding ended. Reliability of the data was increased for all of the interviews by always acquiring the perspective of both youth and adults in each group. The interviews lasted between 20 to 60 minutes. All interviews were recorded on audiocassette and the tapes were transcribed to preserve the words of the interviewees.

When conducting semistructured interviews, the intent was not to follow strictly a predetermined protocol, but instead to allow the interviewees to tell their story in manner that could best describe their group experiences. The protocol (see Appendix) ensured that all the questions were discussed by the end of the interview, if not in the same order. The questions on the protocol consisted of the following: (a) Tell me about how things are going this year with your program and what has changed from last year. (b) What kind of skills and support to youth and adults each need to do this work? (c) What do teachers and students in the school think about your group? Who are the group's biggest allies (principals, teachers, outside nonprofit, and others) (d) Who makes decisions in your group? Who are the leaders? (e) Have you seen any changes in the school as a result of your work yet? Have you seen any changes in yourself? (f) What are your plans for continuing your work after the grant ends?

In addition to interviews, data collection also included gathering group documents of media coverage, internal publications, and pages from group and school Web sites. Observations also were conducted of mandatory meetings that brought potential grant recipients together to learn about the grant process and of subsequent meetings after the funding was awarded that encouraged the schools to share their successes and struggles with each other in order to foster collaborative communication among the grantees. These meetings included small group discussions and collective brain storming on how to improve the work of all of the groups. Data collection at such events consisted of transcribing on a laptop computer the conversations of the attendees and recording all flip chart and other visual forms of communication as well. These opportunities allowed for a comparison of the plans and interaction styles of the 13 groups.

Data Analysis

The coding structure that guided the data analysis was developed using a grounded theory approach (Glaser & Strauss, 1967; Strauss & Corbin, 1990), which is a qualitative methodology that is useful for the purpose of developing theory that is derived from systematically gathered and analyzed data. Although the design of qualitative research is necessarily emergent (Lincoln & Guba, 1985), the grounded theory method provides a process for synthesizing data and creating a set of criteria against which to evaluate results. Moving from raw data to conclusions involved a process of "data reduction" that involved breaking data down, conceptualizing it, and putting it back together in thematic categories that best fit the text (Miles & Huberman, 1994).The data reduction process had three steps: open coding, axial coding, and selective coding (Strauss & Corbin, 1990). The analysis process for this chapter began with *open coding* by examining the ways in which participants articulated the vision and activities of their groups. Based on themes emerging from the data and from the author's previous research on student voice, the main coding bins examined for this study consisted of examining interviewee's conceptions of their work (of student voice overall and their specific project) and the components of their change strategy (vision, actions taken, and partnerships formed).

Next, a process of *axial coding* defined the relational nature of these categories by identifying their properties and dimensions (Becker, 1998). Each school naturally faced unique institutional and community contexts. Nevertheless, through examining the activities and visions of the 13 groups, common patterns were identified among the groups which resulted in defining three levels at which student voice initiatives worked— at the system level looking at broader questions of justice and intolerance, at the organizational level looking at school change, and at the individual level focusing on youth development.

Selective coding involved identifying the central theme around which the hypotheses fit. The three categories were descriptive in nature, but further examination was necessary to examine their relationship to each other. An examination was conducted of whether these three goals were distinct and equal entities or if they were hierarchical or otherwise built upon one another. Moving back and forth between the data from this study and the literature on student voice initiatives and the broader youth-adult partnership literature led to the creation of an *explanatory framework*, which illuminated the relationship between the three categories (Miles & Huberman, 1994, Strauss & Corbin, 1990). All three of the emphases for these schools shared a common thread—that of a social justice focus. The following results summarize the findings of this analysis process. While the grounded theory approach seeks to reduce data into concepts, the quotations provided in the findings offer narratives which allow readers to join in the process of viewing the data in its original, albeit selective, form to share in the interpretive process (Stake, 1995).

FINDINGS

Through an examination of the reasons that individuals participated in these groups, the collective vision of what they wanted to accomplish and the actual activities that the groups pursued, a common theme of social justice emerged across the experiences of these cases. Some of the groups spoke consciously of the intention to address issues of intolerance and equity. For others, this mission was more subtle and instead became clear through follow-up questions in interviews about why they wanted to engage in the activities that they choose. Through these clarifying questions, the values shared by the groups were found to be markedly similar, with common themes of attention to issues of access, voice, equity, and intolerance. Table 9.2 provides on overview of these group goals. It also groups the focus of these groups into three levels—the systemic level focuses on issues of intolerance and injustice, the organizational level focuses on advocating for specific school changes, and the individual level focuses on fostering youth leadership and peer helping. Initiatives are listed in more than one category if their activities were intended to serve more than one purpose. For example, College Center's unity council initiative worked both to relieve administrative problems at the organizational level of the school, and it also was intended to serve as a forum for discussing the systemic racial tensions that were an ongoing source of struggle at the school. At Highland High School, the initiatives sought to develop new skills in individual young people through the creation of new school-wide (organizational) initiatives. The remainder of this section details the vision of change at these three levels and how groups enacted this vision through activities focused on social justice principles.

The visions of other groups fit more solidly into one category, such as McGuire's individual focus of providing peer-to-peer mediation. While this type of program could have some organizational vision as well of how to improve school climate or reduce behavior problems, these possible benefits were not discussed in the interviews and therefore the initiative was classified as having primarily an individual focus.

Change at the Systemic Level

Seven of the groups focused their work on addressing systemic issues of discrimination and inequities, including targeting racism, homophobia, and economic disparities. Midland's Campaigns for Justice and Hillside's Unity of Youth approached their focus on social injustice through a traditional form of organizing, sharing information and, at times, protest. A student leader at Unity of Youth explained, "We've joined the campaign

Table 9.2.   Social Justice Goals of the Youth-Adult Partnerships

Social Justice Focus	Groups	Goals
Systemic	College Center	Fostering dialogue across racial groups
	Hillside	Tempering racial tensions
	Hoover	Educating about gay rights and tolerance
	Latin	Educating peers on racism and student rights
	Midland	Stengthening youth voice in decision-making bodies
	Morgan	Raising awareness of inequities in society through peer education
	Sierra	Examining the structural inequities of their community
Organizational	College Center	Developing a unity council to facilitate within school communication across student groups and with the administration
	Great Valley	Improving school climate through the reduction of bullying
	Hillside	Improving school building conditions
	Highland	Creating a new school lunch program and a school business card program
	King	Creating formal structures for the input of student voice into the school decision-making process
	Whitman	Improve school climate through increasing communications between teachers and students
Individual	Great Valley	Increasing youth leadership and compassion for others to reduce bullying
	High Hills	Improving the self-esteem of Polynesian youth
	Highland	Fostering socially-responsible business skills in youth
	Latin	Providing peer counseling
	McGuire	Providing peer to peer mediation
	Morgan	Valuing the experiences of disadvantaged youth
	Sierra	Increasing youth leadership and sharing youth experiences

to help stop the high school exit exam. We're [also] trying to help some teachers who are getting transferred out of [our school]. And we are trying to get them [the district and state] to stop the budget cuts." Such initiatives were usually coordinated with youth-adult partnerships in other schools. Community-based organizations often took the lead in facilitating communication and planning for such events. Campaigns for Justice also took the importance of student voice and empowerment seriously through creating a series of campaigns aimed at education youth about their rights as citizens, lobbying for a student position on the district's school board, and fighting a community effort to impose a daytime curfew on youth between the times of 8:30 A.M. and 1:30 P.M.

Three of the groups working at the systems level (Hoover's Gay-Straight Alliance, Latin's Peer Support, and College Center's Unity Council) focused their attention on raising awareness of issues of tolerance and discrimination in their own schools. At Latin, the Peer Assistance group spent a semester researching questions of racism, classism, and what they called "nativism" (discrimination against immigrants) and "adultism" (discrimination against youth). The adult advisor explained that they looked at how these issues "connect in our school community and into systems of power." The following semester, these youth would present workshops on these topics to their peers. The shape of the workshop would be the decision of the youth. The advisor explains, "Because it's up to them what direction they'll go from here.... We're looking at doing a school-wide change project based on making presentations and getting a core group of youth talking about racism and classism at school."

College Center focused its efforts on creating a student unity council, which, according to its student leader, would be a "committee of all the clubs" in the school. The youth leader explained that the school has had a "huge problem for the last 30-plus years of African Americans and Latinos getting two or more F's. Last year, two-thirds of the freshman class got two or more F's, meaning they really wouldn't go on to being juniors, or sophomores." The purpose of the council would bring together two undergraduate representatives from each of the clubs in the school—many of which are ethnic clubs representing the incredible diversity in the school. In the words of the student leader of the project, "It's basically started an 'all-student union' on campus—a place to not only unify students, but to protect their rights; and a place where they could come in if they need help of any sort." Through dialogue and a common meeting place, the intention was to increase the voice of students to try to help to address the achievement gap problem in the school, to reduce racial tensions through a source of dialogue, and to provide a focus point for community celebrations.

Hoover High School, along with Morgan and Sierra High Schools created videos and written materials to articulate youth experiences. These personal stories highlighted the injustices experienced by these young people in their schools and their communities, including racism and intolerance. For example, Hoover High School's Gay-Straight Alliance worked on a video to share with their school and other schools. According to a student leader in the group the video is "about stereotypes and what it's like to be gay in high school." Sierra High School instead developed a video about the economic, racial, and social injustices of their neighborhood, specifically focusing on the prevalence of drug and alcohol abuse and domestic violence in their community. The adult advisor explained that the youth also

> want to highlight the lack of grocery stores in [their neighborhood] when there's all kinds of liquor stores. But you walk over the hill to [an affluent neighborhood], they have bakeries and coffee shops and … just the disparity. They ask the question, "How does a child feel when they grow up here as compared to over there?"

A youth member of the group added that the video sought not only to raise awareness of these disparities but also to talk about positive ways to address these inequities head on. The youth commented that they wanted the video "to let everybody know that there's other ways to deal with situations than with violence. Speech is powerful too … and trying to find out a lot of positive things that teens are doing out there."

Change at the Organizational Level

Four groups (College Center, King, Whitman, and Hillside) focused their energies on school reform. For these groups, the unit of change was the organization itself, advocating for improvements in school structures, policies and culture. For example, Hillside's Unity of Youth tackled the problem of inadequate bathroom facilities at their school. A youth leader in the group explained, "First we did a survey on what was wrong here on campus so out [it came three top themes]—security, too many substitutes, and clean bathrooms." The group chose to focus on bathrooms because, according to the student leader, "The bathrooms here at school weren't clean and they were never open.... So we asked students what was it that they needed and what they wanted the principal and staff to do about it." The group felt that the lack of adequate facilities was inappropriate and unfair to young people.

Highland's Free Enterprise group put their socially responsible business skills to work by creating many programs for their school and community including a program that brought local restaurants into the school to offer hot meals at lunch time. A student leader of the group explained,

> It's a completely student run business. Our mission is to provide food alternatives to on-campus meals while supporting local businesses. Because in the school year 2000–2001, we had a 72 percent truancy rate. We have an open campus during lunch but two years ago people weren't coming back.

The program not only increased student attendance, but it also helped to strengthen local businesses by increasing lunchtime sales and it also offered healthier and broader lunch options for the students at the school. Other programs run by the group included income tax assistance for elderly residents in the community and a student-designed business card initiative.

Student Forum at Whitman High School focused its efforts at the organizational level by seeking student participation school reform and to institute new programs and policies. The group eventually narrowed its focus to one school-wide issue—building communication and partnership school-wide between students and teachers. Students joined in the school's reform work, including participating in staff trainings on inquiry-based research and research groups on reading strategies. One student participant explained, "I'm in the 'English as a Second Language group' [where they focus on] trying to help students break into the reading habit. We shared different ways of teaching. I'm willing to give feedback on how this [strategy] doesn't work [and others do]." During these activities, Student Forum members served as experts on their classroom experience by providing teachers with feedback on how students might receive new pedagogical strategies. The students also shared their own experiences, both positive and negative, in Whitman classrooms.

King High School focused specifically on increasing student voice in the problem solving focus of the school by hosting a series of dialogues throughout the school year in which students shared their problems and concerns about the school. A youth leader of the effort explained, "In our school it gives the students a chance to speak their mind without limitations, without holding their breath." As a result of these discussions, the school increased the number of electives offered at the school. Morgan similarly focused on student voice but did so through the creation of a textbook that would reflect the lives and experiences of youth in their school. A youth on the project explained, "We're trying to get everybody's story—like an experience that you had in your life. Something happened to you or you went through something." The advisor explained that this book was needed because a lot of the things that they read in school don't relate to them.... They wanted a way for youth to understand themselves, to understand each other, that they all come from different paths of life and different circumstances. And for teachers to understand youth.

Thus, the sharing of youth experiences could help to both emphasize the value of the youth themselves and to educate their peers and teachers about both the diversity and commonality of the school.

Change at the Individual Level

Seven of the 13 groups emphasized change at the individual student level through such initiatives as peer counseling, conflict resolution, antibullying, and tutoring. Morgan and Latin High Schools worked on peer helping and mediation activities. A youth member of Peer Support at Latin High School explained,

> I'm involved in this program called Peer Theater. Every semester we learn a new topic that has to do with social issues that high schoolers go through, like drugs, peers, identity ... crises, and body image. Then we try to reach out to teach to other people in our school.... We have an assembly day when we perform [skits] throughout that day.

Another youth project leader of the same group described a second program at Latin called Peer Advocates, which pairs up a young person with a student who needs support. She explained that the youth

> meet once a week. They can talk about anything they want and the peer advocate offers support and different choices that they could decide on. They don't necessarily give them advice but listen ... and list options.... It's like a one-on-one kind of help stuff for that person.

Thus, this group worked on both peer education and peer mentoring as ways to help young people work through challenging issues.

McGuire High School's project instead focused on peer mediation and conflict resolution. A youth in the project explained the need for the project by explaining that McGuire "is actually a continuation school, and some of the kids here have a lot of problems ... with their friends and with their family outside of school [because of] drugs, fighting, and stuff like that." Student volunteers for the program received 16 hours of training from an outside organization to serve as mediators. An adult advisor of the group explained the delicate nature of preparing youth for conflict resolution. She explained:

> It's one thing to teach them how to do it. But a lot of it is doing it and making the mistakes. So we do a lot of mock situations and they've been able to see [what] could happen. It's been an excellent opportunity to address issues that already affect them personally and then also to train them how to deal with those things both as a peer but also as a member of a family or [as a] student.

Through direct experience, students both faced their own problems and learned how to help others.

Another group focused on reducing stereotyping and bullying behavior through an intervention approach. Working with a nonprofit organization, the group offered intense all day workshops for 100 or so students with the purpose of breaking down stereotypes and showing the commonalities among youth from different cliques and backgrounds. An adult coordinator of the program explained that the day has a three-step philosophy of "inclusion, influence and affection. You include them by doing an icebreaker that [connects] everybody; you teach them whatever the lesson is; and then you send them off with affection and love them up." Activities throughout the training include, according to the adult advisor, "breaking down those walls and stereotypes of what people think about." The training included opportunities for youth to apologize to others in the school and to acknowledge that they have been hurt by stereotyping themselves. The coordinator explained, "A lot of times kids get up and apologize to teachers, to friends, to kids they've teased. They make amends, and they say what they never want to see in their school again. It's a really, really powerful day."

Almost all of the groups in this study also discussed the need to strengthen the skills of young people in student voice initiatives so that they could work together to make a difference in their own lives and their communities. In this sample, youth in seven of the groups (more than half of all of the cases) received training from external organizations on issues such as leadership, youth rights, parliamentary procedure, conducting research, interacting with adults in power, goal setting, facilitation, and developing a work plan. According to the adult director of Highland's Business Enterprise, the young people learned "socially-responsible business and entrepreneurial skills" from a nonprofit organization whose mission was to foster entrepreneurship and to encourage the development of socially just businesses by training inner-city youth. Unity of Youth students instead received more general training on "how to be more organized and how to organize ourselves … like, 'You're talking to the media. How are you going to speak to them?' " according to a youth member. Five of the seven groups set aside time for internal trainings as well, including hosting all day retreats and weekend meetings at which a longer time could be devoted to building both general community and specific skills.

DISCUSSION

The findings in this chapter describe how school-based youth-adult partnerships worked on social justice issues on three levels—the systemic level by raising concerns about equity and discrimination, the organizational level, by making changes in schools and communities, and the individual level by fostering youth skills. While these three levels were separated in this chapter to articulate the types of goals of youth-adult partnerships, these goals were greatly interrelated for the groups in this study. The levels also appear to have a degree of directionality. While some schools began with an explicit focus on systemic social justice issues, groups focusing on youth leadership or school reform tended to move toward a focus on broader issues of equity and justice. By engaging in collective activities, their understanding of issues became more sophisticated, and their conversations became more honest.

Connection Between Individual and Systemic Issues

The groups experiences in this study suggest that the stronger the focus on fostering youth leadership, the more the work of the group moves toward social justice questions. A great overlap existed in the individual and systemic categories in this study, with four groups fitting in both categories. Indeed, an important lesson from this study is the importance of the social organizing phrase, "the personal is political."

An adult advisor of Morgan High School explained the connection between individual and systemic concerns by stating,

> This is a class where youth take over…. They lead. They decide what projects they want to do and what things they want to change. They want to be change makers. The job of the class is then how to enable these youth to feel that they can change their school and community.

Teaching youth the skills to problem solve and ask questions while bolstering their sense of agency and confidence to ask tough questions inevitably led groups to discussions about injustices and inequities in their community and around the world. According to Morgan's adult advisor, this process is one of enabling youth to find these skills within themselves. She explains,

From the start they understand they don't have ownership. Because we don't teach students to think for themselves or take, take the lead. So you need to ... facilitate for that to happen. You don't teach them; you don't make them. They make themselves.

One step in this enabling process was helping youth make connections between their own personal experiences and issues of race, class, and gender. An adult advisor of Unity of Youth explained her interpretation of how identity formation inherently is related to broader understandings of social structures and inequities. She discussed the importance of helping youth to understand their identity by:

having them learn to be empowered by their race and their class and not having to be ashamed of the fact that they're working class kids. [It's about] being clear about understanding what it is to be a girl in this society, being a young boy having a single mom most of your life. How do all those things affect how you feel power? We work off of community building principles of empowering young people ... to put out the kind of vision of the world that they want to live in. And to live in it.

The adult advisor of the Youth Taking Charge project at Sierra High School also noticed a strong change in the students in the group as they became more aware of the equity questions that arose through the creation of their video project. Sierra is an alternative high school that was in most cases a last chance school for students who were unable to succeed in traditional schools because of discipline problems and other academic concerns. The advisor commented, "The kids involved in it are changing [from] delinquent into activists. [They can see] how they got sucked into being delinquent and the criminal justice system through their upbringing—not just their family, but the community and the policies." The process of open discussion and the encouraging of youth to ask questions that lead to even deeper questions about inequities lends itself naturally to a social justice focus. It also helped young people to understand the connections between their problems and those of others in their community and around the world.

Connection between Organizational and Systemic Issues

For many of the groups in this study, the process of working on school change issues raises awareness of how disparities within a school are inevitably related to injustices in the broader community and in society at large. The principal at King High School noticed, for example, how student dialogues throughout the school year began to broaden from problems with bathrooms to larger inequities that were "political in nature—the distribution of books in the city; [and] why do schools in the hills get better books and better equipment?" Many other school-based projects observed a similar extension from school-focused issues to broader systemic problems. Unity of Youth's bathroom campaign focused on improving the conditions of bathrooms at their school, but it also served as an exclamation point for drawing attention to the marked lack of adequate school facilities in poor communities. Similarly, as a result of Business Enterprise's school lunch program at Highland High School in which they invited local restaurants to sell meals at lunch time, the group extended its focus from school-based concerns to thinking more deeply about the root causes of economic conditions in their neighborhood and the consequences of poor nutrition among their peers. At Latin High school, the Peer Support group's discussion of concerns in the school also extended to a broader examination of youth rights. The group's advisor explained,

> One of the things that [youth] were really frustrated about was [that] when class starts, some teachers would lock their doors. In the process of finding out about student rights we learned that they aren't allowed, because it denies your right to a free public education. They can lock their doors but if you knock they have to let you in, because they can't deny you the ability to be educated.

By looking at specific issues that concerned students in the school, this examination of student rights extended to an investigation of the broader penal code and the types of rights that youth have in society.

CONCLUSION

The 13 youth-adult partnerships in this study demonstrated the potential ways in which students collaborate with adults to examine issues of equity and injustice that they experience in their lives, in their schools, in their communities, and in broader society. The data from this study suggest that social justice conversations tend to begin at either the organizational level or individual level as a stepping stone toward broader discussions at the systemic level. Student voice initiatives therefore could serve an important role in facilitating this progression of thinking about social justice issues in school settings.

The cases further indicate that when youth share in leading efforts to discuss and address social justice issues, they can bring a renewed passion and attention to the process that adults alone rarely do. Youth also bring attention to the need for working on specific projects to address these problems, such as intolerance, bullying, and the inclusion of voices in decision making. While administrators and teachers undoubtedly share in these concerns, the pressing focus on student outcomes, accountability and other important school tasks can tend to relegate such discussions of social justice to the back burner in many schools. This study therefore has important implications for research on distributed leadership (Elmore, 2000; Lashway, 2003) since it points to the specific value of students' contributions to a focus on these matters. Through future connections between educational leadership and student voice/youth-adult partnership research, scholars can strengthen our understanding of the potential for addressing social justice issues by broadening of distributed educational leadership to include youth at the table.

APPENDIX

Interview Protocol for Youth and Adults

Tell me about how things are going this year with your program.
What has changed from last year?
What is the purpose of your organization? (Making change? Youth development? Youth assistance? Something else?)

What kind of support do adults need to do this work?
What kind of supports do youth need to do this work?

What do teachers and students in the school think about your group?
How do they perceive your work?
Who are the group's biggest allies (principals, teachers, outside non-profit, other)

Who makes decisions in your group? Who is a leader?
What types of skills do young people need to engage in the work that you do?
What type of skills do adults need?

Have you seen any changes in the school as a result of their work yet?
Have you seen any changes in the youth involved?

What are your plans for continuing your work after the grant ends?

REFERENCES

Becker, H. S. (1998). *Tricks of the trade: How to think about research while you're doing it.* Chicago: The University of Chicago Press.

Camino, L. A. (2000). Youth-adult partnerships: Entering new territory in community work and research. *Applied Developmental Science, 4*(Supplement Issue), 11–20.

Elmore, R. (2000). *Building a new structure for school leadership.* Washington, DC: The Albert Shanker Institute.

Fielding, M. (2001). Students as radical agents of change. *Journal of Educational Change, 2*(2), 123–141.

Fine, M. (1991). *Framing dropouts: Notes on the politics of an urban high school.* Albany, NY: State University of New York Press.

Ginwright, S. A. (2005). On urban ground: Understanding African-American intergenerational partnerships in urban communities. *Journal of Community Psychology, 33*(1), 101–110.

Glaser, B., & Strauss, A. (1967). *The discovery of grounded theory.* Chicago: Aldine.

Goodwillie, S. (Ed.). (1993). *Voices from the future: Our children tell us but violence in America.* New York: Crown.

Johnson, J. H. (1991). *Student voice motivating students through empowerment* (No. ED337875). Eugene: Oregon School Study Council.

Jones, K. (2004). *An assessment of community-based youth-adult relationships.* Unpublished doctoral dissertation, The Pennsylvania State University.

Jones, K., & Perkins, D. (2004). Youth-adult partnerships. In C. B. Fisher & R. M. Lerner (Eds.), *Applied developmental science: An encyclopedia of research, policies, and programs.* Thousand Oaks, CA: SAGE.

Kirshner, B., O'Donoghue, J. L., & McLaughlin, M. W. (Eds.). (2003). *New directions for youth development: Youth participation improving institutions and communities.* San Francisco: Jossey-Bass.

Kushman, J. W. (Ed.). (1997). *Look who's talking now: Student views of learning in restructuring schools* (Vol. ED028257). Washington, DC: Office of Educational Research and Improvement.

Larson, R., Walker, K., & Pearce, N. (2005). A comparison of youth-driven and adult-driven youth programs: Balancing inputs from youth and adults. *Journal of Community Psychology, 33*(1), 57–74.

Lashway, L. (2003). Distributed leadership [Special issue]. *Research Roundup, 19*(4).

Levin, B. (2000). Putting students at the centre in education reform. *International Journal of Educational Change, 1*(2), 155–172.

Lincoln, Y. S., & Guba, E. G. (1985). *Naturalistic inquiry.* Beverly Hills, CA: SAGE.

Miles, M. B., & Huberman, A. M. (1994). *Qualitative data analysis.* Thousand Oaks, CA: SAGE.

Mitra, D. (2001). Opening the floodgates: Giving students a voice in school reform. *Forum, 43*(2), 91–94.

Mitra, D. L. (2003). Student voice in school reform: Reframing student-teacher relationships. *McGill Journal of Education, 38*(2), 289–304.

Mitra, D. L. (2004). The significance of students: Can increasing "student voice" in schools lead to gains in youth development? *Teachers College Record, 106*(4), 651–688.

National Research Council. (2002). *Community programs to promote youth development.* Washington, DC: National Academy Press.

O'Connor, C., & Camino, L. (2005). *Youth participation in research and evaluation: Outcomes for youth. Youth and adult leaders for program excellence.* Madison, WI: Community Youth Connection, University of Wisconsin Extension.

Rudduck, J., Day, J., & Wallace, G. (1997). Students' perspectives on school improvement. In A. Hargreaves (Ed.), *Rethinking educational change with heart and mind* (The 1997 ASCD Year Book) (pp. 73–91). Alexandria, VA: Association for Supervision and Curriculum Development.

Stake, R. E. (1995). *The art of case study research.* Thousand Oaks, CA: SAGE.

Strauss, A., & Corbin, J. (1990). *Basics of qualitative research: Grounded theory procedures and techniques.* Newbury Park, CA: SAGE.

Thorkildsen, T. A. (1994). Toward a fair community of scholars: Moral education as the negotiation of classroom practices. *Journal of Moral Education, 23*(4), 371–385.

Wehlage, G. G., Rutter, R. A., Smith, G. A., Lesko, N., & Fernandez, R. R. (1989). *Reducing the risk: Schools as communities of support.* London: Falmer Press.

Zeldin, S. (2004). Youth as agents of adult and community development: Mapping the processes and outcomes of youth engaged in organizational governance. *Applied Developmental Science, 8*(2), 75–90.

Zeldin, S., Camino, L., & Mook, C. (2005). The adoption of innovation in youth organizations: creating the conditions for youth-adult partnerships. *Journal of Community Psychology, 33*(1), 121–135.

CHAPTER 10

LEADERSHIP FOR SOCIAL JUSTICE AND MORALITY

Collaborative Partnerships, School-Linked Services and the Plight of the Poor

Anthony H. Normore and Roger I. Blanco

Despite the educational reform initiatives outlined in programs similar to and in the American 2000 plan, conspicuously absent is any in-depth discussion regarding the growing rate of poverty among youth in inner cities. It is a poverty which engulfed one in seven youth in 1970, one in six in 1980, one in five in 1990, and one in four in 2000. Today there are more than 13 million children living in the below-poverty bracket. Among the critical issues that have received some attention about poverty in inner-city schools are: (a) the demographic factors of the disadvantaged students and their urban communities; (b) collaborative efforts for school-linked services and delivery systems; and (c) social justice and moral responsibilities of school leaders and the urban communities which they serve. Drawing from a review of literature, this article posits that leadership for social justice and morality is imperative as advocates commit to collaborative partnerships for integrating services and delivery of programs for poverty-stricken school populations.

Leadership for Social Justice: Promoting Equity and Excellence Through Inquiry and Reflective Practice, pp. 215–240
Copyright © 2008 by Information Age Publishing
215

Poverty among youth has been called the father of social failure, job inse-
curity, emotional imbalance, and social rejection, even though poverty-
stricken parents have high expectations for their youngsters. In 2002, Williams-Boyd reported that there were more than 32 million Americans who
had no health insurance. Further research indicates that there are
approximately 53 million Americans who will face these hardships during
2007 (Jazzar & Algozzine, 2007). Lacking health-care benefits harms individuals and their families. According to Blanco (2003) out of the 48 million school children in the United States, more than 13 million were
living in the below-poverty bracket.

The treatment of poor students in American schools remains an intractable problem of the school reform movement. Brown (2003) maintains
that, along with minorities, students from low income families invariably
crowd the lower-level academic tracks, which has led for community-
based leadership in schools to commit to improving this situation.
According to Brown, "a society stratified by unequal positions of power,
income, and social status can hardly alter social and economic mobility
through its schools. It can merely reproduce the existing inequalities"
(p. 75). Gordon (2004) argues that children who historically have been
economically disadvantaged and undereducated should have access to the
basic human resource development capital that supports development of
academic abilities, including good health, intellectually stimulating life
experiences, and a network of significant people who have the knowledge
and experience to nurture, guide, and support them in their academic
pursuits.

No proposed education reform plans to date have addressed the
differences in levels of family or community capacity to exert aggressive
measures on behalf of culturally-deprived children (i.e., those marginalized by the dominant classes) in urban neighborhoods infested with
destruction, defeatism, and damaging physical and social health. Urban
schools have numerous challenges and social issues that derive from the
high concentrations of families whose social mobility is limited by poverty
and minority status. We contend that America has failed to offer substantive measures regarding the poor beyond remediation and meals as well as
beyond deficiency-oriented rather than school-discriminatory programs.
Cultural and racial diversity and the plight of the poor demand that
schools embrace a revised and enlightened view of true community leadership that advocates and achieves unity and respect for differences. However, in order for such an endorsement to be effective, school leaders and
their communities must engage in leadership where they reconceptualize
their practice based on social justice agendas, specific moral capacities and
responsibilities. If urban schools become more racial, ethnic, and
socioeconomic specific, the major issue for future leaders will be to dem-

onstrate the greatest respect for the parents and nurture the abilities of children in these schools by utilizing the leadership most desired by their respective communities. In other words, it becomes morally imperative to commit to integrating services (i.e., school-linked) whereby the school itself serves as a link between service delivery systems and families. Integrated services occur when these services are available at a school or a nearby site in partnership with a school and involve a coordinated delivery of health, education, prevention, and social services designed to improve the quality of life for individuals and families in order to effectively address the needs of all students.

The purpose of this article is to explore social justice leadership and the moral responsibilities of school leaders and their communities as they advocate for the needs of students from low income families. Combing through common themes and patterns in the literature, a list of implications is provided that can assist leaders in urban education systems to adequately address the social, cultural, and academic needs of all students. We begin by presenting the context of 400 years of historical developments on poverty in America. Since 400 years of history can hardly be captured in an article of this length, we highlight critical events within the 400 year time period to help build the case for community-school-based leadership and education that spans the multiple needs of poor urban children and families. This is followed by a presentation of the demographic factors of disadvantaged school communities. Then we discuss social justice leadership Next, collaborative partnerships and school-linked services, including large-scale full service schools and delivery programs are discussed, followed by a discussion about the need for collaborative partnerships to engage in moral leadership efforts to meet the social, cultural, and academic needs of students. Finally, we offer a summary and conclusion.

HISTORICAL PERSPECTIVES: CONTEXT OF SOCIAL JUSTICE

The fracturing of the American family has resulted in two distinct perspectives on public education: some people believe that schools should do more and provide many of the services heretofore provided by the family whereas others believe that schools should simply return to teaching the "basics." Essentially, children cannot and will not reach their academic potential unless they are reasonably prepared to learn; thus, the concept of full-service schools exemplifies the need to rechannel responsibilities toward local communities, families, and individuals without having to change education through centralized mandates. In support of this assertion, Kowalski (2004) suggests that leaders ought to, therefore, "rekindle a very close relationship between schools and their community of learners;

they need to facilitate rather than dictate; and they need to be respectful and pro-active to public opinion and issues of public concern" (p. 42).

Based on the Poor Law of 1601 in the United States, towns and villages provided support services to local community families and friends in need. The number of transients and poor people grew, as did the lack of concern and care by those who had homes and jobs. Undergirding this construction of social policy lay a profound operational ambivalence regarding the role of society in service to the poor (Kagan, 1993, p. 4). In the late 1800s the Charity Organization Societies were established to coordinate the often overlapping work of hundreds of smaller service groups. In the early 1900s the progressive movement called attention to the plight of the downtrodden, seen as the imperiled generation, by bringing health and social services into the schools. According to Hunter (1905, p. 209), parental rejection of health care was viewed as evidence of ignorance. Curiously enough dentists touted the need for dental hygiene to the extent that like doctors, they saw their work as a "cure-ill, claiming that eliminating caries would bring good health, lessen school failure, and even prevent delinquency" (Tyack, 1997, p. 21). At the time many philan- thropic women's clubs provided free and inexpensive lunches because they felt hungry children were inattentive and could not learn. They pushed schools to provide free or reduced meals, not as charity but rather as part of the service of the school. They also paid teachers to provide experimental learning experiences such as field trips, plays, museum and park visits and trips to the country (Tyack, 1992). However, there is little indication that this level of service was inclusive of all people. The demand soon became far higher than the supply of service.

By 1910 over 300 cities offered medical inspections, and, by 1920, most cities with a large concentration of immigrants provided medical and dental services at the school. In these early days of community-based social services at the school, reformers felt they knew better what the immigrant family needed than the family itself. Therefore, the family was approached from a "deficit model" (Melaville, Blanck, & Asayesh, 1993) indicating that immigrant families were deficient in their knowledge of proper health care for their children, of the civic responsibilities and moral values of their newly adopted country, and even unaware of how to rear their children. By the late 1930s the number of summer school pro- grams began to decrease and health, human, and social services became less important in light of the emphasis placed on school curriculum (Sed- lak & Church, 1982). At the end of this decade, "vacation schools" became institutionalized and changed from enrichment programs for the poor to general population sessions in which students who have failed academic work during the year could repeat courses. Guidance counselors no longer linked students with work opportunities but began to advise them about appropriate courses to take and what academic track to follow. In the 1940s, the government provided child care as women were drawn into the male-abandoned workforce. Yet, following World War II, these services were deemed unnecessary as women returned to the home which left the provision of other services disorganized and sporadic. During "The Great Society" of the 1950s, however, the Civil Rights Movement became the single most influential mobilizer of services and support for the poor and for minorities. School psychologists and social workers were once again added to the school staff in an effort to reduce the high number of high school drop outs.

Many of the services intended for the poor in the period of 1920–1960 disproportionately went to the rich because of local property taxes. During this period of social movement and cultural awareness, when attention was particularly paid to previously ignored groups (i.e., women, Hispanics, African Americans, Aborigines, disabled), education became a dynamic force in the continued War on Poverty. The 1960s saw a flurry of legislation with the establishment of Community Action Agencies intended to coordinate services at the local level leading the forefront. The significant Elementary and Secondary Education Act of 1965, with focus on the poor through Title I (i.e., ensuring that all children have a fair, equal, and significant opportunity to obtain a high quality education and reach, at minimum, proficiency on challenging state academic achievement standards and academic assessments) pushed the creation of Head Start programs. These programs provided health care, nutrition, and preparation for low-income preschoolers which continued to strengthen the participation of parents in compensatory programs (Williams-Boyd, 2002, p. 7).

With a return emphasis on the country's economic competitiveness in the 1970s, the focus was placed on academic standards, heightened graduation requirements, and visible evidence of progress on state-mandated tests. The lack of attention to issues of poverty and equity once again resulted in the muting of the dialogue related to linked-services. In the 1980s, once again, the federal government turned away from parent participation requirements in favor of more state and local government control. Emphasis was placed on the intensification of school requirements rather than on the restructuring of social services. In response to the fragmentation of services of the preceding decade, the number of linked-services initiatives reached new heights in the 1990s. These services represented a holistic, community-based, pro-family perspective with interagency case plans, case management, de-categorized funding, and co-location of services (Williams-Boyd, 2002, p. 8).

In the new millennium, the No Child Left Behind Act (NCLB) of 2002 redefined the role of the federal government in K–12 education. It has been touted as the broadest bill since the Elementary and Secondary Education Act of 1965. Proponents of the bill maintain it will streamline programs and target funds for existing programs for poor children. School personnel, however, experience the bill as "No Child Shall Go Untested" (Blanco, 2004, p. 10). According to Murray (2006), NCLB takes a giant step toward nationalizing elementary and secondary education for holding schools accountable. Murray states:

> It pushes classrooms toward relentless drilling, not something that inspires able people to become teachers or makes children eager to learn. It holds good students hostage to the performance of the least talented, at a time when the economic future of the country depends more than ever on the performance of the most talented. The one aspect of the act that could have inspired enthusiasm from me, promoting school choice, has fallen far short of its hopes. The only way to justify NCLB is through compelling evidence that test scores are improving. (para. 2)

Few would argue that "accountability" is NCLB's favorite word, and the Department of Education is holding school systems accountable for improvements in test scores (see Murray, 2006) with a focus on "proficiency". Murray further reiterates:

> Conceptually, "proficiency" has no objective meaning that lends itself to a cutoff. Administratively, the NCLB penalties for failure to make adequate progress give the states powerful incentives to make progress as easy to show as possible. A pass percentage throws away valuable information, telling you whether someone got over a bar, but not how high the bar was set or by how much the bar was cleared. Most importantly: If you are trying to measure progress in closing group differences, a comparison of changes in pass percentages is inherently misleading. (para. 7)

Research indicates that the federal government continues to reward and punish school systems across the United States based on changes in pass percentages (e.g., Blanco, 2004; Brown, 2003; Murray, 2006). According to Murray:

> It is an uninformative measure for many reasons, but when it comes to measuring one of the central outcomes sought by No Child Left Behind, the closure of the achievement gap that separates poor students from rich, Latino from white, and black from white, the measure is beyond uninformative. It is deceptive. (para. 17)

We now turn to the demographic factors of the disadvantaged. Embedded within the demographics are the complex issues of inner-city communities and factors that marginalize students at schools.

DEMOGRAPHICS OF THE DISADVANTAGED

The "culture of poverty" posits the poor in a microculture which frames its own values and dimensions. As W. E. B. Du Bois predicted in 1958, the line between the "haves" and "have-nots" has become the "real Achilles' heel" of today's society (Gordon, 2004, p. 2). The young become the socially disadvantaged for they are not only imperiled materially but also emotionally and psychologically. Likewise, they are the educationally marginalized, not only due to poverty but also due to minority status, for they cannot take full advantage of available educational opportunities nor are resources afforded to them in an equitable fashion. Research indicates that in 1999, for instance, 20% of Hispanic students, 38% of American Indian/Alaska Native students, 13% of Asian/Pacific Islander students, 35% of Black, non-Hispanic Students, and 15% of White, non-Hispanic students had been suspended or expelled at some point between Grades 7–12. In 2001, approximately 12% of all children were assigned to special education program from which 25% were African American boys. Placement in "special programs" has far-reaching effects. Once children are "labeled" or "expelled," their chances of graduating on time and going on to higher education are greatly reduced (National Center for Education Statistics [NCES], 2003, p. 2). Urban minority and poor students are often overrepresented in special education, and these urban special education classes have been shown to fail to benefit students (Kavale, 1995; Kavale & Forness, 2000; MacMillan & Siperstein, 2002), particularly minority and poor students (Hunter & Donahoo, 2003) who are placed, but may be ill-served.

According to NCES (2003, p. 8), at least one in six children had no health care while nearly 13.5 million children lived in poverty—2 million more than a decade before. Around a quarter of Blacks and 21.8% of Hispanics are living in poverty (Morrison, 2006). Some 17.6% of children under 18 and one in five of those under 6 live in poverty, higher than for any other age group. "Among African Americans the problem correlates primarily to the inner-city and single mothers," said Michael Tanner of CATO Institute, a free-market think tank in Washington. He noted that Black people also suffer disproportionately from poor education and lower quality jobs (see Morrison, 2006). Poverty, socioeconomic class, and deprivation account for poor performances in urban schools to the extent that children from poor families are three times more likely to drop out of school than children from more advantaged homes (Hahn & Danzberger, 1987). Living in substandard housing and foregoing utilities, telephone, plumbing, child care, health care, and transportation, children of the poor often come to school hungry, fatigued, suffering from headaches, dizziness, abuse, and malnutrition leaving them unable to concentrate on learning.

Policymakers in demographically diverse states (i.e., Texas, Georgia, Florida, California, North Carolina) acknowledge that community and school populations are changing. Demographic data in these states highlight a dramatic growth in minorities, second-language learners, recent immigrants, and economically disadvantaged students (see Dantley & Tillman, 2006). This in turn points to the need to address what diverse students need Despite the demographic realities, "racial and ethic minority groups continue to suffer educational disenfranchisement, such as disproportional high dropout rates, educational underachievement in K–12, and inequitable access to and retention in college" (Marshall & Oliva, 2006, p. 6).

Alone schools cannot adapt to the aggressive changing demands in the demographic, economic, political, and social welfare arenas. Alone no single institution has the resources or the capacity to address such issues. Educators recognize that poor children bring more than educational needs to the classroom, needs which left unmet leave little room for learning (Delpit & Kilgour-Dowdy, 2002). The stark reality of today's youth is that children are surrounded and imperiled by drugs, gangs, violence, family dissolution and stress, financial hardship, and social discrepancy. Other factors which place children at-risk include an increase in the enrollment of minority and limited-English-proficiency children in schools. Such is the case of one inner city senior high school in south Florida, whose student body is more than 80% Haitian and to whom the state of Florida has labeled not only as a "failing" school but also as a "quadruple F school" (i.e., 4 consecutive years of receiving an "F" grade) based on the results of the Florida Comprehensive Achievement Test and the State of Florida Department of Education criteria in grading the adequate yearly progress of schools (Miami-Dade County Public Schools, 2005). There are 38 additional low-performing ("failing") schools in the same school district—all inner city. According to Weisglass (2001), these standardized tests can be considered a form of "institutionalized racism" (p. 218) because they lend credibility to policies that have denied, and continue to deny, minorities and poor students equal access to educational and job opportunities. The business of education is not about testing children until they fail but rather a change in family, community, and social structures (Williams & Parker, 2003). We now commonly speak of losing a wide band of poor children to early death, lengthy incarceration, joblessness, or one form of misery or another. Noguera (2004) suggests that "there is a direct link between education and incarceration. The more money the USA government spends on incarceration, the less it spends on education." Noguera raises questions: Why are we modeling schools after prisons? What are schools doing to keep children out of prison? Exclusion, rising rates of poverty, and exploitation of minorities continue to be issues; segregation replaced exclusion—12 million people of color are still considered second class citizens in the United States; anger has resulted out of frustration with confinements; and, incarceration is replacing segregation (Noguera, 2004).

Pluralistic America no longer has a dominant nuclear family. People on welfare are increasingly Black, female, and youthful. Parental engagement with children has been altered by work schedules, salary problems, and family structures. Unfortunately, parental involvement continues to reflect socioeconomic status with higher status parents more likely to be involved. Tillman (2003) suggests that school leaders take an active role as leaders for social justice in facilitating parental involvement so that

> the life chances of disadvantaged children can be significantly enhanced by effective leadership, school leaders who care and are committed to their success, and parents who are given every opportunity to exercise their right to full participation in their children's education. (p. 311)

LEADERSHIP FOR SOCIAL JUSTICE

Recent commemorations of the 50th anniversary of the *Brown v. Board of Education* (i.e., the 1954 decision of the U.S. Supreme Court took scientific research into account in issuing this landmark ruling for desegregation of schools across America) and the 40th anniversary of the Civil Rights Act (i.e., the 1964 Civil Rights Act made racial discrimination in public places, such as theaters, restaurants and hotels, illegal in America, and required employers to provide equal employment opportunities) have emphasized how movements for social justice have helped to define American history. Furthermore, these commemorations have continued to serve as catalysts to refocus thinking on how school leaders have become social justice advocates and activists. According to Dantley and Tillman (2006), discussions about social justice in the field of education have typically framed the concept of social justice around several issues including race, diversity, poverty, marginalization, gender, and spirituality. These authors add age, ability, and sexual orientation to the discourse.

The discourse of social justice and leadership are inextricably linked which begs the question if there exists any one definition for social justice leadership. Some research (e.g., Bogotch, 2005) insists that social justice has no one specific meaning. Rather, "its multiple a posterori meanings emerge[d] differently from experiences and contexts" (p. 7). Bogotch zeros in on a key component of social justice by stating that "social justice, like education, is a deliberate intervention that requires the moral use of power" (p. 2) and concludes that it is "both much more than what we currently call democratic schooling and community education, and much less than what we hold out as the ideals of progressing toward a just and democratic society and a new humanity worldwide" (p. 8). Marshall and Oliva (2006) assert that social justice theorists and activists focus inquiry on how institutional norms, theories and practices in schools and in society lead to social, political, economic, and educational inequities. Furman and Shields (2005) argue the "need for social justice to encompass education that is not only just, democratic, emphatic, and optimistic, but also academically excellent" (as cited in Firestone & Riehl, 2005, p. 123). Starratt (2004) proposes a multidimensional ethical approach for leaders with a social justice agenda. He bases his approach on the combination of ethics of care, justice and critique and posits that school leaders give serious consideration to the ways in which students, particularly those from marginalized groups (i.e., racial and ethnic minorities, poor, gay, lesbian, female students), are socialized in the school setting (more on this further along in the article). Lee and McKerrow (2005) define social justice as "not only by what it is but also by what it is not, namely injustice. By seeking justice, we anticipate the ideal. By questioning injustice, we approach it. Integrating both, we achieve it" (p. 1). The second dimension focuses on the practice of social justice: Individuals for social justice seek to challenge political, economic and social structures that privilege some and disadvantage others in the name of democracy, equity, care, and compassion. They challenge unequal power relationships based on gender, social class, race, ethnicity, religion, disability, sexual orientation, language, and other systems of oppression.

Care and compassion are not enough given the demographics of poverty and its complexities. Coming to school hungry or being abused at home places a child at serious risk of not being successful in school. However, care for the emotional, social, physical, and academic needs of students, parents, and community members can lead to the combined and coordinated partnership efforts of an array of educators and community members who act as advocates for school-linked services. The concept of full-service schools (schools that are prepared to meet the needs of the child, including mental health, medical, dental, social, and nutritional assistance), exemplifies the creation and nurturing of community leadership and collaborative efforts for urban communities in which, as Sergiovanni (1994) suggests, children are provided with human and social capital. Although examples of successful full-service school services exist in part in a few schools throughout the United States (e.g., Wayne County Public Schools in North Carolina), these schools serve only a miniscule fraction of the school children in need of these services across America

(Jazzar & Algozzine, 2007). Throughout the literature, there is no indication that any full-service program meets all the needs of a child, or that this is even possible—at least not in the United States. However, literature indicates that a keen interest in forming full-service schools exists more now than ever (Dryfoos, 2004; Evans, Axelrod, & Langberg, 2004; Hunter et al., 2005; Jazzar & Algozzine, 2007; Nabors, Leff, & Power, 2004).

SCHOOL-LINKED SERVICES

A fundamental question for school leaders and communities to address is how one-in-three "at-risk" youth in school can be reclaimed. How can the precipitating problems such as poverty, premature parenthood, substance abuse, unemployment, and homelessness be addressed so children can learn and be successful in schools? What supports do families need in order to raise their children to be educationally and emotionally ready for school? What is the role of educational leaders in this process? Are there moral responsibilities and obligations of community-based leadership to the family and to the school?

The ambitiousness of the American 2000 Education Strategy (i.e., children coming to schools ready to learn) can only be achieved if schools critically examine the extent to which they serve as catalytic points of contact for children and families in need of support and services beyond the confines of the present school configuration; and whether government provides the resources, authority, and impetus to deal with social justice (Levy & Shepardson, 1992; Levy, Kagan, & Copple, 1992). Goals 2000: Educate America Act established a framework in which to identify world-class academic standards to measure student progress, and to provide the support that students may need to meet the standards. The Act codified in law the six original education goals concerning school readiness, school completion, student academic achievement, leadership in math and science, adult literacy, and safe and drug-free schools. It is the fourth goal of American 2000, however, that charged the community, not just the institution of school, to be the context in which learning takes place. Garvin and Young (1994) maintained that linking delivery systems will help prepare and keep children in school; it will lessen the stigma associated with seeking assistance, and most importantly, it can positively affect the ways in which school personnel interact with families.

According to Evans, Axelrod, and Langberg (2004) and Jazzar and Algozinne (2007) full-service schools ought to be discussed in just about every sector in community as a way of thinking and acting that recognizes the central role of schools in communities—and the power of working together for a common good. It is appropriate that partnerships throughout the learning communities (i.e., schools, colleges, universities, social services, businesses, school districts, parks and recreation departments, child-and-family agencies, museums and zoos, hospitals and health clinics, YM/WCA's, local United Way, Girls and Boy Scout chapters, forestry, police and fire departments, and more) engage moral action and social justice advocacy in diminishing the dividing line between the "haves" and "have nots." Nabors, Leff, and Power (2004) assert that community partnerships and educational leadership are the foundational forces upon which education is perceived as the foundation of democracy. Jazzar and Algozzine (2007) reiterate that when those living in democracy have had needs, education has responded affirmatively. It is only right for educational leaders and their communities to respond as moral leadership role models once again to create a climate, culture and community ethic that exemplifies the very values that they espouse (Fullan, 2003; Furman, 2004; Normore, 2004). As leaders act, so leaders instruct, guide, lead, and commit to delivering adequate services.

Service delivery. The problem is not so much service supply, but rather the service delivery. Rather than being driven by the needs of children and families, too frequently services are regulated by bureaucratic formalities, funding restrictions, legislative mandates, and professional structures. Constrained by funding requirements or by their other obligations schools and helping institutions engage in crisis-intervention and treatment services rather than in preventive assistance, and even then they work alone rather than in force with each other (Crowson & Boyd, 1993; Melaville, Blanck, & Asayesh, 1993). Needs cut across categories of services to embrace health, mental health, education, employment, housing, nutrition, and social services. However, the neediest children are the ones who get "punished" either by humiliation and/or isolation. The fact is that the most severely affected families typically live in a conflicted community, one which presents weak labor markets, substandard schools, unsafe and deteriorating neighborhoods which are characterized by violence, drugs, and dissolution (Blanco, 2004).

Typically, services are built on a deficit-model, or on what is wrong with the family. From the outset, this places the family in a disparaging position, and poses the case worker as the sole expert. The family soon learns the road to assistance is paved with acquiescence to the provider's suggestions rather than laid with the bricks made of the toil and soil of the family's true needs (Melaville et al., 1993). The proponents of school-linked services believe poor education, health and social outcomes for children result in part from the inability of current services systems to respond in a timely, coordinated, and comprehensive fashion to the multiple and interconnected needs of a child and her or his family (Packard Foundation, 1992, p. 8). Tillman (2003) suggests that "there is a direct link between the active involvement of parents and the educational success of students, particularly in large urban school districts" (p. 295). She maintains that leadership for urban school districts should focus on various elements including: (a) community and social service agencies that provide services for children, and particularly those that service urban children and their families, (b) broaden the term parent to include other family members or legal guardians, (c) design ways to communicate with "hard to reach" parents, and (d) get rid of deficit theorizing and replace it with family values and culture applicable to the context and community (p. 302).

As stated by Sergiovanni (1994, p. xiii), "The need for community is universal. It creates a sense of belonging, continuity, of being connected to others and to ideas and values that make our lives meaningful and significant." Society and the public schools are inextricably intertwined, therefore, forces us to consider Epstein's model which suggests that "the highest level of parental involvement occurs when the resources of the community and parents are integrated with those of the school in a total effort centered on the child" (as cited in Casanova, 1996, p. 30).

The United States has enjoyed a rich history of providing noneducational services at school sites. From the aid given colonial-day immigrants and medical and health services provided in the early 1900s—efforts to acculturate the waves of poor immigrant children and families, to the full-service community schools of the early years in the new millennium, the school has served in various forms as the hub of integrated services for the local community (Morrill, 1992). Gomby and Larson (1992) state:

> In a school-linked approach to integrating services for children, (a) services are provided to children and their families through a collaboration among schools, health care providers, and social services agencies; (b) the schools are among the central participants in planning and governing the collaborative effort; and (c) the services are provided at, or are coordinated by personnel located at, the school or a site near the school. Most often, the school-linked approach requires agencies that typically provide health and social services off the school site to move some of their staff and/or services to the school. Although school personnel are actively involved in identifying children who need services, they are not typically the actual providers of the services. (p. 7)

To the degree that integrated services are successful is the amount of success schools experience in forming collaborations. Currently in the United States, schools have begun forming collaborations with families and communities to support school improvement efforts and student achievement. These authors maintain that schools have been linked with a variety of community partners for recreation, presentations, fairs, and other activities. According to Jazzar and Algozinne (2007),

> every professional working with the same child, adult, and family will need to be engaged in cooperative and synchronized efforts ... that the unity of purpose will need to be grounded in an understanding of the value of relationships ... simply put, "working together, works!" (p. 225)

In this capacity, to reiterate earlier messages in this article, it is appropriate for schools, school leaders, their partnerships, and the communities in which they serve, to exercise their moral obligations, responsibilities, and actions to ensure that all students are provided with education of the highest quality and on an equitable playing field. Hence, we argue that this action-oriented leadership is a moral and ethical imperative that supports partnerships and collaborative efforts.

ENHANCING COLLABORATIVE PARTNERSHIPS: ETHICAL LEADERSHIP

Given the decline of traditional social structures (i.e., stable family life, intergenerational influence, introduction of wealth of diversity, and the growth of cities), a shared value system cannot be presumed; if indeed one ever could (Normore, 2004). Due to the breakdown of traditional values we can no longer count on these to guide educational leaders and the communities in which they serve. In a dynamic, globally-linked world, values-systems, moral responsibilities, obligations, and actions involve practices and policies that incorporate their dynamism into the work of school leaders as instructional and transformational.

Important to this component of the discussion is a growing body of research that emphasizes the significance of moral and ethical leadership. This form of leadership can enhance collaborative partnerships if interdependent efforts are to impact the quality of education for all students. Collaborative partnerships are needed because no one educational leader can achieve his or goal maximally and meet the accountabilities efficiently without the collaborative support of others (Jazzar & Algozinne, 2007). Edyburn, Higgins, and Boone (2005) assert that professions and organizations will collaborate out of practical necessity while reflecting their self-interest. As common ground is developed, these collaborators will also develop norms and procedures for reciprocity. For example, according to Jazaar and Algozzine (2007), the school is well served when collaborative partners prepare children and youth to come to school ready and able to learn ... in turn, collaborative partners will be supported and reinforced when children and youth succeed in school ... each system improves and gets stronger because of its new boundary relationships and exchanges. (p. 228)

Few would argue that the business of education is to ethically prepare all children to become responsible adults and productive citizens. Alvy and Robbins (2005) and Brooks and Normore (2005) assert that leaders who are committed to ethical leadership make an unwavering moral commitment to behave justly, encourage and promote student success, facilitate and support teacher growth, and foster quality relationships throughout the school community. Beyond acting on clear-cut issues of right versus wrong (i.e., enforcing discipline policies even-handedly), it is morally and ethically imperative that school leaders facilitate the teaching and learning process to make a positive difference in the life of each student in the school. This moral imperative, according to Fullan (2003), is what makes school leadership a calling rather than just a profession so all students, regardless of race, gender or socioeconomic status, receive the highest quality of education with all students at its heart.

Keeping all students at the heart of education enables leaders first to consider student interests when making important decisions. As a result, leaders at all levels must get in the habit of asking themselves student-centered questions whenever they make decisions or take action concerning school policy, district initiatives, or the everyday activities of the school. They must reflect on whether or not their actions cause any harm to any students; the message that their actions send to the learning community about the importance of student learning; whether their actions support community participation, access and equitability, social justice, effective teaching and learning opportunities, and; the impact of their actions on students. Staratt (1997) explores school and community leadership and how it interconnects with the ethics of justice, care, and critique. He argues that these ethics are mutually inseparable and complimentary to each other. According to Staratt:

the "ethic of justice" concerns the universal application of principles of justice among individuals in society; ... the "ethic of care" compels us to be proactively sensitive to another person, extending ourselves beyond duty and convenience to offer other persons our concern and attention; ... the "ethic of critique" calls upon us to speak out against unjust rules and laws and social arrangements on behalf of those principles of human and civil rights, of brother and sisterhood as human beings, on behalf of a common humanity which is violated through discrimination, disenfranchisement, and an arbitrary denial of equal treatment. (p. 99)

Starratt's ethical paradigm reinforces, for example, that school leaders are morally obligated to lead with integrity in order to make the bold and sometimes agonizing decisions necessary to ensure that all students are receiving a high quality of education. Research indicates that school leaders need to re-commit and exercise constant vigilance about the services they provide for students which in turn reflects their moral actions. Those actions speak volumes about the values they support (Quick & Normore, 2004). It is impossible for a school leader to take an action that does not signify some comment about how things should be done—which, by definition is a moral action.

Preparing children to live and work in the twenty-first century requires very special school leaders who have grappled with their own personal and professional codes of ethics and have reflected upon diverse forms of ethics, taking into account the differing backgrounds of the students who are enrolled in American schools (Shapiro & Stefkovich, 2005). Duke and Grogan (1997) assert that an important step toward more ethical action by leaders is greater clarity concerning personal values and ideals "that an unfortunate consequence of the fast pace of contemporary life has been less reflection on what is truly important in life" (p. 151). O'Keefe (1997) suggests that the importance of including a strong ethical foundation for practice

> promotes philosophical, historical and sociological perspectives through which students can better understand the contexts in which schooling takes place ... where students are encouraged to enter the political arena as agents of educational and social change and prepare for equitable schools. (p. 171)

For the inner city school leaders who may feel overwhelmed by the multitude of educational reform initiatives and the theories available, it becomes critical to translate these theories into actionable strategies for effective practices in order to address their daily realities. As one example, leaders have an ethical responsibility to help the school and the community to thoughtfully examine which initiatives are in the best interest of students and teachers. The ethical leader considers it part of the job to defend staff members and the community against fads that do not help students and waste valuable learning time. A number of other scholars stress the legitimacy of school leaders and communities identifying shared norms, values—and applying these to resolve or manage moral dilemmas (Fullan, 2003; Furman, 2004; Normore, 2004; O'Brien, 2004). Crittenden (1984) argued that general moral values can be upheld objectively and center around "respect for human life" and include such notions as "love, loyalty, justice, honesty, courage, generosity, telling the truth and keeping promises, as well as respect for political authority, property, family and community" (p. 16).

The life chances of poor students can be significantly enhanced by effective leaders who care and are committed to their success, and parents who are given every opportunity to exercise their rights to full participation in their children's education (Tillman, 2003, p. 311). Together, school leaders and their communities can provide the vision, structures, and incentives for initiatives that are intended to improve social, emotional and academic growth of all students. These same leaders model attitudes, behaviors, values, moral purpose, and actions that lead to collaborative and successful partnerships between school and the parent community in order to "to get knowledge of the parent population and validate their cultural frames of reference, values and heritage" (Tillman, 2003, p. 309). Furthermore, as suggested by Delpit and Kilgour-Dowdy (2002), "if we are to invite children into the language of school, we must make school inviting to them." (p. 42)

The crisis in inner-city school systems identifies many of the problems found in inner cities ranging from poor economic conditions for schools and families, personnel shortages and attrition rates, to improper facilities and materials, to political turmoil over issues of structure and control. Urban education is the primary target of the school reform movement and continues to be difficult to assess. The agent of change in this school reform process is the local community, not the school in isolation. Students, teachers, school leaders, parents, community leaders, professionals, and all stakeholders must join with and speak with, not for, those who have been dispossessed. This relational perspective is prudent to developing a respect for differences as part of a common struggle to extend the quality of public life.

SUMMARY AND CONCLUSION

Despite increasing interest to schools to form collaborative partnerships by necessity, the road will not likely be smooth, as this means a departure from past traditions. A school paradigm, as old as industrial America, will be broken during this century. As asserted by Ellis and Hughes (2002), schools need to come to the realization that collaborative partnerships do not form automatically. Fox (2005) states that multiple forms of collaboration ought to be promoted and become part of the planning frame but they will not stand alone. Family-centered collaboration, inter-organizational collaboration, and broad-based community collaboration may add to the complexities of how educational leaders can best form meaningful relationships. Jazaar and Algozzine (2007) reiterate that schools must realize that their strength is found in the services they provide for students, parents, and the community members, not as an exclusive academic island unto themselves. For educational systems to survive the twenty-first century, the school as a stand-alone institution in which educators do it all alone risk extinction—without exception. These authors further assert:

> United schools will stand; divided (non-partnered) schools will fall short in taking care of their students, parents, and community members (their stakeholders) ... that educational leaders must know that if they elect not to take care of their stakeholders, then other educational leaders, in other school systems, will welcome the opportunity. (p. 227)

From the colonial days of the 1600s and the settlement houses of the late 1800s, to the full-service schools of the new millennium, many of the non-educational compensatory programs provided by outside lay people or volunteers soon became part of the operating structure of the school. A vast number of the initial services assumed other forms, as teachers and school leaders shaped the service to the needs of the student in particular classrooms. Essentially, children were, and continue to be, labeled and disengaged with learning. In the 1970s researchers wrote about barriers to their partnerships. In the 1980s they wrote about possibilities which would overcome the barriers and in the 1990s and the beginning years of the new millennium they continue to write about they ways in which any given school can build comprehensive partnerships. Today schools are still multiple service agencies, some with more deliberate linkages to health and social service agencies in the communities than others. Yet, they are all more than academic institutions. Some would see this as a deterrent to the single mission of the school—to prepare students academically to be productive citizens in the world economic market. Back-to-the basics people hold fast to the singular study of numeracy and literacy. Others maintain the school is the single institution, trusted by the neighborhood by virtue and values of its children's attendance, and therefore, should help the whole student and family access all the services they need.

Whereas the Progressive Era attempted to divorce schools from the very communities they were established to serve, the contemporary movement to provide social services through the neighborhood school is an attempt to claim. It is the ethical role of instructional leaders to be involved in a reform movement based on integration versus alienation; citizens with rights and duties versus the consumer awash in a competitive marketplace. The current human services delivery system is divided into three categories: (a) education, which is charged with providing instructional services to children in public and private schools; (b) health, which includes nutrition, medical and mental health; and (c) social services, which support child welfare, day care, counseling, income maintenance, housing, and training. However, education is an irreplaceable element for the future success of our society. It is an enduring, dominant institution which has a history of providing health and social services. Thus, we ought to "engage" our children in their education; they have to understand "who" they are and they ought to have a sense of purpose. Providing sound leadership and services (Irvine, 2004, p. 9) for all children must be seen as a moral act reminiscent of the "lifting as we climb" philosophy. It is our moral and ethical duty to make urban schools safer not by modeling after prisons, but by making teaching and learning meaningful (Blanco, 2004), by providing leadership capacity throughout the community to translate vision into reality, and by defining the craft of education in terms of quality education as a civil right.

The establishment of an educationally sound and focused school community depends on appropriate innovation and change. When communities and educational leaders reflect on the collective vision of what makes a good school, it is essential to view the school within the context of the community. Each school and community has different needs—even schools within close proximity of each other. Thus, deciding how to use community resources and how the school can contribute to the community is a unique project for each school. Today, helping each student succeed is a shared school-community responsibility. Community stakeholder groups—including service agencies, public organizations, and private businesses—expect schools to ask for their support. Effective school leaders need to proactively seek community assistance and distribute the leadership accordingly.

The public schools of inner cities will continue to serve as the "most essential institution in the dissemination of education and assimilation of peoples in forming a nation of vitality, energy, and virtue" (Kern, 2003, p. xx). Community-based leadership might consider the ethical paradigm described by Staratt (2004, 1997) aiding the community in the creation of an institution that is characterized by power-sharing, equitable treatment of all within the community, caring and compassionate interpersonal relationships and purpose driven focus—one that seeks to draw out the inherent potential within individuals and simultaneously address the social, cultural, economic and academic realities and needs of schools and communities. As maintained by research (e.g., Garcia, 2002; Garcia & Hasson, 2004), it is time for urban schools and communities to remember that educational programs, initiatives, strategies, policies, and services that benefit students are equitable, respectful, responsive, responsible, resourceful, and reasonable. When school leaders and their communities engage in a common focus it will likely lead to a movement forward to thwarting the academic failure of students placed at risk. Leadership for social justice and morality is ultimately imperative as school leaders and their communities commit to efforts of collaboration for integrating services and delivery of programs for poverty-stricken school populations.

In times of economic, social, and political change and turbulence it becomes critical that these leaders and their communities not lose sight of their moral obligation and responsibility in support of all children gaining access to a quality education in America, particularly as it relates to the NCLB Act. It takes a strong political skill to bring about the necessary consensus and commitment to make schools work well for everyone. For example, the NCLB Act may well be considered the antithesis of moral leadership and social justice. NCLB sets out with a laudable aim—that narrowing the achievement gap is essential to democracy. However, as asserted by Noddings (1999), such aims must be followed up with reflection, guided by care to see whether the original policy has fulfilled its aims or has introduced new inequities or harm. Since its enactment in 2002, concerns regarding implementation and funding of NCLB quickly emanated from advocates for equality and social justice as it became clear that not all states understood aspects of NCLB. Increased accountability mechanisms lead to affected vulnerability at all levels of the education system. As reiterated by Storey and Beeman (2006), "Not surprisingly, vulnerable people often react with negativity and hostility" (para. 16). The current focus on standardized tests, accountability, and efficiency has caused educational leaders to be more concerned with management rather than leadership and does not "work well for everyone" (Sergiovanni, 2000, p. 166). Surface appearance in the form of student test scores has become the purpose of schooling and what is being lost is the true purpose of education—the drawing out of the inherent potential in all children. It is morally imperative for schools and their communities to establish and communicate high expectations for all students regardless of their skills and ability levels. In advocating for social justice, we must all bring our values and beliefs to the forefront; we must also bring along our prior socialization and present experiences; and gender, race, ethnicity, and class.

Second, the War on Poverty is an issue of morals and ethics. Urban school communities and school leaders need to further engage in meaningful discourse to include an ethic of critique that identifies the power inequities and social injustices, and make them right. This will be precarious work for the leader alone. Political concerns mount as the leader questions current power arrangements. Working to evaluate and discard the old and inequitable and creating new structures, policies, and procedures that are just and fair to everyone involved with education is the purview of ethically and socially just leaders.

Third, community development has to precede school reform (Blanco, 2004; Brown, 2003). Schools are there for parents, students, and communities and it is these very individuals who need to have a voice in how education is practiced demonstrating that the community works together as an interrelated body composed of many parts, teaching the lessons of moral responsibilities. As a moral enterprise education must stay above political power plays and must secure that all individuals have an equal voice in the educational conversation, including the voices of students. The most silent voices in evaluations of schools may well be that of students. Decisions about school-linked services are made based on student needs. These decisions are made for them, but rarely by them. Regrettably, students in low-performing schools are those who seem most shut-out of the shaping of changes in their schools. In the mainstream culture they are often portrayed as dysfunctional illiterates who need "dummied down" curriculum and a climate of control where "sit–down" and "keep quiet" strategies are the instructional norm. Students have great agency in defining school environment, including interaction with teachers and principals and the larger community. These students come to school with positive or negative values or orientations toward education that can override or, hopefully, facilitate any school reform initiative or effort. For example, low income and minority students are often overrepresented in special education, and these special education classes have been shown to fall short of any benefit to students (Hunter & Donahoo, 2003) who are placed, but may be ill-served. The ethic of caring (Starratt, 2004) does not ignore the demands of community governance issues, but claims that caring is the ideal fulfillment of all social relationships (Noddings, 1999), even though most relationships among members of a community might function according to a more remote form of caring.

Finally, a strand of learning should be dedicated to designing and organizing urban schools that are to be "full-service" schools (Melaville et al.,1993; Morrill, 1992). Full-service urban schools is the goal of systemic change and school transformation—schools that will go beyond just providing instruction to students, schools that are opened longer than student hours, and opened to adults and their needs. These schools must serve as the hub of integrated services. For example, schools can be used as places where adults come to learn about house improvements or non-school staff can provide information about legal aid on immigration matters (Wirt, 1993). Schools can be places to host neighborhood association meetings to discuss community-wide issues of concern. Full-service schools can provide space where other community services can be assessed, such as providing free transportation late at night for grocery shopping, emergency babysitting for a single parent household, when the parent has to work late.

Educational leaders' roles and responsibilities will change as they and their schools accept new challenges. Although collaborative partnerships have not traditionally fit into the industrial models of top-down leadership, educational leaders of the twenty-first century will need to transform their practices and form effective relationships with all. As asserted by Jazaar and Algozzine (2007), "all educational leaders will need to form these partnerships with others or watch others depart as increasing numbers of schools will be providing for their children's health, education and wellness" (p. 229). Educators interested in social change and social justice have used an analysis of privilege for some time. Possessing globally privileged citizenship of a safe, stable and, materially comfortable country provides similar unearned assets as does characteristics of dominant groups. The dominant institutional definition of schooling may well be in need of radical change as schools journey through the new millennium. The American public school, as a stand alone organization, will need to open its doors and embrace collaborative partnerships so educators and their colleagues teamed collaboratively at school can focus on children's health, wellness, and academic achievement. As researchers, practitioners, and educators within and outside the United States join ranks and advocate for social justice and the plight of the poor, we need to reflect on ways we might learn from each other in our collaborative efforts to provide socially just and improved educational experiences for all children. We need to critically think about ways to provide a service to the educational leadership profession and to the children in our charge. Collaborative partnerships will share a simple yet compelling logic that school improvement and renewal processes will not accomplish full potentials until the family and the community contexts for children's learning and health and wellness development are addressed simultaneously (Hiatt-Michael, 2001). We contend there is a moral obligation to engage in collaborative efforts to provide school-linked services that address the needs of all children—regardless of political, socioeconomic status, race, or geographical boundaries. In other words, as noted by Jazzar and Algiozinne (2007):

> Today's schools will need to start the factors and forces known to influence and determine children's learning such as healthy development, academic achievement, and success in school and then ask how professional, parents, and other diverse stakeholders, in school communities can work collaboratively to address them. This work will entail institutional change involving schools in building collaborative partnerships. (p. 228)

REFERENCES

Alvy, H., & Robbins, P. (2005). Growing into leadership. *Educational Leadership*, *62*(8), 50–54.

Blanco, R. I. (2003, May). *Social services, public schools and the poor*. Paper presented at the 5th International Conference on Education, Athens, Greece.

Blanco, R. I. (2004, April). *Who's teaching our kids? The transient teacher phenomenon*. Panel presented at the Mis-Education/Incarceration/Re-Education Nexus: Black Communities in the Intersections Conference of the Florida: The State of Black Studies II, Miami, FL.

Bogotch, I. E. (2005, November). *Social justice as an educational construct: Problems and possibilities*. Paper presented at the annual meeting of the University Council of Educational Administration, Nashville, TN.

Brooks, J. S., & Normore, A. H. (2005). An Aristotelian framework for the development of ethical leadership, *Journal of Values and Ethics in Educational Administration*, *3*(2), 1–8.

Brown, F. (2003). Back to the future with the end of *BROWN*: Community control of neighborhood schools, In R. Hunter & F. Brown (Eds.), *Challenges of urban education and efficacy of school reform* (pp. 75–86). Oxford, England: JAI/Elsevier.

Casanova, U. (1996). Parent involvement: A call for prudence, *Educational Researcher*, *25*(8), 30–32.

Crittenden, B. (1984). The moral context of decision making in education. In P. Sola (Ed.), *Ethics, education, and administrative decisions: A book of readings* (pp. 15–35). New York: Peter Lang.

Crowson, R. K. M., & Bioyd, W. L. (1993). Coordinated services for children: Designing arks for storms and seas unknown. *American Journal of Education*, *101*, 140–179.

Dantley, M. E., & Tillman, L. C. (2006). Social justice and moral transformative leadership. In C. Marshall & M. Oliva (Eds.), *Leadership for social justice: Making revolutions in education* (pp. 16–30). Boston: Pearson Education.

Delpit, L., & Kilgour-Dowdy, J. (2002). *The skin that we speak: Thoughts on language and culture in the classroom*. New York: The New Press.

Dryfoos, J. (2004). Full-service community schools: Creating new institutions. *Phi Delta Kappan*, *83*(5), 393–399.

Duke, D., & Grogan, M. (1997). The moral and ethical dimensions of leadership. In L. Beck & J. Murphy, (Eds.), *Ethics in educational leadership programs: Emerging models* (pp. 141–160). Columbia, MO: The University Council of Educational Administration.

Edyburn, D., Higgins, K., & Boone, R. (Eds.). (2005). *Handbook of special education technology research practice*. Whitefish Bay, WI: Knowledge by Design.

Ellis, D., & Hughes, K. (2002). *Partnerships by design: Cultivating effective and meaningful school-family-community partnerships*. Portland, OR: Northeast Regional Educational Laboratory.

Evans, S.W., Axelrod, J., & Langberg, J. M. (2004). Efficacy of a school-based treatment program for middle school youth with ADHD. *Behav Modif*, *28*(4), 528–547.

Fox, E. (2005). Tracking U.S. trends. *Education Week*, *24*(35), 40–42.

Fullan, M. (2003). *The moral imperative of school leadership*. Thousand Oaks, CA: Corwin Press.

Furman, G. C. (2004). The ethic of community. *Journal of Educational Administration, 42*(2), 215–235.

Furman, G. C., & Sheilds, C. M. (2005). How can educational leaders promote and support social justice and democratic community in schools? In W. A. Firestone & C. Riehl (Eds.), *A new agenda for educational leadership* (pp. 119–137). New York: Teachers College Press.

Garcia, E. (2002). *Student cultural diversity: Understanding and meeting the challenge.* New York: Houghton Mifflin.

Garcia, D. C., & Hasson, D. J. (2004). Implementing family literacy programs for linguistically and culturally diverse populations: Key elements to consider. *The School Community Journal, 14*(1), 113–137.

Garvin, J., & Young, A. (1994). Resource issues: A case study from New Orleans. In A. Addler & S. Gardner (Eds.), *The politics of linking schools and social services* (pp. 93–107). London: Fulmer.

Gomby, D. S., & Larson, C. S. (1992). Evaluation of school-linked services. In R.E. Behrman (Ed.), *The future of children, The future of children: School-linked services* (pp. 68–84). Los Altos, CA: The Center for the Future of Children, The David and Lucile Packard Foundation.

Gordon, E. W. (2004). Affirmative student development: Closing the achievement gap by developing human capital. *Policy Notes, Educational Testing Services, 12*(2), 1–4.

Hahn, A., & Danzberger, J. (with Lefkowithz, B.). (1987). *Dropouts in America: Enough is known for action.* Washington, DC: Institute for Educational Leadership.

Hiatt-Michael, D. B. (2001). *Promising practices to connect schools with the community.* Greenwich, CT: Information Age.

Hunter, R. (1905). *Poverty.* New York: Harper & Row.

Hunter, R. C., & Donahoo, S. (2003). Discrimination in tracking and specialized education programs. In R. Hunter & F. Brown (Eds.), *Challenges of urban education and efficacy of school reform* (pp. 87–100). Oxford, England: JAI/Elsevier.

Hunter, L., Hoagwood, K., Evans, S., Weist, M., Smith, C., Paternite, et al. (2005). *Working together to promote academic performance, social and emotional learning, and mental health for children.* New York: Center for the Advancement of Children's Mental Health at Columbia University.

Irvine, J. J. (2004). African American teachers' perceptions of their role as teachers of African American students: The unexamined variable. *Educational Testing Services, 12*(2), 9.

Jazzar, M., & Algozzine, B. (2007). *Keys to successful 21st century educational leadership.* Boston: Pearson.

Kagan, S. L. (1993). *Integration services for children and families: Understanding the past to shape the future.* New Haven: Yale University Press.

Kavale, K. A. (1995). Setting the record straight on learning disabilities and low achievement: The tortuous path of ideology. *Learning Disabilities Research & Practice, 10,* 145–152.

Kavale, K. A., & Forness, S. R. (2000). What definitions of learning disability say and don't say: A critical analysis. *Journal of Learning Disabilities, 33,* 239–256.

Kern, A. (2003). Preface. In R. Hunter & F. Brown (Eds.), *Challenges of urban education and efficacy of school reform* (pp. xvii–xx). Oxford, England: JAI/Elsevier.

Kowalski, T. (2004). *Public relations in schools* (3rd ed.). Upper Saddle River, NJ: Pearson.

Lee, S. S., & McKerrow, K. (2005, Fall). Advancing social justice: Women's work. *Advancing Women in Leadership Online Journal, 19*(1). Retrieved from http://www.advancingwomen.com/awl/fall2005/preface.html

Levy, J., & Shepardson, W. (1992). Look at current school-linked service efforts. *The Future of Children, 2*(1), 44–55.

Levy, J., Kagan, S., & Copple, C. (1992). *Are we ready? Collaboration to support young children and their families.* Washington, DC: Joining Forces, American Public Welfare Association and Council of Chief State School Officers.

MacMillan, D. L., & Siperstein, G. N. (2002). Learning disabilities as operationally defined by schools. In R. Bradley, L. Danielson, & D. P. Hallahan (Eds.), *Identification of learning disabilities: Research to practice* (pp. 287–333). Mahwah, NJ: Erlbaum.

Marshall, C., & Oliva, O. (2006). *Leadership for social justice: Making revolutions in education* (pp. 1–15). Boston: Pearson Education.

Melaville, A., Blank, M., & Asayesh, G. (1993). *Together we can: A guide for crafting a profamily system of education and human services.* Washington, DC: U.S. Government Printing Office, U.S. Department of Education, U.S. Department of Health and Human Services

Miami-Dade County Public Schools. (2005). Retrieved July 24, 2006, from http://www.dadeschools.net

Morrill, W. (1992). Overview of service delivery to children. *The Future of Children, 2*(1), 32–43.

Murray, C. (2006). Acid tests. American Enterprise Institute for Public Policy Research [Electronic version]. Retrieved July 27, 2006, from http://www.aei.org/publications/filter.social,pubID.24711/pub_detail.asp

Nabors, L. A., Leff, S. S., & Power, T. J. (2004). Quality improvement activities and expanded mental health services. *Behav Modif, 28*(4), 596–616.

National Center for Education Statistics. (2003). *Executive summary: Status and trends in the education of Hispanics* [Electronic version]. Retrieved March 30, 2004, from http://nces.ed.gov/pubs2003/hispanics/

Noguera, P. (2004, May). *Who's teaching our kids? Breaking the link between schools and prisons.* Plenary session presented at the Mis-Education/Incarceration/Re-Education Nexus, Black Communities in the Intersections Conference of Florida, The State of Black Studies II, Miami, FL.

Noddings, N. (1999). Introduction. In M. S. Katz, N. Noddings, & K. A. Strike (Eds.), *Justice and caring: the search for common ground in education* (p. 4). New York: Teachers College Press.

Normore, A. H. (2004). Ethics and values in leadership preparation programs: Finding the North Star in the dust storm. *Journal of Values and Ethics in Educational Administration, 2*(2), 1–7.

O'Brien, G. M. (2004). Best interests of the student: An ethical model. *Journal of Educational Administration, 42*(2), 197–214.

O'Keefe, J. (1997). Preparing ethical leaders for equitable schools. In L. Beck & J. Murphy, (Eds.,) *Ethics in educational leadership programs: emerging models* (pp. 161–187). Columbia, MO: The University Council of Educational Administration.

Packard Foundation. (Spring, 1992). School linked services. *The Future of Children*, 2(1), 19

Quick, P., & Normore, A. H. (2004). Moral leadership in the 21st century: Everyone is watching- especially the students, *The Educational Forum, 68*(4), 336–347.

Sedlak, M., & Church, R. (1982). *A history of social services delivered to youth. 1880–1977. Final report to the National Institute of Education* (Contract No. 400-79-0017). Washington, DC: NIE.

Sergiovanni, T. J. (1994). *Building community in schools.* San Francisco: Jossey-Bass.

Sergiovanni, T. J. (2000). *The life-world of leadership: creating culture, community, and personal meaning in our schools.* San Francisco: Jossey-Bass.

Shapiro, J., & Stefkovich, J. A. (2005). *Ethical leadership and decision making in education: Applying theoretical perspectives to complex dilemmas* (2nd ed.). Mahwah, NJ: Erlbaum.

Starratt, R. J. (2004). *Ethical leadership.* San Francisco: Jossey-Bass.

Staratt, R. J. (1997). Administering ethical schools. In L. Beck & J. Murphy (Eds.), *Ethics in educational leadership programs: Emerging models* (pp. 95–108). Columbia, MO: The University Council of Educational Administration.

Storey, V., & Beeman, T. (2006). A New DEEL for an old problem: Social justice at the core. *International Electronic Journal for Leadership in Learning, 10*(31). Retrieved from http://www.ucalgary.ca/~iejll/

Tillman, L. (2003). African American parental involvement in urban school reform: Implications for leadership. In R. Hunter & F. Brown (Eds.), *Challenges of urban education and efficacy of school reform* (pp. 295–312). Oxford, England: JAI/Elsevier.

Tyack, D. (1997, February) Civic education—what roles for citizens. *Educational Leadership, 54*(5), 22–24.

Weisglass, J. (2001). Racism and the achievement gap. *Education Week, 20*(43), 49.

Williams-Boyd, P. (2002). *Educational leadership: A reference handbook.* Santa Barbara, CA: ABC-CLIO Press.

Williams, D. G., & Parker, L. (2003). Standardized testing and assessment policy: Impact on racial minorities and implications for educational leadership. In R. Hunter & F. Brown (Eds.), *Challenges of urban education and efficacy of school reform* (pp. 207–220). Oxford, England: JAI/Elsevier.

Wirt, W. (1993, July). *Ways and means for a closer union between the school and the non-school activities.* Addresses and proceedings of the sixty-first annual meeting of the National Education Association. Washington, DC: NEA.

PART IV

ETHICAL LEADERSHIP AND
PRINCIPLES OF SOCIAL JUSTICE

CHAPTER 11

ETHICS, VALUES, AND SOCIAL JUSTICE LEADERSHIP

Embarking on a Moral Quest for Authenticity

Pauline Leonard

The purpose of this narrative inquiry is to share a story of self-reflection and deliberations about issues of ethics, values, social justice, and educational leadership. It begins as a story of reflections about one College of Education team's struggle for authenticity in the development of a new educational leadership program. However, the story takes a turn in light of the story-teller's renewed deliberations about authenticity in the wake of Hurricane Katrina. In the process, relevant ethical leadership and social justice principles are applied to examine, critique, and evaluate this struggle for authenticity. The narrative is an attempt to capture the multifaceted human dimensions embedded in the successes, achievements, challenges, and frustrations of striving for personal and professional integrity.

Leadership for Social Justice: Promoting Equity and Excellence Through Inquiry and Reflective Practice, pp. 243–256
Copyright © 2008 by Information Age Publishing
All rights of reproduction in any form reserved.

INTRODUCTION

Writing this paper about the problems associated with developing and implementing educational programs during September 2005 in Louisiana was a real challenge. At times I found it difficult to focus. At other times I was drawn so deeply into the vortex of deliberating about values and ethics that I would almost lose sight of myself. This was not an atypical experience for me. In fact, I have found it to be the case whenever I attempt to reflect on the indistinct processes of the human mind and spirit. The reflection becomes a journey, always intricate and often obscure, of grappling with the "overarching ideas, concepts, and theories" (Clandinin & Connelly, 2000, p. xiv) of ethics, values, and social justice in educational leadership. Perhaps not surprisingly, this journey of reflection and deliberation in the lifelong process of becoming authentic, true to oneself, is often considered "the most weighty of life's moral activities" (Starratt, 2004a, p. 5).

Journey Interrupted: Social Context

The difficulty of writing about such matters was at least in part due to the fact that I attempt to explore both public and private landscapes. I am sharing not just my thoughts and experiences about successes, achievements, challenges, and frustrations from an organizational, professional perspective, but from an inner, personal one as well. This was a challenge for me because it required that I take an extended journey inward to a place that required my full attention and sometimes brutal honesty. That type of focus and attention on my own thinking is difficult at the best of times, but the challenge was intensified when, during the writing process, Hurricane Katrina thrust itself upon the Gulf Coast, including many communities in southeast Louisiana. In the wake of the storm, reports of the devastation and destruction to life and property emerged. Writing about my personal experiences with, and the inherent challenges in, developing and implementing educational programs in one university in north Louisiana somehow seemed unimportant in the shadow of this catastrophe, with over a million people evacuated from their homes and communities. It made the issues that I had been writing about seem diminutive, perhaps even trite. Reflecting on the process of my own inner journey began to morph into a self-indulgent one. Better I move away from my computer and go do something of immediate and tangible use. Take action: donate money, donate food, donate blood, or volunteer my services as needed. These are things that really make a difference in times of crisis, aren't they?

Well, yes, they are. Multitudes of people did take action to help; heroic, courageous, self-sacrificing actions. However, alongside the noble acts were also the ineffectual, sometimes ignoble ones. There was also inaction. In the ensuing days after the hurricane, we know that much criticism, blame, and finger pointing took place as the nation and the world began to realize and question the fact that thousands of people were left behind, some by choice, but most as victims of circumstance, to face unimaginable human suffering and anguish in the face of deteriorating conditions. Charges of ineptitude, incompetence, and unpreparedness were leveled against local, state, and federal governments and officials. Along with these indictments, were issues of social justice—more insidious ones comprised of racism, classism, and ageism. What other explanation could there be for why greater resources had not been pre-deployed before the hurricane struck? Would there not have been a ground swell of concern for the people lined up outside of the Superdome if they had been mostly White? Mostly affluent? Mostly strong? Mostly self-sufficient? Would a greater number of people, as bewildered onlookers from the comfort of their living rooms, have been more outraged, more compelled to action, had the demographics of the population standing in line been different? Was there blindness to or denial of the macrocultural values embedded in this picture? Hard questions. And while I do not claim that there are definitive answers to these questions, I do believe that they need asking and considering: at least in my own journey toward authenticity. Moreover, attending to them is not trivial, but rather highly relevant to my deliberation about values, ethics, social justice, and authenticity. For as I continued writing, in the context of this unfolding human tragedy, I realized more fully the importance of not only action, but of reflective action in our endeavors. I asked questions of myself: How can I be sure that my actions are helping to create a better, more just, more caring, more equitable society? How can I, in my role as a professor in an institution of higher learning in Louisiana, acting in the capacity of teacher, researcher, and a servant to the community, better understand and address the social injustices experienced by the marginalized and the disadvantaged, such as those who could not evacuate during the hurricane? While my deliberations were interrupted by Hurricane Katrina and my attention had taken a turn toward the more immediate and urgent matters of doing what I could to help, I eventually returned to my writing with increased fervor in the knowledge, or rather the confirmation that such matters are not trite, nor self-indulgent. Rather they are of great value. The necessity of responding to an urgent situation through our immediate actions does not preclude the need to continue to be philosophical and to consider and reconsider our values, our valuation processes, and the influence of our values on our actions in the pursuit of a morally authentic life. In fact, the two are indeed related, as I hope to amplify as I continue.

REVIEW OF LITERATURE

Journey Continued

As difficult as it was to take this journey, particularly the more personal and private aspects of it, I continued. Parker Palmer (1998) underscores the importance of knowing our inner selves, stating that "the more familiar we are with our inner terrain, the more surefooted ... our living becomes" (p. 5). Palmer, who writes about teachers and teaching, but whose words can apply more broadly to educators in all settings, suggests that our inner and outer reality should "flow seamlessly into each other" (p. 5). In other words, we need to be firmly rooted in a true sense of self—the inner journey—in order to do meaningful work—the outer journey. Although he does not state it directly, Palmer is talking about the journey of authenticity. He couches the journey toward authenticity in terms of the quest for identity and integrity. Identity, he suggests, is a "moving intersection of the inner and outer forces that make me who I am" (p. 13).

Authenticity and Integrity

Examining one's identity as part of the quest for authenticity requires one to take an inner journey, but not in an individualistic sense. The journey is at once personal and public, and requires that an individual think about oneself, one's values and beliefs in relation to one's interactions with others. In that respect, it is a communal process, perhaps in the vein of Furman's (2003) ideas expressed in her deliberations about the ethic of community. Furman writes:

> In its simplest terms, an ethic of community means that administrators, teachers, school staffs, students, parents, and other community members interested in schools commit to the processes of community; in other words, they feel that they are morally responsible to engage in communal processes as they pursue the moral purposes of schooling and address the ongoing challenges of daily life and work in schools. Thus, an ethic of community centers the community over the individual as moral agent—it shifts the locus of moral agency to the community as a whole. (p. 4)

Furman (2002) emphasizes communal processes over community. The sense of community, she writes, "is based in relationships, which depend in turn on the processes of communication, of dialogue, and collaboration, and not on a set of indicators such as 'shared values' and 'shared decision making' " (p. 285). So too, understanding one's identity is not an individualistic process. If we think of identity as transformational and not "fixed essences ... that [do] not change over time" (Butler, 2005, p. 188), but that inform and are informed by the interactions we have with the people we live and work, it is indeed a communal process. It is a journey that cannot be undertaken in an individualistic sense. In other words, identity is inherently social because it is our interactions with other people that help us form a concept of ourselves. Moreover, identity is not static. It is "an evolving nexus where all the forces that constitute my life converge in the mystery of the self "(Palmer, 1998, p. 13). Identity is formed and transformed through our interactions, our relationships, with others.

Implicit in notions of the social nature of identity formation and transformation is "the view of oneself as a moral person, with character, who acts with integrity" (Johnson & Johnson, 2002, p. 36). Integrity, Palmer (1998) asserts, is whatever wholeness one is able to find in that intersection of inner and outer forces as "its vectors form and re-form the pattern of my life.... By choosing integrity, I become more whole, but wholeness does not mean perfection. It means becoming more real by acknowledging the whole of who I am" (p. 13). Conceptualizing integrity as the pathway to wholeness suggests that a person's character remains intact (Cox, La Caze, & Levine, 2005) and that there is congruence in standards, words, and behavior (Branden, 1994). It is also suggests that integrity is a "master virtue, a condition of having others" (Goodman & Lesnick, 2001, p. 162). If one has integrity, then there will be congruence in a person's claim to be honest and in that person's actions. Consequently, having integrity in this sense may not always mean that one's actions are ethical.

DIMENSIONS OF THE EXPERIENCE

Research Design: Narrative Inquiry

Identity and integrity can never be fully defined or known and the pursuit of authenticity as a moral endeavor is a "complex, demanding, life-long process of self-discovery" (Palmer, 1998, p. 13). Begley's (2004) position is similar. In his work on valuational process and educational leadership, he suggests that

the study of ethics should be as much about the life-long personal struggle to be ethical, about failures to be ethical, the inconsistencies of ethical

---

postures, the masquerading of self-interest and personal preference as ethical action, and the dilemmas which occur in everyday and professional life when one ethic trumps another. (p. 5)

Palmer suggests that " 'stories' are the best way to portray elusive realities of this sort" (p. 14). Consequently, I have opted to share a story; a story from my professional world, a story of my interactions and collaborations with others, and what I have learned from these interactions in my moral quest for authenticity. In the manner that Clandinin and Connelly (2000) describe, this narrative inquiry may be defined by its "three-dimensional space" (p. 50) of *continuity, interaction*, and *situation*. In other words, the narrative moves backward and forward in time (continuity of past, present, and future) in this story of my inward and outward journey towards authenticity (personal and social interaction) within the context of living in north Louisiana before and after Hurricane Katrina (situation or notion of place). I will share this story in the context of my deliberations about authenticity and my evolving identity as an educator in Louisiana, particularly in the *aftermath* of Hurricane Katrina. However, first a look at the past in order to understand the present as well as to better prepare for the future.

The Landscape

At the dawn of a new millennium, Louisiana educators were awash in a sea of anticipation, promise, and not a little trepidation, as a result of national- and state-mandated educational reform and accountability efforts. The following excerpt from a 1999 Southwest Educational Development Laboratory report captures the expectations of the time:

> Education is Louisiana's top priority today! There is excitement, energy, and hope about education in Louisiana, a state traditionally ranked near the bottom of the 50 states on educational quality and effectiveness. This state is also near the bottom on measures of the wealth and health of its citizens, but a turnaround is underway. Historically, one common perception of Louisiana has been that of a state defined by opposites which often fall along racial and socioeconomic lines: those who send their children to private schools and those who cannot; those who are powerful and those who are not; those who have professional careers and those who have jobs in agriculture, the service sector, or the oil industry. Today, however, people from these diverse groups are working together to improve education by facing the challenges, barriers, and inertia head-on. ("Progress of education in Louisiana," 1999, p. 5)

The report also announced and applauded Louisiana's new school and district accountability system, which was to have been phased in over the "next several years" (p. 17). These were not hollow promises. The accountability system has been alive and well in Louisiana schools since the year 2000. And while there are many detractors of the accountability system and the approach that Louisiana has taken, the fact that the state education system has made a concerted and extensive effort to improve its status as one of the nation's lowest in student achievement cannot go unrecognized. Indeed, it has recently been receiving considerable national acclaim for actually doing so ("Quality Counts," 2005). Moreover, the PK–12 education system was not the sole benefactor of this "new-found excitement, energy, and hope." In the year 2000, all universities in Louisiana were required by the Board of Regents and the Board of Elementary and Secondary Education to redesign their teacher preparation programs. Following that, in 2003, the universities were mandated to redesign their postbaccalaureate programs to

> expand knowledge gained in redesigned teacher preparation programs, address new requirements for the No Child Left Behind Act and other federal legislation (e.g., Individuals with Disabilities Education Act), focus upon school improvement and student achievement, and address the recommendations of the Blue Ribbon Commission. (Louisiana Teacher Quality Initiative, 2003, p. 2)

In effect, what this means as it relates to my story is my colleagues and I, along with other stakeholders, have been redesigning various programs of study for the past five years. As already stated, the intent in sharing this story is not so much to discuss a specific program, but to share insights pertaining to authenticity and ethical leadership theory. In January 2003, the Master of Educational Leadership team, or the MEL team, as we later began to call ourselves, began the task of designing a new educational leadership program. The MEL team was the university redesign team for the new leadership program and we worked with three advisory teams to develop the program. Following are a few highlights from that experience that have resonated with me in light of my deliberations about authenticity, justice, and moral leadership.

Accountability, Authenticity, and Moral Responsibility

There is considerable debate about the perceived benefits, consequences, challenges, and goals of current accountability efforts in American education. And while this is worthwhile discourse for scholars, policymakers, educational practitioners, parents, and the general public to engage, those directly involved in the efforts must find a way to digest and implement accountability policies and their directives in a manner that will allow them to meet the demands of these diverse external forces in a way that will bring "wholeness and life rather than fragmentation and death" (Palmer, 1998, p. 13). In other words, teachers, principals, university faculty, and so forth, must find a way to maneuver this landscape in such a way that their personal and professional standards remain congruent with their words and actions so that they maintain their integrity—if that is their quest. We can imagine those who deliberate about such matters as embarking on an inner and outer journey toward authenticity—a journey which requires each of us to weave "the major strands of [our] identity into [our] work" (p. 16). In working with the MEL team, I believe many of us were on such a journey. And while I cannot speak on behalf of each team member, I can share some of my experiences in the process. What was quite interesting, upon reflection, is that as a committee I would say we took our responsibility very seriously, but the nature of that responsibility often differed. To explain this phenomenon I use Starratt's (2004b) work on ethical leadership and the ethics of responsibility.

Starratt (2004b) suggests that educational leaders must be morally responsible, not only in a preventative sense but in a proactive one as well. Responsibility in the latter sense is three-dimensional in that the leader is: (a) responsible as; (b) responsible to; and, (c) responsible for. As stated, upon reflection, the MEL university team members as a unit seemed to have been responsible in all three of these ways, with each member being responsible in different ways on different issues. One example that comes to mind was the issue of meeting the redesign guidelines, particularly the request for identifying the empirical basis for educational practices and teaching methods covered in the newly developed courses for the program. There was considerable deliberation about which research studies to include with some of MEL team members placing considerable importance on integrating studies from journals and organizations that were reportedly considered to be embraced by the Board of Regents and the state Board of Education, suggesting they felt a primary responsibility:

- as state employees
- to state governing agencies
- for developing an educational program based on strict adherence to state guidelines.

On the other hand, other committee members expressed dismay at such an approach, and advocated that there was enough expertise on the committee to locate, examine, and utilize empirical studies that were deemed most appropriate for meeting course and program goals and objectives. This stance appears to suggest they felt a primary responsibility:

- as program developers
- to prospective program candidates
- for developing an educational leadership program informed, but not constrained, by state guidelines.

As might be expected, there were other issues for which MEL committee members held differing positions throughout the year-and-a-half collaborative endeavor. Since much of my research and writing has been in the area of professional collaboration (e.g., Leonard, 2002; Leonard & Leonard, 2005; Leonard & Smith, 2004), not from an ethical standpoint, but from the perspective of benefits and challenges in developing professional learning communities, I will elaborate on that issue. In my work as a committee member on the MEL team, I was able to experience first-hand the challenges of working collaboratively to develop the new leadership program. As addressed previously, there were differences in how we conceptualized our responsibilities as, to, and for when developing the program. Consequently, important questions to consider are: How did we work out our differences? Did we collaborate and in what manner? How did this process affect the outcome—the educational leadership program? Was this a collaborative and democratic process? Was it a communal process?

Begley (2005) purports that "the essential, and often absent, component that would make adherence to a value genuinely democratic is dialogue" (p. 1). I believe in resolving most of our differences, but certainly not all, the "dialogic deliberation" (p. 2) did occur and toward the end of the process, we began to compromise, and in some cases approached collaboration in the fashion advocated by Friend and Cook (2000). This may have occurred because as a group we began what Starratt (2004a) describes as the process of authentically knowing or

> putting aside one's own sense of superiority or importance, leaving one's own self-centered agenda aside, submitting oneself to the message of the subject, letting the subject re-position the self in a new or clearer set of relationships (natural, social, cultural), allowing the self to be humbled by the integrity of the known. (p. 18)

Again, this is not to suggest that the entire process was communal. In some instances it was not. Personal egos and agendas emerged as we discussed various aspects of the program, manifesting themselves in a variety of styles of interaction—competitive, avoiding, compromising, withdrawing. However, through some of these discussions new and better

ideas for shaping the program and the internship began to emerge. The
process emerged as collaborative and the leadership distributed and, in
the manner that Furman (2003) describes, was grounded in our
"interpersonal and group skills ... [and] ... ongoing dialogue ... that
allow[ed] all voices to be heard" (p. 4). And while, the ethic of community
may be an ideal difficult to explain and challenging to create given the
many constraints under which collaborative educational endeavors usually take place, I believe that when people come together to work and
share ideas in pursuit of mutual goals, and each is sincere in the process,
then we are at least approaching community in the sense that Furman
describes. The experience and reflection upon the experience has helped
me realize the important of knowing who we are, of clarifying our identity, and of understanding who we are responsible as, to, and for. The
quest for authenticity demands that we participate in this process.

WAKEFULNESS OF THE EDUCATIONAL LEADER WITHIN

Striving for Authenticity in the Aftermath of Katrina

The inner and the outer struggle for authenticity is one which involves
making sense of the world in which we live and work in ways that acknowledges, nourishes, but also challenges our inner realities. It requires that
we take stock of who we are and what we stand for and that we understand
the cultural, social, political, geographic, and additional influences on
our identity. It means putting into context all of what we do—the pursuit
of aligning our inner and outer realities so that they might flow seamlessly
together. Being authentic is not easy. What it means for me is that I must
find ways to align my professional responsibilities with my personal and
professional values as a teacher, as a researcher and scholar, and as a servant to the community. I must also be sensitive to the context in which I
live and work. Sometimes this process requires that I reconsider my personal and professional values—not to sacrifice my integrity, but to examine these values from the vantage points of others.

For example, my ideals of my role as a professor in higher education
were put to the test when I moved to Louisiana and began working with
teachers faced with the challenges of meeting state accountability measures while working with insufficient resources and support and often with
students who come to school with many strikes against them. While I have
over 15 years of experience teaching in public schools, I have not had the
experience of teaching in an atmosphere infused by the kind of hysteria
that accompanies comprehensive accountability plans, high-stakes testing, school report cards, measures of adequate yearly progress, all of

which have potentially grave consequences for teachers and students, particularly those in diverse, high-poverty settings. Talking about the ideals and values of collaboration just does not "cut it" with these teachers in this type of environment. While I concur wholeheartedly with Palmer's (1998) assertion that "the most practical thing we can achieve in any kind of work is insight into what is happening inside us" (p. 5), I have found it difficult to help teachers in the PK–12 setting to see this perspective. I suspect that, in the wake of Katrina, and subsequently Hurricane Rita, this struggle will not only continue, but perhaps intensify. Hurricane Katrina, in particular, has struck a severe blow to the nation in general, and to numerous communities in the south in particular. The effects of this blow are widespread, with the education system in Louisiana being one of the areas that has been deeply affected. Education in Louisiana has experienced severe turbulence "with structural damage ... to normal operations" (Gross, 1998, p. 20). Katrina destroyed or damaged schools in at least six Louisiana parishes, displacing more than 135,000 students, most of whom were poor and Black, in the PK–12 system as well as many students in post-secondary institutions. Thousands of teachers were also displaced. At our institution in north Louisiana, the university president stated that the university was utilizing every possible resource to provide stability and a first-class education to all students and comfort and assistance to displaced students and their families affected by this disaster.

A first-class education is a high standard in times of extreme turbulence. I suspect that there will continue to be a "chasm between the school's learning agenda (state defined curriculum standards) and the students' learning agenda (the existential task of becoming a somebody in the drama of everyday life with all of its ambiguities and challenges" (Starratt, 2004a, p. 14) in these turbulent times. However, it's a standard worth striving to reach. To strive for professional authenticity will require that I know who I am and what I stand for and be able to articulate that in both words and actions within the professional community.

Striving for Professional Authenticity

It will require a continuous clarification and in some cases revision of who I am as a human, as a teacher, as a researcher, and as a servant and ongoing evaluation of my words and actions within my professional community. As a human I am responsible to the community for contributing to the creation of a just, caring, equitable, democratic society. Any aspects of my professional identity must be congruent with this aspect of my being. As a *teacher leader* in higher education, I have the privilege of working with preservice and in-service teachers and administrators completing baccalaureate, advanced, or alternative teacher and leader-ship certification programs. To that end, I am obligated to creating authentic learning environments for program candidates so that I may "practice what I preach." As a *researcher leader*, I can select research projects that are congruent with my personal and professional values. For example, I intend to continue to investigate ways to help teachers and administrators engage in real collaboration for the creation of authentic learning environments that are informed, not restricted by curriculum standards and accountability measures so that their students are success-ful in a holistic sense. As a *servant leader* in a professional learning com-munity I can continue to reflect on my personal and professional identities and the potential impact of my services on this community. What I have confirmed in my involvement in and deliberations about pro-gram development, particularly with the new MEL program, is that col-laboration, while rarely a smooth process, is a highly important aspect in the endeavor to be authentic. Consequently, I must recognize and seize the opportunities to collaborate with my colleagues through my service on department, college, and university committees. In doing so, I recognize and embrace my responsibilities as a human and as a professional work-ing in a university setting *to* faculty, staff, and students in a professional learning community for helping to create and sustain a just, caring, equi-table, and democratic society. In the interest of authenticity, I must engage in "mutually affirming relationships" (Starratt, 2004b, p. 71) in my collaborations.

CONCLUSIONS AND IMPLICATIONS

In presenting my story and discussing aspects of it in light of particular ethical and values leadership theories, I acknowledge that the story of MEL, as well as any additional clips of my professional life that I have shared, are told from my perspective, and are therefore partial and "con-ditional on [my] interests and surrounding circumstances" (Clandinin & Connelly, 2000, p. 179). I also acknowledge that, while I may not be guilty of creating the " 'Hollywood plot' ... [where] everything works out well in the end" (p. 181), there has been some "narrative smoothing" (p. 181) in the interest of omitting details which might negatively reflect on persons and places described in the story. To address this in my attempt to attain authenticity I will need to acquire a "language of wakefulness" (p. 182), where I am more fully alert to the risks of oversimplification, of creating simplistic plots and interpreting the world and people's actions through my own limited lens. At the same time, however, I am mindful of what Maya Angelou's response to bell hooks (1998) question: "Do you simply write for your own inner purposes or do you have a conscious didactic purpose?" Angelou replies:

> I will tell the truth. I may not tell the facts; facts can obscure the truth. You can tell so many facts you never get to the truth. So I want to tell the truth as I see it, as I've lived it. I will not tell everything I know. But what I do say is the truth. (p. 3)

Similarly, I believe I tell the truth, as I know it, in striving for authenticity. Becoming authentic is a process, a journey, not an end in itself; it is an inner and outer journey and requires a continual examination of one's multiple identities within the context of the communities in which one lives, works, and interacts. It involves wakefulness to the dialogue, actions, and values of diverse others within those communities. It demands what Starratt (2004b) describes as "presence", where one is "wide awake to what's in front of [us]" (p. 88), requiring us to "remove ourselves from the center of the universe" (p. 90) in ways that are affirming, critiquing, and enabling. Considering the global interconnectedness that increasingly characterizes our schools and communities, removing ourselves from the center of the universe is necessary on both an individual level and a societal one. Achieving authenticity also requires an understanding that there is much to be learned as we navigate the road of authenticity, particularly as we attempt to make sense of the interruptions we encounter along the way, from the casual to the catastrophic.

REFERENCES

Angelou, M., & hooks, b. (1998, January). There's no place to go but up. *Shambhala Sun*. Retrieved September 22, 2005, from http://www.shambhalasun.com/Archives/Features/1998/Jan98/Angelou.htm

Begley, P. (2004). Understanding valuational processes: Exploring the linkage between motivation and action. *International studies in educational administration, 32*(2), 4–17.

Begley, P. (2005). *Ethics matters: New expectations for democratic educational leadership in a global community*. University Park, PA: Rock Ethics Institute.

Branden, N. (1994). *The six pillars of self-esteem*. New York: Bantam.

Butler, J. E. (2005). Transforming the curriculum: Teaching about women of color. In J. A. Banks & C. A. M. Banks (Eds.), *Multicultural education: Issues and perspectives*. Hoboken, NJ: Wiley.

Clandinin, D. J., & Connelly, F. M. (2000). *Narrative inquiry: Experience and story in qualitative research*. San Francisco: Jossey-Bass.

Cox, D., La Caze, M., & Levine, M. Integrity. (2005). *The Stanford encyclopedia of philosophy*. Retrieved August 24, 2005, from http://plato.stanford.edu/archives/fall2005/entries/integrity/

Friend, M., & Cook, L. (2000). *Interactions: Collaboration skills for school professionals*. New York: Longman.

Furman, G. C. (Ed) (2002). *School as community: From promise to practice*. Albany, NY: SUNY Press.

Furman, G. (2003). Moral leadership and the ethics of community. *Values and Ethics in Educational Administration, 2*(1), 1–8.

Goodman, J. F., & Lesnick, H. (2001). *The moral stake in education: Contested premises and practices*. New York: Longman.

Gross, S. J. (1998). *Staying centered: Curriculum leadership in a turbulent era*. Alexandria, VA: The Association of Supervision and Curriculum Development.

Johnson, D. W., & Johnson, R. T. (2002). *Introduction to multicultural education and human relations: Valuing diversity*. Boston: Allyn & Bacon.

Leonard, L., & Leonard, P. (2005). Achieving professional community in schools: The administrator challenge. *Planning and Changing, 36*(1&2), 23–39.

Leonard, P. (2002). Professional collaboration: Setting standards of support. *Leading and Managing, 8*(1), 46–59.

Leonard, P., & Smith, R. (2004). Collaboration for inclusion: The "principal" challenge. *Leading and Managing, 9*(2), 117–123.

Louisiana Teacher Quality Initiative. (2003). *Guidelines for the redesign of postbaccalaureate education programs*. Baton Rouge: Louisiana Board of Regents and the Board of Elementary and Secondary Education.

Palmer. P. J. (1998). *The courage to teach*. San Francisco: Jossey-Bass.

Progress of education in Louisiana. (1999). *Southwest Educational Development Laboratory*. Retrieved August 24, 2005, from http://www.sedl.org/pubs/pic01/progress-LA.pdf

Quality counts 2005: State report cards. (2005). *Education Week, 24*(17), 119.

Starratt, R. J. (2004a, Sept. 30–Oct. 2). *The ethics of learning: Learning to be moral by engaging the morality of learning*. Paper presented at the 9th annual Leadership and Ethics Conference, Christ Church, Barbados.

Starratt, R. J. (2004b). *Ethical leadership*: San Francisco: Jossey-Bass.

CHAPTER 12

(RE-)CONSTRUCTING A MOVEMENT FOR SOCIAL JUSTICE IN OUR PROFESSION

Steven Jay Gross

The purpose of this article is to describe the emergence of the New DEEL (Democratic Ethical Educational Leadership) and the role it is attempting to play in confronting the excesses of the current accountability movement typified by massive standardized testing and No Child Left Behind (NCLB) legislation in the United States. This article depicts the choice facing the field of educational leadership that pits a top-down control regime, modeled after corporations on the one hand against a progressive, democratic-ethical alternative on the other hand. A brief account of the historic traditions of the latter and its ties to the cause of social justice is also offered. Representing the democratic-ethical tradition in this era, the New DEEL movement, originating in university departments of educational leadership and policy studies in the United States, Canada, Australia, is portrayed. This account includes the New DEEL' s mission, emerging set of educational leadership skills, and recent accomplishments.

Leadership for Social Justice: Promoting Equity and Excellence Through Inquiry and Reflective Practice, pp. 257–266
Copyright © 2008 by Information Age Publishing
257

INTRODUCTION

While the turn of the millennia was only 8 years ago, we seem to be in a dramatically different world today. The dominance of the bubble economy is a mere memory yet the corporate metaphor looms greater than ever in our schools thanks to the accountability movement, massive standardized testing, and NCLB. Countering this hierarchical, bureaucratic, and alienating direction, is a democratic-ethical tradition in the field of educational leadership. The purpose of this article is to describe the emergence of the New DEEL and the role it is attempting to play in reviving that tradition, thereby helping to move educational leadership closer to the goal of social justice.

THE END OF AN ERA

Each of us likely remembers where we were late in the evening of December 31, 1999. For years we had spoken about the dawn of the new century and the new millennium. Books, articles, and conferences seemed fixated on the transition to the new era. In those glory days of the dot-com bubble economy, corporate metaphors were all the rage and the biggest worry seemed to be our software's readiness to accept a date beyond the twentieth century.

How little actual time has passed between those days and these and yet, how dated those images now appear. We *have* crossed the metaphoric bridge into the twenty-first century, but what a different time it is from the one we were told to expect. Some worries, like the clocks in our computers, never materialized. Titans of that era, such as Michael Eisner of the Disney Corporation, have faded, and some of the giants of the supposed new economy, such as Enron, turned out to be little more than swindlers on a gigabyte scale. Given the collapse of the fantasy-driven technology economy, the hit television show, *Who Wants to be a Millionaire?* might more accurately be called, *Who **Used** to be a Millionaire?*

We have sustained tribulations that are far more serious in the last 8 years. The tragedy of September 11, 2001 and its global aftermath will forever be frozen in our minds, coloring our view of life. We now live in a world stressed by war and the threat of greater war. We have come to accept global warming and the destruction of ecosystems as a sickening part of human existence. Social distinctions and the gap in wealth in the United States are greater now than in any time since 1929. At the same time, we have gone from budget surpluses to record budget deficits that imperil the economic future of our children and grandchildren. With all of America's advantages in medical knowledge, 45 million of our fellow citizens are without adequate health care, 18 million of which are children in our schools. War, environmental ruin, economic inequality, and mushrooming social injustice were far from our minds on that remarkable New Year's Eve but they are facts that we live with every evening now as we anticipate the future. The dichotomy between the euphoric promise and the disquieting reality of the intervening years since 2000 has clear implications for educational leadership.

A CLEAR CHOICE FOR EDUCATIONAL LEADERSHIP

In the field of educational leadership, the story also features a series of twists and turns making the imperatives of the 1990's seem dated and inadequate. While that decade started with the promise of serious innovation and transformation in schools, the relentless drumbeat of a politically zealous accountability movement brought on a new wave of mistrust of public education in North America that now echoes in places as far away as Australia. Ironically, just as consensus builds on the need for adoptive, creative, and socially just forms of organizations around the world (Aiken, 2002; Begley, 1999; Begley & Zaretsky, 2004; Boyd. 2000; Davis 2003; Gross, 2004; Reitzug & O'Hair, 2002, Sernak, 1998; Shapiro & Purpel, 2004; Shapiro & Stefkovich, 2005; Starratt, 2004; Young, Petersen, & Short, 2002), the forces of the accountability movement thrust our schools, their leaders, and our own institutions into more bureaucratic, more top-down, and more alienating forms of control that resemble hierarchal corporate life. Since the passage of federal NCLB legislation, this trend has only escalated, narrowing the curriculum and forcing ever-greater attention to standardized testing. Educational leadership is faced with a choice: continue to embrace a corporate model or design an alternative that may be more appropriate to our field, our times and the cause of social justice.

Before advocating for a move away from the corporate model, some reflection on why we find ourselves imitating business culture is in order. One major reason for our current condition is a narrow definition of school reform typically referred to as school improvement. In the past, we have been told that the choice for educational leadership programs was simple. We could either opt for school improvement or democratic schools or social justice as our organizing principles (Murphy, 1999). While there is a surface logic to this construction, framing the problem of priorities in this way falsely separates social justice from democracy and pits both against school improvement. The limits of school improvement when alienated from social justice and democracy are not difficult to see. School improvement, in isolation, has too often meant the over use of corporate culture, mores and metaphors that are ill suited for education, and insufficient for our purposes. By imposing business models and values, educators find themselves running scared, reducing learning to scores on a test, and ceding the field (literally and figuratively) to the forces of privatization—including our field of educational leadership.

In a country like the United States, where the bottom line and commercialism are pervasive, it is not surprising to find some educators and many from large businesses advocate a corporate model for schools and school leadership. While this is hardly a new circumstance (Cubberly, 1916), it is a flawed proposition, often carried to extremes. There may be some overlap between the work of educational leaders and business leaders, yet applying Morgan's (1997) proposition that metaphors both illuminate and obscure quickly shows the severe limits of this comparison. In this case, the little that the corporate metaphor illuminates for our field is eclipsed by what it obscures. Simply put, those who have committed their careers to education have a very different set of values from those who focus on corporate life. Our fiduciary obligation is not to stockholders, it is to our students, their families and their communities. We do not look at our students as mere customers who exchange money for services rendered. Finances certainly are a part of our work, but our responsibilities to our students go much deeper. A corporation counts its development in quarterly earnings reports. As educators, we count development in the lives that our students live, as well as the society that those whom we have the privilege to influence build. Our project is not simply a summary of short-term profits designed to impress the investment community. It is the pursuit of a democratic-ethical world. While business is transactional, our work is transformational. Given the challenges and threats of our times, transformational work, in the cause of a more democratic and just world seems ever more critical.

For those aspiring to educational leadership coming to us for answers the question is clear: Will we prepare a generation of obedient functionaries serving a bureaucratic accountability regime, or will we prepare a new kind of leader who can build a democratic-ethical vision for the school and the surrounding community? Put differently, do we believe enough in the ideal of social justice to act upon our principles, even against great odds? Upon whose shoulder might we stand?

REDISCOVERING THE TRADITION OF SOCIAL JUSTICE IN EDUCATIONAL LEADERSHIP

While many have justly criticized the field of educational leadership for its tendencies to reinforce social hierarchies (Rapp, 2002), that is not the whole story. There is rich historical precedence for taking a different position in educational leadership than the current trend toward corporate imitation and top-down accountability control. Over the past century, educational leaders have recoiled from scientific-management and the creation of factory-like schools wherein leadership was a matter of top-down control. Ella Flagg Young, John Dewey's colleague and the first woman to become superintendent of a major American city school system, promoted teacher councils that empowered classroom faculty to share in power and decision making (Webb & McCarthy 1998). Dewey's (1903) work, of course, centered on the vital connection between education and democratic life. George S. Counts' (1932) classic, *Dare the School Build a New Social Order?*, challenged the limits of the progressive's vision of education, asking them to aim at the construction of a more just society. During the 1930s and 1940s, as the world faced and then fought fascist Italy, imperial Japan, and Nazi Germany the future of democracy was in grave doubt. Responding to this crisis, educational leaders such as Alice Miel and Harold Rugg of Teachers College helped to build a new movement in our field called democratic school administration (Kliebard, 1987). The point of this endeavor was to help the schools of their era buttress democracy by teaching leaders to model democratic behaviors. These are not mere examples of democratic-ethical administration in the past; they represent a rich tradition built by the leaders with lessons to teach us today.

Progressives and social meliorists pursued a more democratic society with passion and scholarship. Now an energized emphasis upon ethical reasoning needs to be added to the mixture to meet the dynamic challenges of the early twenty-first century where critical and complex dilemmas are a daily element in the lives of educational leaders. This priority follows the lessons learned from noted current scholars (Shapiro & Stefkovich, 2005; Starratt, 2004). In his recent book, *God has a Dream*, Archbishop Desmond Tutu (2004) shares the concept of *ubuntu*, which captures the spirit of a new perspective on society and illustrates the potential of democratic-ethical educational leadership:

> According to ubuntu, it is not a great good to be successful through being aggressively competitive and succeeding at the expense of others. In the end, our purpose is social and communal harmony and well-being. Ubuntu does not say, "I think, therefore I am." It says rather, "I am human because I belong. I participate. I share." Harmony, friendliness, community are great goods. Social harmony is for us the *summum bonum*—the greatest good. Anything that subverts, that undermines this sought-after good is to be avoided like the plague. Anger, resentment, lust for revenge, even success through aggressive competitiveness, are corrosive of this good. (p. 27)

Facing the upheavals of this century—while drawing upon a democratic tradition in educational leadership, and adding a new emphasis on deeply grounded ethical reasoning—laid the groundwork for action by reframing the debates in our field.

LAUNCHING OF THE NEW DEEL

In response to the dilemma facing the field of educational leadership, colleagues from leading University Council for Educational Administration (UCEA) institutions joined committed practitioners to take action. During the 2004–2005 academic year faculty and department leaders from Temple University, Penn State, the University of Vermont, Rowan University, the University of Oklahoma, the University Council of Educational Administration, and the University of North Carolina at Greensboro as well as U.S. and Canadian practitioner leaders launched a new movement in the field of educational leadership. This movement, called the New DEEL, aims to change the direction of our field away from an overly corporate model toward the values of democracy and ethical behavior.

New DEEL members believe that the first job of the school is to help young people become effective citizens in a democracy. Learning how to earn a living is crucial, but it is a close second, in their opinion. Democratic citizenship in any era is a complex task but it seems especially difficult in our era where international conflict and growing economic and social inequality are the rule. New DEEL members consider the either/or choice among school improvement, democracy, and social justice critiqued above to be a false dilemma. They believe instead, that there is no democracy without social justice, no social justice without democracy, and that these mutually inclusive concepts are indispensable ingredients to school improvement worthy of the name. The New DEEL's mission statement focuses on these values:

> The mission of the New DEEL is to create an action-oriented partnership, dedicated to inquiry into the nature and practice of democratic, ethical educational leadership through sustained processes of open dialogue, right to voice, community inclusion, and responsible participation toward the common good. We strive to create an environment to facilitate democratic ethical decision-making in educational theory and practice which acts in the best interest of all students. (Gross & Shapiro, 2005, pp. 1–4)

EMERGING SKILLS OF A NEW DEEL LEADER

High on the group's agenda is the development of a profile for educational leaders who live the values of the New DEEL mission statement.

Clearly, this means a different kind of educational leader from those cast in the corporate mold including a new set of skills as well as a broader definition leadership itself. The New DEEL leader's skills and values stand in contrast the characteristics promoted by the accountability movement as illustrated in Table 12.1. Included in the New DEEL perspective are the skills of community building, deep ethical understanding, a theoretical and practical knowledge of turbulence driven by the internal desire to lead from an ever-expanding sense of mission and responsibility. While the traditional leader seeks to climb the existing power structure, largely for the sake of greater power and prestige, the New DEEL leader may be at the top of a given system but is never satisfied with that. Rather, the goal is one of a transformed community through education that will likely include working through turbulent conditions and knotty ethical dilemmas. Whereas the traditional school leader shies away from such responsibilities, the New DEEL leader understands that these challenges are part of the work of leadership in our era and has a clear educational

Table 12.1.   Comparison of New DEEL Vision for Leaders With the Behavior of Traditional School Leaders

New DEEL Vision for Leaders	Behavior of Traditional School Leaders
Transformational	*Transactional*
Guided by inner sense of responsibility to students, families, the community and social development on a world scale.	Driven by an exterior pressure of accountability to those above in the organizational/political hierarchy
Leads from an expansive community-building perspective. A democratic actor who understands when and how to *shield* the school from turbulence and when and how to *use* turbulence to facilitate change.	Bound by the system and the physical building. a small part of a monolithic, more corporate structure.
Integrates the concepts of democracy, social justice and school reform through scholarship, dialogue, and action.	Separates democracy and social justice from guiding vision and accepts school improvement (a subset of school reform) as the dominant perspective.
Operatives from a deep understanding of ethical decision making in the context of a dynamic, inclusive, democratic vision.	Operates largely from perspective of the ethic of justice wherein obedience to authority and current regulations is largely unquestioned despite one' own misgivings.
See one's career as a calling and has a well developed sense of mission towards democratic social improvement that cuts across political, national, class, gender, racial, ethnic, and religious boundaries.	Sees one's career in terms of specific job titles with an aim to move to ever greater positions of perceived power within the current system's structure.

foundation for this reality. In sum, the traditional leader is a functionary of a system that is becoming ever more centralized, corporate and removed from the influence of students, families and communities. The New DEEL vision promotes democratic life growing from the heart of the community toward the wide world.

FROM CONCEPT TO ACTION:
RECENT NEW DEEL ACCOMPLISHMENTS

In their first year New DEEL members conferred and presented papers at national and international scholarly meetings including UCEA and the American Educational Research Association, initiated an international study of high school student engagement, and held two winter strategy sessions at Temple University. The group also grew in size numbering representatives from over two-dozen universities and K–12 school systems in North America, Canada, Australia, and the United Kingdom. Projects for 2006–2007 build upon these to include technology support, curriculum development, sharing an organically developed code of ethics, expanding research into student engagement, funding, and the development of a scholarly basis for the New DEEL through publications. The group has also committed to an annual conference of its own where scholarship and strategy will be shared. This conference, now in the planning stages, will encourage scholarly debate on pivotal issues facing the New DEEL including: What kind of curriculum best moves the field toward democratic-ethical leadership at all levels? How might this movement adapt itself to regional and national conditions where differing concepts of democracy and ethics exist? How can departments of educational leadership prepare students for the demands of the current accountability-centered system and still prepare them to bring about serious changes embodied in the New DEEL mission?

Scholarship, activism, and a compelling, positive vision for the future seem required ingredients if the ideals of the New DEEL are to take root and move educational leadership and education itself away from today's alienating values of corporate control from above toward democratic-ethical community building social justice around the world. It is appropriate that this movement includes colleagues from a growing list of nations and continents since the challenge of raising a new generation of leaders dedicated to these goals transcends national boundaries and parochial limits. Those in opposition to direction taken by the New DEEL certainly utilize a world view. Our perspective needs to be equally broad. It may be a daunting challenge but we are equal to it. One day, decades from now, we will reflect on this violent and dangerous time with the benefit of historical perspective and better understand our impact when our influence mattered and the field looked to us for wisdom and guidance. We will either look back with pride knowing that we took an ethical stand or in despair mourning a lost chance to make a critical difference when we were most needed. By their actions, New DEEL colleagues show confidence in our community and have faith that now, when the moment for leadership is at hand, those teaching educational leadership will act. This turbulent century demands no less of us.

REFERENCES

Aiken, J. (2002). The socialization of new principals: Another perspective on principal retention. *Educational Leadership Review, 3*(1), 32–40.

Begley, P. T. (Ed.). (1999). *Values and educational leadership*. Albany: State University of New York Press.

Begley, P. T., & Zaretsky, L. (2004). Democratic school leadership in Canada's public school systems: Professional value and social ethic. *The Journal of Educational Administration, 42*(6), 640–655.

Boyd, W. L. (2000). The r's of school reform and the politics of reforming or replacing public schools. *Journal of Educational Change, 1*(3), 225–252.

Counts, G. S. (1932). *Dare the schools build a new social order?* Carbondale, IL: Southern Illinois University Press.

Cubberly, E. P. (1916). *Public administration*. Boston: Houghton Mifflin.

Davis, J. E. (2003). Early schooling and the achievement of African American males. *Urban Education, 38*(5), 515–537.

Dewey, J. (1903). *Democracy and education*. New York: The Free Press

Gross, S. J. (2004). *Promises kept: Sustaining school and district leadership in a turbulent era*. Alexandria, VA: The Association for Supervision and Curriculum Development.

Gross, S. J., & Shapiro, J. P. (2005). Our new era requires a New DEEL: Towards democratic ethical educational leadership. *The UCEA Review, XLVII*(3), 1–4.

Kliebard, H. M. (1987). *The struggle for the American curriculum: 1893–1958*. Boston: Routledge & Kegan Paul.

Morgan, G. (1997). *Images of organization*. Thousand Oaks, CA: SAGE.

Murphy, J. (1999). *The quest for a center: Notes on the state of the profession of educational leadership*. Columbia, MO: University Council for Educational Administration.

Rapp, D. (2002). Social justice and the importance of rebellious oppositional imaginations. *Journal of School Leadership, 12*(3), 226–245.

Reitzug, U. C., O'Hair, M. J. (2002). Tensions and struggles in moving toward a democratic school community. In G. Furman-Brown (Ed.), *School as community: From promise to practice* (pp. 119-142). New York: SUNY.

Sernak, K. (1998). *School leadership-balancing power with caring*. New York: Teachers College Press.

Shapiro, H. S., & Purpel, D. E. (Eds.). (2004). *Critical social issues in American Education: Democracy and meaning in a globalizing world* (3rd ed.). Mahwah, NJ: Erlbaum.

Shapiro, J. P., & Stefkovich, J. A. (2005). *Ethical leadership and decision making in education: Applying theoretical perspectives to complex dilemmas* (2nd ed.). Mahwah, NJ: Erlbaum.

Starratt, R. J. (2004). *Ethical leadership*. San Franscisco: Jossey-Bass.

Tutu, D. (2004). *God has a dream*. New York: Doubleday.

Webb, L., & McCarthy, M. C. (1998). Ella Flagg Young: Pioneer of democratic school administration. *Educational Administration Quarterly, 34*(2), 223–242.

Young, M. D, Petersen, G. J., & Short, P. M. (2002). The complexity of substantive reform: A call for interdependence among key stakeholders. *Educational Administration Quarterly, 38*(2), 36–175.

CHAPTER 13

A NEW DEEL FOR
AN OLD PROBLEM

Social Justice at the Core

Valerie A. Storey and Thomas E. Beeman

New DEEL (Democratic Ethical Educational Leadership) does not refer to a
specific policy or reform, but rather to an ideology, unencumbered by international borders and domestic politics. In this chapter, we first endeavor to
identify the rhetoric of New DEEL and social justice, and the reality of its
implementation in schools today; spending time on No Child Left Behind
(NCLB) which we postulate is a major current impediment to New DEEL
and social justice. We identify steps to scaffold strategies which facilitate the
movement toward Democratic-Ethical Educational Leadership (DEEL) in
schools today. By default, this ensures that social justice is the major priority
of our education system. To achieve this end, we propose implementing a
structure which expands the notion of pedagogy from the four walls of the
classroom to a personalized, school-wide strategy.

"Greater than the tread of mighty armies is an idea whose time has come."[1]

Victor Hugo, 1802–1885

*Leadership for Social Justice: Promoting Equity and Excellence Through Inquiry and
Reflective Practice*, pp. 267–285
Copyright © 2008 by Information Age Publishing
All rights of reproduction in any form reserved.

INTRODUCTION

The knowledge base, research, and professional culture of the educational administration professorate and practitioners face acute pressure in the current era of high-stakes testing and standardization. Furthermore, pressures to conform to federal and state-wide education reform are forcing many educators to question their *raison d'etre*. As Fullan (1991) points out, the process of educational change often requires individuals to confront philosophical beliefs and values. May Sarton reminds us all that, "crisis may be one of the climates where education flourishes-a climate that forces honesty out, breaks down the walls of what ought to be, and reveals what is, instead" (Sarton, as cited in Katz, 1999, p. 138).

In *Teaching Democracy: Unity and Diversity in Public Life*, Walter Parker (2003) argues that in societies working toward democracy, the role of education is to help make citizens who are deeply engaged in the service of the public good, not merely in their own self interests. Following a pathway that "recognizes individual and group differences and to unite them horizontally in democratic moral discourse" (p. 25) education is thus charged with fostering a discourse of authenticity, responsibility and duty, thereby enabling citizen participation in the public arena. There has been a permeation of unease growing amongst educators committed to this viewpoint as they see the emphasis in schooling moving away from service and the personalizing of education to a more standard view of one fit for all. The unease is further reinforced by a feeling among the profession that there is a loss of voice at the grassroots level as the drive towards standardization gains increasing impetus. For some, this unease has had a tangentially, beneficial effect. It acts as a catalyst, causing them to reflect, not only on what their students need to learn, but also on what they as teachers now feel compelled to teach in order for their students to succeed in the international arena.

Concerns and issues about social justice that have been articulated during informal sessions at national and international conferences have been increasingly marginalized. These have served to unite previously disparate voices within educational administration to confront issues of inequality and injustice in our field. Ensuing collaborations served to build momentum to such a degree that representatives from university faculty, administration, Superintendents and school practitioners representing the United States, Canada, Australia, and the United Kingdom have united under an umbrella of shared concerns to demonstrate how research, status, and influence can be utilized to transform our profession, taking Democratic-Ethical-Educational-Leadership (DEEL) into schools and the wider community.

New DEEL does not refer to a specific policy or reform but rather to an ideology, unrestricted by international borders and domestic politics. The aim of New DEEL is to transform the profession. It may seem a daunting task but ideology is what moves people forward. It inspires actions which we might never have thought ourselves capable of. It requires vision, trust, confidence, stamina and indeed bravery as the New DEEL is likely to make some professionals uncomfortable. It demands that individual values and beliefs are questioned. It entails a commitment to proselytize the message through conference presentations, journal publications, and policy papers to ensure a growing and supportive network. Finally, it compels all those committed to the New DEEL vision to ensure that the values, voices, and scholarship of social justice permeate all actions, both personal and professional.

An understanding of New DEEL, however, requires that we move beyond the abstract to paint a picture of New DEEL in practice. In this chapter we first endeavor to identify the rhetoric of social justice and the reality of its implementation in schools today. Spending time on NCLB which we postulate is a major current impediment to New DEEL and social justice in our current education system. Second, we identify steps to scaffold strategies which facilitate the movement toward the goal of DEEL in schools today. This by default ensures that social justice is the major priority of our education system. To achieve this end, we propose a model (see Figure 13.1) based on harnessing distributive leadership. This model contends that distributive leadership in the field of education should extend well beyond the principal's (headteacher's) office, the school corridor and even the classroom but to the student learner.

Rhetoric: New DEEL and Social Justice

Contrary to experiences of educators in the field, research evidence suggests that social justice has reached the top of the education agenda in many Western industrialized societies. According to Furman and Shields (2003) the concepts of social justice and democratic community have become major concerns for educational scholars and practitioners at the beginning of the twenty- first century. As Furman (2003) notes, the increasing attention given to social justice is part of a general shift in the field toward a focus on the moral purposes of leadership in schools and how to achieve these purposes. Current awareness is motivated by several factors, including the growing diversity of school-age populations, the increasing awareness of the achievement and economic gaps between mainstream and "minoritized" children and the increasingly sophisticated analyses of social injustice as played out in schools, including those

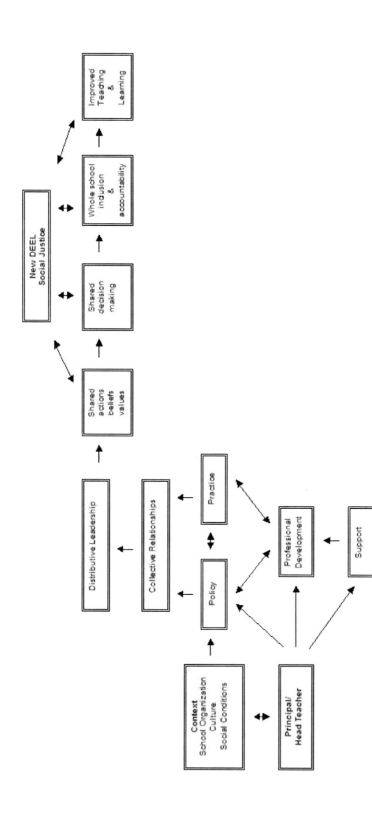

Figure 13.1. Facilitating the movement towards the goal of democratic—ethical educational leadership in schools.

that may arise from the high-stakes accountability movement (e.g., Larson & Ovando, 2001; McNeil, 2000)

Furman and Gruenewald (2004) note that there is increasing evidence of ongoing dialogue in the educational subfields of curriculum theory and cultural studies. Recent literature specific to educational leadership also marks the growing interest in this topic, including several chapters in the 2002 yearbook of the *National Society for the Study of Education* (Murphy, 2002) and two special issues of the *Journal of School Leadership*. They point out that social justice has become so prominent a topic that Murphy (1999) recently identified it as one of "three powerful synthesizing paradigms"[2] (p. 54) embedded in the "shifting landscape" of the field.

Reality: New DEEL and Social Justice

We are reminded by Shapiro and Stefkovich (2001), Katz (1999), and Noddings (1984), that teaching is a moral responsibility, that it is complex and that at the core of this moral complexity is the challenge of balancing care and justice. If we accept the truth of this construct, how do we ensure balance between a just education system and care for our students when the twenty-first century curricula being delivered in American classrooms today still tends to represent and promote the values and beliefs of the majority culture? Furthermore, the very constructs of school—timetables, policies, assessment methods, discipline, physical design, and so forth—are often quite foreign to students' experiences. While these problems appear to be entrenched norms due to being culturally and contextually based, they are not intractable.

In an effort to address this imbalance it is imperative that we move beyond the rhetoric and address social injustice pragmatically within our education system. First, we must look at the microlevel—at the student, classroom culture, school culture—and second at a macrolevel the values-aims and priorities of the state. This worthy aim cannot be achieved by maintaining the status quo but by critical reflection on current practices.

So what do we mean when we refer to social justice in the classroom? Many teachers have considerable trouble explaining what social justice is and what it looks like but can wax verbosely about everyday social injustices visible in their schools. With not a little embarrassment, countless teachers say that the classroom today has become a place in which learning is focused around the test, that its value has been narrowed, creativity and ingenuity has been replaced by instrumental and calculative pedagogy, and students rewarded for conformity rather than initiative. The ability to think critically has been surpassed by the need to regurgitate learned facts in the desired sequence. Personalized learning has gone out of the window and the philosophy of "one fit for all" predominates.

Students have become insular in many of their pursuits by using the Internet, listening to their iPod, text messaging the friend standing next to them. Their thoughts tend to focus more on the individual than concerning themselves with the responsibility of citizenship. On the other hand many students are involved in school or community service but this is often seen as discrete from what happens in the classroom. The curriculum delivered by schools today offer students few opportunities for self reflection. It is therefore not surprising that young people are becoming more used to absorbing knowledge from the "expert," whether a teacher in the classroom or through current technology. The ability to critique, empathize, and develop personal viewpoints should not be left purely to the domain of advanced placements classes. All students should be presented with such opportunities.

Social Justice: Pedagogical Issues and New DEEL

While text books may refer to pedagogy as educational methodology and technique; educators know that it embraces the social, cultural, and political context of the institution of schooling. It seeks to engage members of the school body at all levels in the act of reexamining their educational assumptions to ensure that their school utilizes the capacity of all their members. Educators embracing the New DEEL, while actively critiquing current education policy cannot be regarded as "Luddite," as they are involved in dialogue and empirical research aimed at presenting to policymakers alternatives to current education policy. According to Bogotch (2002), this is essential. Bogotch argues that it is necessary for all social justice/education reform efforts to be deliberately and continuously reinvented and critiqued.

It is such a critique of the educational system as advocated by scholars (Gross, 2006; Gross & Shapiro, 2006; Shapiro, 2006) that is required if schools are to foster equitable and socially responsible learning. It is a reasonable expectation that curriculum changes and newly implemented accountability systems have this as their aim. But according to Brown (2004), though scholars tend to have conflicting views of social justice, of the sources of injustice in schools and society, and of educators' obligations to committed action there is general consensus that the evidence is clear and alarming; various segments of public school population experience negative and inequitable treatment on a daily basis (Valenzuela, 2002). Gaps between sex, race, and socioeconomic groups are persistent and pervasive.

NCLB: The Paradox

For many advocates of New DEEL the culprits behind the current ret-rograde focus in the classroom are recent state and federal reforms, most notably NCLB, signed into law by President Bush in early 2002. This law requires schools and districts to break down achievement data by racial, demographic, and socioeconomic subgroups in every grade, and show progress for each group. The affect of this policy focuses attention on reducing and eliminating the achievements gaps between minority and White students; low income students attending schools that fail to meet academic performance targets for three straight years are eligible for free tuition from public or private providers that have been approved by state education officials. Districts are required to set aside a portion of the fed-eral Title 1^3 (the largest of the federal education programs, providing fed-eral funding for schools to help students who are behind academically or at risk of falling behind. Services can include: hiring teachers to reduce class size, tutoring, computer labs, parental involvement activities, profes-sional development, purchase of materials and supplies, prekindergarten programs, and hiring teacher assistants or others) money they receive for disadvantaged students to pay for the tutoring and school choice provi-sions of the law.

NCLB sets out with a laudable aim, that closing the achievement gap is essential to democracy, but needs to be followed up with reflection, guided by care to see whether the original policy has fulfilled its aims or has introduced new equities or harm (Noddings, 1999). Concerns regard-ing implementation and funding of NCLB quickly emanated from advo-cates for equality and social justice as it became clear that not all states understood aspects of NCLB. The increasingly, transparent accountability affected vulnerability at all levels of the education system. Not surpris-ingly, vulnerable people often react with negativity and hostility.

NCLB has now been around for 4 years and research is being pub-lished that has longitudinal grounding. The fundamental question to address is: Has NCLB fostered social justice? The answer is of course complex as each state has created its own set of academic standards indi-cating what a student should know and learn at each grade level. This lack of consistency between states currently negates direct state by state comparisons. Each school and district is expected to show adequate yearly progress (AYP) toward meeting required participation and proficiency levels on state assessments. According to NCLB, such progress is mea-sured for all students in each of the following categories of students:

1. American Indian
2. Asian/Pacific Islander

3. Black (non-Hispanic)
4. Hispanic
5. White
6. Limited English proficiency (English as a second language)
7. Special education
8. Free/reduced price lunch
9. Entire student population of school or district

In reporting AYP, a school or district must have at least 40 students in a category for it to count for participation; 20 students are required for proficiency, except special education which requires 40 students.

Research conducted by the U.S. Department of Education[4] (2006) found that most subgroups of students measured by the NCLB had made small but distinctive achievement gains in the fourth and eighth grade reading and math from the 2000–01 to the 2002-03 school year. State assessments also indicated slight reductions in the achievement gap between students from low-income families and other students[5] These are positive, welcomed gains, but more negatively, the report also projected that based on current data only Delaware, Kansas, North Carolina, and Oklahoma are likely to get their poor-student subgroup to state proficiency level by 2013–14 school year as mandated NCLB.

The reality is that there is a lack of consistency as to how NCLB has been implemented in states and school districts, much being dependent on the commitment of resources both in the terms of dollars and personnel. Many parents remain unaware of the fact that their children are eligible for this additional tuition because by law, it is the school districts that have the responsibility of notifying parents and this is not always happening. Consequently, the beneficiaries of NCLB tend to be those who are strong in political and social capital while for many students NCLB actually contributes further to their perceived exclusion, conflict which has yet to be resolved. A survey from the Education Industry Association (EIA)[6] (February, 2006) revealed that many districts do not offer timely or clear enough notification to parents of children who are eligible for additional tuition and resources. The *National Assessment of Title 1: Interim Report to Congress* (U.S. Department of Education, 2006) confirmed the EIA findings. The report found that only 17% of eligible students nationwide signed up for the free tutoring that Title 1 schools are required to offer after not meeting educational targets 3 years in a row. However, the number of students receiving those supplemental educational services increased more than fourfold in the 2-year period from the 2002–2003 school year through the 2003–04 year. Statistics from the Center on Education Policy (2006) in their report *From the Capital to the Classroom* (their fourth published report, comprehensively studying the implementation of NCLB at the federal, state, and local level) indicated that the percentage of students participating in school tutoring programs has remained constant for the last 2 years at 20%.

Districts known for successfully communicating educating policy to parents are experiencing a different problem in that in some districts (i.e., Chicago) demand is outstripping resources. The district has worked aggressively to ensure that all eligible students and parents are aware of the service and this is reflected in the relatively high participation rate. The district estimates that 200,000 students are eligible for free tutoring, Elizabeth F. Swanson, the director of the after-school and community-school programs said in an interview[7] and of those, 43,000 students received tutoring at the start of this school year.

Yet, a further tension exists in relation to additional tuition, which McNeil (2000) points out. Educational reforms designed to increase equity in achievement through testing often translate into regimes of remediation and segregation that have a record of putting further behind the very populations they were supposed to serve. More empirical data is required to see whether NCLB is indeed impacting disadvantaged groups in this way.

Nevertheless, this disparity in participation rates needs addressing. Even the "relatively high" participation rate in Chicago should not be acceptable. Currently there are no real statutory consequences at either the state or district level for failing to meet student needs. Some states have found several aspects of NCLB to be unacceptable; primarily, the financial imposition on their education budget. Other states have cited the further assessment of students in reading and mathematics annually in Grades 3–8 and at least once in high school, and determining whether schools are making AYP toward ensuring that all students are proficient in reading and math by the 2013–2014, as unacceptable. Some states are openly rebelling (e.g., Connecticut).[8] To combat this action by the state, civil rights groups, including the Connecticut National Association for the Advancement of Colored People (NAACP) and the national office of the NAACP have joined the U.S. Education Department in defending NCLB. The general counsel for the national NAACP explained that allowing states to opt out of the federal law's test requirement would set a dangerous precedent for other states. The Connecticut NAACP, acting on behalf of three minority students in high-poverty schools, filed papers in federal courts in New Haven, Connecticut (January, 2006) asking the judge in the *Connecticut v. Spelling* case to allow the group to intervene on the side of the U.S. Department of Education.[9]

The Center on Education Policy (2006) found that while NCLB is having the positive effect of encouraging schools and districts to more closely aligning teaching and learning with states' curriculum standards, and that test scores are rising, it is doing so at the detriment of subjects such as social studies, music and art, to make more time for the main subjects being tested (i.e., reading and mathematics), thereby "diminishing activities that might keep children in school" (p. 7). The in-depth study also found that districts have become more restrictive in what teachers are supposed to teach. This quantitative study is the first published, empirical research from an independent body, to confirm what teachers have been saying anecdotally for the last 4 years. As yet, the implications of the ad hoc approach by school districts have yet to be fully understood. While the rhetoric of most school districts and states place strong emphasis on the curriculum principles of breadth, balance, and progression, there is recognition of the tension that exists in maintaining these principles and, at the same time achieves manageability and sufficient emphasis on developing skills and knowledge in the tested subject areas.

Teachers' frustration and negative views in relation to the effect of NCLB on subjects taught, and their opposition to NCLB is becoming more overt and explicit. Over the past 2 years, the U.S. Department of Education has made so many compromises in implementing NCLB that the law's legitimacy is in serious question according to a recent study by the Civil Rights Project (n.d.) at Harvard University. They found that state accountability has weakened as a direct result of the comprises being made by education department officials on NCLB implementation (contrary to American history where education was considered a more local responsibility). The department has felt pressurized on two sides. First, there has been increasing political and professional criticisms of its requirements, and second there are an increasing number of schools and districts identified for improvement. This is very much an ongoing issue.

There is no doubt that high stakes testing has a major impact on which curriculum values are considered most important. Greater attention should be given to the way in which dilemmas might be resolved, at both a local, state, and federal level. While we have pointed the finger at the NCLB, and accused it of hindering pedagogical development within schools, it may also be argued that it is the catalyst by which interest groups previously outside the mainstream domain are welcomed into the system as coalitions develop to fight, not the inequities of NCLB but the inequities and justice issues of implementation and delivery.

DEEL: HOW DO WE RECOGNIZE IT?

The key to positively implementing policy mandates often lies in the specific contextual responses of school leaders. Recent literature supports the view that the capacity for leadership exists, and must be developed throughout schools. Murphy (2006, p. 50) points out that "while at first glance it may seem a bit paradoxical, evidence indicates that the head-teacher occupies the critical position in ensuring that teacher leadership takes root and flourishes in schools."

Observing current developments, Fullan (2000) comments that

> the scientific study of leadership has never been greater, nor has the recognition that broad-based leadership is the only way forward.... We are force-fully reminded that the notion of leadership must not be confined to those holding formal leadership positions. All leadership, if it is effective, must have a strong component of sharedness. (p. xx)

Only through actively engaging in shared dialogue can colleagues agree on a shared value system and thereby speak as one voice, ensuring that school leadership becomes and remains democratic and ethical.

Fostering a democracy within every school will help ensure the full participation of all community members within the school building and the local community working for a consensually agreed common "moral good" of social justice. "If school leadership comes not only from the front of a classroom but from within the classroom itself, then the behavior of such leaders as observed by members of the organization and their constituents must mirror their rhetoric" (Storey & Beeman, 2006). In reality this means that many decisions on collective actions are context based being constructed by members of the community in the midst of their unique local context (Furman & Shields, 2003).

Twenty years ago Gutmann (1987) asked the pertinent question, "how much internal democratization of schools is desirable in a democracy?" (p. 93). The question is critical and as valid today. In attempting to answer the question Gutmann reflects on the Laboratory School at the University of Chicago lead by John Dewey from 1896–1903. Students were given responsible roles outside the classroom and participated in reviewing and planning their learning. "It was an embryonic democratic society because it elicited a commitment to learning and cultivated the prototypically democratic virtues among its students, not because it treated them as the political or intellectual equals of its teachers" (p. 93). Despite the fact that students were not involved in curriculum planning and assessment and that many decisions were determined by teachers and administrators, Gutmann does not see the internal structure of the school as a failure in democracy. She makes the point that "an ideal democratic school is not as democratic as an ideal democratic society should not disenchant us either with schooling or democracy, since democracies depend on schools to prepare students for citizenship" (p. 94).

School Leadership

To ensure that schools are being lead in a democratic and ethical manner we propose that the leadership model adopted within a school is distributive among many actors. In other words, leadership is not the purview solely of administrators, but also exercised by people in many positions (Smylie, Conley, & Marks, 2002). There are many different models of distributive leadership, but taken together, they suggest that, not only is leadership distributed throughout the school, but that leadership "multiplies" through the type of interactions. Smylie and Shields (2003) advocate the use of a second leadership lens, that is, constructivist leadership theory which purports that leadership aims at the construction of meaning and purpose by members of a community through their communicative relationships, or "the reciprocal processes that enable participants in an educational community to construct meanings that lead toward a common purpose about schooling" (Lambert et al., 1995, p. 29).

We now turn our attention onto processes that we believe facilitate these communal relationships by explaining how democratic leadership becomes constructed and "distributed" across a school community.

Teacher Leadership

The classic bureaucratic model of leadership is one where knowledge and expertise resides with those with power and authority who then transmit to those on the lower rungs of the hierarchical ladder. An alternative model of leadership is based on relationships and collaboration. Prominent school reformers are focusing on how opening the leadership relationship to all and focusing collective work on learning generate broad, collective leadership (Barth, 1990; Macbeath, 1998; Macbeath, Demetriou, Rudduck, & Myers, 2003; Harris & Lambert, 2003; Fullan, 2000) As teachers take on roles that might previously have been seen as beyond the scope of the regular classroom for which they were prepared new understandings are evolving. Yet the transition from teacher to leader involves a shift in 'cultural positioning' wherein processes and procedures normally associated with the role of classroom teacher change, and subsequently, the teacher's own perception of self, changes. Unobservable barriers among colleagues such as lack of trust or lack of respect may foster a negative school culture and may hinder such a transition. Barth suggests that something deep and powerful within school cultures seems to work against teacher leadership.

Teacher leadership has the potential to upset the status quo within a school as roles become blurred or merged as evidence of sharedness become more avert. The potential for rivalry or exclusion is obvious. Many teachers may find safety in the heroic leader model believing that this is the stronger route to academic freedom. Confusion regarding new roles and the fear of change may lead to feelings of negativity and distrust. In the United Kingdom, support for teachers has come from the voluntary program, Networked Learning Communities[10] (NLC) which is one of the largest projects of the National College of School Leadership[11] (NCSL), drawing to a close in August 2006. McGregor (2006) found that "those schools closely engaged in this voluntary NLCs programme, with its emphasis on joint practice development, enquiry and distributed leadership might be those where such supported risk-taking is likely to take place" (p. 16).

Teacher/Student Leadership

Democratic education requires empowering children to participate in, and take responsibility for, their own learning (Shields, 2004). "It is argued that a perception of leadership as a relational process of influence rather than of hierarchical power strengthens the possibility of recognizing the potential of students as leaders" (McGregor, 2006, p. 1). This alternative way of conceptualizing leadership includes active teacher/student dialogue outside the classroom. While not totally eliminating the perceived power roles collaborative dialogue does allow the student a degree of freedom (seldom experienced) to participate in school strategy and planning as an equal partner (Fielding, 2004; Rudduck & Flutter, 2004; Mitra, 2004). Giving students a voice at the leadership and management (i.e., the decision making) table on strategic planning augments the focus on equity; presenting opportunities to raise and discuss contentious issues hopefully reducing issues of dissonance between teacher and student.

Work on student voice in schools and communities is a rapidly growing research literature (Fielding, 2001). New practice and emerging research knowledge indicates the potential for the student voice movement to transform education processes but in order to achieve this potential Fielding believes that educators need to embrace a view of education which understands that the means of engagement cannot sensibly be separated from the nature of aspirations. However, his review of the literature leads him to the conclusion that" work on student voice is at an interesting crossroads" (p. 100). He suggests that the movement to increase student voice has a dual capacity to either reinforce the current status quo, or "develop genuinely transformative practices that offer the possibility of more creative, more fulfilling alternatives" (p. 100). He presents two different scenarios for increasing the advocacy of student voice:

In the first scenario: the student becomes the voice of the customer disciplining the teacher into the pre-ordained, imperfectly internalized competences of government edict and market responsiveness. Here the rigors of performance culture deepen the accountability and responsiveness of teachers as pedagogic technicians and sustain a notion of students as the collectors of educational products (test results, certificates, saleable skills) that "add value" to their employment prospects. (Fielding, 2001, p. 107)

In the second scenario: teachers and students: go beyond what is currently required to create a quite different present, a present that has within it a future that is more securely centered on the development of persons in and through community, rather than the growth of consumers in and through the market. Insofar as students and teachers do this together, their practices are "transitive," transgressive, emancipatory, creative of quite different realities to those we are currently required emulating. (Fielding, 2001, p. 108)

Fielding (2001) cites research currently being conducted in the United Kingdom, funding of a major ESRC (Economic & Social Research Council) Network Project—*Consulting Pupils About Teaching & Learning*[12] that forms part of the wider ESRC Teaching & Learning Research Program and in North America, South America, and Australasia, all of which has within it the possibility of new communities of democratic practice. While Fielding advocates strongly for a communal transformative model of student voice he suggests that the need for implementation of supporting systems maybe an inhibiting factor and that in the era of accountability the model of student quality management will dominate.

Mitra (2006) in her advocacy of student voice envisages students working with administrators and teachers to cocreate school reform. Recent evidence from her research suggests that such involvement enables students to meet their own developmental needs and strengthens student ownership of the change process. It is envisioned that an outcome of the developing synergy will be to enhance pedagogy, curriculum, assessment, teacher training, and school culture; ultimately enabling students, teachers, and administrators to co-create school reform.

Involvement in the dynamic process of pedagogy enables the student to develop an enhanced understanding of the ideological underpinnings of the curriculum. A relevant example of student input into curriculum development is the reviewing and adopting text books. Particularly controversial for specific cultural groups is what they perceive as inaccuracies and biases in text books' portrayal of racial, religious or ethnic groups. For example, California, the largest text-book adoption state, recently put off voting on over 500 revision changes requested by the Hindu Education Foundation in the San Francisco Bay area on the grounds that the revisions were of a religious-political nature. The volunteer curriculum commission review felt unequipped to respond to the vocal interest group.[13] There is evidence of similar efforts by groups that want to revise the portrayal of Islam in text books.[14]

Students can provide insights and contribute to the conversations on improving teaching and learning in their school. For example, The Best Practices (BP) club at Lexington High School in Lexington, Massachusetts is a student-run club that works with teachers to improve teaching and learning at the high school. BP was created as an outlet for positive student feedback on teaching and learning. It is now a place that has started three different kinds of dialogue at the high school: (a) student-student; (b) student-teacher; (c) teacher-teacher. BP student members have used student observers in the classroom, facilitated student-teacher meetings, and conducted workshops on best teaching practices used in the classroom.[15] The workshops have the dual purpose of improving curricula delivery and engaging students in the "in language" of the teaching profession. They contribute to the mutual "respect" that BP students recognize as essential to the success of their initiative. Students also expressed the hope that teachers would respect what they were doing, respect their opinions, and also respect their viewpoints.

DIRECTIONS AND CHALLENGES

Our discussions of democratic-ethical-educational leadership underscore the fact that education in twenty-first century schools has a moral purpose. Schools in the earlier days of the republic were truly reflections of the local community teaching core values and the basics considered by the local community to prepare youth to become good citizens and lead a productive life. As the roles of parents, teachers and local citizens were usurped, first by the state and then by the federal government, more emphasis on measurement than developing a moral citizenry has evolved. Instead of creating educated and motivated young people, the increased federal involvement is having a reverse sobering and leveling effect. Suggesting that young people today are less able to take on roles of good citizenship, a sense of competition and not collaboration is affecting the social milieu. To rectify the situation schools must again take on the mantle of the moral agent, facilitating the energizing of a democratic community; based on agreed common values; promoted by school curricula and pedagogy; reinforced in the home. By building student capacity for leadership young people are able to work with teachers, administrators and members of their local community to cocreate the path of reform, it enables students to meet their own developmental needs, and strengthens the understanding of the community for the values espoused by the school. Implementing such a model enhances a democratic, socially just, and ethical organization.

HAS THE DIALOGUE REACHED STALEMATE?

Is this a "Pollyanna-ish ideal?" A paradigm shift in ideology, most certainly, but feasible within current education contexts. New DEEL advocates articulate the need for a radical review of the system and structure of schooling, and to reconceptualize pedagogy as learner-centered. We propose constructing new organizational possibilities to enhance active involvement for the whole school body to ensure all feel involved or represented in the leading and forward strategic planning of their school, personalizing teaching and learning to the student body. Each student will be presented with the opportunity to become involved in the process of decision making relating to their school and their personal learning, and of critically examining choices in their learning process, personal expectations, interpersonal relationships, and personal lives. Such a reflective and participative culture will assist students to view ethical choices as a vital part of their future lives, both as professionals and in their daily living. While this may be regarded as transformational it is not unrealistic. The implementation of such structures will expand the notion of pedagogy from the four walls of the classroom to become a personalized, school-wide learning strategy. There is however a sense of urgency as a worrying concern is whether teachers entering the profession today, under the umbrella of NCLB, are equipped with the necessary skills and mindset to implement New DEEL ideology. Transformation unfortunately is hard work and often the tyranny of the urgent impedes collective thinking. Advocates of New DEEL have a shared responsibility to make their voices heard. As international collaborations continue to grow and develop, research and emerging new practices are likely to challenge existing education structures demonstrating how research, status, and influence can be utilized to transform our profession, and reassign democratic values to their rightful place, the heart of education.

NOTES

1. Victor Hugo, French author, 1852, *The Book of Political Quotes*, p. 166.
2. The two other powerful synthesizing paradigms according to Murphy are school improvement and democratic community.

3. Title I, the cornerstone of the NCLB, is the largest federal education program. It is intended to help ensure that all children have the opportunity to obtain a high quality education and reach proficiency on challenging state academic standards and assessments. Many of the major requirements in NCLB are outlined in Title I–AYP, teacher, and paraprofessional requirements, accountability, sanctions for schools designated for improvement, standards and assessments, annual state report cards, professional development, and parent involvement.

4. National Assessment of Title 1: Interim Report to Congress.

5. National Assessment of Title 1: Interim Report (April, 2006) from the U.S. Department of Education.

6. Washington-based association, a trade group representing a range of private-sector education businesses, commissioned the survey. The independent American Institutes for research analyzed and reported the results from 216 respondents.

7. *Education Week*, February 22, 2006.

8. Connecticut officials, argue that NCLB duplicates many of their own accountability measures, which were put in place long before the federal law and provide ample information about how students are performing. Several other states have also mounted protests against the 2002 law. Utah says its laws will take priority over federal laws.

9. *Education Week*, February 8, 2006.

10. NCSL's NLC program was launched in 2002. It is a coordinated reform initiative involving over 130 school-to-school networks drawn from over 1,500 schools. Each NLC comprises a group or cluster of schools working collaboratively in partnership with local authorities, higher education institutions and the wider community to improve opportunities and raise standards for their students. Retrieved from http://www.ncsl.org.uk/networked/index.cfm.

11. NCSL provides learning and development opportunities and professional and practical support for school leaders at every stage in their career. NCSL's core purpose is to develop individuals and teams to lead and manage their own schools and work collaboratively with others. Retrieved from http://www.ncsl.org.uk/

12. ESRC Network Project—Consulting Pupils About Teaching & Learning raises a number of issues and concerns that must be addressed. Primarily, the creation of new/different student elites comprised of the voices of those who find it easiest to speak coherently and those who adults find it easier to hear.

13. *Education Week*, February 6, 2003

14. *Education Week*, February 8, 2006

15. http://www.bestpracticeslex.org/

REFERENCES

Barth, R. S. (1990). *Improving schools from within*. San Francisco: Jossey Bass.

Bogotch, L. E. (2002). Educational leadership and social justice: Practice into theory. *Journal of School Leadership, 12,* 138-156.

Brown, K. M. (2004). Leadership for social justice and equity: Weaving a transformative framework and pedagogy. *Education Administration Quarterly, 40*(1). 79-110.

Center on Education Policy. (2006). *From the Capital to the classroom: Year 4 of the No Child Left Behind Act.* Washington, DC: Author.

Civil Rights Project at Harvard University. (n.d.). Retrieved July 18th 2007 from http://www.civilrightsproject.ucla.edu/

Fielding, M. (2001). Beyond the rhetoric of student voice: new departures or new constraints in the transformation of 21st century school? *FORUM 43* (2) 100-109.

Fielding, M. (2004). Transformative approaches to student voice: Theoretical underpinnings, recalcitrant realities. *British Educational Research Journal, 30*(2), 295–311.

Fullan, M. (1991). *The new meaning of educational change.* New York: Teachers College Press.

Fullan, M. (2000). *Introduction. The Jossey-Bass Reader on Educational Leadership.* San Francisco: Jossey-Bass.

Furman, G. (2003). The 2002 UCEA presidential address: Toward a new scholarship of educational leadership? *UCEA Review, 45*(1), 1–6.

Furman, G. C., & Gruenewald, D. A. (2004). Expanding the landscape of social justice: A critical ecological analysis. *Educational Administration Quarterly, 40,* 47–76.

Furman, G. C., & Shields, C. M. (2003, April). *How can educational leaders promote and support social justice and democratic community in schools?* Paper presented at the annual meeting of the American Educational Research Association, Chicago.

Gutmann, A. (1987). Democratic Education. Princeton: University Press.

Gross, S. J. (2006, February 16 & 17). Key note speech made at the New DEEL, Winter Strategy Session at Temple University, Philadelphia.

Gross, S. J., & Shapiro, J. P. (2005). Our new era requires a New DEEL: Towards democratic ethical educational leadership. *UCEA Review, XLVII*(3), 1-4.

Harris, A., & Lambert, L. (2003) *What is leadership capacity?* Cranfield, National College for School Leadership. Retrieved from http://networkedlearning.ncsl.org.uk/knowledge-base/think-pieces/what-is-leadership-capacity-2003.pdf

Lambert, L., Walker, D., Zimmerman, D. P., Cooper, J. E., Lambert, M.D., Gardner, M. E., et al. (1995). *The constructivist leader.* New York: Teachers College Press.

Larson, C., & Ovando, C. (2001). *The color of bureaucracy: The politics of equity in multicultural school communities.* Belmont, CA: Wadsworth.

Katz, M. S. (1999). Teaching about fairness and caring. In M. S. Katz, N. Noddings, & K. A. Strike (Eds.), *Justice and caring: The search for common ground in education* (pp. 59–74). New York: Teachers College Press.

Macbeath, J. (Ed.) (1998) *Effective school leadership: Responding to change.* London: Paul Chapman.

Macbeath, J., Demetriou, H., Rudduck, J., & Myers, K. (2003). Cambridge, England: Pearson.

McGregor, J. (2006, May). *Pupil voice and participation: Promises, pleasures, pitfalls.* Paper presented at Conference Pupil Voice and Participation, University of Nottingham, England.

McNeil, L. M. (2000). *Contradictions of school reform: Educational costs of standardized testing.* New York: Routledge.

Mitra, D. (2006). Increasing student voice and moving toward youth leadership. *The Prevention Researcher, 13*(1), 7–10.

Murphy, J. (1999). *The quest for a center: Notes on the state of the profession of educational leadership.* Columbia, MO: University Council for Educational Administration.

Murphy, J. (Ed.). (2002). *The educational leadership challenge: Redefining leadership for the 21st century. One hundred-first yearbook of the National Society for the Study of Education.* Chicago: National Society for the Study of Education.

Murphy, J. (2006). Some insights on shared leadership and communities of practice. In *National College for School Leadership: International Perspectives on Networked Learning.* Retrieved from http://networkedlearning.ncsl.org.uk/collections/network-research-series/reports/international-perspectives-on-networked-learning/nlg-some-insights-on-shared-leadership-and-communities-of-practice.pdf

Noddings, N. (1984). *Caring: A feminine approach to ethics and moral education.* Berkeley: University of California Press.

Noddings, N. (1999). Introduction. In M. S. Katz, N. Noddings, & K. A. Strike (Eds.), *Justice and caring: The search for common ground in education* (pp. 1–7). New York: Teachers College Press.

Parker, W. C. (2003). *Teaching democracy: Unity and diversity in public life.* New York: Teachers College Press.

Rudduck, J., & Flutter, J. (2004) *How to improve your school: Giving pupils a voice.* London: Continuum.

Shapiro, J. P. (2006, February 16 & 17). Presentation made at the New DEEL, Winter Strategy Session at Temple University, Philadelphia.

Shapiro, J., & Stefkovich, J.A. (2001). *Ethical leadership and decision making in education Applying theoretical perspectives to complex dilemmas.* Mahwah, NJ: Erlbaum.

Shields, C. M. (2004). Dialogic leadership for social justice: Overcoming pathologies of silence. *Educational Administration Quarterly, 40*(1). 109–132.

Smylie, M. A., Conley, S., & Marks, H. M. (2002). Exploring new approaches to teacher leadership for school improvement. In J. Murphy (Ed.), *The educational leadership challenge: Redefining leadership for the 21st century* (pp. 162–188). Chicago: National Society for the Study of Education.

Storey, V. A., & Beeman, T. (2006). The New DEEL: A path toward more authentic leadership. *The Beacon: Pennsylvania School Study Council, 2*(3), 1–8.

U.S. Department of Education. (2006). *National Assessment of Title 1: Interim Report to Congress.* Washington, DC: National Center for Education Evaluation and Region Assessment

Valenzuela, A. (2002). Reflections on the subtractive underpinnings of education research and policy. *Journal of Teacher Education, 53*(3), 235–241.

CHAPTER 14

ETHICS AND SOCIAL JUSTICE WITHIN THE NEW DEEL

Addressing the Paradox of Control/Democracy

Joan Poliner Shapiro

This chapter addresses the ethical and social justice implications of an educational movement called, the New DEEL (Democratic Ethical Educational Leadership). In particular, this chapter emphasizes the ethical underpinnings of this movement by focusing on a paradox in the form of the dyad of control/democracy. This important paradox is developed through a discussion of the profound contradictions between the accountability thrust and the democratic emphasis in schools, particularly in the United States. The chapter attempts to grapple with the inconsistencies within the paradox and provides some suggestions for coping with the challenges of blending these two very different and opposing concepts together during a very turbulent era. It also attempts to illuminate what a New DEEL moral educational leader might value, especially in the area of social justice, as well as how he or she might guide an organization.

Leadership for Social Justice: Promoting Equity and Excellence Through Inquiry and Reflective Practice, pp. 287–301
Copyright © 2008 by Information Age Publishing
All rights of reproduction in any form reserved.

INTRODUCTION

This chapter focuses on the ethical and social justice implications of the New DEEL. This is a movement that promotes democratic action using a moral framework focusing on leadership in schools, in higher education, and in the wider community.

In response to the challenges facing the field of educational leadership today, colleagues from leading University Council of Educational Administration's (UCEA) members joined committed practitioners to take action. During the 2004–2005 academic year, faculty and department leaders from Temple University, The Pennsylvania State University, the University of Vermont, Rowan University, the University of Oklahoma, the University of North Carolina at Greensboro, and UCEA, as well as United States, Canadian, Australian, British, and Taiwanese practitioners, launched a new movement in the field of educational leadership. Since its inception more than 20 universities and colleges have joined the group and more and more educators across the globe are responding to its call. The New DEEL aims to change the direction of educational administration away from an overly corporate and controlling model towards the values of democratic and ethical behavior (Gross & Shapiro, 2005).

Those who are part of this movement believe that the first job of the school is to help all young people become effective citizens in a democracy. Democratic citizenship, in any era, is a complex task but it seems especially difficult at this time when international conflict and growing economic and social inequality are the rule and not the exception. The spirit of the New DEEL is towards a liberating education enabling students from different social classes, ethnicities, races, and even genders, to make intelligent and moral decisions as future citizens.

The mission of the New DEEL is to create an action-oriented partnership, dedicated to inquiry into the nature and practice of democratic, ethical educational leadership through sustained processes of open dialogue, right to voice, community inclusion, and responsible participation toward the common good. The group strives to create an environment to facilitate democratic ethical decision making in educational theory and practice which acts in the best interests of all students.

What the New DEEL hopes to stimulate is a focus on educational leadership and not educational management. One difference in creating these kinds of leaders is that they have been prepared, through the study of ethics, to appreciate a difficult paradox or inconsistency when they meet it, and then know how to deal with it in ways that are not purely managerial in nature, but, instead, are morally sound.

This chapter will focus on the ethical underpinning of the New DEEL. To accomplish this, the emphasis will be on a paradox that seems to play a central role in the working lives of school administrators in the United States in this current era. It is framed using the dyad of control/democracy. In this chapter, then, there will be a discussion of these two differing and opposing concepts followed by an attempt to blend them together, taking into consideration the turbulence of this period.

AN IMPORTANT PARADOX

Purpel (1989), in his inspiring and classic book, *The Moral and Spiritual Crisis of Education*, provided some excellent examples of paradoxes. In particular, he dealt directly with the inconsistencies that he felt existed between control and democracy. Purpel wrote that most of us wish to control our destinies. He went on to say that this is hard to do in a world riddled with terrorism, nuclear bombs, and internal violence; where there are economic depressions, tidal waves, famines, pollution, volcanoes, and hurricanes. He continued that because of this desire for control, in our bureaucratized, computerized culture, we value "work, productivity, efficiency and uniformity over play, flexibility, diversity and freedom" (p. 48).

Then Purpel (1989) turned to democracy. He spoke of how bureaucracy "sharply conflicts with our dedication to democratic principles which stress self-determination and a process for both sustaining autonomy and adjusting conflicts" (p. 49). Purpel continued by discussing John Dewey's conceptualization of the school as a "laboratory" of democracy where students and teachers could wrestle with the challenges of the democratic experience" (p. 49).

Currently, in U.S. public schools, accountability is very much in vogue. Discipline and school policies are of major concerns. Meeting standards through the raising of test scores are a central focus. Student government is lying low. Debating societies are not emphasized. Controversy and critique are not desired nor is there really any time for it in a curriculum that is driven by high stakes testing. While schools can and should be the way to encourage democracy, by teaching young people to be good citizens, this is clearly not the case in this era. Civics education seems to be missing in many schools that are focusing on testing and a very basic education.

Despite the trend, there is a counter movement in America. For example, there is at the very least an increasing cry for more service education (Keith, 1999, 2005). Service learning does ask students to go beyond the school and help organizations within society. In addition, there are a number of scholars (Aiken, 2002; Boyd, 2000; Crow, 2006; Driscoll, 2001; Furman-Brown, 2002; Gutmann, 1999; Gutmann & Thompson, 2004; O'Hair, McLaughlin & Reitzug, 2000; Mitra, 2004; Reitzug & O'Hair, 2002; Shapiro & Purpel, 2004) who maintain that students should have a strong civics education to be prepared to play important, assertive, and meaningful roles in the democratic process.

Not too long ago, I talked about this paradox of control versus democracy in my ethics class with graduate students. These students were also administrators and teachers from urban, suburban, and rural schools in the mid-Atlantic region of the United States. I asked them about student government, as we had just finished discussing Lawrence Kohlberg's (1981) *Just Community,* in which students with their teachers actually made some decisions relating to important school issues. Interestingly enough, in this class of 25 graduate students, none of their schools had active student governments that provided young people with decision-making opportunities in areas that mattered.

ACCOUNTABILITY: A CONTAGIOUS DISEASE?

Schools have been captured by the concept of "accountability," which has been transformed from a notion that schools need to be responsive and responsible to community concerns to one in which numbers are used to demonstrate that schools have met their minimal requirement—a reductionism which has given higher priority to the need to control than to educational considerations (Purpel, 1989, p. 48)

Despite many of the positive arguments that are made regarding accountability today (Scheurich, Skrla, & Johnson, 2000; Skrla, Scheurich, & Johnson, 2000), there are a considerable number of negative aspects associated with this concept. *Accountability: A Contagious Disease?* was a paper that I wrote in the late 1970s. The article (Shapiro, 1979) was published in a journal in the United Kingdom when I was doing postdoctoral work at the University of London's Institute of Education. At that time, I was able to view the U.S. educational scene from a distance and realized that the time had come to warn British educators about a movement developing in America that could have profound effects on them. In particular, I wrote about a taxpayer's revolt that began in California with Proposition 13. In one sweeping decision, in 1978, California voters rejected local school district support of public education. This trend followed in Massachusetts with Proposition 2 ½. I also noted that, in Michigan, "blanket" testing was in place and that there was an attempt to utilize those test results as vehicles for dismissals and promotions of teachers. A form of *payment by results* had become a reality. In the area of teacher training, at that time, performance-based standards were required in seventeen states. Back to basics was the slogan used for curriculum development.

In that period, accountability occurred for two major reasons. Bowles and Gintis (1976) explained one motive when they described the public's increasing disdain for the American Dream in which the majority of the young people in the country could graduate from college and find excellent jobs. In that period, there was a restricted employment market for youth. Another reason had to do with the instability of the social reforms and progressive education that occurred in the 1960s. Control, through accountability and through a back to basics curriculum, was thought to be the panacea. In the late 1970s, in the United Kingdom, educators were hearing the term, accountability, for the first time. In the United States, the movement had begun in earnest. The *accountant's ledger* was just becoming the bottom-line in education. This movement was seen as a way to put educators in their place by making them produce measurable results through testing. Underlying accountability, at that time, was attribution theory or blaming, and it was very much a part of the discourse.

In the United States, *A Nation at Risk* (National Commission on Excellence in Education, 1983), *America 2000* (1991), *Goals 2000* (1993) and No Child Left Behind (2002) were documents that developed the concept of accountability in education. These reports from various commissions, departments, governors, and even presidents, made it clear that holding educators accountable was essential. Deconstructing *America 2000*, for example, my colleagues and I (Sewell, DuCette, & Shapiro, 1998) discovered that the term, accountability, was mentioned 23 times—the same number of pages as the report.

Although discussed in general terms initially in the earlier reports, accountability has proven to be far more complicated concept than we thought initially. For example, Darling-Hammond and Snyder (1992) discovered five types of accountability—*political, legal, bureaucratic, professional,* and *market.* Later on, my colleagues and I (Gross, Shaw, & Shapiro, 2003) added four other forms of accountability that we discovered in scholarly journals, practitioner journals, and newspapers. They were *parent, fiscal, student,* and *personal.* Gold and Simon (2004) contributed a tenth type, *public accountability,* to append to the list.

Returning to the title of my paper in 1979, I still believe that accountability could be classified as a disease that has metastasized over time. In fact, Leithwood (2001) calls this era the "accountability age," while Normore (2004), when discussing the plight of school administrators today, refers to the current situation as "the edge of chaos" (p. 55). The major difference in the form of accountability that I wrote about in the 1970s is that it has changed from one overarching concept into, at the very least, 10 types, and most of these, but not all, have increasingly been used to blame educational leaders and teachers for not doing their jobs.

While accountability tends to blame educators for all kinds of problems, the term, responsibility, is something quite different. It comes from the heart rather than from the head, and is an ethical concept. Responsibility asks everyone to become a part of the process and help to educate the next generation (Gross & Shapiro, 2002). Since responsibility comes from within, blaming others is not its focus. Thus, Gross and Shapiro are urging educators to reconsider the term, accountability, and substitute the word, responsibility, in its place.

DEMOCRACY AND PUBLIC SCHOOLING

The barrage of accountability measures aimed at schools has caused educators to focus on varied and questionable purposes, such as teaching to the tests and "dumbing down" the curriculum (McNeil, 2000) rather than preparing students to become useful and productive citizens. (Kochan & Reed, 2005, p. 71)

Kochan and Reed (2005), in the above quote, addressed directly the control/democracy paradox currently being played out in schools and warned educators that accountability, at its extreme, can hurt students by not preparing them to be useful and productive citizens. Unfortunately, as the authors cautioned, the continuing focus on accountability, with its emphasis on high stakes testing, places social studies and civics education off to the side. A major reason for this is that reading, writing, and arithmetic (the three Rs) figure prominently on the tests while social studies and many other subjects are too often treated as peripheral disciplines within the curriculum. Even if social studies is included on the tests, the citizenship piece is something that requires much more than answering questions on a high stakes exam. It requires dialogue, debate, and decision making.

Recently, a social studies teacher from an affluent suburb in the Northeast told me that she feels as if her area is inconsequential because it is not part of the major areas to be tested. While there is a fairly strong debating society and a student government at her school, she is dismayed that it is only the same very bright students who take part in these activities. She lamented that all students needed to take part in these outside experiences and, above all, that the school needed to make citizenship education central in the curriculum.

At a more global level, Madeline Albright, when she was Secretary of State, discovered that if she "ran down the list of challenges faced by the world—from terrorism and war to poverty and pollution—democracy was the surest path to progress" (Albright, 2003, p. 561).

Although it is clear that democracy is extremely powerful and important and needs to be taught in schools, Amy Gutmann (1999), in *Democratic Education*, raised what she considered to be the central question of the political theory of education: "How should citizens be educated and by whom?" (p. xi). She framed her discussion around two paradoxes. The first inconsistency that she described was between multiculturalism/ patriotism. This paradox rests on the assumption, by some, that those who are different from the norm cannot become good citizens. The underpinning of this belief focuses on the issue of social justice or the lack of it. Difference, then, can be defined in the all-encompassing term of diversity that would include categories such as social class, race, ethnicity, gender, disability, sexual orientation, and exceptionalities, as well as cultural variations (Banks, 2001; Cushner, McClelland, & Safford, 1992; Shapiro, Sewell, & DuCette, 2002). Brown (2004), Larson and Murtadha (2002), Marshall (2004), Shields (2004) and many others would argue that those who are different from the majority can add a great deal that is positive to a society. By keeping the hopeful aspects of differences in mind, and by providing excellent citizenship education and opportunities to children within a democracy, many scholars believe that all of them can develop into outstanding citizens.

The other tension Gutmann (1999) turned to was the dyad of parental control/public control. In her discussion, she spoke of civic minimalism that some parents thought was appropriate for public schooling. These parents believed that they should "have the right to exempt their children from any part of the school curriculum as long as the education that they wish to substitute satisfies the civic minimum" (p. xii). Gutmann also discussed the democratic educationalists who offered "a principled defense of schooling whose aim is to teach the skills and virtues of democratic deliberation within a social context where educational authority is shared among parents, citizens, and professional educators" (p. xiv). Gutmann made a sound case for what she called deliberative democracy.

Deliberative democracy asks all parties to come together to discuss in depth controversial issues and attempts to deal with them in such a way that their problems can be resolved. Gutmann (1999) requested a more principled educational debate on the difficult problems related to education. She further asked for education that teaches students to handle complex problems. She wanted them to learn about the civic values that made up their own country and the moral purpose of other nations.

Gutmann's (1999) approach requires a great deal from teachers and from educational administrators. She emphasized tolerance as well as critical discussions of the concept itself. To teach this kind of democracy, there is really no place for the back to basics movement. Gutmann's curriculum is comprehensive and broad-based. She advocated a kind of democracy where the process itself—the deliberation—is significant and must be taught and practiced.

In our own work, Gross, Shaw, and Shapiro (2003), which we wrote on accountability, the focus was very much on the concept of democracy as well. In fact, we accepted a complex view of both accountability and democracy. To accomplish this, we explored different forms of account-ability using the lenses of three democratic philosophies—progressive, free market, and essentialist. To define progressive education, we turned to the work of John Dewey (1902), who asserted that education should be student-centered, exploratory, and collaborative. Another exemplar of this kind of education was Maxine Greene (1978), who argued for an edu-cation that would not make students feel powerless. Turning to the free market approach to democracy, we discussed how it is often associated with Milton Friedman and Chester Finn's beliefs. This philosophy places schools in the same category as other institutions in our economy—that is, organizations competing for customers who have free choice. Our exemplar for the essentialist movement was William Bagely from Teachers College who, during the early decades of the last century, believed that schools must prepare students for a harshly competitive world. His belief was that the curriculum should become much more standardized with lit-tle local design and should above all be rigorous. So-called soft subjects, like social studies, were suspect, while Latin, algebra, and geometry were emphasized.

Through the review of 36 articles, published in the early 2000s in academic journals, practitioner journals, and the popular press, we discovered that relatively few of them had an underlying progressive democracy emphasis that was student-centered. We also noted that the free market form of democracy was not very much a part of the accountability articles. This form of democracy aims to choose the best educational product for children. There is little sense of community in this argument and there is little hope for the common good. However, we did find that the essentialist philosophy of democracy was clearly underly-ing the majority of the papers on accountability—this form seemed to be driving the debate. Unfortunately, although the strongest philosophy, with its standardized curriculum, it is a type of democracy that does not have the ability to respond quickly to rapidly changing conditions and to turbulence (Gross, 1998, 2004; Shapiro & Gross, 2008).

ETHICAL LEADERSHIP FROM THE HEART

Moral leadership, therefore, is broader than traditional school manage-ment. It demands a deep investment of the genuine or authentic self of the educational leader. Moral leaders have the courage to locate their work in a broader as well as deeper space as they work to bring about societal transformation. (Dantley, 2005, p. 45)

In this complex and chaotic era, to educate leaders and not just managers, it is important that morality or ethics is at the center of educating leaders. The New DEEL treats ethical decision making seriously. Educational leaders need to know when they meet paradoxes, such as control versus democracy, and then must learn ways to solve or at least resolve them. Modeling rational and intuitive decision making abilities is powerful as it is bound to have an effect on staff and students. Hopefully, at its best, this kind of decision making can lead over time to the societal transformation that Dantley (2005) mentions in the above quotation.

It is important to realize that ethical leadership is not always rational. There is a need for the kind of leadership Sergiovani (1992, 2006) speaks of that is not just with the head and the hand, but also with the heart. Emotions enter the picture where good leadership, not management, is concerned. It is important for leaders to be aware of their own emotions as well as other people's reactions, and know how to channel them appropriately. This kind of leadership takes into account issues of motivation and self-knowledge that is so much a part of Begley's (1999) and Begley and Zaretsky's (2004) onion model of educational leaders that places "self" at the center. This kind of leadership should take into consideration Gross' (1998, 2004) turbulence theory, that asks leaders to gauge the level of upheaval when making an ethical decision, and to determine, in advance, if the decision that will be made will increase the level of turbulence or decrease it.

ETHICAL LEADERSHIP FROM THE HEAD AND THE HANDS

Not only does ethical leadership take into account emotions, but it especially turns to the moral groundwork laid by Starratt (1991, 1994, 2004), in his writings about ethical schools, and the thoughtful work of Noddings (1984, 1992) and Sernak (1998) on the ethic of care. It also takes into consideration the writings of Davis (2000, 2001), Shapiro and Purpel (2004), and Young, Petersen, and Short (2002), who turn to the ethic of critique to highlight issues of social justice. In addition, this type of leadership relates well to the model designed by my colleague, Jackie Stefkovich and myself (Shapiro & Stefkovich, 2005; Stefkovich & Shapiro, 1994, 2003) focusing on the ethics of justice, critique, care, and the profession.

This kind of leadership asks us to prepare individuals who can deal with the hard questions such as: What is the law? Is it appropriate in this particular ethical dilemma? Could the law be wrong? Who will I hurt by my decision? Who will I help? Above all, what is in the student's best interests? And, finally, what happens if my decision is in the best interests of some students but not all?

Because this is leadership preparation, the ethic of the profession requires particular attention. In this ethic, students are placed at the center instead of focusing on budgets, efficiency, accountability, and control. It means that educational leaders will think of what is good for their students throughout the decision making process.

THE NEW DEEL: CONTROL VERSUS DEMOCRACY

The paradox of control versus democracy has become somewhat more complex in public education in the United States at the beginning of the twenty-first century, but it is still very much with us. Kochan and Reed (2005) wrote:

> Recent trends in education suggest two possibilities: Either greater control will be exerted over public schools and schooling, or conversely, educational autonomy will be expanded in the form of charter and independent schools, which would be unfettered by external controls and perceived as an alternative to public education (Goldring & Greenfield, 2002). No matter what the requirements or configurations of schools, educational leaders in the public sector will likely face greater stresses and increased demands for the successful performance of all students and for outcomes established by governmental and community groups. (pp. 71–72)

Kochan and Reed (2005), in the above quote, point out that charter and independent schools may allow for some relaxation and freedom from external controls for public education. However, they also speak of the problems that educational leaders will still face because of increasing accountability.

The New DEEL (Gross & Shapiro, 2005) does not focus on restructuring some public schools by turning them into charters or independent institutions. Instead, this concept asks educational leaders to return to the historical mandate of the public schools to prepare citizens for participation in a democratic society (Retallick & Fink, 2002). It also goes beyond that mandate by asking educational leaders to create schools that prepare *all* students to be intelligent and thoughtful citizens who are able to make wise, ethical decisions.

The New DEEL, while innovative and broad in its scope, still aligns well with the current version of the U.S.'s Interstate Licensure Standards (ISLLC) that were developed for educational administrators to uphold. In particular, Standard 5 within ISLLC states: "A school administrator is an educational leader who promotes the success of all students by acting with integrity, fairness, and in an ethical manner" (Interstate School Leaders Licensure Consortium, 1996, p. 18). To meet this standard, an administrator, among other things, must: (a) possess a knowledge and understanding of various ethical frameworks and perspectives on ethics, (b) have a knowledge and understanding of professional codes of ethics, (c) believe in, value, and be committed to bringing ethical principles to the decision-making process, and (d) believe in, value, and be committed to developing a caring school community. While this standard is well written, it could go further by asking for more than a caring school community— which would be a fine start—but also for a democratic school community.

CONCLUSION

In this chapter, the paradox of control/democracy is illuminated. This profound contradiction highlights the ethical underpinnings of the New DEEL. It focuses on both the hierarchical management style and attribution of blame that are noticeable in this era of increasingly diverse forms of accountability in public education. It speaks to the importance of creating more empowering and engaging experiences for all young people, no matter what their social class, race, gender, or other categories of difference might be. Therefore, social justice is at the very center of this paradox. It also advocates the importance of using deliberative democracy, as well as avoiding the Back to Basics curriculum that occurs because of high stakes testing. In addition, this chapter considers the importance of leadership that emphasizes not just the head, but also the hands and the heart. Knowing how to make sound ethical decisions, taking into account both the rational and emotional contexts, is essential for educational leaders, especially in this challenging time.

With the inconsistencies, complexities and turbulence in this early part of the twenty-first century, it is imperative that those of us who prepare educational leaders throughout the world keep a dialogue going to widen the discussion of the New DEEL so that we begin to have common understandings. Already, the New DEEL has attracted international interest. Canadian, Australian, British, and Taiwanese practitioners are involved in this endeavor. Consensus should be achieved as educators work together to create new kinds of educational leaders. Hopefully, this broad-based group of educators can move towards implementation of the ideas inherent in this new movement—that is to develop educational leaders who are knowledgeable of diverse students and different communities, who are compassionate and supportive of their intellectual and emotional needs and their dreams, and who prepare all of them to be democratic and moral citizens.

REFERENCES

Aiken, J. (2002). The socialization of new principals: Another perspective on principal retention. *Educational Leadership Review, 3*(1), 32–40.

Albright, M. (2003). *Madam secretary.* New York: Hyperion.

America 2000: An education strategy. (1991). Washington, DC: U.S. Government Printing Office.

Banks, J. A. (2001). *Cultural diversity and education: Foundations, curriculum and teaching* (4th ed.). Boston: Allyn & Bacon.

Begley, P. T. (Ed.). (1999). *Values and educational leadership.* Albany, NY: State University of New York Press.

Begley, P. T., & Zaretsky, L. (2004). Democratic school leadership in Canada's public school systems: Professional value and social ethic. *The Journal of Educational Administration, 42*(6), 640–655.

Bowles, S., & Gintis, H. (1976). *Schooling in capitalist America.* New York: Routledge & Kegan Paul.

Boyd, W. L. (2000). The r's of school reform and the politics of reforming or replacing public schools. *Journal of Educational Change, 1*(3), 225–252.

Brown, K. M. (2004). Leadership for social justice and equity: Weaving a transformative framework and pedagogy. *Educational Administration Quarterly, 40*(1), 77–108.

Crow, G. (2006). Democracy and educational work in an age of complexity. *UCEA Review, XLVIII*(1), 1–5.

Cushner, K., McClelland, A., & Safford, P. (1992). *Human diversity in education: An integrative approach.* New York: McGraw Hill.

Dantley, M. E. (2005). Moral leadership: Shifting the management paradigm. In F. W. English (Ed.), *The sage handbook of educational leadership: Advances in theory, research, and practice* (pp. 34–46). Thousand Oaks, CA: SAGE.

Darling-Hammond, L., & Snyder, J. (1992). Reframing accountability: Creating learner-centered schools. In A. Lieberman (Ed.), *The changing contexts of teaching* (pp. 11–36). Chicago: University of Chicago Press.

Davis, J. E. (2000). Mothering for manhood: The (Re)production of a black son's gendered self. In M. C. Brown II, & J. E. Davis (Eds.), *Black Sons to mothers: Complements, critiques, and challenges for cultural workers in education* (pp. 51–70). New York: Peter Lang.

Davis, J. E. (2001). Transgressing the masculine: African American boys and the failure of schools. In W. Martino, & B. Meyenn (Eds.), *What about the boys?* (pp. 140–153). Philadelphia: Open University Press.

Dewey, J. (1902). *The school and society.* Chicago: University of Chicago Press.

Driscoll, M. E. (2001). The sense of place and the neighborhood school: Implications for building social capital and for community development. In R.

Crowson (Ed.), *Community development and school reform* (pp. 19–42). New York: JAI/Elsevier.

Furman-Brown, G. (Ed.). (2002). *School as community: From promise to practice*. New York: SUNY Press.

Goals 2000: Educate America Act. (1993). Washington, DC: U.S. Government Printing Office.

Gold, E., & Simon, E. (2004). Public accountability: School improvement efforts need the active involvement of communities to succeed. *Education Week, XXIII*(11), January 14, Reprint Department.

Goldring, E., & Greenfield, W. (2002). Understanding the evolving concept of leadership in education: Roles, expectations, and dilemmas. In J. Murphy (Ed.), *The educational leadership challenge: Redefining leadership for the 21st century* (pp. 1–19). Chicago: University of Chicago Press.

Greene, M. (1978). *Landscapes of learning*. New York: Teachers College Press.

Gross, S. J. (1998). *Staying centered: Curriculum leadership in a turbulent era*. Alexandria, VA: Association for Supervision and Curriculum Development.

Gross, S. J. (2004). *Promises kept: Sustaining innovative curriculum leadership*. Alexandria, VA: The Association of Supervision and Curriculum Development.

Gross, S. J., & Shapiro, J. P. (2002). Towards ethically responsible leadership in a new era of high stakes accountability. In G. Perrault & F. Lunenberg (Eds.), *The changing world of school administration* (pp. 256–266). Lanham, MD: The Scarecrow Press.

Gross, S. J., & Shapiro, J. P. (2005). Our new era requires a New Deel: Towards Democratic ethical educational leadership. *The UCEA Review, XLVII*(3), 1–4.

Gross, S. J., Shaw, K., & Shapiro, J. P. (2003). Deconstructing accountability through the lens of democratic philosophies: Toward a new analytic framework. *The Journal of Research for Educational Leadership, 1*(3), 5–27.

Gutmann, A. (1999). *Democratic education*. Princeton, NJ: Princeton University Press.

Gutmann, A., & Thompson, D. (2004). *Why deliberative democracy?* Princeton, NJ: Princeton University Press.

Interstate School Leaders Licensure Consortium. (1996). *Standards for school leaders*. Washington, DC: Author.

Keith, N. Z. (1999). Whose community schools? Discourses, old patterns. *Theory into Practice. 38*(4), 225–234.

Keith, N. Z. (2005, Spring). Community service learning in the face of globalization: Rethinking theory and practice. *Michigan Journal of Community Service Learning, 11*(2), 5–24.

Kochan, F. K., & Reed, C. J. (2005). Collaborative leadership, community building, and democracy in public education. In F. W. English (Ed.), *The SAGE handbook of educational leadership: Advances in theory, research, and practice* (pp. 68–84). Thousand Oaks, CA: SAGE.

Kohlberg, L. (1981). *The philosophy of moral development: moral stages and the idea of justice* (Vol. 1). San Francisco: Harper & Row.

Larson, C., & Murtadha, K. (2002). Leadership for social justice. In J. Murphy (Ed.), *The educational leadership challenge: Redefining leadership for the 21st century* (pp. 134–161). Chicago: University of Chicago Press.

Leithwood, K. (2001). School leadership in the context of accountabilility policies. *International Journal of Leadership in Education*, *4*(3), 217–236.

McNeil, L. M. (2000). *Contradictions of school reform: Educational costs of standardized testing*. New York: Routledge.

Marshall, C. (2004). Social justice challenges to educational administration: Introduction to a special issue. *Educational Administration Quarterly*, *40*(1), 3–13.

Mitra, D. L. (2004). The significance of students: Can increasing "student voice" in schools lead to gains in youth development? *Teachers College Record*, *106*(4), 651–688.

National Commission on Excellence in Education. (1983). *A nation at risk: The imperative for educational reform*. Washington, DC: U.S. Government Printing Office.

No Child Left Behind Act of 2001. Pub.L. No. 107-110, 115 Stat. 1425 (codified as amended at 20 U.S.C. 6301 et. seq.) (2002).

Noddings, N. (1984). *Caring: A feminine approach to ethics and moral education*. Berkeley, CA: University of California Press.

Noddings, N. (1992). *The challenge to care in schools: An alternative approach to education*. New York: Teachers College Press.

Normore, A. H. (2004). The edge of chaos: School administrators and accountability. *Journal of Educational Administration*, *42*(4), 55–77.

O'Hair, M. J., McLaughlin, H. J., & Reitzug, U. C. (2000). *Foundations of democratic education*. Cambridge, MA: Thomson Wadsworth.

Purpel, D. E. (1989). *The moral and spiritual crisis in education: A curriculum for justice and compassion in education*. New York: Bergin & Garvey.

Retallick, J., & Fink, D. (2002). *Framing leadership: Contributions and impediments to educational change*. International Journal of Leadership in Education, *5*(20), 91–104.

Reitzug, U. C., & O'Hair, M. J. (2002). From conventional school to democratic school community: The dilemmas of teaching and leading. In G. Furman-Brown (Ed.). *School as community: From promise to practice*. New York: SUNY Press.

Scheurich, J. J., Skrla, L., & Johnson, J. F. (2000). Thinking carefully about equity and accountability. *Phi Delta Kappan*, *82*(4), 293–299.

Sergiovanni, T. J. (1992). *Moral leadership: Getting to the heart of school improvement*. San Francisco: Jossey-Bass.

Sergiovanni, T. J. (2006). *The principalship: A reflective practice perspective* (5th ed.). Boston: Pearson.

Sernak, K. (1998). *School leadership-Balancing power with caring*. New York: Teachers College Press.

Sewell, T. E., DuCette, J. P., & Shapiro, J. P. (1998). Educational assessment and diversity. In N. Lambert & B. L. McCombs (Eds.), *How students learn: Reforming schools through learner-centered education* (pp. 311–338). Washington, DC: APA.

Shapiro, H. S., & Purpel, D. E. (Eds.). (2004). *Critical social issues in American education: Democracy and meaning in a globalizing world* (3rd ed.). Mahwah, NJ: Erlbaum.

Shapiro, J. P. (1979). Accountability—A contagious disease? *Forum: For the Discussion of New Trends in Education, 22*(1), 16–18.

Shapiro, J. P., & Gross, S. J. (2008). *Ethical educational leadership in turbulent times: (Re)solving moral dilemmas.* Mahwah, NJ: Erlbaum.

Shapiro, J. P., Sewell, T. E., & DuCette, J. P. (2002). Reframing diversity in education. Lanham, MD: Rowman & Littlefield.

Shapiro, J. P., & Stefkovich, J. A. (2005). *Ethical leadership and decision making in education: Applying theoretical perspectives to complex dilemmas* (2nd ed.). Mahwah, NJ: Erlbaum.

Shields, C. M. (2004). Dialogic leadership for social justice: Overcoming pathologies of silence. *Educational Administration Quarterly, 40*(1),109–132.

Skrla, L., Scheurich, J. J., & Johnson, J. F. (2000). *Equity-driven, achievement-focused school districts.* Austin, TX: The Charles A. Dana Center.

Starratt, R. J. (1991). Building an ethical school: A theory for practice in educational leadership. *Educational Administration Quarterly, 27*(2), 185–202.

Starratt, R. J. (1994). *Building an ethical school.* London: Falmer Press.

Starratt, R. J. (2004). *Ethical leadership.* San Francisco: Jossey-Bass.

Stefkovich, J. A., & Shapiro, J. P. (1994). Personal and professional ethics for educational administrators. *Review Journal of Philosophy and Social Science, 20*(1&2), 157–186.

Stefkovich, J. A., & Shapiro, J. P. (2003). Deconstructing communities: Educational leaders and their ethical decision-making processes. In P. Begley & O. Johansson (Eds.), *The ethical dimensions of school leadership* (pp. 69–106). Boston: Kluwer.

Young, M. D, Petersen, G. J., & Short P. M. (2002). The complexity of substantive reform: A call for interdependence among key stakeholders. *Educational Administration Quarterly, 38*(2), 136–175.

ABOUT THE AUTHORS

Dr. Judy A. Alston is an associate professor in the Center for Education at Widener University. Her research foci include gender and educational leadership with a focus on Black female school superintendents; urban education and educational leadership highlighting administrative reform in urban schools; and diversity and educational leadership exploring how the intersections of class, race/ethnicity, gender, sexual diversity, and ability affect leaders. E-mail: JAAPSUPHD96@aol.com

Thomas E. Beeman is the president and chief executive officer of Lancaster general health system and hospital (United States). He is also deeply connected to the Naval Reserves, where he serves as a commanding officer of a medical unit in San Diego. His interests are leadership and moral decision making. E-mail: thomasebeeman@yahoo.com

Roger I. Blanco, a former curriculum specialist for the Division of Mathematics and Science Education, Miami-Dade County Public Schools, Dr. Blanco is currently manager of school partnerships at Carnegie Learning, Inc., Pittsburg, Pennsylvania. Dr. Blanco holds a doctor of unity theology and divinity degree from Unity-Fillmore Seminary as well as an educational specialist degree from Florida International University. He is a well-known state, national, and international (People's Republic of China, Japan, Canada, Venezuela, Brazil, Singapore, Greece, Guatemala, The Grand Bahamas, Thailand, Australia, and Barbados) presenter in the areas of school reform and secondary mathematics education. He has 11 years of successful teaching experience in the field of urban education as well as over 16 years of managerial involvement. E-mail: RBlanco@carnegielearning.com

Ruth. S. Britt has worked in museums for over 20 years—in exhibit design and planning, exhibit evaluation, and as a writer of exhibit text. She was codesigner of the Civil Unrest exhibit and a writer on the exhibit team. She also observed visitor behavior while serving as a docent in the exhibit throughout its 3-month run.

Jeffrey S. Brooks is an associate professor of educational leadership in the Department of Educational Foundations, Leadership and Technology at Auburn University. His research interests include school reform, teacher leadership, ethics, and sociocultural dynamics of leadership practice and preparation. He has completed ethnographic and case study research in the United States and the Philippines and his work has been published in *Educational Administration Quarterly*, the *Journal of School Leadership*, the *Journal of Educational Administration*, *Educational Policy*, the *Journal of Cases in Educational Leadership*, the *International Electronic Journal of Leadership for Learning*, and the *Journal of Values and Ethics in Educational Administration*. Dr. Brooks is author of *The Dark Side of School Reform: Teaching in the Space Between Reality and Utopia* (Rowman & Littlefield Education, 2006) and is a contributor to the forthcoming edited volume, *Radicalizing Educational Leadership: Toward a Theory of Social Justice* (Sense Publishing, 2008). E-mail: jeffreysbrooks@mac.com

Lionel H. Brown, EdD, received his educational doctorate in urban educational leadership from the University of Cincinnati where he is currently an assistant professor. He served as a principal and as deputy superintendent in the Cincinnati public schools and continues to provide consulting services to schools and community organizations concerning issues such as youth violence and African Americans in government. His awards include: Diversity Merit Award, Mary McCloud Bethune Outstanding Educator Award, and James N. Jacobs Public Education Award. E-mail: Lionel.Brown@uc.edu

Steven Jay Gross is a professor of educational leadership and policy studies at Temple University, Philadelphia, Pennsylvania. Gross' teaching, books, articles and research activities focus on initiating and sustaining deep, democratic reform in schools and turbulence theory. His books include: *Leadership Mentoring: Maintaining School Improvement in Turbulent Times* (2006), *Staying Centered: Curriculum Leadership in a Turbulent Era* (1998) and *Promises Kept: Sustaining School and District Leadership in a Turbulent Era* (2004). Gross served as editor of ASCD's Curriculum Handbook series and is a senior fellow at the Vermont Society for the Study of Education. Along with colleagues across North America and Australia, Gross is a leading figure in a movement called the